# TRAVEL
## in the
# MIDDLE
# AGES

# Travel
## in the Middle Ages

JEAN VERDON

translated by
GEORGE
HOLOCH

UNIVERSITY OF NOTRE DAME PRESS · Notre Dame, Indiana

English Language Edition Copyright © 2003 by
University of Notre Dame
Notre Dame, Indiana 46556
www.undpress.nd.edu
All Rights Reserved

Manufactured in the United States of America


Translated by George Holoch from *Voyager au Moyen Age* by Jean Verdon,
© Librarie Académique Perrin, 1998.

The publisher is grateful to
THE FRENCH MINISTRY OF CULTURE—CENTRE NATIONAL DU LIVRE
for support of the costs of translation.


*Library of Congress Cataloging-in-Publication Data*
Verdon, Jean.
[Voyager au Moyen Age. English]
Travel in the middle ages / Jean Verdon ; translated by George Holoch.
p.   cm.
Includes bibliographical references and index.
ISBN 0-268-04222-5 (cloth : alk. paper)
ISBN 0-268-04223-3 (pbk. : alk. paper)
1. Travel, Medieval.   2. Voyages, Imaginary—History and criticism.
I. Title.

G89 .V4813    2003
910.4'09'02—dc21

2002155286


∞ *This book is printed on acid-free paper.*

# CONTENTS

# INTRODUCTION

S ETTLED OR MOBILE?

A journey in the current sense, with its philosophical implications suggesting both "the movement of a person who travels to a fairly distant place" (Robert) and ideas of distraction and flight from the self, did not exist in the Middle Ages.

The concept had so little substance that at first it was identified with the concrete elements that made it up: the road itself (*via*—way or journey), or the money needed to carry it out (*viaticum*). Later came the sense of movement, especially as carried out by pilgrims, and then by those armed pilgrims, the Crusaders. In fact, in the early fifteenth century, the term "to journey" was understood to mean to make military expeditions. It was only in the late Middle Ages that the terms "journey" and "travel" began to take on the meaning with which we are familiar.

Indeed, nothing either in the means of communication (which defined a restricted space) or in the landscape encouraged travel.

## A Narrow Horizon

Most travel involved short, indeed very short distances. For example, in Poitou in the late fourteenth century, Jean Le Pelletier and his brother-in-law Jean Croissons traveled to the market in

Pouzauges, bringing with them two animals loaded with earthen pots to sell. Once they had sold their goods, they ate and drank heartily in a tavern before setting out on the road back at nightfall. There would be a stop along the way if the distance to be covered seemed too great. Nicolas Voyer, from Poiré-sous-La-Roche-sur-Yon, left his home to go to a village six leagues away, but he decided to spend the night at the house of Jean de Pont-de-Vie, a relative of his wife. If the distance was greater than fifteen kilometers, a traveler was unlikely to return home the same day.

The letters of remission studied by Claude Gauvard show that in France in the late Middle Ages approximately 40 percent of the supplicants had committed their crimes in the place where they lived and 15 percent at a distance less than five kilometers away. Given the fact that 5 percent of criminal acts took place within the home, the proportion of journeys made outside of familiar surroundings seems to be small. This observation is not enough to establish that people did not leave their villages, but the men of the Middle Ages remained attached to their native soil. Of course, once their crime had been committed, many criminals fled, for justice was harsh and swift. To secure their letters of remission, many exiles asserted that their families would not survive outside their land of origin. A man in the jurisdiction of Amiens who had been sentenced to banishment three years earlier solicited a pardon, because he "went to a foreign country and deserted his wife and his children, so that he has been and is now in great poverty and want and on the path to end his final days in misery and his wife and children to become beggars in their country." There is of course an element of special pleading in such remarks—some made their fortune in distant regions—but attachment to one's native soil was undeniable. Criminals returned to live not far from their native village despite the danger of a denunciation, evidence that this danger was not as great as the danger of adventure.

Gauvard's study is valid not only for those who committed crimes, for the majority of supplicants, approximately 70 percent, left their homes with no idea that they were about to commit a crime. Work, leisure, and religious life unfolded in an enclosed space of about five kilometers in diameter. And this was true even for the young.

Professional activity seems to have had an effect on the length of journeys. Only 2 percent of farm laborers ventured beyond thirty kilometers. The percentage rises to 10 percent for craftsmen, and as high as 28 percent for men at arms, and 17 percent for the clergy. It is not at all surprising to find greater mobility among warriors than among farm laborers. It is also to be expected that women, even more than men, remained confined to their localities, unless they emigrated to get married.

## A Hostile Landscape

The forest predominated, occupying a much larger space than it does today. But in the course of the Middle Ages, a long period extending over a millennium from the fall of the Roman Empire to the Renaissance, important changes took place.

From the Mediterranean regions to central Europe, the soil and the climate produced a great variety of forest cover. In the early Middle Ages, Aquitaine, like the Pyrenees and Alps regions, seems to have been heavily wooded, not only in the Massif Central but also in the regions of the Garonne. This forest continued into the Loire region; documents from Le Mans indicate that there were only modest farms among vast woods and stretches of fallow land. What the vegetation was in the Beauce is uncertain, but the Paris region offered to Merovingian and Carolingian monarchs large wooded areas that were good for hunting. To the north and east of the Seine, the forest gradually grew denser and became a real frontier. The traveler would then enter the old Hercynian forest that stretched from the Rhine to Bohemia.

The Benedictine Lambert of Hersfeld (c. 1033–c. 1080), describing Henry IV's fight against the Saxons, mentions in passing the great primitive forest that still covered vast areas of Germania. In the heart of the forest that separated Franconia from the southern cantons of Thuringia, Henry inhabited a castle located on the top of a hill that could be reached only by a very difficult path. The slopes of the mountain were plunged in the shadow of the woods that stretched for thousands and thousands of paces. The king could thus quietly slip away with a few companions. For three days without eating, it was said, they walked through this immense forest, following a narrow and little-known path.

Some years earlier, in 991, Richer, a monk of the abbey of Saint-Remi in Reims, traveled to Chartres. After a stop at the monastery of Orbais, he set out on the road to Meaux. But, he wrote, "having, with my two companions, taken the twisted paths of the woods, many misfortunes befell us. For, losing our way at a crossroads, we made a detour of six leagues."

To judge by literary texts, in the twelfth century the forest still seemed to be a place that one could enter only with a great deal of difficulty. Real and imaginary dangers alike inhabited it. The knights of the Round Table went there seeking adventure, like the valiant Calogrenant. "Chance led me into the middle of a dense forest where the trails, obstructed by brambles and thorns, hid many dangers. Not without trouble, nor without injury, I managed to follow a path. I rode along it for almost an entire day, until in the end I finally came out of the forest."

The forest, however, no longer resembled the forest of the Carolingian epoch. It was not as unpopulated as one might suppose, for hermits found refuge there. Geoffroy, a monk of the Benedictine abbey of Tiron in the early twelfth century, described vast wooded areas south of the Sélune separating Normandy from Brittany, with many anchorites living there in separate cells. Among them was Pierre, who knew neither how to cultivate the fields nor how to garden; young shoots of trees and his work on the lathe allowed him to survive. He had built his house with the bark of trees. Although this forest had some similarities to the German forest, the vegetation appears to have been not at all primitive. And it did not have the solitude of the German forest. An important phenomenon had occurred, beginning in the late tenth century and continuing through the thirteenth: clearances. France, and England, which was more wooded than France, no longer had entirely virgin forests. Although fallow land and forest had a resurgence during the Hundred Years' War, the landscape of western Europe was no longer what it had been in the course of the first millennium: moors and forests as far as the eye could see with a few scattered clearings where men gathered together.

But an adventure that happened to the powerful duke of Burgundy, Philip the Good, suggests that not everything had changed. Philip decided to leave his house in secret and arranged one night to meet a few lords who were his friends. The days were short and it was already "basse vesprée" when he mounted his horse. The thaw following a long and bitter freeze and the dense mist that had held on all day before changing into light rain soaked the ground. Nevertheless, the duke rode off, thinking that he would easily find his way. Daylight disappeared and the night was upon him, but there was no question of returning to Brussels. "Now, he had entered a dense forest, wide and deep, neither the entrance nor the exit of which he knew," wrote the chronicler Chastellain. The weather was rainy and the paths iced over. The duke wandered hoping that he would in the end find a way out. He struggled up hillocks, went down into deep and swampy ditches, broke the ice covering the ground in spots. While he thought he was following a firm path, he sank into the mire from which he could barely extricate himself. He ran into brambles, turned once to the left, then to the right, went up and down, turned and turned again, often dismounted and touched the ground with his hand looking for some trace of a horse or wagon, wandering where no one had ever been. Philip nevertheless kept up his courage, paying no heed to either cold or darkness, awaiting the break of day and telling himself that a night, even a hard one, is soon over. His shouts produced no reply. His horse stumbled three or four times.

He finally saw a distant light, but it was a lump of earth with flame coming out of all sides. It could have been midnight. He took up his way again. Long he wandered. Finally, he heard a dog barking and reached a cottage where a poor man and his wife were sleeping. In spite of shouts and violent blows on the door, the man was in no hurry to answer, "for he thought it was brigands of the woods or wicked people since, at that hour and in such weather and so far from any road, they were out and about." "Go away, it is now after midnight, let us sleep and go away." The duke managed to persuade the fellow to let him into his little house. He had the duke sit by the fire and brought him a frugal meal and then, in exchange for good hard currency, went with him to show him the right way.

On the whole, the idea that the forest was dangerous was established in the Middle Ages. For Suger, counselor of King Louis VII of France, the image owed a good deal to biblical memories, for it suggested that the robbers haunting the forests of the kingdom resembled the merchants of the Temple. The myth persisted after the clearances. In 1400, a squire from Saintonge still feared "to come and go through the said forests by reason of the presence of several murderers and thieves who had their lair in that place." The fact that he had to justify carrying forbidden weapons—for purposes of a punitive expedition—no doubt encouraged the petitioner to appeal to the imagination. It is nevertheless true that, even if the reality did not correspond to the fear expressed, the argument was still admissible. However, many peasants at the time were not afraid to lead their cattle to pasture in the woods. One has to go to the Holy Roman Empire to encounter fearful forests. When a crime in France really took place in a dense forest, the letter of remission took on an epic cast, reporting for example the wild ride of a pair of lovers fleeing their pursuers at top speed, a distant echo of the story of Tristan and Iseut.

On the whole, aside from the stereotyped image of the Crusades, which was not immediately identified with a journey, the Middle Ages seems to have been a time of stagnation between Antiquity and its world travelers, mythical like Ulysses or real like the Phoenicians, and the Renaissance of the great discoveries.

And yet, the world of the Middle Ages was a world of unceasing movement.

## A LIFE IN PERPETUAL MOTION

Some people's occupations forced them to be constantly on the move. This was the case for Eudes Rigaud, who is well known for his *Registre des visites,* extant for the years 1248–1268. From a family of the minor nobility, Rigaud entered the Franciscan order in Paris. A renowned preacher, barely had he been appointed superior of the Franciscan monastery in Rouen when, in 1247, he was elected as archbishop of the city. He was obliged to accept the position at the urging of King Louis I and Pope Innocent IV. Wishing to eradicate abuses and to put into effect the decisions promulgated at the Fourth Lateran Council in 1215, he constantly traveled through the suffragan bishoprics and particularly through his own diocese.

Consecrated bishop in March 1248, Eudes immediately began his pastoral visits. The earliest extant record is from the priory of Graville at the edge of his diocese, dated July 17, 1248, but since the first page of the manuscript has been lost, he had certainly been on the road for several days. He was making a circuit of the deaneries of the diocese of Rouen.

On April 21, 1249, Rigaud interrupted his pastoral visits to embark at Wissant for England in order to lay claim to revenues that Henry III had seized; he returned on May 7 and resumed his visits. We find him on September 23 officiating at the funeral of Bishop Gautier of Paris and then with Pope Innocent IV in Lyon at the end of the year. In 1250, he traveled to the six Norman dioceses, exhibiting intense activity, but still finding the time to visit the pope in Lyon twice and to make long journeys in the interest of the kingdom.

It would be tedious to list all the travels related in the diary. However, we know from other sources that Eudes was with Louis IX in July 1270 off the coast of Sardinia, where the king appointed him as one of the executors of his will. He probably resumed his pastoral visits on his return. In 1273, he and two other prelates were appointed by Pope Gregory X as inquisitors for the possible canonization of the deceased king. In 1274, the same pope named him as a participant in the general council of Lyon. He died in Rouen in July 1275.

This activity may seem insignificant to our contemporaries, who can travel by TGV from Paris to Bordeaux in three hours. It is therefore necessary to consider the time devoted to travel. In order to do this, following Yves Renouard, we will examine in more detail Rigaud's journey to Rome in 1253–54. Concerned with reforming the clergy of his province, the archbishop came up against suffragan bishops who tolerated many abuses. He wished to hear in person the complaints and appeals of the clergy and laity of the whole province, which removed from the six suffragans a part of their jurisdiction, revenues that they derived from it, and some of their authority. Since they had appealed to the pope, Eudes decided to go to Rome to present his case to the sovereign pontiff, Innocent IV. He left immediately after Christmas 1253, accompanied by a dozen people. This was his first journey to Italy, and because he was in no particular hurry, he did not take the most direct route so that he would be able to visit places in which he was particularly interested.

The register provides details about the places he stayed each night. Although he was still in Rouen on December 29, 1253, by the evening of December 30 he was in Auffray, a town located about forty kilometers from the archiepiscopal city. Then, passing through Paris (January 11 and 12, 1254), Dijon (January 23), Lausanne (February 1 and 2), Milan (February 12 and 13), Bologna (where he arrived on February 21 and left on February 25), he reached Rome on March 11. He left the eternal city on July 12 and slept that evening in Sutri, forty-five kilometers distant, then passing through Genoa (July 27), Turin (August 2), Lyon (August 17), Paris (August 31), and Beauvais (September 5), he made a ceremonial entry into Rouen on September 9.

Eudes Rigaud covered 1,845 kilometers in fifty-six stages on the way to Rome, and 1,740 kilometers in fifty-one stages on the way back. The length of each stage obviously varied depending in part on the nature of the terrain, but also on the traveler's wishes. On the way up mountains, stages were from twenty to thirty kilometers, on the way down from thirty to forty. There was much more variation on level ground, ranging from ten to sixty kilometers. The average came to thirty-three kilometers, but if stops are taken into account, a day's journey on the way was twenty-five kilometers, and on the way back twenty-nine kilometers. Because of stops, the journey from Rouen to Rome required seventy-three days, while the journey from Rome to Rouen was accomplished in sixty. In all, he was absent for eight months, because the prelate had to wait a long time for the pope's decision.

Beyond the notation of stages of the journey, the diary indicates only major holidays and the traversal of mountain passes. Because of snow, the travelers had to wait three days before crossing the western slope of the Jura, the Revermont. They almost drowned crossing the Adda. The journey was not a pleasure trip, but was carried out for administrative and spiritual reasons. This is why Eudes left in winter, so that he could meet the pope before he replied to his suffragans. And he left Rome the day after the promulgation of the bull that resolved the question, no doubt eager to return to his archdiocese. Such long journeys were not unusual in the Middle Ages, but travelers tried to avoid the rigors of winter as well as the heat of summer.

Even women, or at least great ladies, had no hesitation in traveling the roads. The journeys of Countess Mahaut of Artois were constant. Every year and often twice a year, she left Paris for Artois; while there, she traveled several times through her domains. Less frequently, she went to Burgundy and took advantage of the trip from time to time to meditate at the abbey of Cherlieu where her husband's body had lain since 1310. She often went from Paris to Fontainebleau, to Saint-Mandé, to the woods of Vincennes, to Conflans, to Pontoise, or to the abbey of Maubuisson where her father was buried. The accounts for the period from May 21, 1327 to October 31, 1328 show that out of 536 days, Mahaut stayed at her city houses or her castles on only 300 of them, or a little more than half. Winter reduced these journeys to some degree, but did not eliminate them. For example, she made a long trip from Burgundy to Paris between December 25 and January 7.

Travel was thus not an anomaly in the Middle Ages. Although a sedentary life was acceptable to many peasants, large numbers of people were constantly traveling.

*Clergy*. Popes and their curia were divided between Rome and other Italian cities, not to mention their voyages through France. Bishops and deans visited circumscriptions under their jurisdiction. Members of provincial councils, high dignitaries of the region, came together for meetings. Monarchs sometimes used clergy as ambassadors. Abbots carried out inspections of the priories dependent on their abbeys. Monks traveled from monastery to monastery carrying scrolls announcing the death of an important personage, not to mention the wandering monks.

*Laity*. Merchants, required by their work to travel, went to fairs to sell their goods and to branch establishments located in major towns, made contact with makers of wool and other cloth, and returned to their towns to occupy political office. The king's agents were constantly on the road to conduct investigations or collect taxes. Traveling players went from castle to castle to enliven the lords' feasts. Pilgrims traveled not only the roads of the West, but also those of the Holy Land. In times of war or plague, peasants took refuge in the cities.

The medieval world does thus not appear to have been a motionless one.

## Mixed Feelings

Literature, a more or less faithful reflection of reality, demonstrates in the realm of thought how complex the understanding of travel was in the Middle Ages.

At the beginning of *La Chanson de Roland*, everyone wishes to go to King Marsile in Saragossa.

> "Allow me to go," replies Duke Naimes;
> "Give me the glove and the staff!"
> . . . . . . . . . . . .
> Roland answers: "I can very well go!"
> "Oh no, not you!" says Count Olivier,
> "Your spirit is fierce and very dangerous;
> I would greatly fear that you would quarrel.
> If the king wills, I can go."
> . . . . . . . . . .
> Turpin of Reims has risen from his seat,
> And says to the king: "Leave your Franks in peace!
> In this country you have stayed seven years;
> They have had much pain and suffering.
> Give me, Sire, the staff and the glove,
> And I will go, I, to see the Saracen of Spain!"

Going on an expedition could be a source of joy. At the beginning of *Le Charroi de Nîmes*, Guillaume undertakes the conquest of a fief. He recruits knights with enthusiasm and it is with enthusiasm that they join him. The reasons for this fervor can be easily understood: there were conquests to be carried out at the expense of pagans, and glory to be won in battles where one's value as a warrior could be demonstrated.

The hero cannot remain sedentary. Erec is living the perfect dream of love with Enide but she has heard malicious gossip about her husband:

> Everyone blamed him, squires
> And knights alike, until
> Even Enide heard them
> Saying her husband was now
> Too lazy for chivalry and had thrown up
> His knighthood; he led a new life.

What does Erec do?

> "Lady," he said, "you were right,
> And the things they said were true.
> Quickly, prepare yourself

For a journey. Rise and put on
The most beautiful dress you own,
And have your saddle put
On your very best palfrey."[1]

All the heroes of Chrétien de Troyes are in movement, for
a journey will bring them adventures and therefore renown. Not
to go means to refuse assuming one's responsibilities or playing
one's role in society, and finally to fail in the realm of morality.
At its best, the road strewn with ordeals leads to God. This is
the meaning of the quest for the Holy Grail.

Some characters, however, have little desire to travel. In *La
Chanson de Roland*, Ganelon does not volunteer for the embassy to Saragossa. His attitude appears shocking and yet, his
reasons are not without basis. Like Naimes, he wishes to make
an agreement with King Marsile; a different decision is made
and he is asked to apply it. He also recalls what the volunteers
have forgotten, that the preceding messengers have not returned.
Thus, when he is chosen, he gives free rein to his anger. He
leaves, but against his will. His later conduct is not at all surprising. Hesitating to leave is thus not an attitude worthy of a
knight.

Medieval literature contains a more realistic strand, that of
the fabliaux; they represent the journey as a trying, dangerous,
and tiring thing. For example, in the *Dit des Marchéans*, Phélip-
pot shows that the merchants deserve the recognition of men as
well as eternal happiness, because they wear themselves out
and incur grave dangers to get everyone what they need.

The poet Eustache Deschamps, a contemporary of King
Charles VI of France, writes in a ballad devoted to journeys:

Those who do not leave home
To go to various countries,
Do not know the mortal sorrow
That assails the people who go:
The evils, the doubts, the perils
Of seas, of rivers and of steps,

---

1. Chrétien de Troyes, *Erec and Enide*, tr. Burton Raffel (New Haven,
Conn.: Yale University Press, 1997), 2462–67, 2575–81.

The languages they do not understand,
The pain and the fatigue of bodies.
But how weary they are of all this,
He who does not venture forth knows nothing.

There was fear of danger and difficulty, but also knowledge of the world gained from encounters and the sight of foreign ways. This was a curiosity compounded of suspicion and attraction.

Mobility and stability perhaps corresponded in the end to real and ideal. If men's mobility in the Middle Ages is undeniable, it was subordinated to stability, as the Benedictine Rule shows. According to Gregory the Great, the dead themselves, condemned to the pains of purgatory, suffer punishment in the places of their sins. Material and intellectual insecurity led to the closing of the gates of the cities and to the rejection of dreams. However, beginning in the middle of the twelfth century, a secularization of life and thought led the Christian West to an opening to the world.

How did these journeys, that were hard by definition, unfold? Can we imagine what they meant for people not aware of current concepts? Will we recognize an evolution or a revolution from their time to ours? Can the Middle Ages enlighten us on the meaning of the journey in the contemporary world?

PART ONE

# methods

# ONE

# on the continent

When the Crusaders went to Jerusalem in the late eleventh century to deliver it from the Infidels, most of them chose to go by road. Medieval man, in general, felt safer on land than on water.

## THE ROADS

### The Legacy of Antiquity

In the late Roman Empire, the network of roads seems to have been excellent, including public roads and secondary roads that were periodically repaired. Because roads had primarily military purposes, they were laid out in straight lines. Military distance markers were set at regular intervals. Relay stations every nine to twelve kilometers and resting places every two or three relays made it possible for travelers to move relatively quickly. Rutilius Namatianus, a high Roman official born in Gaul and author of a poem *On His Return* in which he describes a journey from Rome to Gaul in the autumn of 416, notes that "the tired traveler has the impression of making progress when he sees the many miles inscribed on the stones." Michel Rouche, to whom these pages owe a good deal,[2] notes that the

---

2. See also the works of Robert-Henri Bautier.

last known reconstruction of a road dates from 469, work done on the road from Toulouse to Javols.

The state thus played a role in the organization of means of transportation and consequently in the organization of travel. Written authorizations for free transport were granted, particularly to couriers and officials who had to travel within the Roman Empire. These journeys at state expense therefore turned out to be quite comfortable, for it was a great advantage to be sure of finding predictable places to change horses or to spend the night.

We have the itinerary of a fourth-century pilgrim from Bordeaux to Jerusalem, who very carefully noted the distances between post houses where he stopped, the towns he traveled through, and the places where he slept. He recorded thirty relay stations and eleven stops from Bordeaux to Arles; from Arles to Milan, sixty-three relay stations and twenty-two stops; from Milan to Aquileia, twenty-four relay stations and nine stops. The same ratio between relay stations and stops continued through the rest of the journey. Intervals varied as a function of the nature of the land traveled through or from accidental causes, such as the ravages of the barbarians.

When it was not possible to use public vehicles, individuals had to organize their own travels. Praising the worthiness of Abraham who had to find his own way from Mesopotamia to Palestine, John Chrysostom compared this to the ease of travel on military roads: the way went through inhabited places that were close together; the large number of travelers increased security; and town magistrates had organized provincial police.

In general, the Roman world contained roads essentially of political and military interest, in a sense ignoring geography and aiming principally at finding the most direct route. Economic needs seem to have been secondary, because heavy goods were transported by sea or river.

Difficulties of Repair and Maintenance

In the Merovingian era, the population used the old roads, which still had a military function. When there were battles, they took place on or near the roads. In 732, the second battle of Poitiers occurred at Moussais-la-Bataille on the Roman road between Poitiers and Tours.

Journeys at state expense persisted, as attested by the formulary of Marculf composed in Saint-Denis before 735. Relay stations were also maintained. In the sixth century in the region of Famars, an inn located near the Roman road was the usual stopping place for a slave merchant.

The Roman roads had, however, suffered the consequences of the Germanic invasions. With reference to the Aurelian Way, Rutilius Namatianus noted that inns had been burnt down, which increased the length of stages in the forest, and that bridges had been destroyed, forcing travelers to ford rivers. Kings had no hesitation in interfering with road travel, evidence that they still had some political and military power. "Irritated, the king [Gontran]," writes Gregory of Tours, "had the roads blocked throughout his kingdom." Further, there was a change in capitals. In the fifth century, from Trier to Arles, the principal axis of roads connected the Rhine to the Mediterranean. In the Merovingian era, the centers of political power were located in Paris, Orléans, Soissons, and Reims, so that the hierarchy of means of communication was radically transformed.

The Carolingian era was marked by a restoration of the old Roman roads. Milestones were replaced by simple stones without inscriptions, but Charlemagne and his successors endeavored to restore the ancient roads. The king's envoys were required to see to it that the bridges were well maintained. For example, in 821, they forced recalcitrant peasants to rebuild the twelve bridges over the Seine to permit travel from Meaux to Sens and on to Troyes. In 853, Charles the Bald declared that where bridges had existed from ancient times, they would be restored by those who held the titles under whose authority they had been built in the past. Thus, not only peasants were called upon, but also those who had been granted lands. The kings reminded these landholders that money derived from taxes on merchandise was to be used to maintain bridges and roads. When an ancient network did not exist, as in Germania, the Carolingians managed to create roads that made it possible particularly for merchants and soldiers to travel.

The need for rapid transmission of news and ease of travel for tax collectors and troops even led to the maintenance of a veritable postal network for the king's purposes, similar to the Roman system. At the judicial assembly of Quierzy, before leaving for Italy, Charles the Bald declared, "May our son and our other faithful followers see to it that nothing new or evil comes about in this kingdom that we do not know of, by means of riders or couriers on foot."

Nevertheless, because the centers of decision remained the same, few new roads appeared. Moreover, old roads shrank. The life of Théodulf shows him encountering a farmer plowing the public way. "It is not good to cut the road with your plow," he told him, "for it has to be trod by travelers with unoffending feet." Much more seriously, some roads turned out to be unusable.

Let us follow a traveler who wants to go from Germania to Spain. The first part of the journey, up to the Rhine, will require some effort. Once he has reached the river, he will take the road from Cologne to Senlis, and from there through Paris, Tours, Saintes, Bordeaux, and the pass of Roncevaux, he will end up at Pamplona. If he does not want to deal with the Basques, he will follow the right bank of the Rhône to Nîmes. Then, through Narbonne and the pass of la Perche, he will arrive in Barcelona. This was the route used by the slave merchants from the Slavic countries who traveled through Mayence and Verdun on their way to the court of Córdoba.

By the middle of the ninth century, new waves of invaders showed up. The earthen castles that then stood to stop them were generally set along the old roads. The monarchs had little time to build new ones. Furthermore, to resist the Normans, the inhabitants cut the roads and destroyed the bridges. In 854, Charles the Bald ordered the opening of roads that had recently been closed by flooding, the repair of bridges, and a reduction in taxes paid by refugees displaced by the Normans. This was a genuine break from the old Roman network, especially when the Carolingian empire was succeeded by territorial principalities. There was no longer a central political authority to make decisions for the empire as a whole. The tenth and eleventh centuries were really the last time that the Roman roads were used.

The journey of the historian Richer from Reims to Chartres makes this clear. There were still relay horses, inns, and mileposts. "After passing through Château-Thierry, the mount, who until then had seemed a Bucephalus, began to move at the pace of a donkey. The sun had left the meridian and was going to set; it was rainy weather when our vigorous Bucephalus, exhausted by a supreme effort, collapsed between the legs of the servant who was riding him and expired, struck down six miles from the town." His servant's horse was a real nag supplied by a relay station. The organization of roads thus turned out to be hardly effective, whereas the roads themselves were still passable. We should add that, in order to reach Meaux, Richer had to cross a very dilapidated bridge.

> Accompanied only by the rider from Chartres, I arrived in Meaux. I could hardly distinguish in daylight the bridge I crossed; but, contemplating it, I was seized by new emotions. It was full of so many large holes that those who had dealings with the inhabitants of the town had had trouble crossing it during the day. The man from Chartres, who was an active and experienced traveler, looked everywhere in the neighborhood for a boat. Not finding one, he came back to attempt the dangers of the bridge and, heaven be praised, the horses crossed it without accident. At the gaping spots, under the horses' hoofs he placed either his shield or planks that were lying on the ground and, sometimes bent over, sometimes erect, sometimes moving slowly, sometimes running, he succeeded in crossing the bridge with me and the horses.

But a few years later, in 1004, Abbon de Fleury did not use the Roman road to go from Poitiers to La Réole. He preferred to use a new road. Old roads and recently constructed ones thus coexisted.

It is obvious that roads dating from the Roman Empire were not suited for an age in which, under demographic pressure, major clearances were being carried out. The Roman roads were abandoned for the most part in the tenth and eleventh centuries. A new network was put in place, created by private initiative. The purpose was no longer to cover distances as quickly as possible, but to connect all inhabited spots with one another.

A Certain Disorganization (Eleventh and Twelfth Centuries)

With the dismantling of authority, the situation turned out to be rather anarchic. The network of everyday local transport was extraordinarily complex. The smallest village, as Bernadette Barrière has shown in the case of the Limousin, was connected to the parish seat, to the neighboring market, and to the castle by a whole series of foot paths, horse trails, and cart roads, which sometimes overlapped with portions of the main road. But connections were affected by social categories. Whereas it was important for villagers to be able easily to reach their parish church, the castle of which they were dependents, and the market, the religious community needed to control the lands that were its source of wealth, and the local noble was primarily interested in the routes that linked the principal fortresses under his command. Various passages of the *Chronique de Geoffroy de Vigeois* demonstrate the importance of horse trails. For example, in the second half of the eleventh century, learning that his lord, Bernard de Comborn, is in grave danger, Guy III de Lastours slips away from the duke holding him hostage in Poitiers. He leaves the town dressed as a squire and gallops day and night. After changing horses at Lastours, he arrives in Pompadour as dawn is breaking.

These roads made some kinds of transport difficult. The same Geoffroy de Vigeois reports that, sometime between 1030 and 1040, a certain Simplicius brought the stone intended for the main altar of the abbey of Saint-Martial from Narbonne. The stone had to be transported on the road through Capdenac. When the local lord was informed, not only did he tear down town walls to broaden the way, he provided oxen to pull the cart.

The location of roads of local interest inevitably gave rise to conflict. For example, in 1298, the court of the viscount of Limoges issued a ruling on the decision of the prior of Aureil to condemn and block, on his own authority, a *via publica* passing near a field belonging to him. He had replaced it with a new road that was inappropriate according to the viscount, without having asked for his authorization.

In addition to roads of local or regional interest, there were interregional connections. Certain routes were of ancient origin: the one connecting Bourges to Bordeaux and bypassing Limoges and Périgueux is documented without interruption from the Bronze Age through the end of the Middle Ages and perhaps even later. The route, which tended to follow an interfluvial path, nevertheless had to cross a few rivers. At those points there were castles and towns, showing that this ancient road was constantly used during the Middle Ages.

There were many reasons for the existence of particular roads: economic, political, administrative, and particularly religious. Let us consider the latter.

## On the Roads to Santiago

There is an invaluable work dating from the twelfth century, *Le Guide du pèlerin de Saint-Jacques-de-Compostelle*. According to recent research, this work was rather little known for centuries, for there seem to be few manuscripts. Because the author praises at length Poitou and its inhabitants, it is thought that he came from that province. He might be Aymeri Picaud, from Parthenay-le-Vieux. Although the Spanish part of the route is described in much more detail than the French part, and many towns or roads permitting passage from one route to another in France are not mentioned, this guide constitutes a basic source for knowledge of the routes leading to one of the most famous pilgrimage destinations in Christendom.

The first chapter indicates: "There are four routes running to Santiago which come together into one at Puente la Reina, in Spanish territory." The first route went through Toulouse. The pilgrims who had come from the east and from Italy, those who crossed the Alps and traveled toward Avignon or Aix, and those who had followed the Mediterranean coast took this route. But the route really began in Arles. There, pilgrims had to visit the body of Saint Caesar, bishop and martyr, and seek the relics of the bishop Saint Honorat in the cemetery. The history of the most holy martyr Genès is presented in detail, as is the cemetery of Aliscamps. In no other cemetery anywhere can be found so many marble tombs, nor such large ones, set in rows on the ground. They are of varied workmanship and bear ancient inscriptions carved in Latin letters but in an unintelligible language. The more one looks in the distance, the longer the line of sarcophagi one sees. Continuing to the west, the pilgrims then went through Saint-Gilles-du-Gard. After Montpellier, they venerated the body of Saint Guillaume in Saint-Guilhem-le-Désert, crossed the northern slope of Black Mountain, and followed the banks of the Garonne to Toulouse, an important city with many sanctuaries, in particular that of Saint-Sernin where the martyr was buried. Through the countryside around Toulouse and the Béarn region, through Gimont, Auch, and Oloron, the pilgrims reached the pass of Somport, and then rested in the hospice of Sainte-Christine. There they met up with those from Montpelier who had preferred the road through Catalonia to the Languedoc route. Beginning their descent toward Jaca, at Puente la Reina they met up with the pilgrims who had taken the three other routes.

The second route went through Le Puy. After passing through this town in a region of volcanoes, pilgrims from Lyon and Clermont stopped at Conques, where they "must venerate the relics of Saint Foy, virgin and martyr." Then, passing through Cahors, with a view of the cathedral of Saint-Étienne and the Valentré bridge, and through Moissac with its abbey, they reached Ostabat. A variant of this route left from Brioude and brought other travelers through Aurillac and the sanctuary of Rocamadour.

The third way, called "Limousine," came from Burgundy. Pilgrims from the east and northeast honored Mary Magdalen in her magnificent sanctuary in Vézelay. In Limoges, they venerated Saint Martial in the abbey bearing his name, then "in the town of Périgueux you must visit the body of the blessed Front, bishop and confessor." The road through La Réole and Mont-de-Marsan led the pious travelers to Ostabat.

For the fourth route, pilgrims from northern Europe, namely, from the Low Countries and northern France, passed through Paris and continued on through Orléans, where they were urged to see the wood of the Cross and the chalice of Saint Euverte; Tours, made illustrious by the memory of Saint Martin; and Saintes, where was located the body of the blessed Eutrope. Then, through the Bordeaux region and the Landes, by stages evoking the memory of Roland, they reached Spain.

*Le Guide* teems with tasty details about the territories it passes through. For example, Poitou is "fertile, excellent, and full of pleasant things. The Poitevins are vigorous people and good warriors, clever in the handling of bows and arrows and lances in war, courageous in the face of battle, very fast runners, elegant in their dress, with handsome faces, witty, very generous, and most hospitable." In the Bordeaux region, "the wine is excellent, fish abundant, but the language crude." It takes a three-day walk for already tired people to cross the Landes. The country is not very hospitable.

It is a desolate country, lacking in everything; there is neither bread, nor wine, nor meat, nor fish, nor water, nor springs; there are few villages in this sandy plain which, however, abounds in honey, millet, panic [a kind of millet], and pigs. If you happen to cross the Landes in summer, take care to protect your face from the enormous flies that are especially abundant there and are called wasps or horseflies; and if you do not watch your feet with caution, you will quickly sink up to your knees in the invasive ocean sand.

After crossing this country, you come to Gascony, rich in white bread and excellent red wine, covered with woods and meadows, rivers and pure springs. The Gascons are flighty of speech, talkative, mocking, debauched, drunkards, ill dressed in rags, and lacking in money; however, they are trained for battle and remarkable for their hospitality to the poor.

Several other routes supplemented this one. In particular, pilgrims coming from England and the west reached Tours through Chartres and Vendôme or through Le Mans. They might get to Poitiers through Angers.

The second, third, and fourth routes came together in Ostabat. The road continued through Saint-Jean-Pied-de-Port and the ports of Cize. The pilgrims then reached Pamplona, the capital of Navarre, and then Puente la Reina.

Basques and Navarrese are depicted in dark colors. The Navarrese are

a barbarous people, different from all other peoples in its customs and its race, full of wickedness, dark in color, ugly of face, debauched, depraved, perfidious, disloyal, corrupt, voluptuous, drunken, expert in every violence, fierce and savage, dishonest and lying, impious and rude, cruel and argumentative, incapable of any good feeling, and brought up in every vice and iniquity.

From Puente la Reina to Santiago de Compostela, the travelers took the "French road," so called because it was the route that had been used for centuries by pilgrims from France. They reached Estella and then turned toward Burgos.

León, capital of the kingdom of the same name, was an important stop before crossing partly wild regions with dangerous passes and hostile populations.

The end of the journey took place in the heart of a welcoming country.

> Here, the landscape is wooded, watered by rivers, well furnished with meadows and excellent orchards; the fruits are good and the springs clear, but towns, villages, and cultivated fields are rare; wheat bread and wine are not plentiful, but you can find plenty of rye bread and cider, cattle and horses, milk and honey; the fish that come from the sea are enormous but small in number; as for gold, silver, cloth, the fur of forest animals, and other riches, they are abundant, along with sumptuous Saracen treasures.

Finally, Compostela appeared.

The pilgrims, who had access to many hospices, did not necessarily follow one of the routes from one end to the other. On the way, they changed direction for reasons of curiosity or piety. In addition, some routes not indicated were close to the seashore: English pilgrims landed at Soulac and continued their journey along the coast.

## The Reorganization

From the middle of the twelfth century to the beginning of the fourteenth a network of roads was organized in France as a consequence of a rapidly expanding economy. Fairs attracted merchants who sometimes came from distant regions. Routes were specified in order to avoid disputes. In 1218, the lord of Maligny agreed to restore eight *toises* of the width of the road connecting Chably to Fouchères that he had narrowed to prevent the passage of the flocks of the abbey of Pontigny; in addition, he allowed the monks to restore the ditches of the road that he had filled in. The first mentions of paved roads appeared at around this time. For example, in 1203, Blanche de Navarre hired contractors to pave a portion of the road between Troyes and Sézanne within seven years. To recover their expenses, the contractors would receive the revenue of tolls for a certain period of time. The procedure is analogous to what is done for our modern highways!

The network of roads inherited from the Roman epoch had been profoundly changed by the growing activity of Paris in political and administrative matters and by the use of horses, particularly in northern France. It was appropriate to set out new routes and to broaden the old ones.

Philippe de Beaumanoir, author of a work entitled *Coutumes de Beauvaisis,* composed in the late thirteenth century, distinguishes five types of roads.

- The path (*sentier*), 1.2 meters wide, allowing travel from one major road to another or from one locality to another; carts should not use it because they would risk damage to fields or goods.
- The cart road (*charrière*), 2.4 meters wide, on which two carts could not travel next to one another, but could pass one another; the cattle should be held by the bridle.
- The way (*voie*), 4.8 meters wide, on which two carts could move next to one another leaving a path on either side: cattle are driven from behind from one village to another or from one market to another, but with no stops for grazing; it made it possible to connect rural towns and castles with one another.
- The road (*chemin*), 9.6 meters wide, on which animals have the right to graze and to stop, and merchandise may go through; here, transport taxes are collected.
- The royal road (*grand chemin royal*), 19.2 meters wide, laid out in a straight line insofar as possible, except when high mountains, rivers, or swamps prohibit it. "Why were they made so wide? So that all the products of the earth and the animals, on which men and women feed themselves to live, might be led and transported there; so that everyone might go and come, have all necessary comfort thanks to the width of the road, and go through towns and castles to carry on his business."

Such definitions are obviously situated on the conceptual level and did not always correspond to reality. In the region of Chartres, the width of roads varied greatly: 2.9 meters between

Châteaudun and Allaines, 6.5 meters between Chartres, Blois, and Tours by way of Châteaudun.

As a good lawyer, Philippe de Beaumanoir examined problems that might arise. As a general rule, all roads belonged to the lord of the land, whether they were part of his own domain or of that of his subjects. Anyone who broke up the roadway, removed the stones and planks set over rough places, or cut down trees planted as resting places or for shade damaged the road. Even if the doer of such deeds had justice on his side, the ruler should not stand for these misdeeds, but should levy a fine and have the road repaired. If a wagon, a cart, a beast of burden, or an aged person met at a narrow spot, whoever was bearing the lightest load and that least subject to damage was to give way. It was the custom in many places to make crosses of stone or wood at crossroads, outside of consecrated places. These crosses would not protect malefactors; otherwise, murderers, thieves, and the disorderly would get off too lightly for their crimes.

Whereas in the past the Roman network starting from Lyon created traffic that ran essentially east and west, more and more in France roads came together in Paris, giving rise to north-south traffic. The roads to Santiago already showed this in the twelfth century. More precisely, two axes appeared: one, running from southwest to northeast, connected Gascony, Languedoc, and the Bordeaux region to Flanders, passing through Berry and Paris; the other, running from southeast to northwest, connected the Alpine passes to Flanders through Burgundy and Champagne. The west of the kingdom and the Massif Central were much less endowed with means of communication. Unlike the network in France, the English network developed in the final centuries of the Middle Ages as under the Roman Empire from the same kernel of roads from London.

Medieval roads seemed capable of sustaining considerable traffic. Armies and princes traveled with many carts with four wheels ringed with iron or reinforced with metal plates; four, six, or eight horses pulled such vehicles. On many important roads, an average of one thousand tons of merchandise moved each year. The major building projects of the town of Troyes used stone that came from quarries located about fifty kilometers away. Drivers of teams living in villages located halfway had to cover the distance in two days. Each cart could transport two or three tons of stones.

The end of the thirteenth century and the beginning of the fourteenth saw the completion of the development leading to the creation of major royal roads. The princes had an interest in this road policy, because they collected tolls and contributed to the economic development of their states. The network thus became dense enough to allow travel from one point to another by various routes. As for the notion of *conduit,* it tended to disappear in France insofar as all the roads of the kingdom were placed under the responsibility of the king.

The Hundred Years' War put an end to the golden age that had been recognized in the early fourteenth century. In 1359, when Edward III decided to ride from Calais to Reims and Paris, he provided for five hundred valets with shovels and axes to go before the army to level the road and cut down thorn bushes and brambles. It took some time in the second half of the fifteenth century for the road network to be reconstituted in France, with some changes due to the installation of popes in Avignon, the growth of the fairs of Geneva and then Lyon, and the fact that Paris again became the capital under Louis XI.

Europe was covered with a communication network that was more or less dense depending on the region, a network that varied throughout the Middle Ages either in the routes followed or in its appearance. Travelers following major roads could easily reach cities, but, because there were still many forests and certain roads were known only to local inhabitants, it was sometimes useful to rely on a guide. The *Miracles de saint Hubert,* which deals with the period 950–1050, recounts that Erluin, count of Givet, having lost his way in the Ardennes, finally came to a little locality called Bure. He started looking for a guide to get back on the right road; not finding a real one, he forced a herdsman, a serf of Saint-Hubert, to play that role. To get what he wanted, he had no hesitation in having the herdsman beaten. The troop came to Masbourg, six kilometers from Bure, that is, the spot passed by the Roman road from Trèves to Bavai, allowing the count easily to return to Givet.

In distant countries, the Holy Land for example, the presence of a guide turned out to be even more necessary. The *Miracles de sainte Foy de Conques,* an eleventh-century text, tells how an abbot from that establishment went to Jerusalem. In Ephesus, he met a clerk named Pierre, who became his companion. This character, who came from Puy-en-Velay and had emigrated to the east to make his fortune, knew, on land as well as at sea, routes and great roads, more modest roads, and even paths, as well as the laws, customs, and languages of the populations.

In the late Middle Ages in the West, reliance on guides had principally military motives. During the campaign of Charles VI in Gueldre in 1388, the French army moving north had to cross a zone of deserted heath, and then a region covered with early snow. For days it advanced without crossing a village, led by inhabitants of the country.

## RIVERS

A traveler would not move only on solid ground. In the course of his journey, he might encounter water in the form of rivers. He might cross them by bridge or by fording. But a river might also be used as a "road."

The river network was more or less developed depending on the country. The Greek geographer Strabo (c. 63 B.C.–19 A.D.) who claimed to have traveled throughout the Mediterranean world, marveled at the number of waterways contained in Gaul, with rivers flowing in every direction, generally in plains or through hills whose gentle slopes posed no obstacle to navigation. They were, in addition, so well distributed that it was easy to move goods from one sea to another. It is therefore not surprising that river traffic in France was dense throughout the Middle Ages.

There was an obvious complementarity between road and river, thanks to geological formations that were easy to cross. The longest of these lay between Toulouse on the Garonne and the Aude valley and allowed for easy travel between the Atlantic and the Mediterranean. This was true for goods as well as people. After following the Yonne, the Seine, and the Oise, wine from Beaune was carried on carts from Compiègne or the environs of Noyon to Péronne, and then reached England by means of the Somme, or Flanders on the Lys and the Schelde. Under Philippe le Bel in 1295, Genoese sailors, who had come to Aigues-Mortes on their way to Rouen, boarded five ships and sailed down the Loire; they then reached the Seine and arrived in the Norman city by boat.

As in the Roman period, there was significant activity on navigable rivers during the early Middle Ages, apparently without major difficulties, if we are to judge by an anecdote related by Gregory of Tours. A merchant from Trier who is in the salt trade in Metz lands near that town's bridge, commending himself, his small children, and his boat to Saint Martin. He goes to sleep on the boat. He wakes up the next morning before the gates of Trier. Emperor Charlemagne, grown old and unable to ride, traveled by boat on the Rhine, the Meuse, and the Danube and planned (preliminary work was even done on the project) a canal connecting the Rhine and Danube basins.

Let us travel for a while with Sidonius Apollinaris on his journey from Lyon to Rome. After crossing the Alps quickly and easily over a road that had been dug for him through the snow, and crossing a waterway by convenient fords or passable bridges, he continued by river.

> At Pavia, I boarded the *Mail* (the name given to this boat); it soon took me to the Po. . . . The swampy Lambro, the azure Adda, the swift Adige, and the lazy Mincio, which have their source in the mountains of Liguria and Eugania, I saw each of them flow because I went a little upstream from their confluence. Their banks are all covered with forests of oak and maple. . . . Continuing on my way, I reached Cremona whose proximity once caused much grief to Tityrus of Mantua. Then we entered the town of Brescello, but immediately left it, with just enough time for our Venetian rowers to give way to the Emilian sailors who took their place, and soon afterward, taking the right fork, we reached Ravenna.

Information on the succeeding period turns out to be scanty. But in the late eleventh century and during the first half of the twelfth, tolls on rivers, like those on land, proliferated, which indicates an expansion of traffic. In 1171, King Louis VII of France confirmed the privileges of the "water merchants," prohibiting anyone else from transporting goods between the bridges of Paris and the bridge of Mantes, unless he shared half the profits with the Parisian water merchants. Whoever violated this rule would have the transported goods confiscated. This guild of the Water Merchants of Paris, governed by a provost and aldermen, was to give rise to the municipal government of Paris.

River traffic grew considerably from the thirteenth century on, probably in conjunction with large public works carried out at the time. According to Christine de Pisan, Charles V conceived of the plan of linking the Seine and the Loire by having "the earth dug so widely and deeply and in such a clever way that the Loire river might follow its course to the Seine river and carry a ship to Paris."

It is difficult to evaluate the relative size of land and river traffic. Rivers were used primarily to transport heavy products, such as wine, grain, salt, wood, and construction materials. Individuals generally used the roads. However, a change took place in the fifteenth century, when many travelers used rivers, like Louis XI going from Lyon to Tours in 1446. Means of transportation designed especially for people were created in the late fifteenth century, and pleasure and use were sometimes combined. Charles d'Orléans liked to drift with the current, joining this pleasure with that of good food.

> Supper in the bath and dinner on a boat,
> In this world there is no better company.

## Means of Transportation

### On Foot

Walking was the simplest way of moving from place to place. It was obviously used for small distances and particularly by members of the lowest social categories, or by pilgrims and others who wished to make a journey an occasion for penance. Unlike Saint Martin and Saint George, Saint James is always represented on foot with a staff in hand. Some documents indicate that a pilgrimage had to be carried out not only on foot, but barefoot—the term could be applied to walking in open sandals. Sometimes an entire journey was accomplished in that way. A hagiographer speaking of a perpetual pilgrim indicates that he is always barefoot, that the soles of his feet are blackened, and that he cannot bear to wear any kind of shoes. In the late twelfth century, a monk with leprosy decided to go to Canterbury to ask Saint Thomas à Becket to cure him. He was set on a horse, but the horse refused to move; the monk understood that he had to walk.

A pilgrim sometimes had to give up her mount because of natural conditions. In the late fourth century, Egeria was able to scale only a part of Mount Nebo on muleback. Before Sinai, she had to dismount. Melanie found Mount Modicus covered so deeply in snow that the animals refused to go any further on such a rough road. The two women did not hesitate. The ascent of Sinai did not frighten Egeria, and yet, the difficulties were great, for the mount was in the midst of hills that had to be climbed one by one—"not," notes Egeria, "by following the contours or, as they say, snail-wise, but in a straight line and over steep trails." It was thus a good idea to set out early in the cool of morning. Egeria got up very early and reached the summit of Sinai at ten o'clock in the morning. After dismounting, Melanie walked "at such a virile pace," according to Gerontius, to whom a life of the saint is attributed, "that you have to have seen her to believe it." As she seemed exhausted, she was invited, in spite of everything, to continue her journey on muleback. But she refused and climbed the mountain on foot, to the astonishment of the caravan.

Conversely, for the pious, the use of even a modest mount constituted a refinement to which they resigned themselves only under duress. Saint Jerome says of Hilarion that, planning to reach the deep solitude of Egypt, he had a donkey brought because, worn out by fasting, he no longer had the strength to walk. He usually went on foot, and three days in a row in the desert did not frighten him.

However, what was most important was to walk at the moments of departure and arrival in order to show clearly the penitential nature of the journey. Thus a pilgrim reaching his destination would leave his horse, or even his litter if he were infirm, and finish his journey on foot. The chronicler Roger of Hoveden points out that King Henry II of England, wishing to expiate the murder of Thomas à Becket, made a pilgrimage to Canterbury. He began on horseback, but three miles from his goal he dismounted and walked the rest of the way, leaving bloody marks on the sharp stones of the road.

On Horseback

Animals were frequently used: mules, donkeys, and horses. The horse plays a great role not only in narrative sources but also in literary texts. The *chansons de geste* present it as the knight's most faithful companion and give it a name. Veillantif is Roland's horse, Renaud de Monauban's is Bayard; and Broiefort, the horse of Ogier the Dane, weeps for joy on finding his master again after seven years of separation.

Writers name horses differently depending on the role assigned to them. The palfrey is the horse of aristocrats: ladies and prelates always ride them, and nobles do so for ceremonies. The charger (*destrier*) is the battle horse; during journeys, it is led by a squire, who rides a *roncin*, a work horse normally used for plowing. The pack horse (*sommier*) is used to carry baggage.

Poetry and romances as well as the accounts of noble houses provide many descriptions that offer glimpses of the way in which horses were distinguished by using the color of their coats and particular marks. The most valued were all white or all black; then came the *baucents*, that is, of no particular color, but with a good deal of white, then the variously dappled grays. Brown bays and tawny chestnuts were less prized.

Prices provide information about this hierarchy. In 1299, the count of Artois paid 20 livres parisis for a horse that was "bay, with a star on its forehead, and with a white spot on its right rear leg." Mahaut, countess of Artois, bought horses, either directly or through brokers. For example, "a large black horse with white on the right rear leg"—a battle horse—for 230 livres tournois from a Milan merchant in 1313, and "a bay palfrey for Robert, acquired by Jacquemart, the stable master, in the presence of Madame" for 95 livres in December 1316, a palfrey probably intended to serve as a mount for her son Robert at the coronation of Philip V.

Feed for horses consisted of straw, hay, vetch, rye, and oats. If they were ill and the stable hands were unable to cure them, the blacksmith, who played the role of veterinarian, was called in.

Harnessing changed in the course of the second half of the twelfth century. The pommels of the saddle became wider, particularly the rear one, the *troussequin*, which was changed into a little back rest. The saddle rested on a rectangular rug, the cover, which, by the end of the century had grown into a covering that protected the neck, body, and legs of the animal. A piece of leather or metal protected its head. Spurs, originally made of a metallic shaft with a conical point, were later furnished with a moving rowel that was less painful for the animal.

For great nobles, saddles were often veritable works of art, made of cordovan, velvet, or other valuable material and decorated with embroidery.

The *sambue* was the ladies' saddle, on which they sat with their legs hanging on the left flank of the horse; but by the early fourteenth century, some of them are depicted with their right leg thrown over the pommel or at least folded on the front of the saddle. Mahaut d'Artois and her maidens had their *sambues*, whereas servants such as Perrinette the washerwoman rode astride on padded saddles. This way of traveling was more suited to the young than to those of a riper age. Nevertheless, despite her girth, Isabella of Bavaria, queen of France, seems still to have been riding in 1416, when a tailor supplied her with riding trousers. However, as she feared the sun that ruined the complexion and dust, she bought material to make a large hood "to put over her eyes when she rides."

Great nobles traveled with many companions. In March 1491, Louis II de la Trémoïlle, viscount of Thouars, went from Amboise to Nantes. In Amboise, there were twenty-seven or twenty-eight horses, as well as mules, a cart, and many people, including several carters and mule drivers. In Nantes, there were still twenty-eight horses, but the documents tell us that the viscount had made the journey with five horses. Thus, baggage and servants did not travel with the master and covered the distance at a slower pace.

It happened that a mount was a sign of humility. Melanie the Ancient took pride in never having traveled in a litter since she had retired from the world. Very significant on this point was her attitude when she arrived in Naples on her return from Jerusalem. Illustrious figures from Rome had come to greet her with great solemnity, with luxurious traveling carriages. To rich litters, Melanie preferred "a skinny little horse, more lowly than an ass." She judged that this modest mount was more fitting for "her old black rags." Martin of Tours accomplished his journeys around Gaul on a donkey.

Caravans crossing deserts used dromedaries. Their number appears to have varied a good deal. Hans Tucher, who went to the Holy Land in 1479, noted on September 21 that his caravan included eleven camels for the baggage, led by four Arabs, and thirteen mules for the pilgrims and their food supplies. During his second pilgrimage to the Holy Land, Felix Faber looked for

German companions in Jerusalem in order to continue the adventure, that is, to reach Sinai through the desert, to sail up the Red Sea, return to Cairo through the desert, and go down the Nile to Alexandria to meet up with the Venetian fleet. A contract was drawn up on July 22, 1483. The caravan included twenty-five camels, thirty donkeys, six donkey drivers, seven camel drivers, two Arab guides, two interpreters with a young Ethiopian slave, and eighteen pilgrims, and probably some other travelers as well, because Faber writes that it contained in all sixty men. Joos van Ghistele, who undertook a journey to the Holy Land on November 15, 1481, also decided to continue on beyond Jerusalem. After his preparations were complete, and he had hired an interpreter and good guides and procured camels, mules, and provisions, he learned that a caravan was about to leave. It included between 1,500 and 1,600 beasts of burden, such as camels, dromedaries, mules, donkeys, and horses. He waited for the caravan with his companions two miles from Cairo, so that he could travel with it as far as possible and thereby escape from the dangers threatening smaller groups.

Bertrandon de la Broquière, an advisor to Philip the Good, duke of Burgundy, reports having asked how to ride a camel. Indeed, he wanted to buy some donkeys and some camels. The latter, he writes, gave a great deal of trouble to those who were not accustomed to riding them, because they "swayed too much."

## In Carriages

Carts generally had two wheels and were used to transport baggage and people of modest status. Wagons with four wheels and luxurious appointments were the ancestors of carriages. The carriages of Mahaut, countess of Artois, seem to have had no suspension; the expression "swaying carriages" appears only in the late fourteenth century. Hence, Mahaut had to use instead a litter, resting on two long shafts between which were set two horses. In 1328, Guillaume the cartwright made one for her. It was painted and covered with tanned cloth. Robert Le Pelé supplied an armchair and a ladder for this litter, which was very expensive.

In her own household, the viscountess of Thouars employed one person for the litter, two for the wagon, two for the carts, and one for the mules, as well as a rider. She traveled in a wagon, so that she was greatly dependent on the condition of the roads. Thus, during the winter of 1493–94, she was on her way as usual in a wagon to Rochefort-sur-Loire, but the high winter waters blocked passage, so she returned on horseback and the wagon was not brought back to Thouars until April.

The litter was also known in the East. According to Ibn Battuta, born in Tangiers in 1304, a tireless traveler, it was widespread in India.

> Some days later the eunuchs from the palace . . . brought a *dula,* that is a litter in which women are carried, though men also use it for journeys, resembling a couch. The roof of the litter is made of braids of silk or cotton and on top of these there is a curved piece of wood like that on the top of parasols in our country, made of curved Indian bamboo. It is carried by eight men in two lots of four, who rest and carry in turn. These *dulas* in India are like the donkeys in Egypt, it is on them that most people go about on business; if a man has slaves of his own they carry him, and if he has no slaves he hires men to carry him. . . . The *dulas* of women are covered with silk curtains. . . .[3]

## By Boat

All kinds of boats could be found on streams and rivers. The fourth-century poet Ausonius speaks in a letter of his steward sailing on the Tarn and the Garonne "in dinghies, rowboats, small craft, smacks, and barges."

Rich landowners had luxurious ships which they sometimes used to transport their guests. Writing to his beloved Trygetius, Sidonius Apollinaris describes the boat that a Bordeaux nobleman named Leontius planned to send to the port of Langon to bring Sidonius to him.

> There awaits you a bed made of cushions, a chess board with pawns of two colors, many dice eager to bounce on the ivory sides of their cups; to keep your dangling feet from

---

3. Ibn Battuta, *The Travels of Ibn Battuta,* tr. H. A. R. Gibb (Cambridge: Hakluyt Society, 1958–1994), v. III, p. 740.

being soaked by the sloshing of the dirty water of the hold, the curved sides of the ship will be topped by a bridge of pine planks; there you will be protected from the perfidies of the winter damp by the screen of a tent cloth sloping over your head. What more could be done for your refined leisure than to surprise you by arriving when you have barely noticed the journey?

In another passage, Sidonius mentions a light, solid felucca able to carry a bed that his friend Agricola had sent him.

In the Merovingian period, the transportation of people was often carried out under less favorable conditions. Jonas of Bobbio, author of the life of Saint Amand, tells of sailing with the saint and soaking his feet in the Scarpe.

Owning a boat was often an economic necessity. The correspondence of Loup, elected abbot of Ferrières toward the end of 840, provides an example. Around 859, the abbey felt the need for a boat. When the abbot could not find one that suited him, he decided to have one built by the monastery's carpenters. He asked Abbot Odon of Corbie to give him twenty trees from the woods of Marnay and to supply him with some clever carpenters. The construction of the boat, which went on despite the Norman threat, lasted for about four months. Veritable flotillas were traveling on the Seine at the time. In 841, the army of Charles the Bald crossed the river over twenty boats at anchor at Saint-Denis. At around the same time, the merchants of Rouen were able to procure twenty-eight ships.

Thanks to the work of Jacques Bernard, we can examine the shipping on the Garonne a few centuries later. Whereas the barges of Bordeaux carried wine, the *couraux* carried wheat or woad. The boats were different in appearance and character: the Bordeaux boats had undergone change, while the up-country barges had retained certain characteristics. They had to navigate streams with stable beds and unchanging rates of flow. The average high water levels in autumn and spring as well as the less rainy winter were best for sailing on the river and its tributaries. The *couraux* made no stops, traveling even at night, with members of the crew resting in turn. Extra time was usually allotted for unforeseen risks, because the time at which ocean-going vessels were to be loaded was sometimes set in advance. Economic considerations and the characteristics of the river restricted the time periods when the *couraux* sailed, so that they made up veritable flotillas that could be broken down into flotillas from the same towns or little groups owned by a single merchant. The barges of the lower Garonne and the estuary were of various types, and even the pure type had variants. Unlike the *couraux*, they had many functions, chief among them the transportation of passengers, either from one bank to the other or up or down the river.

Nine centuries later, recalling the luxurious vessels of Sidonius Apollinaris, there are the ships of the cadi of Lahore. "He had fifteen ships with which he had come on the river of Sind, carrying his baggage train," writes Ibn Battuta,

> so I set out with him. [He] had amongst his vessels one called by the name of *ahawra*, somewhat like a *tarida* in our country, but broader and shorter. In the centre of it there was a wooden cabin to which one climbed up by steps, and on the top of this there was a place prepared for the governor to sit in. His suite sat in front of him and the mamluks stood to right and left, while the crew of about forty men rowed. Accompanying the *ahawra* were four vessels to right and left, two of which carried the governor's "honours," i.e., standards, kettledrums, trumpets, bugles and reedpipes . . . and the other two carried singers. First the drums and trumpets would be sounded and then the musicians would sing, and they kept this up alternately from early morning to the hour of the midday meal. When this moment arrived the ships came together and closed up with one another and gangways were placed from one to the other. The musicians then came on board the governor's *ahawra* and sang until he finished eating, when they had their meal and at the end of it returned to their vessel. They then set off on their journey in the manner described until nightfall. When it became dark, the camp was set up on the bank of the river, the governor disembarked and went to his tents, the repast was spread and most of the troops joined in the meal.[4]

---

4. *The Travels of Ibn Battuta*, tr. H. A. R. Gibb, v. III, pp. 600–601.

## Difficulties

Difficulties were of two orders, related either to natural conditions or to human obstacles.

### Nature

In winter, rain too often changed roads into muddy paths. Cold created ice that made horses slip. Although the cold was moderate in France, this was not true for some regions, particularly in Asia, where the temperature might fall as low as -50°C. According to Ibn Fadlan in the tenth century, the Gurgan region, west of the lower branch of the Amu Darya, was "a gate to the great cold of hell." One day after taking a Turkish bath, he noticed when he returned home that his beard was a single block of ice; he had to come close to the fire to make it melt. When he and his companions were preparing to go to the land of the Turks, the inhabitants told them to dress warmly. Each of them wore in layers a tunic, a caftan, a cloak, a felt jacket, a hood, and plain and lined underpants; they wore slippers and leather boots, with another pair of boots over them. It was thus impossible to move once they had mounted their camels. As he was about to reach central Asia, Ibn Battuta wrote:

> This was in the depth of winter, and I used to put on three fur coats and two pairs of trousers, one of them quilted, and on my feet I had woolen boots, with a pair of boots quilted with linen cloth on top of them, and on top of these again a pair of boots of . . . horse-skin lined with bear-skin. I used to perform my ablutions with hot water close to the fire, but not a drop of water fell without being frozen on the instant. When I washed my face, the water would run down my beard and freeze, then I would shake it and there would fall from it a kind of snow. The moisture that dripped from the nose would freeze on the moustache. I was unable to mount a horse because of the quantity of clothes I had on, so that my associates had to help me into the saddle.
> [W]e travelled for three nights on the river Itil and its joining waters, which were frozen over. Whenever we needed water we used to cut out pieces of ice, put the ice in a caul-

dron until it turned into water, and then use this for drinking and cooking.[5]

Similarly, some journeys became ordeals because of the heat. Some Czech noblemen traveling through the West between 1465 and 1467 suffered greatly from the scorching heat that prevailed in Biscay and Castile. "I remember that pine forest very vividly because the horses were so exhausted that two of us went through it on foot, and when we were seized by thirst because of the great heat, wherever we looked for something to drink, we could find nothing."

The desert combined heat by day and cold by night. Felix Faber recounts that his group of pilgrims left the Magareth desert shortly after midnight. The travelers then entered an extremely harsh desert and reached a region that was so cold that their feet, hands, and noses were numb and their teeth were chattering. The cold was all the more painful because until then they had been subject to great heat, and now they had to deal with extreme cold without suitable clothing. They therefore moved quickly through the region, hoping that the sun would soon rise to warm them, whereas before they had wished it to set so they could feel the cool.

There were several topographical features that posed obstacles to travel.

*Mountains.* Crossing the Alps in particular posed great difficulties. Sedulius of Liège recounts how Bishop Hartgar and his retinue crossed "the snowy fields and icy roads." This was a matter both of geography and of climate. You had to be in a hurry to confront the Alps in winter. When Arab ambassadors arrived at Ivrée in October 801, bringing with them an elephant intended for Charlemagne, they decided to wait until spring in Verceil before crossing the mountains. Returning from Rome, Raoul, a monk from Saint-Trond, found himself at the foot of the mountains on Christmas 1128. Great quantities of snow had accumulated and avalanches were frequent. On January 1, 1219, the pilgrims arrived in the village of Saint-Remy, led by guides

---

5. *The Travels of Ibn Battuta,* tr. H. A. R. Gibb, v. II, pp. 514–15.

known as *marons*. After waiting for several days, the guides proposed to go on: they would lead the way, followed by the pilgrims on foot, and then by the horses. The way would thus be leveled for the high-ranking travelers who would bring up the rear. The *marons,* their heads wrapped in felt because of the cold, wearing gloves and boots with crampons, carried long poles to estimate the depth of the snow. Another avalanche occurred, and the pass could not be crossed until good weather returned.

Mount Sinai had to be crossed on foot, because the paths were narrow and dangerous, and camels could take them only if they were carrying nothing. As for the Hindu Kush, a vast mountain range in northern Afghanistan, Ibn Battuta writes:

> Another reason for our halt was fear of the snow. For upon this road there is a mountain called Hindukush, which means "the slayer of the Indians," because the slave-boys and girls who are brought from the land of India die there in large numbers as a result of the extreme cold and the great quantity of snow. [The passage of] it extends for a whole day's march. We stayed until the warm weather had definitely set in. . . .[6]

*Rivers.* A ferry service was provided on large rivers, and bridges were built. On the Seine, Charles the Bald had wooden bridges maintained in Charenton, Paris, and Pitres. But it was a difficult task, and the men who reconstructed the Charenton bridge were promised that they would not be called on again. When bridges were out, they could be provisionally replaced by boats attached to one another. For example, the chronicler Nithard recounts that in the spring of 841, the Seine having overflowed its banks, "the fords had everywhere become impassable and the river guards had broken or sunk all the vessels. Moreover Count Gérard (of Paris) had destroyed all the bridges he had come upon. Thus the extreme difficulty of passage caused deep anxiety to those who intended to cross. . . . It was reported that merchant vessels, driven by the tide, had been carried from the mouth of the Seine as far as Rouen. . . ." Charles reached Rouen, requisitioned the boats and, with his army, crossed the river downstream from the city.

---

6. *The Travels of Ibn Battuta,* tr. H. A. R. Gibb, v. III, p. 586.

The simplest thing was to find a passable ford. If its precise location was unknown, the best solution was to call upon the local inhabitants. Froissart recounts that, three days before the battle of Crécy in 1346, King Edward III of England was vainly seeking a ford to cross the Somme downstream from Abbeville. One of his prisoners pointed out a passage that he knew very well, where he had crossed back and forth several times during that year. At some places, twelve men could cross abreast. Once the operation had succeeded, the king freed the prisoner and his companions and gave him one hundred gold *nobles* and a good work horse. Military convoys might include amphibious vehicles. In the capitulary *De Villis*, Charlemagne ordered the overseeing of the construction of vehicles called *bastarnes*. Their openings had to be covered in leather and so tightly sealed that they could cross rivers without water getting in.

In the late thirteenth century, abbeys controlling tolls stressed the expenses of maintaining bridges. Perhaps they had earlier been motivated by the hope of new profits. It has been noted that many bridges were built in the eleventh and twelfth centuries. According to Jean-Marc Bienvenu, the ones built in Anjou were almost all made of wood. In Le Mans, the Perrin bridge seems to have been of stone, but the expression "stone bridge" should not always be taken literally, because it meant only that the piers were stone. For example, in a charter of 1028, Foulque Nerra mentions a stone bridge that he had just built in Angers. But a chronicle of the next century notes that the bridge is largely made of wood. Moreover, it was ravaged by fire three times in the twelfth century, and early in the thirteenth century, King John the Landless of England deliberately burned it in his flight from Philip Augustus. Water, as well as fire, could cause damage. In 1175, floods destroyed several of the neighboring houses. Fifty years later, ice swept away the bridges of Saumur and Tours. This is why, in 1075, when Guillaume, the lord of Juvardeil, made an agreement with the monks of Saint-Nicolas who were settled on his lands, and the construction of a bridge on the Sarthe was planned, it was specified that the profits from tolls and the cost of repairs would be shared between them. The situation turned out to be more complicated when, as frequently happened, the arches of a bridge contained mills that did not belong to the owner of the bridge. How could the bridges of Cé be maintained, when the nuns of Fontevraud received the tolls and the monks of Saint-Aubin in Angers owned four mills and fishing grounds under four of the bridge's arches? It was not until 1230—the bridges and their tolls had been given to the order of Fontevraud more than a century earlier—that the question was settled. The monks would have to maintain the four arches at their expense. If they collapsed, they would have nine weeks to rebuild them; thereafter they would pay the abbess 20 sous for each day's delay. All the possibilities were considered: partially damaged arches; impossibility of carrying out repairs because of the freezing of the Loire; total destruction of the bridge. Finally, maintenance of the bridge in good condition must have turned out to be a heavy burden, because Abbess Marguerite de Pocé willingly gave up her rights to Count Charles of Anjou in 1293: "Such thing was very costly, harmful, and perilous for us and our church, that is, maintaining this bridge that spans the entire Loire."

In the East, another natural obstacle awaited travelers, the desert. In 1470–71, Anselme Adorno made a journey to the Holy Land, an account of which was compiled soon thereafter by his son Jean Adorno. A small caravan containing seven men led by Anselme left Bruges on February 19, 1470. After a short stay in Pavia where Jean, who was a student in the city, joined his father, the pilgrims went to Rome. Then five of them reached Genoa where they embarked on May 7. They were at Mount Sinai on August 24.

*L'Itinéraire d'Anselme Adorno* indicates the precautions to be taken in order to cross deserts.

> Deserts are dry, arid, sandy, lacking in water, uncultivated, almost everywhere uninhabited; only savage Arabs sometimes live there in a few scattered spots near springs. Thus it is necessary for anyone who is going to traverse these regions who wants to survive to take as thorough and careful precautions as possible, not only against hunger but also against the thieving and rebellious Arabs who despoil men in deserts. First and above all, you have to provide yourself with a loyal and sensible intermediary or interpreter to accompany the pilgrims, take faithful care of all their affairs, defend and guide them, as the good shepherd leads his sheep. . . . In the second place, it is important that you buy the food needed in the desert. . . . It is, moreover, indis-

pensable to have skins in which to keep and carry fresh water. . . . In the third place, to carry goods and people, you have to rent animals with *moucres*, leaders and keepers of these animals. I would not advise you to take horses or donkeys, but camels who eat little and can walk for three or four days without drinking. They are, in addition, strong animals that carry large burdens.

Despite all these precautions, crossing the desert is not a pleasure jaunt:

The days are scorching, and the nights are correspondingly cold and humid because of the dew falling from the sky. It happened several times that we found ourselves soaked in the morning as though rain had fallen on us all night long. Another danger of the desert is sand. Like the sea, whose waves and swells move from one place to another, in certain parts of the desert, the sands are carried from place to place by the wind and grow, like the waves of the sea, to form sandy mountains and hills, under which there is a great risk of being smothered. But this peril is especially great in times of winter storms. There is no more appropriate and propitious time to traverse in safety these deserted expanses and to avoid excessive heat and shifting sand than the months of August and September.

Central Asia held the same difficulties in store. "From this place we went on for thirty days by forced marches," writes Ibn Battuta,

halting only for two hours each day, one in the forenoon and the other at sunset. . . . Everybody eats and sleeps in his wagon while it is actually on the move, and I had in my wagon three slavegirls. It is the custom of travellers in this wilderness to use the utmost speed, because of the scarcity of herbage. Of the camels that cross it the majority perish and the remainder are of no use except a year later, after they are fattened up. The water in this desert is at certain known waterpoints, separated by two or three days' march, and is rainwater [in surface pools] and shallow wells under the sand.[7]

---

7. *The Travels of Ibn Battuta*, tr. H. A. R. Gibb, v. III, pp. 539–41.

Marco Polo says of the Gobi desert:

This desert is reported to be so long that it would take a year to go from end to end; and at the narrowest point it takes a month to cross it. It consists entirely of mountains and sand and valleys. There is nothing at all to eat.[8]

Caravans had to stop during the heat of the sun. During the hottest times, the journey even went on at night. In the late twelfth century, this is how Ibn Jubayr made the two-day trip from Ra's al-'Ayn (a town now on the border between Syria and Turkey) and Harrân:

At sunset on Saturday, June 12, we resumed our journey to benefit from the dark and cool of night, thus avoiding the blistering heat of day. . . . We walked on into the morning, then we stopped in the desert near a well to rest a little. . . . We traveled until morning to arrive in the town of Harrân at sunrise on Monday, June 18.

Sandstorms were capable of burying caravans. Ibn Battuta recounts that in a large desert of central Asia that would take two weeks to cross, a "poisonous" and mortal wind blows that causes such putrefaction that when a man dies there his limbs fall off his body. In 1497, Arnold von Harff mentions the death of Arabs, camels, and two traveling companions in three days of extremely difficult travel in the desert, adding that he saw in the sand fifty corpses half eaten by birds of prey or other animals.

Some regions were unhealthy, such as southern Italy. The Tuscan swamp also had a bad reputation. Sidonius Apollinaris mentions the "poisonous airs" breathed in that "pestilential region." Sudden changes in temperature weakened the organism and made it less resistant. Fever and unquenchable thirst ensued, and Sidonius fell victim to these symptoms. "Fever and thirst consumed my body," he writes. "To assuage them, I promised to their ferocity not only the delicious water of fountains or hidden springs but also all the water that was near or

---

8. Marco Polo, *The Travels*, tr. Ronald Latham (London: Penguin Books, 1958), 84.

might come into view. . . . But it did no good." Ravenna as well left him with a very bad memory, so that he was unable to understand how his friend Candidianus, who had just moved there, could like it. What charms could there be in a city "where the cousins of the Po shatter your ears," in "that fetid marsh of stagnant water, where patients walk the streets while their doctors are confined to bed, where the baths are icy and the houses roasting, where the living die of thirst"?

## Men

Just as natural conditions might interfere with travel, men did not always make it easy either. Taxes and particularly insecurity were common experiences.

In our day, customs duties are on the wane. In the Middle Ages, on the contrary, it was difficult to travel without paying duties, particularly if you were transporting merchandise. The formulary of Marculfe provides a negative example. It set forth an exemption from indirect taxes on transport. The king allowed a church or a monastery to pay no tax for a fixed number of carts carrying products intended for lighting. This was valid in all places and in all ports.

> We decide by the present precept and We order that it remain in perpetuity that neither you, nor your dependents, nor your successors request or demand a duty for so many carts belonging to this bishop . . . wherever in Our kingdom duties are demanded, whether they be taxes on transport by boat or by cart, on wheels, for crossing a bridge, for the dust raised, or for the grass consumed, or any other tax that Our revenue service usually collects.

Collected in principle to cover the costs of the protection and maintenance of roads, from the eleventh century to the thirteenth, tolls made up one of the principal sources of revenue for the nobility in a changing economy. Landri le Gros acknowledged that he had stopped merchants from Langres passing through his lands and had seized their goods. It took all the persuasive force of the bishop of Langres and the abbot of Cluny to bring him to return a part of his booty. In order to cross his domain in complete safety thereafter, merchants agreed to pay him a certain sum. Landri then decided to impose on travelers through his lands, for purposes of trade or pilgrimage, a charge called a toll. The lords of Cluny, aware that this was a novelty, asked him to give up this charge. They purchased it by giving him 300 sous. To attempt to remedy abuses, canon XXII of the Lateran Council of 1179 threatened to excommunicate anyone who created new tolls or increased the size of old ones without the authorization of kings and princes.

Because the Church secured exemptions, taxes fell princi-pally on merchants. In Anjou, duties most of the time had to be paid in cash and depended on the mode of transport of goods: porters, beasts of burden, or vehicles. For example, in Saumur, a merchant carrying his own goods paid nothing; but if he trav-eled with a porter, the latter was required to pay "as a beast of burden." When the tax was on goods, the charge varied accord-ing to quantity, or was calculated by weight or size. Fresh fish—herring, cuttlefish, eels—were taxed per thousand or hundred. Charges were very variable. A Jew paid 12 deniers at the Ponts-de-Cé but only 1 denier in Saumur, and then only if he was transporting goods.

The temptation to cheat was obviously great. A letter of remission from 1460 recounts that Louis Blanchart was engaged by the monks of the abbey of Moreilles to collect duties on the route that merchants from Poitou took to go to La Rochelle. One day when he was at the port to carry out his duties, he saw in the distance five or six individuals coming from that town with their mounts loaded with iron and other merchandise going toward the port of Moreilles. When they were about an eighth of a mile away, he saw them take an uncustomary route skirting the port. He came up to them and told them that there was no road at that spot "and that to traverse and pass through there would be to destroy and demolish the said canal, which is built and maintained to receive the water that is abundant there because it is a swampy country." The discussion degen-erated into a brawl.

The study of tolls helps us to imagine the bustle on the roads, with carts, troops, riders carrying food on their saddles, porters, not to mention mere travelers. Collection of tolls was sometimes carried out with excessive zeal. Ibn Battuta notes that in India, at the spot where the road reached the Ravi, a tributary of the Indus, both travelers and baggage were carefully searched. The custom was to collect one quarter of the goods imported by traders. The narrator, with a somewhat inflated view of himself, found the searching of his baggage intolerable. "I was disgusted that they stuck their noses into it!" Luckily, a superior officer arrived and ordered that he be left alone. Not many merchants would pay tolls—that would be included in the cost of goods—unless they could travel in peace. Nobles who wanted to collect duties therefore had to take care of that.

*Safety.* Deep forests, the slow pace of travel, and often ineffective policing explain the fear that led people to travel together.

The barbarians invaded the West in the fifth century. Travelers were exposed to many troubles and even to grave dangers. Sidonius Apollinaris praises Constantius, bishop of Lyon, for having, despite his age and infirmity,

> broken down all the obstacles and all the barriers, overcome all the hindrances in the way of his journey: the length of the road, the shortness of the days, the abundance of snow, the dearth of forage, the solitude of the countryside, uncomfortable inns, roads that had become impassable because of water or ice, piles of stone blocking the way, dangerous frozen rivers, harsh and steep hills, valleys dotted with rock slides.

What a relief when "the perfidious nation having withdrawn behind its borders, there are no more obstacles to the safety of travelers."

Brigands remained fearsome throughout the Middle Ages. In the Merovingian era, Gregory of Tours provides many examples of travelers despoiled or worse, assassinated, even when precautions were taken. King Chilperic of Neustria entrusted his daughter Rigonthe to the ambassadors of the Goths, whose king she was to marry. He gave her treasures, to which her mother Frédégonde added an immense quantity of gold. The young woman set out with a large retinue, and this is what happened:

> After leaving Paris, she had tents set up eight miles from the city. Fifty men rode up in the night and seized one hundred of the best horses and as many golden bits, as well as two great bowls. . . . Then, because the king suspected that his brother and his nephew wanted to set ambushes for the

47

young woman during the journey, he ordered her to continue on her way under a troop's escort.

Rigonthe reached Toulouse. Realizing that she was close to the territory of the Goths, she slowed the pace. Her companions asked her to stop for, tired by the journey, their clothes were dirty and their shoes tattered; the horses' harnesses and the fittings of the carriages carried on carts were also dilapidated. It was fitting to set things to rights so that she could present herself to her fiancé in elegant dress. While they were thus delayed, word of the death of Chilperic reached the ears of Duke Didier. "Assembling around him very vigorous men, he entered the city of Toulouse and, having discovered treasures, he removed them from the queen's control and placed them in a house under seal and guarded by vigorous men."

Travelers on water, like those on the roads, were at the mercy of brigands. In 861, the Normans pursued and captured merchants trying to escape from them by sailing up the Seine. In the same year, Loup, the abbot of Ferrières, expressed his worry to a correspondent about the dangers he and his men might encounter on the Seine and the Oise.

Peace did not put an end to banditry. In 1446, Vincent Gautereau stopped Christine Bretin from Fontenay-le-Comte on the main highway as she was coming back from Machecoul where she had gone to consult a doctor; he extorted a promise of marriage from her by using force and threats. While he was going through some woods, seeing a man and woman pursuing him, "he went to meet them, drew his sword, and told them that if they did not go away, he would grow angry." They obviously took flight.

In distant countries, the situation turned out to be even more delicate. In Alexandria, as soon as the emir learned that Anselme Adorno and his companions had arrived, he summoned them and demanded a large sum of money to provide them with a safe-conduct. They managed to leave the city in the company of a mameluke and an interpreter. Also traveling with them were four mamelukes on horseback, armed with bows and arrows, who were supposed to see to their safety as far as the Nile, because of Arabs whose presence in the vicinity of Alexandria had been noted. Indeed, despite the expeditions launched against them by the mameluke sultans, the Bedouin nomad tribes persisted in their banditry as far as the delta, particularly during periods of interregnum. When Adorno visited the country, one of those troubled periods had just ended. In order to travel in greater safety, the little troop rode all night until noon the next day over sandy terrain, usually by the seashore. "The mamelukes went along this shore with some fearfulness, because they were afraid of sea pirates, but we had to go this way, which was the best, because the other road was occupied by Arabs." The travelers thus threaded their way between Scylla and Charybdis. Catalan and Italian corsairs anchored very near the coast, where they hid in ambush to attack caravans.

At Fuwwah, the sailors attached ropes to posts on the shore in order to anchor the boat. Returning from a walk, the pilgrims saw their sailors chased off by others, who then took them onto a large boat—the sultan had given these sailors the privilege of loading their ships before all others.

> On this boat there were some mamelukes who that night took by force our fine malmsey wine. . . . But, to tell the truth, the change of ship, which at first had alarmed and annoyed us, turned out in the end to be very useful, and it saved our lives. In fact, Arabs tried to seize our great ship. We barely escaped from their savage attack on that ship; what would we have done on the original little vessel? We would all have been captured, or killed, or sent into slavery.

In Cairo, the travelers went to see the sultan's representative, who received them hospitably: "He was always delighted by the arrival of people that he thought he could not only swindle but completely devour." Pleasantly surprised, Adorno notes, "We suffered fewer insults and blows in Cairo than elsewhere."

A good interpreter was needed to cross the desert, but there were few trustworthy interpreters and even fewer good ones. The Arab who was supposed to protect the little group was a clever man: "He had white hair and had been aged not only by time but by deceit and perfidy, for every day of his life he had pillaged and robbed travelers in the desert. He knew all the scoundrels and bandits and how to avoid their roads and camps." This Arab belonged to a tribe whose members robbed travelers, but when they saw one of their own with a group, they spared them out of respect for him. So it was that, every evening, he was in the habit of calling out the names and nicknames of all the bandits of all the families to notify them of his presence.

On August 19, the little troop set out in the company of a caravan.

> So we rode without fear of highway bandits, but we were afraid of the Moors, the Arabs, and the men at arms in the caravan, who subjected us to many troubles. They constantly importuned us with their demands. In the course of that day, we encountered many Arabs who would probably have robbed us if they had found us alone. They came close to starting a battle with the Moors in our caravan.

The travelers finally reached Mount Sinai, where there was a monastery. While they were resting, a band of Arabs approached several times to threaten them and demand payment of customs duties; otherwise, they would be unable to cross the Sinai safe and sound and to visit the Holy Places.

Despite the opinion of the *moucres,* who advised them to delay their departure for a few days, because they claimed to have seen recent traces of at least twenty bandits, the pilgrims left Mount Sinai on August 30, very early in the morning. The first five days, they traveled through hilly and stony deserts, frequently noticing traces of bandits, but meeting no one, except on the third day, when they came across an Arab, who was apparently exhausted, but had in reality come to reconnoiter the size of the group. "So, in order to escape from these Arabs, we immediately abandoned the direct route and went off on foot at an angle to cross a very high mountain." But after this ascent, the guide told Adorno that he no longer wanted to continue the journey for the agreed amount. He went off with his baggage.

> Considering his past as a scoundrel and a bandit, we feared that he would, or already had, set traps for us. Besides, our *moucres* told us that, without the guide, they could not find the direct route that we had left under his leadership to flee the bandits. Driven by necessity, we reached a new agreement with him. Trickery of this kind was constant, with the purpose of lightening our purses.

After many terrors, and several meetings on the road with Moors who threatened them and struck them with their bows, they finally reached Jerusalem.

It was the duty of the king, and also in his interest, to ensure the safety of anyone who traveled through his kingdom. The safe-conduct played an important role insofar as it encouraged travel and trade by providing protection to an individual or a group of people crossing through a region or heading for a particular place. It might be a simple escort, effective because of its armed force, an escort provided for an official figure, or quite simply a document prohibiting harm to the bearer. According to Gregory of Tours, in 587, when Bishop Egidius of Reims was suspected of the crime of lèse-majesté, he came with great gifts to King Childebert to beg for forgiveness, after having secured a promise under oath that no harm would come to him during his journey. In the same period, Gondovald, a usurper, sent two ambassadors to King Gontran with consecrated rods following the Frankish ritual, so that no one would harm them and so that they might return with an answer to their message.

In 779, Charlemagne prohibited harm to anyone traveling in his kingdom, wherever he might go. In a celebrated document of 828, Emperor Louis the Pious took measures to see to it that traveling merchants could come and go without fear.

> We decree and order that neither you, nor your dependents, nor your successors, nor your traveling *missi* dare to trouble the said loyal subjects on any legally foreseen occasion, whatever it may be, and that you neither denounce them nor take or damage unjustly any of their goods, nor seize their ships, by claiming to do so for our service, nor that you put pressure on them or try to collect the *hériban* or demand payments of any other kind.

Under the Carolingians, it was the monarch who had the right to ensure the safety of travelers. His solicitude was particularly extended to ambassadors, merchants, and pilgrims. Most of the time, measures of protection were provided for categories of person.

In the course of the second half of the ninth century and during the following century, troubles were frequent because of the weakness of monarchs, internal struggles, and invasions, particularly by the Normans.

It was not until more solid authority was reestablished, although it was only regional, that protection of travelers once again became the order of the day. The safe-conduct then took on a more specific form. It no longer protected a general category, but the inhabitants or merchants of a town, the monks of a monastery, or people going to a specified fair. Nobles became aware of the importance of trade and tried to attract merchants to their domains, granting commercial privileges and guaranteeing the safety of people and property. Their protection was not free. Safety on the roads was thus of just as much interest to princes as to merchants.

Albert of Hapsburg declared in 1305:

> In consideration of the loyal, pleasing, and honorable services they have rendered and will render to us and to the Empire, both for the repair of roads and for the safety and trustworthy armed protection of travelers, and especially merchants, by our royal authority, we have granted as a fief to the said Dukes Otto, Ludwig, and Heinrich and to their heirs, the customs duties at Lueg, Töll, and Bolzano, that they will hold, receive, and collect as follows. . . . We also wish, and the aforementioned dukes have solemnly promised that they will provide, within the borders of their rule noted below, for the defense and protection of roads and paths, so that all may pass without danger and unharmed . . . protection to which the aforementioned dukes are held as much by their rule as by the said customs duties. We have in addition decreed and prescribed in favor of the ecclesiastical and secular princes and prelates of churches that they will not pay, as such duties, any charge, toll, or imposition on the wine coming from their own vineyards and intended for their households.

When the count of Forez created the fairs of Montbrison in 1308, after a lengthy exposition of the fees that the merchants had to pay, he declared:

> We will protect all the merchants, their associates, and their goods, who come to the said fairs, with safeguards and safe-conducts, in good faith, going, coming, and in place; and the goods that they lose on our land and under our juris-

diction, by violence or rapine, we will replace with our own goods; and what they lose outside our land and our jurisdiction we will do everything possible to help them recover, following the custom of the fairs of Champagne.

The fairs of Champagne were essential meeting places in the thirteenth century, where trade was carried on by the merchants of the two major economic regions of the age, Flanders and Italy.

It remains to find out whether safe-conducts always turned out to be effective. In the feudal period, some nobles turned into bandits, making their castles into staging posts for attacks on travelers. In 1288, Duke Jean I of Brabant, who wanted to ensure freedom and safety on the road between Bruges and Cologne, laid siege to the castle of Worringen, because the archbishop of Cologne had made it a refuge for bandits who pillaged merchants. When he was informed, the archbishop assembled a large army, but had to abandon the battlefield. The duke finally seized the castle and destroyed it, thus making traffic on the royal road free and safe.

Reprisals allowed princes to exercise pressure on the authorities responsible for actions taken against their subjects or associates. In 1342, King Edward III of England ordered the seizure of goods in his kingdom belonging to inhabitants of Cologne, Lorraine, and Liège, because one of his subjects had been imprisoned in the Cologne region. In the early fourteenth century, inhabitants of Malines were arrested at the fairs of Champagne and Brie because of the debts of the duke of Brabant. And yet, the king of France had promised them that they would have no trouble for that reason.

Safety was, however, not really certain. In the course of the weeks preceding the cold-weather fair of Chalon-sur-Saône in 1363, a company of Bretons established in La-Roche-de-Nolay prevented merchants from reaching the fair. During the entire fair, the Bretons remained a threat on the outskirts of the town, putting the merchants "in great fear." The situation did not improve during the course of the summer. It was probably before the warm-weather fair that Jean de Chauffour captured some merchants near Dijon. In the month of September, cloth sellers stuck in Troyes needed an escort to go to Chalon, and the opening of the fair was once again delayed for two weeks. Armed groups in the area prevented the collection of taxes.

It was a good time for highway robbers. Mérigot Marchès, who was executed for his countless misdeeds, expressed his memories and regrets in these terms:

> There is no time, diversion, gold, silver, or glory in this world that can compare to men at arms battling as we have done in the past. How delighted we were when we rode off on adventures, and we might find in the fields a rich abbot or a rich prior or a rich merchant or a string of mules from Montpellier, Narbonne, Limoux, Fanjeaux, Béziers, Carcassonne, or Toulouse, loaded with cloth of gold or silk, from Brussels or Montivilliers, and skins coming from the fairs of Lendit or elsewhere, or spices coming from Damascus or Alexandria! Everything was ours, or ransomed at our will. Every day we had new money. . . . And when we rode, the whole country trembled before us; everything was ours, going and coming.

No matter. Countless travelers went on the roads, and they went by sea.

# by sea

And your sea is so deep
That it is rightly to be feared.
—RUTEBEUF

EAR

For a land civilization like that of the Middle Ages, the sea could
only provoke fear, anxiety, and repulsion. Of course, the men of
the age were acquainted with water through river navigation,
but on rivers they could see the banks, *terra firma*. Once they
had left the continent, there was nothing solid to hold onto. The
traveler saw an enormous liquid expanse. The imagination and
reality joined to make the sea an object of fear.

Fiction

Gervaise of Tilbury, who composed *The Book of Marvels* around
1210 for Emperor Otto IV of Brunswick, later defeated at Bou-
vines, writes that in the English sea, sirens sit on rocks; they
have women's heads and blond hair, and down to the navel they
have female forms; the rest is in the shape of a fish. "They in-
sinuate themselves into the hearts of passing sailors with their
very sweet song whose delicacy deliciously tickles their ears;

completely enchanted, they neglect their duty and, for lack of attention, are often drowned."

Legends of this kind about the treacherous sea circulated in the Middle Ages, and medieval romances often pictured it raging. At the last minute, a storm separates Iseut from Tristan:

> Everyone was gay and the sailing pleasant. Suddenly, a wind from the south assails them and strikes the sail head on. It makes the whole ship keel over.
> The sailors run to windward and turn the sail. Against all expectation, they are pushed back. The wind strengthens and raises the waves. The sea rumbles to its depths. The sky clouds, the air thickens, the waves swell, the sea darkens. It rains and hails, the gale increases. Bowlines and cables snap. The sailors take down the sail and the ship drifts off tossed by wind and waves. They had just put their launch to sea for they had almost reached port, but unfortunately they forgot it; a wave broke it in pieces. Moreover, they suffered so much damage and the storm became so violent that even the most experienced sailors could not keep their footing. All were crying and all lamenting. Fear drove them to show great terror.

Iseut fears drowning and thus being separated forever from Tristan. Finally after five days of storm, good weather returns:

> Heat rises and the wind falls so that they can go no further. The sea is calm and flat. The ship goes neither one way nor another, except where the waves lead it and they no longer have their launch. And now, great is their anguish.

The monotony of images in literary works is striking. To characterize the sea in fury, writers use the same expressions. A storm is a literary device that makes it possible to change the course of events. The separation of Iseut and her lover authorizes the poet to set down the heroine's songs. In Chrétien de Troyes, thanks to a storm, William of England and his wife are reunited after many adventures.

"Is there a more banal theme," writes Gaston Bachelard in *L'Eau et les Rêves,* than the anger of the Ocean? A calm sea is taken with sudden anger. It rumbles and roars. It carries all the metaphors of fury, all the animal symbols of furor and rage. . . . The number of psychological states to be projected is much larger in anger than in love. The metaphors of the cheerful and benevolent sea are thus less numerous than those of the bad sea. . . . Violent water is one of the earliest schemata for universal anger. Hence, there is no epic without a storm scene.

A literary *topos*, to be sure, but the sea that, through its movements, contrasts with ideal stability is at the forefront when it comes to the end of the world. A fourteenth-century preacher, author of a collection of sermons, reports under the title *Sleep in peace* that when the first trumpet sounds the highest mountains will be submerged, at the second trumpet ships and thieving merchants will be destroyed, at the third the sea will swallow one third of humankind. The sea, dispenser of justice, punishes sinners. As soon as Huon de Bordeaux and Esclarmonde have fallen into one another's arms, a terrible storm bursts; the two guilty ones, hanging onto a plank, wander in the water, before landing on a desert island.

Michel Mollat, however, has noted a certain evolution, with repulsion dominating fear, the fear of certain seasickness prevailing over the terror of an uncertain shipwreck. Even further, the literary theme of the sea became a subject for amusement. Mystery plays used ships; carnival carts had the shape of galleys in 1382 in Salins. Eustache Deschamps imagined a dialogue between earth and sea in which the sea shows its usefulness.

A Source of Evils

The imagination was moreover reinforced by reality. In the Middle Ages in the West many evils arrived by sea. There were men such as the Normans who came from the North on their ships. "The sea," writes Abbot Hariulf of Saint-Riquier, in a rather turgid style,

> brings no end to its desolations. It constantly terrifies the inhabitants of the earth by some unforeseen catastrophe. In our time, it vomits on the shores the monsters fed by its

fish. No doubt it is obeying the laws of nature when it devours living beings and swallows them in impetuous tor-
rents. But the idea we had developed of its barbarity was
greatly exceeded when, instead of providing its usual benefi-
cent gifts, it brought us horrible assassins; when the delicious
food we gather on its shores was followed by the messengers
of death, bringing with them hunger with a gaunt and livid
face. Who has not seen the cruel hordes of Danes covering
afar the plains of the sea with their ships? These barbarians,
in the midst of their high masts, represent for us wild beasts
in a forest.[9]

These invasions produced an exodus of populations. The Norman poet Wace (twelfth century) declares in the *Roman de Brut*
that no one dares live near the coasts because of pirates and buccaneers.

The sea also brought epidemics. Gregory of Tours recounts
how a ship and its cargo were the origin of the inguinal plague
that ravaged Marseille in particular around 587:

A ship coming from Spain, with its usual cargo, had anchored in the port of that city, unfortunately bringing with
it the germ of that sickness. Many inhabitants bought various goods from the ship; a house with eight people was
quickly emptied, because all the inhabitants had died of the
contagion. This fierce epidemic did not spread immediately
to all houses, but after pausing for a certain time, it reignited
like a flame in the midst of a haystack and set the whole city
ablaze with the fire of disease.

The black plague had the same origin. Genoese coming from the
Black Sea brought the terrible disease to Messina in September 1347.

Storms

The dangers created directly by the sea were in the minds of all
sailors. Toward 700, when Willibrod wanted to bring thirty young

---

9. Text quoted by Michel Mollat.

catechumens from Denmark to Frisia, he baptized them before leaving, contrary to the custom of the time, for he feared that they would have to endure "the dangers of such a long voyage" and that they might risk eternal damnation. And in fact, travel narratives abound in terrifying events, particularly about the Mediterranean.

In 1254, when Saint Louis was returning to France with the queen, Joinville, and the survivors of the Seventh Crusade, the travelers had to confront a violent storm off the coast of Cyprus. There was a first incident, in the end without serious consequences: the ship struck a sand bank, which allowed it to avoid the rocks covered by the sea. The master mariners then advised the king to leave the ship for another.

> We give you this advice, for we are told that the planks of your ship are all coming loose. This is why we fear that, if it reaches open sea, it will not withstand the blows of the waves and will fall to pieces. This is what happened to one of the ships when you came from France. . . . All who were on it perished, except one woman and her child who escaped on a piece of the ship.

The king refused, not wishing to abandon the other passengers, who would be obliged to remain in Cyprus, perhaps forever. Joinville also mentions the case of a very bold knight who had conducted himself very well in the Holy Land but who did not dare to stay with them for fear of drowning. It took him a year and a half to rejoin the king despite his rank and his wealth. All danger, however, was not removed.

> From this peril, from which God saved us, we fell into another, for the wind that had blown us to Cyprus . . . grew very strong and very horrible; it drove us with force on the island. The sailors dropped their anchor against the wind, but to stop the ship they had to lower five of them. They had to knock down the walls of the king's room, where no one dared stay for fear of being blown overboard by the wind.

In 1270, on the way back from the crusade to Tunis where Saint Louis died, there was a terrible storm that so struck contemporaries that many chronicles mention it. With hostilities at an end, the new king Philip of France left on Thursday November 20 and without difficulty reached Trapani, a port situated at the western extremity of Sicily on Friday at around three in the afternoon. The galley of Charles of Anjou, king of Sicily had arrived the preceding midnight. "But," reports Pierre de Condé, the king's clerk, in a letter dated January 30, 1271,

> God, who had granted a fortunate crossing, allowed on Saturday night for the sea to be troubled by such a violent wind that on Sunday morning it was very difficult to get on or off the vessels; and, throughout the day, the storm so increased that it became absolutely impossible for those who remained on board to disembark. How can we forget! What a memory! All this same Sunday night and all Monday, day and night, the storm raged at sea with such violence that the sailors swore they had never seen its like. The masts were broken, the anchors snapped, even the largest vessels swallowed like stones in the depths of the sea. And by the way, it is not so much their loss nor the loss of everything that they contained that should be deplored, but the disappearance of so many people, noble or not, men and women, young and old, that witnesses of this disaster estimate at about four thousand. Even a great number of those who managed to escape from this disaster alive died shortly thereafter from sorrow and anguish. In the vessel of the bishop of Langres alone nearly a thousand people were lost, I have been told, and this is likely enough, for the vessel was large and very few managed to get off. . . .
>
> What more can be said? In this storm were lost eighteen large, strong, and new vessels, with many people and countless things, not to mention the smaller boats about which I say nothing.

Pierre de Condé describes the disaster only in part, for the rest of the army shared an equally terrible fate. When they reached open sea, the sailors saw the sky darken. Their efforts to resist the storm turned out to be futile. The winds broke the masts and the rigging and shattered the rudders. "They made the vessels fly so high that they seemed to be raising them to the clouds, and then brought them so low that they seemed to want to plunge them into the abyss." Water poured into the ships from every direction; passengers were drowned. These vessels then encountered the ones that had remained empty at Trapani and that the storm had driven out of the port.

> Among them was one named *Montjoie* that had been specially made for the king of France, with very strong seals and very fine appearance, nobler than all the others, large and marvelous and strong: the ropes were broken, the anchors torn off; it began to run on the sea like an enraged savage beast charging the others; so it ran straight on the vessels and struck them with such great violence that it made them sink into the sea; it ran from side to side and back and forth, as though devils were steering it.

Once calm had returned, the port of Trapani presented a lamentable spectacle, encumbered with ship debris, and corpses of men and horses.

Two centuries later, Jean Adorno stressed "the dangers of the waves, countless especially in winter. Storms are violent beyond measure, the winds of great bitterness, rain and bad weather frequent; the nights, almost always dark, are extremely long, which makes it necessary to go out on the open sea to avoid striking any submerged land hidden from the navigators."

The other seas turned out to be just as dangerous.

One event that marked contemporaries was the shipwreck in 1120 of *Blanche Nef,* whose frightening story was told by Orderic Vital and later by Wace. After subduing the Norman barons, Henry I wished to return to his kingdom of England and, to do so, decided to embark at Barfleur. He arrived in port along with his two sons, including the heir William, and a large retinue. His usual ship was there, but a certain Thomas proposed to take him, following the example of his father who had transported William the Conqueror. Henry refused, but accepted the proposition for his sons, his nieces, and their companions, who came from the best Norman families.

The two vessels set out. The ship carrying the king quickly took the lead. It headed northeast in order to be able to quickly avoid any shoals. Thomas decided to take the short way, parallel to the land, straight north, in order to cover a shorter distance and to take advantage of a stronger current. He knew the rocks.

Did the heavy vessel refuse to obey the rudder? Did the darkness make it hard to judge distances? Or else had the pilot had too much good cheer? In any event, *Blanche Nef* ripped open its hull on the rock of Quillebeuf. The lifeboat was put to sea, but so many people threw themselves into it that it sank. Only a butcher from Rouen, hanging onto a floating spar, was able to reach land. And Wace concluded: "Never again did King Henry smile."

*The Atlantic.* After reaching America, Christopher Columbus was returning to Europe. On February 14, 1493, a storm broke off the Azores.

> That night, the wind stiffened; the waves were terrible, crashing into one another; they came abeam, blocking the movement of the ship, which could neither go forward nor get out of the waves that crashed against it. . . . After sunrise, as the wind had become more violent and the sea more terrible by the beam, he [the admiral] had set only the main sail, and that very loosely, so that the ship could get out of the waves coming by the beam, and so that they would not send it to the bottom.

On the evening of March 3, there was a burst of wind that tore all the sails. The *Niña* had to move forward "with only masts and rigging, because of the strong storm wind and the sea that attacked them from both sides." Not far from Lisbon, during the night of March 3–4, "they met with a terrible storm, to the point that they thought they were lost because of the waves coming from both sides and the winds that were so violent that they seemed to raise the caravel into the air, and because of the rain and lightning falling everywhere." The inhabitants of Cascais, a town located at the mouth of the Tagus, were astonished to see the sailors safe and sound. In Rastelo, the port of Lisbon, Columbus learned from sailors that twenty-five ships had been lost in Flanders and that others had been unable to leave port for four months.

In sum, nature was the origin of a first category of dangers, either when a strong wind and foul weather unleashed a storm capable of sweeping away passengers and dashing a ship against the coast, or because lack of wind immobilized the ship placing the passengers at risk of hunger and thirst or attack by pirates. Maritime contracts in the late Middle Ages allude to envious Fortune that symbolizes the inconstancy of the wind, as well as to God "who ordains, and we arrange." Particularly when voyages had no intermediate stops, charters made exceptions for "fortune," "misfortune," or "rough seas."

Pirates

Passengers and sailors also lived in fear of pirates. These pirates might take on an inoffensive appearance, because they knew how to disguise themselves. Sidonius Apollinaris thought it necessary to give wise advice to the captain of a ship engaged in pursuing pirates on the Atlantic coast:

> As many oarsman as you see among them you should count as so many corsairs; for they all organize, commit, teach, and learn banditry. So I have good reason to warn you to take great care. The pirate is the fiercest of all enemies. He attacks unexpectedly; he escapes when you think you have caught him; he has contempt for those who expect him; he slays those who do not. If he pursues, he catches you quickly; if he flees, he escapes.

Nothing bothered these bandits, neither storm nor shipwreck. Even more frightful, they had the habit of "putting one tenth of their captives to death with horrible tortures." According to Saint Jerome, sailors should expect surprises of every kind. "If the wind is too violent, the storm is to be feared; if it hardly blows and barely wrinkles the surface of the water, the traveler is threatened by an attack of pirates. In sum, carried on a fragile boat, he passes his time in fearing or going through the sad experience of danger."

Throughout the Middle Ages, travelers by sea were the prey of attacks by buccaneers. Historians have discussed at length the extent to which Muslims hindered Mediterranean commerce in the Carolingian period. There was chronic piracy from the ninth century on, which turned into a veritable institution with the expansion of Italian and Catalan fleets. Political authorities, in the name of their superior interests, could declare this illicit activity legal. From the eleventh century on, Pisan, Genoese, Catalan, Greek, and Muslim privateering became a permanent element in the existence of sailors. People and goods were the prey of corsairs. Complaints from plundered merchants and captured and ransomed travelers who appealed to the authorities proliferated. The authorities variously issued warnings, conducted arbitrations, allowed privateering, or protected their own citizens.

Although privateering and privacy were not confined to any particular ports, it is nonetheless true that the major Mediterranean ports established an official organization for privateering. Ibn Khaldun provides a precise description of the technique used in Bejaia:

> Privateering is done in the following way: a more or less numerous company of corsairs is organized; they build a ship and choose men of proven boldness to man it. These warriors carry out raids on the coasts and islands inhabited by the Franks; they arrive without warning and carry off everything that comes to hand; they also attack the ships of the infidels, very often seize them, and return to port loaded with booty and prisoners. In this way, Bejaia and the other western ports (of Ifriqiya) are filled with captives; the streets of these towns echo with the sound of their chains, especially when these unfortunates, loaded with irons and shackles, spread out in every direction to work at their daily tasks. The price of their ransom is set so high that it is very difficult, and often impossible, for them to meet it.[10]

Commercial losses and diplomatic incidents resulting from these practices led the authorities to take measures that gave rise to an international maritime law in the late Middle Ages. The Office of Piracy in Genoa attempted to remedy the damages suffered by merchants, even when they contravened the orders of the Church by trading with Muslims. This is how it was done. The palace of the commune of Genoa contained a chest with three locks guarded by three agents. Anyone, Christian, Jew, or Saracen—on the condition that he was not from a country at war with Genoa and was not complaining against a Genoese—could introduce into this chest, without being seen, a slip of paper

---

10. Text quoted by Georges Jehel.

containing his complaint, if he considered himself wronged. The officers in charge opened the chest at fixed intervals, read the notes, and summoned the plunderers, who were forced to make restitution.

The same dangers existed in the North and the West. Rimbert, archbishop of Bremen and Hamburg in the second half of the ninth century, recounts in the *Life of Ansgar* that, engaged in establishing a church in Denmark in 829, he was given a mission by Emperor Louis the Pious to do the same in Sweden. Accompanied by a disciple, he embarked on a merchant ship that sailed with a convoy toward Birka. On the way, pirates attacked the vessel. The merchants defended themselves, momentarily repelled the attackers, but finally surrendered. Ansgar and his companion managed to reach shore and continued on their way on foot, using ships only to cross gulfs.

In the late Middle Ages, like highway robbers, pirates and soldiers deprived of a livelihood by peace or truces attacked ships in peacetime as in war. The northern seas harbored frightful and well-organized looters, such as the Frisian Jehan Stortebeker, known as the "Swallower of glasses," and his "Pirate Brothers." In the Baltic, piracy grew considerably after 1381, and the period of great insecurity lasted at least until 1430.

Pirates often took up positions not in open water, but at crossing points, in straits, and sometimes before ports, taunting the authorities who were incapable of hunting them down. They thus remained close to their dens and attacked sailors exhausted by long voyages. At the entry to the English Channel, both Bretons and English lay in wait for ships. Coasts and ports were thus often more dangerous than the high seas.

Fishermen sometimes turned themselves from victims into pirates, opportunity making the thief. Around 1450, the crew of the *Marie* from Bristol, which was fishing off the coast of Ireland, captured a Spanish ship, which was soon taken away from them by the inhabitants of Kinsale, attracted by such a great prize.

As in the Mediterranean, the border between piracy, letters of marque, and private reprisals or privateering appeared to be uncertain. The seizure of a ship might be justified by challenging the validity of a safe-conduct or by unawareness of a treaty.

Attacks were sometimes accompanied by acts of cruelty. In the late thirteenth century, the Normans, engaged in naval warfare with Bayonne, hung a ship's boy from the yardarm. In 1458, despite their safe-conduct passes, the inhabitants of Bordeaux drowned sailors and even English merchants whom they had caught in nets. But the enlightened self-interest of brigands led them to ransom rather than kill their victims.

To defend themselves against a piracy that had become almost endemic in the late Middle Ages, even ships of small tonnage carried artillery pieces. In addition, pirates were subject to the harshest treatment. The great monarchies could not let their misdeeds go unpunished. But procedures were lengthy and punishment uncertain. Shipmasters, lacking confidence in their safe-conduct passes, took supplementary precautions. And they had reason to do so, as shown by the adventure of some large English vessels in Bordeaux in 1459. The ships entered the river armed with safe-conduct passes, but they were arrested. One of them fled and its sailors sank a Breton ship in the river and committed other offenses on land. Soon thereafter, there was a naval battle between another ship, also under safe-conduct, and a ship that Bordeaux had sent in pursuit, in which some were taken prisoner and others drowned.

Reprisals should not be forgotten. The victim or his agents had in particular rights of pursuit that allowed them to repossess the stolen goods even from someone who held them in good faith. For example, in 1456, men of Bordeaux who had bought the *Saint-Eustache* of La Rochelle captured by English pirates from Bayonne had to return it.

The best defense against piracy was in the end to sail in convoys. In the eighth century, when the Frisian merchant Ibbo decided to leave Trier on a ship for England, he joined a group of six ships that had the same destination. In the fourteenth century, convoys of Venetian galleys might comprise nine, ten, or even more ships, and they provided so much protection that merchants did not have to insure themselves against risk at sea. Froissart relates in his *Chronicles* that in 1350, after loading their vessels with cloth and other merchandise in the Flemish port of Sluis, some Spanish merchants embarked on their ships, which were well provided with artillery pieces. When the wind became favorable, they weighed anchor despite the presence of English ships blocking the port. Their fleet comprised forty large vessels. The foremasts had fortified tops and soldiers armed with stones. In Brittany, under Jean IV, probably in 1372, it was decided to put a convoy to sea. In return for a contribution, merchants taking the wine route were given an armed escort. In 1483, a convoy comprised five vessels and two small boats, all together with a capacity of 720 barrels. There were 513 fighting men ready to intervene. La Rochelle was the principal destination, with another group of vessels heading for Bordeaux or Bayonne with a reduced escort. Once loading was complete, the fleet headed back to its home port.

Because of risks at sea, some merchants preferred land routes despite their elevated costs. In 1450, Guillaume de Varye, an associate of Jacques Cœur in Normandy, commissioned a businessman of Bourges, Étienne Caillat, to go to Scotland to buy leather, cloth, and wool, the leather to go to La Rochelle, and the cloth and wool through Flanders to Rouen. Once the goods had been unloaded, whatever the location, they were not to go back on ship; Caillat received a formal order to use a land route to bring them to Rouen. However, considering that the costs of carriage transport were comparable to the value of the wool and cloth, he loaded the goods on a ship.

This was a fearful world and a world in motion. To the dangers threatening travelers can be added anecdotes about seasickness. John Mandeville advises those "who cannot endure the *carroier* of the sea" to go by land to Jerusalem. Taken ill in 1531, Dom Loupvent was given a jar of wine by the shipmaster to soothe him, but he did not recover: "I could not stand sailing for I was very ill in the head and the stomach, because of the movement of the ship, that I was not accustomed to. This is why I vomited the little I had eaten the day before, and thought I would probably die without the care of my companions."

This fear of the sea lasted well beyond the Middle Ages. One senses behind the lines of Victor Hugo's *Oceano Nox* a repulsion that stretches back to the beginning of time.

Influence on Religious Life

Fear of the sea was also fear of death, that opened the gates to eternity. Hence the religious life of both passengers and sailors had specific characteristics.

The miracle books of Gregory of Tours cannot imagine a sea voyage without a storm; but the peril is averted by the intercession of a saint whose power is thereby demonstrated. In the work entitled *Of the Glory of Martyrs*, Gregory recounts that, after receiving from Pope Pelagius relics of several martyrs and confessors, a deacon took ship to return home. As they were sailing toward the port of Marseille, the ship came close to a point on the coast where there stood a mountain of rocks. The wind drove the ship forward at great speed, so that the hull was about to be shattered. But the deacon lifted up the reliquary and a stronger contrary wind carried the ship back into the open sea.

Saint Maximin of Trier saved the Frisian merchant Ibbo and his companions from shipwreck as they sailed toward England; the other ships in the convoy sank, no doubt because their sailors had not thought of asking for the saint's intercession. Grippo the prefect of Quentovic, returning from England where he had carried out a successful diplomatic mission sometime between 858 and 868, had to cross the Pas-de-Calais to reach home; the storm was so violent that the boat had to be allowed to drift. After long being tossed about by the waves, it came close to the Boulogne lighthouse. At that point, Grippo had a vision of the basilica containing the relics of Saint Wandrille. His prayers were followed by the calming of the sea.

Chronicles and travel narratives corroborate the testimony of hagiographic works. When Saint Louis was returning from the Seventh Crusade, in the course of the storm described earlier, the queen went to the king's chamber. Joinville, who was there, asked her what she had come to do.

> She wanted, she answered, to speak to the king, to tell him to promise God or his saints to make a pilgrimage for our deliverance, for according to the sailors we were in danger of drowning.
>
> "Madame," I answered, "promise a pilgrimage to his grace Saint Nicholas of Varangeville, and I guarantee on his behalf that God will return you to France with the king and your children."
>
> "Seneschal," she said, "truly I would willingly do it, but the king is so strange that, if he knew that I had promised without him, he would never let me go."
>
> "Here is what you will do. If God returns you to France, you will promise him a vessel of silver worth 5 marks, for the king, for you, and for your three children, and I guarantee you that God will save you. For I promised Saint Nicho-

las that if he allowed us to escape from the danger we were in this night, I would go from Joinville barefoot to pray to him."

She told me that she would promise the vessel to Saint Nicholas and that I would be her guarantor. I willingly agreed. She left but soon came back and said: "Saint Nicholas has saved us, the wind has dropped."

When a violent squall came upon the ship carrying Anselme Adorno and his companions home in the Gulf of Venice, the first reaction of the passengers was to pray.

We began to call on the Lord in a miserable voice, as though we were at the end of our lives, and to pray fervently, for we had no further hope of succor, except from the grace of God. Indeed, all of us were certain that we had reached our final hour. How pitiful were our cries! Each of us looked at his neighbor in torment, and we lowered our eyes. My father grasped me as though to say; "Son, I wish it, let us die together." He nevertheless continued to call on the blessed Catherine and placed his confidence and his hope in her, and even more in Our Lord Jesus Christ, even though the master and the sailors had lost all hope. But the very blessed Lord Jesus delivered us from that monstrous storm. . . .

There were even specific prayers. A fourteenth-century manuscript in the Vatican provides a weapon against storms: "Against thunder and against storm, while making the sign of the cross, you will say this prayer: Here is the cross of Our Lord Jesus Christ, fly, hostile elements and withdraw. . . ." This is an incantation attempting to remove the danger by a series of namings as complete as possible, accompanied in the manuscript by signs of the cross that have an immunizing value. Some passages seem hardly orthodox, in that sometimes bizarre formulations take precedence over the invocation of Christ. It is more a matter of averting a danger "by virtue of all the things that can be said" than of submitting with confidence to the goodness of God.

As for the sailors in particular, their devotion was fed from the same sources as that of the passengers. Official iconography initiated them into the teaching of the Church. In the preambles to their wills, they commended themselves to God, to Christ, to the Virgin, to the saints. But at sea, they were in such great danger that they were in a sense condemned men, and for this reason their piety had certain particular characteristics. They risked dying without receiving the final sacraments and their bodies might very well not rest in consecrated ground if they died at sea. The least they could hope for was the prayers of their families. The possessions of the drowned whose heirs could not be found were in addition to be used for pious works designed to comfort the souls of the dead, according to the prescriptions of the *Rôles d'Oléron*. The sailors and merchants of the *Warry*, the *Gost*, and the *Anne*, who had suffered serious harm in 1458 from the servants of the seneschal in Gironde, requested the foundation of a chapel and three weekly perpetual masses. But above all they wished a search to be made for the bodies of the missing so they could have Christian burial. Rest in consecrated ground, however, did nothing to prevent the cruel fate of sailors and travelers who died and were buried far from home.

The life of the sailor, much more exposed than that of other men, expressed the adventure of the soul and the dangers awaiting it on the path to salvation.

Sailors could not accomplish their religious duties with any regularity. In storms at sea, their first act was to try to save the ship. Then, when all means had been exhausted, nothing was left but prayer. In autumn 1498, the *Trinity* from Newcastle broke up on a shoal in the North Sea; the sailors, "seeing that no remedy could prevent the sea from swallowing them, if they were not saved by the ineffable goodness of God and the pious intercession of the saints," begged that God would save their lives. When terrible waves threatened to sink his ship, Christopher Columbus ordered that straws be drawn to choose one sailor who would carry a candle of 5 livres to Our Lady of Guadalupe, to select a pilgrim to Our Lady of Loreto, and to send another on a mission to conduct a vigil one night at Santa Clara de Moguer and to have a mass celebrated there. Finally, Columbus and all his men promised that as soon as they landed they would go in their shifts to a church consecrated to Our Lady. In addition to general and common vows, each sailor made a particular vow, because they all thought they were lost. From experience, sailors knew that prayers were not always answered, but although they attributed fortunate outcomes to God, they felt a certain repugnance to hold Him responsible for misfortune. They reached port "with the help of God," but difficulties came from "the fortune of weather and sea." In immediate danger, they turned toward Jesus, the Virgin, and the saints, closer to them in their humanity. Besides, the ship was often placed under the protection of the Virgin or a saint whose name it bore. A study carried out on approximately three hundred ships active in Normandy, Brittany, and Gascony between 1200 and 1460, shows a progression of religious names; in Brittany, the proportion of secular names sank from 24 percent to none. Devotion to intercessor saints seems to have been quite remarkable. Some were chosen because of a connection to maritime life: Saint Peter, protector of fishermen; Saint Clement, his successor, who drowned at sea tied to an anchor; Saint Nicholas, who saved a child who had fallen overboard. As for names associated with Mary, they progressed from 16 to 21 percent in Normandy, and from 15 to 30 percent in Brittany; and they were extremely varied: *Sainte-Marie, Notre-Dame, Ave Maria, Étoile de la Mer, Notre-Dame-de Miséricorde, Notre-Dame d'Espérance. . . .*

The practice of the sacraments was occasional, because merchant ships did not have priests on board; the obligation of the Sunday mass gave way before the constraints imposed by wind and tide.

On land, the religious practices of people of the sea seems not to have differed from those of others. It seems, according to Jacques Bernard, that the particular dangers that sailors confronted did not lead them, when they were back with their families, to pay more attention to the salvation of their souls than their sedentary neighbors.

Indeed, a certain laxity in morals seems to have affected sailors when they were far from home, in foreign ports, if we are to believe Jacques de Vitry, bishop of Saint-Jean d'Acre in the early thirteenth century. In a sermon addressed to sailors, he stigmatized alike the seaman who squandered his money on prostitutes and in taverns, the merchant who speculated, and the pirates and crews who extorted money from passengers. A *Manuel de confesseur* of the fourteenth century contains advice on the manner of dealing with a penitent sailor:

You, the confessor, if you happen to hear some sailor in confession, do not fail to question him with care. You must know that an entire pen would hardly suffice to write down all the sins into which those men are sunk. So great indeed is their wickedness that it goes beyond the names of all the sins. . . . Not only do they kill clergy and laymen when they are on land, but at sea they give themselves over to the abomination of piracy, pillaging the wealth of others and especially of merchants. . . . In addition, they are all adulterers and fornicators, for in all the lands and regions in which they live, either they have liaisons with various women, believing that it is permitted, or else they give in to debauchery with prostitutes.[11]

But confessors' manuals, like the penitentials of the early Middle Ages, had a rather negative vision because of the purposes they served. Indeed, despite moral failings (men on land did not always lead a life in conformity with the precepts of the Church), and despite a rather utilitarian conception of the relationship between man and God (but how many men on land said prayers of thanksgiving before prayers of petition?), men of the sea did have a sense of the spiritual. The chapels and crosses that they erected indicate not only the carrying out of a vow or the wish to ensure divine protection against the perils of the sea, they also demonstrate a concern for the salvation of their souls.

The attitude toward the sea involved a certain ambivalence. Even if fear did not disappear, it was overcome, to judge by the number of pilgrims to the Holy Land. The sea, in addition, made it possible to glimpse other shores, to discover wonders. The documents never speak of a fine and lovely sea, for it always caused fear, but it grew increasingly attractive as it made it possible to know other worlds.

## THE SHIPS

Throughout the Middle Ages, many ships[12] circulated on the seas, of diverse shapes and sizes, depending on the task assigned: transport of passengers or goods, fishing, coastal navigation, etc.

---

11. Passage quoted by M. Mollat.

12. See in particular the works of Régis Boyer (the Viking ship), Jacques Bernard (great sailing vessels), and Jean Merrien.

## The Viking Ship

From the folk of the Geats the good man had chosen warriors of the bravest that he could find; one of fifteen he led
the way, the warrior sought the wooden ship, the sea-skilled
one the land's edge. The time had come: the ship was on the
waves, the boat under the cliff. The warriors eagerly climbed
on the prow—the sea-currents eddied, sea against sand; men
bore bright weapons into the ship's bosom, splendid armor.
Men pushed the well-braced ship from shore, warriors on a
well-wished voyage. Then over the sea-waves, blown by the
wind, the foam-necked boat traveled, most like a bird, until
at good time on the second day the curved prow had come
to where the seafarers could see land, the sea-cliffs shine,
towering hills, great headlands. Then was the sea crossed,
the journey at an end. Then quickly the men of the Geats
climbed upon the shore, moored the wooden ship; mail-
shirts rattled, dress for battle. They thanked God that the
wave-way had been easy for them.[13]

The epic of *Beowulf,* from which this passage comes, a verse
epic at first transmitted orally and set down in writing before
750, is known to us from a single manuscript from the tenth
century. We see here the leader of a Scandinavian maritime
people undertaking a military expedition, using few men, fifteen in all. The warriors row a good part of the voyage; the ship
uses its sail only in open sea and for a short period of time, since
the journey lasts barely more than twenty-four hours. The joy
they feel on seeing the cliffs is evidence that sailing in a straight
line was still infrequent in the eighth century.

But let us examine this ship more closely. The Vikings, incidentally, spent much more time on land than at sea: a few days
of coastal navigation or crossing open water before engaging in
military or trading activities.

The Viking boat did not have great capacity. With no bridge,
a long voyage was not possible because of limited space.
Nevertheless, this ship enabled the Vikings to come to the

---

13. *Beowulf,* tr. E. Talbot Donaldson (New York: Norton, 1966), 5.

West, striking fear into an entire population. It is natural that it played an essential role in their existence. A good deal of know-how went into its making. After a slow development— the ship of Nydam in Denmark which might go back to the fourth century is a distant ancestor—it was for three centuries, from the ninth through the eleventh, a kind of ideal. Its appearance is familiar; a prow and a poop that are identical and similarly raised, a large mast carrying a rectangular sail, long oars extending from the hull, and shields set along the planking.

It took a long time to build such a boat. Using an ax, they began by shaping the keel in a single piece. In general, it was of oak, but this was not the only wood used. Metal rivets or wooden dowels attached it to the stem and the stern-post. The planks were set so that they partially overlapped. These planks were riveted together and the interstices sealed with hemp previously soaked in tar. Varangs, curved or forked pieces carefully placed on the keel along its axis gave the whole some stability. Transversal beams that kept the varangs apart, longitudinal pieces that crossed the insides of the frames, and the gunwales enclosing the planks completed the ship. The foot of the mast was set on or into the planking. A small platform forward, and possibly another at the stern, fixed the dimensions of the hold where cargo and horses were stowed. It remained to sculpt the prow-head which could be removed and replaced at will. This was usually the head of an animal or a monster which probably at first played a religious role, namely, to frighten the spirits of enemy places.

The sail, which was rectangular and usually higher than it was broad, was made of vertical strips. The uppermost plank had holes for the oars. The Viking ships had to be long in order to carry the oarsmen. Considering that most of the time there were between six and thirty-six benches, that the interval between benches was about a meter, and that there had to be free space at each end as well as for the mast, their length varied generally from nine to thirty-five meters.

The mast, which was ten to thirteen meters high, was attached to the hull by a piece of wood allowing both longitudinal and lateral movement. Thus, to a certain extent, mast and sail could follow the wind. A clever system made it possible quickly to strike the sail, which was eleven meters wide and a little higher, and to fasten it to the main yard; mast and sail were then set down lengthwise without interfering with the oarsmen.

The ship of Gokstad in Norway, which dates from the ninth century, measures 23.3 meters in all, its greatest width is 5.25 meters, its height from keel to planking is 1.95 meters. It weighs nine tons, eighteen when laden. It can hold a maximum of seventy men. This ship, very wide since the ratio of length to width is 4.4, thus has good lateral stability. Even filled with water, it is difficult to capsize. In addition, it is surprisingly flat. It draws only 90 to 95 centimeters, making it easy to beach. But in open sea, since the ship has no bridge, high waves and violent rain bring in large quantities of water. In bad weather, if using the sail, the crew would have to be constantly bailing, and if rowing, some of the crew would have to give up their oars to undertake this exhausting labor. In fact, after scooping the water, they would have to throw it over a gunwale 2.5 meters away and about 2 meters high.

This ship is surprisingly supple. It can reverse direction very quickly and in a very narrow radius. It lends itself to the movement of the waves, does not hit them head on, but matches them, gives in to their power while simultaneously maintaining its course. It is not surprising that poems compare it to a serpent undulating on the sea. This handling made surprising speed possible, around ten knots, which allowed the Normans often to devastate with impunity the countries of the West, because Carolingian vessels were certainly unable to rival such ships. And thanks to this speed, the Vikings covered long distances, for it was not necessary to carry very large quantities of provisions and fresh water.

There were several types of Viking ship. Régis Boyer points out that the term *drakkar* is a monstrosity in grammatical terms. The prowhead frequently designated the ship as a whole: Bison, Serpent, Ram, depending on the animal sculpted. Most often it was a dragon, *dreki* in Old Norse, plural *drekar*. This is no doubt the origin of the word *drakkar*, which contains errors in number, morphology, and spelling.

The typical Viking ship bore the name *knörr*, with slight variants according to size or purpose. It was very costly, so that several people had to come together to finance its construction, and it was an object of pride; in the saga of the Norwegian king

Olaf Tryggvason, the *Long Serpent* brings out adjectives applicable to a beloved person. It was sculpted, gilded, and the shields covered with shining metal or painted in bright colors hanging along its side gave it a proud appearance.

The dimensions of the *knörr* did not allow it to transport many people—the crew was normally between forty and seventy men—or heavy goods. It could hold only luxury items that took up little space. Moreover, because of the cost, few of them were made. The immense fleets spoken of in the Western chronicles existed only in the imaginations of their authors. As evidenced in the tapestry of Queen Mathilde in Bayeux, the Viking ships sometimes carried horses. Excellent horsemen, the Normans could thus carry out raids on land once they had reached their destination.

Round Ships

On the Atlantic Ocean, the vessel (*nef*), still rather long in the thirteenth century, gave way in the course of the following century to a ship with high sides and heavy tonnage, because increasing economic activity necessitated the transport of large cargoes. Among the technical improvements of the thirteenth century, a prominent place is occupied by the stern-post rudder. For a long, low ship, a steering oar is preferable. In contrast, the stern-post rudders are more adapted to round and broad ships. We should recall that the stern-post is a piece of construction continuing the keel that rises at the stern of the ship. This now became the location of the rudder. It was difficult to manipulate and the steersman did not always have a clear view. Nevertheless, it was the only device capable of keeping a large ship on course without the pilot having to show exceptional talent. This fact should not lead us to forget other improvements concerning the construction of the hull, which made it possible to put cargo ships to sea, with the *cogue* its Nordic version, while the *nef*, at the head of a kind of hierarchy including barges, whalers, and other minor types, made up the Atlantic contingent.

It is easier to form a picture of this vessel from iconography than from documents. In the fourteenth and fifteenth centuries, it had become a potbellied, wide, and short ship, with the ratio of length to width of the order of three or four to one. Capacity and security were the qualities sought above all. The characteristics of this kind of ship fit well with navigational conditions in the shallow seas of northern Europe and the state of the ports in the Middle Ages.

This transformation of the *nef* made secondary adjustments indispensable. Because the hold was deeper, pails were replaced by pumps. A bridge became necessary for the security of the ship and the preservation of the goods being carried. On large vessels, there were even several bridges which prevented adequate aeration of the hold. In order not to diminish the resistance of the hull, however, few openings were made.

Castles were considered fundamental elements of the Gothic vessel. At first intended for military purposes, they were enlarged, consolidated, and elevated. Situated in the interior of the vessels in the thirteenth century, they were more closely linked to the structure in the course of the following century. In the fifteenth century, completely incorporated into the ship, they formed a projection fore and were doubled at the stern where they became lodgings. On the sides, under the corridors, places for passengers were installed.

The rigging had to evolve with the changes in the ship. In the fourteenth century and during a large part of the fifteenth, the vessel still had only one mast, set in the center. With the increase in the ship's dimensions, the mast was made stronger. All in one piece, on warships it had a topcastle, that is, a platform from which soldiers could shoot arrows. The yard—the long piece of wood set crosswise on the front of the mast—carried a square sail.

The larger dimensions of the vessel made it necessary to increase the number of mast supports as well as the instruments likely to help in heavy maneuvers. Despite all these improvements, there was a difference only in degree not in nature, with respect to rigging, between the thirteenth-century vessel and that of the early fifteenth century. It was then that a change took place. The rigging was divided, and the two masts that Mediterranean ships had long had made their appearance in the Atlantic. The second mast appeared sometime in the second decade of the century, soon followed by a third between 1430 and 1440. The development took place slowly. Until the mid-fifteenth century, many large vessels still had only a single mast.

The way of reducing or increasing the surface of the main sail improved. This was not a secondary detail, because the quality of navigation with the wind and the safety of the ship depended on this operation. The problem could be resolved in two ways: expand a small sail or reduce a large one. To increase the surface of the square sail, strips of canvas called studding sails had to be added when there was little wind. In the fourteenth and fifteenth centuries, one or two horizontal studding sails were placed under the main sail. This system had a drawback; since lacing was not continuous, the wind could pass through the holes. To reduce the surface of the sail, all that had to be done was to fold it up from the bottom. Two small sails, aft a mizzen, and fore a foresail, might complete the rigging.

The ships used by the Hanseatic League, the association of Northern European merchants, went through several changes. When Lübeck was established in the mid-twelfth century, the northern seas had only two kinds of ship, the Viking ship and the Western sailing ship, wider and more stable, with a cargo capacity no greater than thirty tons. Toward the end of the century, the *cogue,* able to carry two hundred tons, made its appearance. About thirty meters long and seven wide, and drawing three meters, it carried a single sail and could reach ten or fifteen knots an hour in a good wind.

In the fourteenth century the *hourque,* a transport vessel of reduced size with a flat bottom, became widespread. As its dimensions expanded, the *cogue* disappeared. The *hourque,* indeed, had a cargo capacity of three hundred tons, sometimes more.

After 1450, the caravel made its appearance; it was of Italian and Atlantic origin and had three masts and a smooth hull with sealed planks. The Hanseatic League became acquainted with this new ship in a fortuitous way. In 1462, the *Saint-Pierre-de-La-Rochelle* was abandoned by its captain in the port of Danzig. The *hourque,* however, remained the ship most used in the Hanseatic seas.

Caravels were the ships that Christopher Columbus used for his 1492 voyage to the American continent, at least the *Pinta* and the *Niña.* The third ship, the *Santa-Maria,* heavier than a caravel, was originally named the *Gallega,* the Galician, but Columbus was intent on placing it under the protection of the Virgin Mary. The heavy *Santa-Maria,* which had a capacity of a hundred tons, was the flagship.

Finally, the largest ship used in the Middle Ages was the carrack. The carracks of the late fifteenth century with their three masts, as they appear in miniatures of the time, had a striking appearance. A carrying capacity in excess of five hundred tons, a longer hull, and a powerful rudder distinguished them from the vessels of the thirteenth century. On either side of the hold, the castles contained two floors of sleeping spaces. The masts had huge yards furnished with platforms large enough to carry artillery pieces. However, they still belonged to the same category as their predecessor vessels.

To what extent were these ships able to carry out their assigned tasks quickly and safely? On average, vessels (*nefs*) had a speed of five or six knots. In 1386, it took an English fleet five days to sail from Brest to La Corogne. When the wind was favorable, London was ten to twelve days' sailing from Bordeaux. Such direct journeys, when the elements were favorable, often differed from the usual merchant's voyage. The wind was not always favorable. Although it was possible to go from Dover to Calais on a single tide in favorable conditions, this was not the case in 1475, when King Edward IV of England wanted to cross the Channel. "King Edward being at Dover," we are told by Commynes,

> the Duke of Burgundy sent for his crossing five hundred ships from Holland and Zeeland, which are flat and low-sided, very suitable for carrying horses, and are called *suites*. And notwithstanding this great number and everything that the king of England was able to do, he took more than three months to cross. There are only seven leagues between Dover and Calais. But see how difficult it was for a king of England to cross to France.

A fleet took thirty-six hours to go from Royan to Penmarc'h but two weeks to cross the few miles of narrows of Brest. Finally, it took about a month to reach Falmouth from Bordeaux. Thus, it can be seen that improvements in navigation did not appreciably shorten the length of voyages, dependent primarily on wind and weather.

If we cross the Strait of Gibraltar and enter the Mediterranean, we also find round ships of substantial size, *naves*, that had been in use for a longer time. The Mediterranean climate was more propitious than that of the Atlantic for the sailing of large ships. And passenger transport, particularly of pilgrims, was a profitable activity, so that shipmasters were inclined to take more and more on board. We shall see in what conditions they traveled. The size of ships therefore had to be increased, all the more because the cost of the return voyage was covered by booty and merchandise brought back from the East. When a ship became wider and longer, provided it remained solid, it was possible to increase its height. This made it possible to have two bridges set one above the other, and connecting the two extremities of the ship. There was thus created between the hold and the upper bridge a steerage space, which remained badly ventilated until scuttle holes for artillery made their appearance; but the steerage was level and better suited for passenger transport than a curved hull. This airless and noisy steerage was the place for impecunious passengers.

From around 1380 to 1460, very large Genoese ships were used on the Eastern routes for the transport of alum. Their tonnage was frequently between 18,000 and 20,000 *cantares* (a *cantare* was a little less than 105 pounds) thus much greater than Provençal, Catalan, or Atlantic vessels.

The increase in size of ships was indispensable at the time of the Crusades because of the need to carry horses. Lowering these animals into the hold after having led them onto the upper bridge was obviously an arduous and delicate task, and the reverse operation turned out to be even more difficult. As a consequence, a bold solution was adopted: just above the waterline a large door was cut in the hull (a *huis*, which gave the name *huissiers* to these ships) through which the horses entered directly into the hold or the steerage. But the presence of a door made the hull less solid and sometimes caused ships to sink in storms. Penetration of water through the joints was remedied by nailing or pegging the panel that formed the door and caulking the gaps. In addition, the horses were supported from above so that their hoofs rested lightly on the bottom.

These general considerations do not make it possible to imagine all the complexity of medieval fleets. For example, Venetian sailors in the twelfth and thirteenth centuries used a Latin vessel, generally with one mast, such as the *Roccaforte*, a ship with two bridges, 38.19 meters long, measuring 14.22 meters at its widest point, 9.35 meters high in the middle of the hull, but 13.7 meters high under the castles. The tonnage must have been as high as 600. Supplied with Latin-style sails, the ship was steered by two powerful oars located on either side of the poop. This *nave* was in competition with the *taride*, a round vessel designed to carry voluminous goods, with a length to width ratio of 2.5 making it close to the *nef*. But it had only one bridge. Around 1300, when the *coque* made its appearance in the Mediterranean, the *taride* was given another bridge and the rigging was probably modified. It disappeared in the course of the second half of the fourteenth century.

The *coque*, provided with square rigging and a stern rudder, had a much smaller capacity than the *nef* and the *taride*. It was only during the last quarter of the fourteenth century that Venice adopted it as a long-distance vessel; also during this period it became considerably heavier, and it replaced the *nef*. Although the *coque* offered certain advantages, such as ease of maneuvering the stern rudder and the square sail on the yard, on the other hand, the lack of Latin sails which made sailing by tacking possible hindered navigation, so that its success was short-lived. In the course of the fifteenth century, it gradually disappeared from the Venetian vocabulary which soon retained only the term *nef* to designate the large cargo ship.

The new Mediterranean *nef*, supplied with three, four, or even five masts, resembled the *coque* with its square sails and its rudder. The mainmast and the small foremast were square rigged, while the mizzen and Bonaventure masts had Latin sails. Running and maneuvering the ship were made easier by these changes. This was functionally identical to the Atlantic carrack, but Venetians and Genoese continued to call it a *nef*.

Long Ships

The galley, which was found principally in the Mediterranean, was a long, narrow ship that rode low in the water and was low in height. It was long to accommodate a large number of oars, narrow to move quickly, low to be light and easy to maneuver, and low in the water to move lightly and facilitate the use of oars. The reverse of these advantages was a lack of capacity to transport either heavy or voluminous goods. To attempt to remedy this disadvantage hybrid ships were sometimes used, but with little success.

Such a narrow ship could not be very stable. Thus, despite the advantages of a relatively large number of sails that would have allowed the oarsmen to rest and the ship to move more quickly, the galley had only one or two short and easily dismantled masts and one or two small sails. And they could only be used if the wind was gentle or blowing in the right direction.

The ship contained a bridge left exposed for reasons of security; at the stern of the bridge, a simple tent provided shelter for the officers. On the bridge were benches separated by an elevated straight walk enabling supervision of the oarsmen and movement from stern to bow. It was wide enough to permit two officers to pass, but because it had no railing it was unstable. Forward, there was a platform for soldiers and for sailors charged with manipulating the sails. In the stern, the bridge ended in a little raised space to which the ladders that were the way on board were attached.

The bridge had hatches that provided access to the hold. In merchant galleys, the hold provided storage for goods or lodging for pilgrims. In military galleys, it held navigational equipment and provisions, and provided a few uncomfortable living spaces.

To secure the advantages of such a ship without its drawbacks, the technicians of the Venice Arsenal perfected the large galley that married the cargo capacity of the round ship to the speed and maneuverability of the long ship. This vessel, which reached its greatest development in the late fifteenth century, had two or three square-rigged masts and a large number of oarsmen, who became fighting men as the need arose. At the same time a specialized war fleet was established. But the changes in trade routes, the high cost of crews, and improvements in the round ship soon brought about the decline of the large galley as a merchant ship. It then began a new career in the sixteenth century as a warship.

Hence, the traveler had a choice among several types of ship to reach his destination. He decided on the basis of the weather, his plans, and his social situation.

Anselme Adorno had just arrived in Genoa, one of the major ports of the West, with three *moles* on which lanterns burned all night to permit ships to sail in and out. To get from Genoa to Alexandria, he had to go by sea. What ship should he choose? The Genoese friends from whom Anselme asked advice recommended that he sail in summer on a large *nef* rather than a trireme.

On the other hand, in winter, when the sea swells because of the many gales, when violent winds are constantly blowing and bring on many long storms, galleys are safer because, in case of imminent danger at sea, they can always take refuge in a port. Large *nefs*, in contrast, do not head for port in a strong storm, but head for open sea for greater safety. In summer, these perils of the sea are not frequent and if they do arise, their violence is short-lived. This is why in that season you should choose a large *nef* on which you will be much more comfortable than on a trireme. . . . Well advised by knowledgeable friends, on May 7 in Genoa, we embarked on a large *nef* of 15,000 *cantares*, well supplied with bombards, bows, spears, cannonballs, and other weapons, and with a crew of 110 men to resist the Turkish enemies and the pirates that very often attack sailors.

This ship carried the pilgrims to Tunis, from which a larger Genoese ship took them to Alexandria.


## LIFE ON BOARD

On the Viking ship, given the small available space, life could not have been easy. Food consisted of fish, meat, dried seaweed, salted butter, and coarse bread. Sailors ate in pairs. Hygiene was limited, but voyages were usually short. The Vikings principally carried on coastal navigation. They stopped frequently, and when landings were not for military purposes, they unloaded their wooden-framed tents and set up camp on land. When their intentions were warlike, they conducted efficient raids to seize precious goods, but above all provisions and cattle.

A frequent ploy was to go into hiding not far from the mouth of a river near a wealthy spot. On the occasion of a festival or a fair, the sailors would land, using their own or captured horses, rush and pillage the place and quickly return to their ship, setting fires to cut off any pursuit. But the Vikings were also, and perhaps more than anything else, clever merchants who made war when the circumstances warranted.

Let us turn next to the great ships that, with a sometimes large crew, carried passengers and goods.

The Sailors

Travel writers mention above all the discomfort suffered in their crossings. Fortunately, legal documents, such as the *Rôles d'Olé-ron* and the *Maritime Law of the Hanseatic League* provide more plentiful information, but unfortunately this is of a normative order, because the regulations were not necessarily applied. Documents preserved in the archives contain invaluable details, too often succinct, but better reflecting reality.

The precise hierarchy maintained on modern ships did not exist in the Middle Ages. At the head of the ship was the master, rather infrequently accompanied by men able to replace him, which meant that a death at sea had dramatic consequences. When a military action was planned, soldiers were on board. But generally sailors themselves did the fighting. Felix Faber provides a fairly precise enumeration of the seamen aboard the galley of Agostino Contarino taking him to the Holy Land. He mentions the master himself, assisted by advisers, a person in charge of weapons, the man responsible for provisions, the caulker who kept the hull in good condition, the pilot who knew the sea, and astronomers able to use navigation instruments and charts. The boatswain carried out maneuvers and maintained good order on board, assisted by men responsible for the rigging, the sails, and the anchors. Nine agile young men climbed on the rigging and the yard; older sailors took care of maneuvers. Galley slaves handled the oars; but when oars were not in use, they performed other tasks: they were tailors, barbers, cobblers, laundry men. The ship also carried two surgeons, officers of justice, trumpeters, three or four ship's boys, several cooks, and finally a scribe.

In his study of seamen of Bordeaux, Jacques Bernard points out that the term 'master' should not be confused with 'captain', a figure whose title and role were connected to military matters: Berthomieu Ydron, master of a barque, became a captain when his ship was armed for privateering. Thus, while there was no captain on large trading vessels, there might be one on ships that also had been given a military mission.

The notion of master, however, turns out to be complex insofar as he might join to his role as navigator those of ship owner and merchant. But he was a sailor. He was expected to remain on board, he ordered maneuvers, regulated the speed of the ship, and proposed to merchants and "companions," when he did not decide himself, to lighten the ship, that is, to jettison part or all of the cargo. However, he was not necessarily an expert navigator. He would then rely on the pilot, a well-paid figure, engaged for a single voyage, whose possible incompetence would be customarily punished. But many ships had no pilot, either because the master knew how to use navigation instruments, or because the ship belonged to a fleet and each individual ship had no need of its own pilot.

Attaining the status of master was not accomplished without difficulty. In the early sixteenth century, a Breton merchant declared that he had been going to Bordeaux for ten years, but "it was only this year that he became shipmaster." It was not until 1584 that an official examination guaranteed technical competence on the French coasts. But it is obvious that merchants recruited, although they might be in error, clever men with good reputations. In short, masters appear to have earned their status.

Next to the master were the companions. This term, coming from the vocabulary of guilds, set them in the framework of a trade, a social structure that fostered bonds of solidarity. Sometimes, the ship owner imposed certain sailors, but the master generally hired the members of the crew. He only had to be sure that there were enough men on board to sail the ship and to defend it if necessary. Finally, corresponding to apprentices on land, the ship's boys made up the lowest degree of the hierarchy. These three categories, master, companions, and ship's boys, made up the foundations of the society of the ship.

The master had to conduct himself as a leader aware of his responsibilities and not allow himself to lose his temper. Besides, custom protected companions from blows, from attacks on their dignity, and from the dramatic consequences of being discharged. The *Rôles d'Oléron* authorized discharge only if all other means had been exhausted. And in foreign ports, members of ships' crews felt solidarity with one another: in 1467, the master of a carrack from Venice prevented the authorities of Sluis from arresting some of his sailors. A settlement was worked out because it was impossible to lay hands on the delinquents. Custom also protected the companions in financial matters, because

it required payment of sailors' wages as a priority. Disputes sometimes arose, because some masters did not pay wages until after
goods had been sold.

But what principally bound master and companions together
was their common interest, since a number of them had shares
in the ship. Because of their knowledge and experience, some of
them were able to take command of the ship. Finally, the same
geographic origin and sometimes family connections knit relations among these people who made up a small society within
the larger society represented by the fleet.

The company sometimes made up an assembly deliberating
under the leadership of the master, discussing in particular safety
problems for the ship and its cargo. According to the second ar-
ticle of the *Rôles d'Oléron:*

> When a ship is in harbor awaiting a favorable moment to
> leave, the master cannot set sail without consulting his com-
> panions and saying to them: "Gentlemen, see what weather
> we have." If some say: "The weather is not fair," and others:
> "The weather is fine and good," the master must follow the
> opinion of the majority. And if he were to do otherwise, and
> if the ship were lost, he would be personally obligated to in-
> demnify the owners of the ship and the cargo.

Of course, mutinies might break out, but in this context they
would appear to be the conclusion to a long process. For example,
the English sailors of the *Marguerite d'Aurouelle,* whose ship
had been sequestered for several months in Bordeaux in 1459,
imprisoned the master who had come to pacify them, threw
him into the hold, and threatened to drown him if he did not
take them back to England; they obtained satisfaction.

Solidarity among sailors made it possible for them to put up
with often difficult material conditions. The room at their dis-
posal was extremely limited, because ship owners had an interest
in carrying the largest possible quantity of goods. On ships of
from ten to thirty tons without bridges, the members of the
crew could take refuge only in the stern room, more precisely
under a canvas stretched over arches. It hardly needs mention-
ing that rain and high waves ensured that nothing on board remained dry.

On large ships, the noble section was located in the stern,
where the aftercastle was reserved for the merchants, the mas-

ter, and the pilot. When it was double, it provided a room and a refuge underneath for the master or for noteworthy personages. This was where chests containing precious objects, account books, and various papers were kept. But cautious merchants preferred other hiding places for these chests that were easily discovered by pirates. As for the crew, it was housed in the forecastle, the extreme end of the upper bridge, where it had spaces provided with large openings that had to be blocked in bad weather or when the sun was too strong. Most sailors had a chest and a straw mattress in these recesses. They did not undress for sleep, because they had to be ready at a moment's notice.

The ship owners or the master were obligated to feed the men. Bread, generally sea biscuit, and smoked or salted meat and fish made up the basis of the diet on board. In 1459, the *Anthoine,* sailing between Hull and Bordeaux, loaded six months of provisions, namely, five barrels of flour and biscuit, ten barrels of salted meat, and thirteen barrels of salted fish. Fresh vegetables were lacking, but on ships from the Mediterranean, the diet was supplemented with oranges, lemons, and raisins. Fresh fish caught on the voyage sometimes improved the diet. Fresh water was a precious drink, but on long crossings it became putrid. The *Anthoine* from Hull carried twenty barrels of it, while for other beverages, notably wine, there were thirty.

All in all, although a sailor's existence had some similarities to that of an artisan or a peasant, the conditions under which he worked were unquestionably harsher. In bad weather, there were no limits but those imposed by physical resistance; and Sundays and holidays barely existed for the sailor. But there were family visits between voyages, and long stays in port. Sometimes, as Froissart writes, "for these days the weather was so fine and pretty and the air so calm and so gentle that it was a great pleasure to go by sea." But did sailors have the leisure or the desire to enjoy such moments?

Let us turn from this relatively stable and cohesive little society and make our acquaintance with the true travelers.

The Passengers

On ships where available space was limited, the problem of housing was a crucial one. On board the *nave,* passengers had several types of berth. The most important passengers occupied the aftercastle or sometimes the forecastle, which was much less pleasant; they were sheltered there but did not have individual rooms. Others settled on the upper bridge and on unenclosed spaces under the castles, but they risked being displaced, at least temporarily, during certain maneuvers. The poorer passengers stifled, some in steerage, others in the stable.

The berth was a frame designed for two in which was set out bedding brought by the passengers. During the day, the bedding (generally mats) and the blankets (often coats) were hung on the sides of the ship. The master removed the extra frames, forbidden but customary, that were set in the passages every night. Let us imagine the life of the many pilgrims wishing to go to the Holy Land, such as Felix Faber, whom we have already met; Pierre Barbatre, a priest from Vernon; Sancto Brascha from Milan, chancellor of Frederico Sforza; and an anonymous cleric from the Paris region, all four of whom traveled on the same ship, the *Contarina*, in 1480, and all four of whom recounted their adventures.

In Venice, "the best city in the world for taking ship," the pilgrim was taken in hand by specialists. They were supposed to help him find lodging, to make his purchases, to exchange his money. They then conducted him to master-owners of ships that the Republic had allowed to sail to Jaffa. In 1480, only one, the *Contarina*, had received that authorization.

The Venetian State in fact very strictly regulated the transport of pilgrims to the Holy Land, fitting out ships that were particularly intended for them, the pilgrim galleys. From 1470 on, there was only one sailing in June with a fleet of two or three ships. Only pilgrims had the right to use them; the pilgrims could bring with them a chest of provisions, a barrel of fresh water, and one of wine. Because Venice and the Turks had engaged in fierce battles in the preceding years, these precautions were intended to give an international character to the pilgrim galley; hence, the annual convoys had not been interrupted. It was forbidden to take a merchant on board and to carry goods other than the provisions intended to feed the crew and the pilgrims, who had to come from different countries. The galley had defensive armaments and its course could be changed depending on circumstances. To show its particularity, it was not escorted by a warship, and its prow carried a flag bearing the cross of Jerusalem.

However, Anselme Adorno advised against sailing on Venetian galleys:

> I advise against it, both because of the narrowness and the crampedness of the space and because of the number of people of diverse nations who spread disease to one another by their breath. In fact, this year, in one of those galleys, forty-nine or more pilgrims died.

It was elementary to choose a solid ship able to resist a storm. Still more prudent, for his 1480 voyage, Felix Faber made a contract with the master: he would have the right to a glass of malmsey on rising, two meals a day, would be authorized to bring living chickens that would be fed, would be guaranteed (but what was such a guarantee worth?) against unforeseen stops, and that they would not land in Cyprus.

The pilgrim, walking up a shaky plank, came on board. He was greeted by the scribe who noted his name and reserved a place for him. Then he brought on his baggage.

They were ready to set sail. "When the horses had come on board," reports Joinville,

> our master sailor cried to his men who were in the beak-head of the ship:
> "Is your work ready?"
> "Yes, Lord. Let the clerics and the priests come forward."
> When they had come, the master cried out to them:
> "Sing, by God!"
> And they all intoned in a single voice:
> "*Veni, creator Spiritus.*"
> Then he ordered his sailors:
> "Set sail, by God!"
> Which they did. In a little while, the wind struck the sails and removed us from sight of land, so that we could see only sky and water. Every day, the wind moved us away from the countries where we had been born.

And Joinville adds: "He is a bold madman who dares to place himself in such peril with the goods of others, or he is in mortal sin. For at night he goes to sleep not knowing whether he will find himself at the bottom of the sea the next morning."

Imagine our pilgrim sailing far from any land, perhaps not yet thinking of gales, because the rolling has made him seasick. Let us hope he has brought a sedative. Soon, hunger returns. Thus, when the trumpets sound the meal, twice a day, he hurries toward the tables set under the aftercastle and fastened to the bridge so they will not be shifted by the rolling. Because the dishes are not plentiful, he has brought a few supplements, unless he buys them from the sailors. Ibn Jubayr, returning to the West, embarked on a large ship on October 6, 1184, after gathering provisions of water and food. He estimated the number of pilgrims to Jerusalem at more than two thousand, not including the Muslims. On the ship, he writes, there were many things to buy: bread, water, condiments, fruits (pomegranates, quinces, melons from Sind, pears), chestnuts, walnuts, chickpeas, raw and cooked beans, onions, garlic, figs, cheese, fish, and various other products. But many Christian pilgrims disembarked in Calabria because of the lack of food on board. Passengers were reduced to a ration of one pound of dry bread to be shared among four of them, moistening it with a little water. The ones who left sold, at a high price, the provisions they had left. The Muslims bought everything they could. Indeed, the crossing lasted two months, whereas the passengers had estimated it at ten days to two weeks at most, so that the most prudent had brought food for thirty days, whereas most had provided for only fifteen or twenty.

In the course of the voyage of the *Contarina* in 1480, improvements were made in the food on various occasions. In Jaffa, the pilgrims obtained from the inhabitants eggs, figs, red and white grapes, and bread. This was on the way there. On the way back, as they were leaving Rhodes, compatriots gave them cheese and ham. When they embarked from Crete, several passengers were drunk because they had consumed too much malmsey wine. To pass the time after meals, they played games. They played chess, cards as soon as they appeared in the late fourteenth century, and especially dice. Everyone threw them, from the poorest pilgrim to the greatest lord. And this went on no matter what the circumstances. Although the court was in deep mourning on the return from Egypt, Saint Louis found one of his brothers playing dice; in his anger, he threw the dice and the table overboard. Music, singing, and for some, reading passed the time in an atmosphere that varied, according to Felix Faber, with the climate and the conditions of the sea. Various incidents caught their attention. When a diver repaired a broken rudder, Faber was astonished, wondering how he could breathe so long underwater, handle the hammer, and replace the nails.

Pilgrims also spent the time singing litanies and reciting prayers. More often than not, the prayers were to ask for divine grace for someone who had died: sailors who had had accidents or passengers who had succumbed to disease. The *Contarina* left Venice on June 6, 1480. On the 15th, a sailor, who was between twenty-eight and thirty, died. He was sewed into a coat, weighted with sand, and thrown overboard. A few days later, in Curzola, they buried a sailor who had been killed in an accident. On July 6, another accident ended more happily. A sailor's shirts fell overboard. Their owner tried to recover them but, although he was a good swimmer, he would have drowned if his companions had not launched the lifeboat. On the return voyage, in August, two pilgrims died of illness: a Franciscan and a layman, both of whom were buried. Soon thereafter, a German knight who died was thrown overboard, since the ship had left port. And Sancto Brascha, on his return from Nicosia, noted the poor condition of many pilgrims "because of the very bad air of the island": a German knight, Sigismund, who had been made mad by fever, gave himself three mortal knife wounds; another German knight who threatened to do the same, was bound in ropes and died like that; a ship's officer tried to throw himself overboard in a fit of madness, but was held back in time. Sancto Brascha himself had a high fever for six days. On August 30, while sails were being repaired, the largest of them fell on the second in command, who was immediately killed; he was buried on the island of Cyprus. The same day, after the galley sailed, a German knight died, and his body was quickly carried back to land.

There were dramatic events on board ship, but also events of an entirely different magnitude on land. When the governor of Corfu informed a German delegation that the sea was infested with Turks and advised against continuing the voyage, there were vigorous discussions among the pilgrims. There was great disappointment, because many of them had come from distant lands, and the voyage had cost them dearly. Felix Faber, who wanted to go on, was violently criticized; pilgrims objected that it was easy for him to die because he had neither relatives, nor friends, nor fortune. It was then decided to let each one make his own decision and, in the meantime, to lead a more pious life on board, to no longer play dice or cards, and to stop blaspheming and quarreling. But the decision was not implemented, and relations grew tense between the Germans and the French, "proud and passionate men." A Bavarian priest was wounded in an altercation and it was decided from then on to separate the French and the Germans. In the end, nearly one fourth of the pilgrims decided not to go on, and among them were some important figures, including the bishops of Geneva and Le Mans.

The day had passed more or less well. After reciting prayers, the pilgrims chatted for a few moments, then went to their sleeping quarters, each one carrying the lantern he had had to bring to light the way.

They slept, but their sleep was troubled by their neighbors' movements, by odors, by heat or cold depending on the season, and by the pitching and rolling of the ship. Sometimes large rats ran over their bodies. Above all, lack of privacy offended modesty when they had to satisfy natural needs. Felix Faber describes this with great realism:

> Each pilgrim has near his bed a urinal—a vessel of terra-cotta, a small bottle—into which he urinates and vomits. But since the quarters are cramped for the number of people, and dark besides, and since there is much coming and going, it is seldom that these vessels are not overturned before dawn. Quite regularly, in fact, driven by a pressing urge that obliges him to get up, some clumsy fellow will knock over five or six urinals in passing, giving rise to an intolerable stench.
>
> In the morning when the pilgrims get up and their stomachs ask for grace, they climb the bridge and head for the prow where on either side of the spit privies have been provided. Sometimes as many as thirteen people or more will line up for a place on the seat, and when someone takes too long it is not embarrassment but irritation that is expressed. . . .
>
> At night, it is a difficult business to approach the privies owing to the huge number of people lying or sleeping on the decks from one end of the galley to the other. Anyone who wants to go must climb over more than forty people, stepping on them as he goes; with every step he risks kicking a fellow passenger or falling on top of a sleeping body. If he

bumps into someone along the way, insults fly. Those without fear or vertigo can climb up to the prow by climbing along the ship's gunwales, pushing themselves along from rope to rope, which I often did despite the risk and the danger. By climbing out the hatches to the oars, one can slide along in a sitting position from oar to oar, but this is not for the faint of heart, for straddling the oars is dangerous, and even the sailors do not like it.

But the difficulties become really serious in bad weather, when the privies are constantly inundated by waves and the oars are shipped and laid across the benches. To go to the seat in the middle of a storm is thus to risk being completely soaked, so that many passengers remove their clothing and go stark naked. But in this, modesty suffers greatly, which only stirs the shameful parts even more. Those who do not wish to be seen this way go squat in other places, that they soil, causing tempers to flare and fights to break out, discrediting even honorable people. Some even fill their vessels near their berths, which is disgusting and poisons the neighbors, and can be tolerated only in invalids, who cannot be blamed: a few words are not enough to recount what I was forced to endure on account of a sick bedmate.[14]

And when a gust of wind came up: "By day, storms are bearable. . . . But at night! The spectacle goes beyond any human conception," writes the same Felix Faber. And one dark night, when he and his companions found themselves in the midst of waves and stuck in the mud in Egypt, he declared that he had had no greater distress in all his wandering, except for one night in the desert. Nor did he remember "ever having noticed with such precision the seven hours of the night as I did that night."

Day breaks. The sailors clean the bridge. A new day begins. Hans von Mergenthal, who accompanied Duke Albert of Saxony to the Holy Land in 1476, concludes: "In short, we had very little opportunity to rest, and I think that on board ship there was little else to do but to be patient."

---

14. Passage quoted by Philippe Braunstein, "Toward Intimacy: The Fourteenth and Fifteenth Centuries," in *A History of Private Life*, II, *Revelations of the Medieval World*, ed. Georges Duby, tr. Arthur Goldhammer (Cambridge, Mass.: Harvard University Press, 1988), 587–88.

Voyages were long. Pierre Barbatre left Venice on June 6 and did not reach Jaffa until July 24, forty-nine days later. But this was an exceptionally long voyage, since the *Contarina* took only twenty-six days to make the same trip in 1483. Of those forty-nine days, the pilgrims spent only sixteen on land at ports of call; for a week, the ship lay at anchor off the coast. Hence, actual sailing lasted only twenty-five days. Return voyages always took longer because the winds were less favorable. Pierre Barbatre left Jaffa on August 13 and arrived in Venice (having changed ships in Parenzo) on October 23, almost two and a half months later. Even so, as soon as he returned to Ulm, Felix Faber announced his intention to return to the Holy Land.

Rich merchants traveled in better conditions, although not without weariness and discomfort. In Muslim countries, customs agents sometimes showed excessive zeal directed particularly against them. Ibn Jubayr, passing through Alexandria on his way to Mecca, reports:

> The first scene we witnessed on the day of our arrival was the boarding by customs agents, in the name of the governor of the city, to inspect the entire cargo.
>
> All the Muslim passengers appeared in turn; the agents recorded their names, descriptions, and countries of origin. Each one was questioned about the goods he was transporting and the currency he was carrying, in order to collect the *zakât* [tax for charitable purposes levied against certain possessions of Muslims that had not been used for a year], without bothering to find out whether or not a year had passed since he had taken possession. Most of the passengers had undertaken this voyage only to fulfill the obligation of pilgrimage and had only brought along provisions for the voyage. . . . Then the Muslims were ordered to disembark their baggage and their remaining provisions. On shore, they met agents who took charge of bringing them to customs and carrying all their things. They were then called one by one, and each one presented his baggage in the crowd. All the baggage was searched, whether it was of any value or not, and it was all jumbled together. Agents stuck their hands under belts to find anything that might be hidden there. Passengers were asked to swear that they had nothing besides what had been found. In the midst of this crush, a good deal

of baggage disappeared, either stolen or lost in the crowd. Finally, the Muslims were released after this terribly humiliating and degrading process.

The Alexandria customs agents were just as zealous at the time of Felix Faber. And the pilgrims were well aware of it. "On the 24th [of October 1483]," the Dominican from Ulm reports, "at daybreak, we gathered our things together and prepared bags and baskets, arranging things inside so that any one searching us would find nothing precious at the top of all this baggage." Some pilgrims placed ducats inside loaves of bread, others in the lining of their clothing, in a flask of oil, in butter or cheese, everyone trying to hide some in various ways, because the collectors of Alexandria demanded a combined tax and passage fee for everything that came into or went out of Alexandria.

As for the merchants:

The sun had risen shortly before, and those who wanted to go in with loaded camels were making a great uproar, yelling in front of the outer gate. The guards of the gates finally arrived with the customs men and the tax collectors. . . . They made all the camels kneel, and throwing the bags to the ground, they searched everything, including the camel drivers, their co-religionists, and, before our eyes, they made the Saracens, the Egyptians, and the Moors undress to make sure they were not concealing anything. . . . If we had been merchants, we would not have escaped such treatment [the pilgrims were better treated]; they strip them down to the skin and, something that is inhuman and shameful even to mention, they search even in the anus, the mouth, and the ears for gold and precious stones that might be hidden there.

*A more optimistic note.* Chinese ships appear to have been comfortable, to judge by the description of them by Ibn Battuta:

On the ship [the junk] there are four bridges with sleeping berths, cabins, and rooms for merchants. The cabin may contain several berths and privies. It has a door that can be locked. The merchants travel with their concubines and their wives. It often happens that a merchant stays in his cabin and no passenger knows that he is on board until they reach port.

When Ibn Battuta was in Calcutta on his way to China, a junk was fitted out. He asked for a cabin for himself, because of his concubines, since he usually traveled with them, but the steward told him that Chinese merchants had hired the cabins for the round trip, although his son-in-law, who had one, would agree to give it to Ibn Battuta; however, he added, it had no privy. Nevertheless, Ibn Battuta ordered his baggage embarked. But one of his young female slaves told him that the cabin he had rented was too cramped. Then the master of the junk suggested that he embark on a smaller ship where suitable cabins were available.

At sea, the traveler did not have to worry about lodging, even though he might have little room. On land, things were not the same, unless he slept in the open. In any event, whatever the means of transport, the question of the expenses of travel had to be faced.

# material considerations

## ℒODGING

At nightfall, if he had not already solved the problem, the traveler was seized with the concern of where to stay. Solutions varied according to his social situation and from century to century.

We can deal briefly with the great personages who owned various properties, such as the kings of the Carolingian era arriving in their palaces made ready by special servants. Failing that, they invoked the right of shelter that required bishops, abbots, and vassals to receive them and to cover the costs. Notker of Saint-Gall depicts the ardor of a bishop who had just learned of the emperor's arrival and who had churches, lodgings, and even streets prepared to receive him. It was indeed not a small matter to receive the monarch, since his retinue might include several hundred people. The right to shelter obviously gave rise to abuses. This is why, in Meaux in 845, the bishops asked the king's men to behave properly in the bishop's house and to allow no women to come in. Many protested against the great expense involved, but in vain, for it was easy and economical for the prince to stay with members of the nobility. Most of the charters of Charles the Bald were signed during his stays in major abbeys, such as Saint-Denis and Saint-Martin in Tours. The heavy expenses created by such stays were not balanced by the advantages that the abbots might draw from them.

In his work *On the Organization of the Palace*, which concerns the age of Charlemagne, Archbishop Hincmar of Reims indicates that taxes should be enough to feed the court, in Aix and when it traveled, as well as to ensure that the army lacked for nothing. But needs had to be foreseen.

> The three ministers: the seneschal, the wine steward, and the constable, according to the nature and importance of their offices, each one with respect to what concerned him but in agreement with the others, was required to inform immediately all the agents of the State when and for how long the king would stay in any particular place so that transport and preparation of whatever was necessary could be carried out. Thus the royal personnel would not be needlessly troubled by a delay in providing information, nor would provisions be required to be made at inopportune times or with too much haste. . . . Also included among these ministers was the steward (*intendant*) who, as his name indicates, was charged, along with the others, to ensure that the agents mentioned above and the revenue collectors would know at the right moment that the king was coming to their territory at such and such a time and to such and such a place.

During the same period, aristocrats required to attend the king or wishing to visit relatives or friends tried to take advantage of an institution of Roman origin that lasted until about 865, that is, securing lodging and requisitioning everything their retinue might need. For example, a bishop had the right to demand daily forty loaves of bread, three casks of drink, one pig, three chickens, fifteen eggs, and fifteen casks of fodder, whereas a vassal had the right to only seventeen loaves of bread, one cask of drink, and two of fodder. Relay stations provided fresh horses.

The custom assimilating popes to monarchs allowed them to use the right to shelter, for example during their stays in France in the twelfth century. But this right had two drawbacks: it could only be used in a fixed location and authorized only brief stays. Hence, popes stayed little more than two weeks in episcopal cities and for even shorter times in abbeys. However, the expenses incurred by a visit of the sovereign pontiff burdened episcopal finances only in part. Around 1127, in a dispute between Bishop Étienne de Senlis of Paris and his archdeacon Thibaud about their respective powers, the arbitration conducted in Rome stipulated that the bishop would not take collections in his parish himself, without the archdeacon, except in order to receive the pope. According to a decree of King Louis VII of France, "the abbot [of Tournus] will impose the *taille* on *bourgeois* only for our aid and lodging, or for the lodging of the lord pope or one of the cardinals."

There might be a formal agreement in the case of a long stay. The Roman curia, for example, entered into conventions with the town of Viterbo in 1266 and 1278. Since the town knew that the arrival of the pontifical court was favorable to economic activity, it benefited from this fact. According to the agreement accepted by Clement IV in 1266, the town had to enlarge the apartment built a few years earlier under Alexander IV. It was also to build at its expense a large room in the episcopal palace next to the cathedral and supply housing for the cardinals and their retinue. The number of members of the curia having the right to free lodging was, in addition, substantial. It applied not only to the most important, but also to a swarm of chaplains, cooks, messengers, and servants, everyone for whom the Apostolic Chamber (the ministry of finances) normally paid rent.

In a Private House

More generally, hospitality granted might not be a matter of obligation. People were frequently well received by relatives or friends.

Sidonius Apollinaris, a high official, had no problems, thanks to his many connections. When he came to Bordeaux, his many friends vied with one another to welcome him in their homes, and he had merely to send them a message to have a comfortable apartment immediately available. After he became bishop, he received the same welcome from his colleagues.

Writing to Donidius, he explained why, although he had left for Nîmes some time ago, he had still not arrived. He had had a delightful stay in the pleasant homes of two very agreeable men. "It remains for me to unveil the lovely organization of the hospitality I received. . . . Every morning there arose a first friendly dispute between the two about their guest to determine which of the two kitchens would be the first to light its fires for our meals."

But generous hospitality might turn out to be importunate, by limiting freedom and causing delays. Writing to Herenius to narrate his journey from Lyon to Rome, Sidonius Apollinaris declared:

> From the moment I left the ramparts of our city on the Rhône, being summoned by imperial letter, I used the official post, which by the way took me through the homes of my comrades and friends; what caused delays on the way was not the lack of post horses, but the great number of friends who, grasping me firmly in their arms, vied with one another in attentiveness to wish me a pleasant journey and return.

Arriving in Rome with a high fever, Sidonius was glad to avoid the noisy festivities for the marriage of the patrician Ricimer and the daughter of the emperor and to rest in a rented lodging. "I found refuge in a hotel apartment that I had rented, and today as I write you these words in my bed, I am still giving myself a little more time to rest."

Throughout the Middle Ages, staying with an individual, relative, friend, or even stranger was a common practice. The welcome of a knight errant at night in a hospitable, though unknown, dwelling was a veritable *topos*. In Chrétien de Troyes's romance *Erec and Enide*, written around 1170, Erec, a knight of the Round Table, has gone in pursuit of a dwarf and a knight who have affronted him. He comes before a fortified city.

> And Erec followed the knight
> Straight across the courtyard,
> Till he'd shut himself in a room.
> Seeing him safely housed,
> Erec could not have been happier.
> Going a little farther,
> He saw an elderly man
> Of the lower nobility reclining

On the steps of a shabby house,
A good gray-bearded, honorable
Man, fine-featured, courteous.
He was sitting all alone,
Obviously lost in thought.
He had the look of a sensible
Man, who'd offer a visitor
Shelter. Erec approached,
And the old knight turned to meet him.
Before Erec could speak,
The old man bowed in greeting.
"Good lord," he said, "be welcome!
And be my guest, if you will:
My house is ready to receive you."
Erec answered, "My thanks.
I come seeking shelter
For the night, a bed and a roof."
Erec dismounted and the old man
Himself took in his horse,
Led it in by the bridle,
Knowing his household honored.
And then he summoned his wife,
And his daughter wonderfully lovely;
They'd been busy, off in a workroom;
I've no idea what they made.
The lady came out, and her daughter
With her. . . .
. . . . . .
The old man said to his daughter,
"My sweet good child, take
This horse and lead it straight
To the stable where my own are kept.
Make sure it lacks for nothing,
Unbuckle its saddle and bridle,
Set out oats and hay,
Curry and brush it well,
See it has all it needs."
The girl then took the horse,
Unlaced its armored breastplate,
Took off its saddle and bridle.

The beast was in very good hands:
She devoted herself to its care,
Covering its head with a halter
And a padded collar, curried
And combed it, tied on a feedbag
And filled it with plenty of hay
And oats, all clean and fresh.
And then she came back to her father,
Who said, "My dear daughter,
Now take this knight by the hand
And honor his presence in our house
By showing him up to his room."
The girl was courtesy
Itself, and never held back.
She led him off by the hand.
Her mother had gone up first
To see that the room was readied,
And covered over the bed
With embroidered quilts and blankets,
On which the three of them sat,
Erec, his host to one side,
His host's daughter on the other.
A hot, clear fire was burning.
The good old man had only
A single servant, no chamber-
Maid, no groom, no boy,
And this servant was in the kitchen,
Cooking meat and fowl
For dinner. She was wonderfully deft,
Able to quickly and carefully
Boil beef and roast
Fowl. And when the meal
Was ready, she brought them water
In a pair of basins, laid out
Cloths and napkins, bread
And wine, quickly and well.
They seated themselves at the table.
Whatever they wanted and needed
Was waiting ready to hand.

. . . . . . . . . .

They sat up late, that night.

> White sheets were put on the beds,
> And down-soft quilts, and they finally
> Stopped talking and all went happily
> Off to sleep.[15]

Without hesitation and despite his poverty, the old man takes Erec in and treats him as well as he can. Of course, not everyone was as hospitable, but a passage like this is evidence of a certain state of mind.

A state of mind that could be found in all social categories: let us remain in the world of literature with the seventh of the *Cent nouvelles nouvelles*, a collection of bawdy tales dating from the middle of the fifteenth century. A carter delivers willow charcoal to a goldsmith of Paris. Once the charcoal has been unloaded and his horses installed in the stable, he takes his time eating supper. When the diners are quite satisfied, the bell sounds midnight, which surprises everyone.

> Since it was so late, the goldsmith invited his carter to sleep there, fearing for him an encounter with the soldiers of the watch who, if they had found him in the street at that hour, would not have failed to lodge him in the Châtelet prison. But, given the circumstances, our goldsmith had so many people who worked for him that he was obliged to have the carter share the bed he occupied with his wife.

The carter, as a man of common sense, begins by refusing the offer and insists with all his might on sleeping on a bench or in the barn. But he must give in to the insistence of his host. You can guess the sequel.

However, having someone sleep in your own bed even when your wife is there is not pure fiction. For example, a letter of remission of September 1398 recounts the following anecdote. The Tuesday before Lent, Jean Jourdain, a tailor established in Parthenay, was visited in his workshop by a young Englishman named Guillemin, a clothing worker passing through the town. Jean Jourdain hired him and, the following Wednesday, after eating and drinking in several places in town until nightfall, they

---

15. *Erec and Enide*, tr. Burton Raffel, 367–401, 449–99, 690–94.

went to a combmaker who had lodged the Englishman the night before; but the worker and his wife refused to welcome him again. Seeing that it was night, Jean Jourdain brought him home and put him to sleep in his own bed with his wife who was already asleep, with himself in the middle. During his sleep, Guillemin attempted to rape the wife, who defended herself.

Here are a few examples of lodging gleaned from letters of remission in Poitou in the fifteenth century. With a relative: Guillaume Cado, a saddlemaker living in Lusignan, who went to Poitiers to commit a theft from a rich priest, spent the night at his mother-in-law's (the document does not say whether she was aware of his intentions). With a person with whom one has business relations: Guillaume Perault slept near Poitiers in the home of the man who had rented him an animal; Renaud Chabot, lord of Jarnac, having come to Clairvaux, half of which belonged to him through his wife, stayed with his steward. Members of the clergy often spent the night with a colleague or in a monastery. Sometimes it was a matter of obligation, with individuals providing, more or less willingly, beds for soldiers.

It happened that lodging was provided for payment, along the lines of the good man in Boccaccio's *Decameron*. Living in the plain of Mugnone, he was accustomed to putting up people he knew for payment.

In Muslim countries, hospitality was the rule to judge by the narrative of Ibn Battuta. In Maqdishû (present-day Mogadishu, capital of Somalia), the inhabitants had the following custom. When a ship arrived, it was met by little boats carrying young men. Each of them had a plate of food and offered it to a merchant on the ship, saying: "You will be my guest!" Thus when each merchant debarked, he had a house to welcome him, unless he came often and knew the inhabitants of the city; in that case, he stayed where he liked.

In Ladhîq (the former Laodicea of Phrygia), when Ibn Battuta and his companions went through a market, men came out of their shops to greet them and took their horses' reins, but other men challenged their right to do so and a quarrel broke out. While they were afraid of being robbed, an inhabitant explained to them that these were members of two brotherhoods both of which wanted to offer them lodging. "We were all surprised by the generosity of these people. But they made peace on condition that we draw lots to determine with whom we would stay first."

## Thanks to the Church

If the Church wished to be faithful to the teaching of Christ, it had to come to the aid of the most deprived. And among them were poor travelers journeying for pious reasons or afflicted with disease. The Church thus had a particular duty to pilgrims and to the sick. Monks in particular practiced hospitality. A guest house, a *xenodochium*, became a required addition to every monastery.

Chapter 53 of the Rule of Saint Benedict treats all phases of accommodating strangers, from their arrival and first meal to their lodging if they wish to stay. "All guests who appear will be received like Christ, for He Himself is to say: 'I was a stranger, and ye took me in.' Suitable consideration will be shown to all, especially to brothers in the faith and to pilgrims." Once welcomed, the guest is led to prayer, then the monks sit in his company to listen to an edifying reading, and finally he is shown all possible generosity. The superior breaks his fast, except if it is a privileged day; the brothers observe the usual fasts. The abbot washes the guests' hands, and then, with the whole community, he washes their feet. It is recommended to take particular care in greeting the poor and pilgrims. The kitchen serving the abbot and guests is set apart so that guests arriving at unexpected hours will not trouble the monks. Two brothers are assigned to serve in this kitchen; help is given them if need be, evidence that guests are generally numerous.

Whereas in the older rule of Le Maître, measures were taken to avoid theft, such precautions disappeared in the rule of Saint Benedict. On the contrary, it was stressed that beds were to be provided with sufficient coverings. A change of attitude had taken place, with suspicion giving way to solicitude. What was now important was to receive strangers fittingly. In the rule of Le Maître, two monks with no particular qualifications were given the duty; in the Benedictine rule, a "wise" manager "imbued with the fear of God" was given the duty of administering the lodging of guests. The length and the dignity of the office had been so enlarged that it can be considered something new. With rare exceptions, monks were not to mingle with guests or speak to them. Whereas Le Maître feared that the guests might be thieves, Benedict was concerned that they might disturb the monks by interfering with their fasts and their silence. What

Benedict wished for primarily was that all men be honored. If certain guests were owed particular respect, this was because as poor strangers they bore more resemblance to Christ; "the very fear of the rich forces us to grant them honor."

Throughout the Middle Ages, the Church was thus concerned with the poor traveler, particularly if he was on the way to give thanks to God. In its canon 11, the Council of Mâcon in 585 reminded bishops of their duty of charity and hospitality. Canon 19 of the Council of Paris in 1213 contained the same recommendation.

To provide a clearer picture of reality, let us examine the lodging provided for pilgrims to Santiago de Compostela. The *Guide du pèlerin* mentions only one hospice, probably the most important one, the hospice of Saint Christine at the pass of Somport, described as one of the three largest in the world, the other two located in Jerusalem and at the Saint Bernard pass. But all along the route, many foundations welcomed pilgrims. For example, by the twelfth century Paris had a hospice located on the present-day rue Saint-Jacques. From a bull of Alexander III, we learn that the Church of Compostela owned a certain number of religious buildings to which hospices were connected in the northern Pyrenees. The crossing of the Pyrenees was probably the most dangerous part of the journey. According to the founding charter of the hospice of Roncesvalles, thousands of pilgrims had died stranded in snow storms and even more had been eaten by wolves. This establishment then expanded a great deal because of its location as well as its reputation, as evidenced by a curious document from the early thirteenth century that praises its comfort:

> There is no road comparable to that one, for those on the way to Santiago; there is none more heavily traveled. . . . The door is open to all, sick or healthy; not only to Catholics, but also to pagans, to Jews, to heretics, to the lazy, to the frivolous, in a word, to the good and the unbelievers. In this house, they wash the feet of the poor, wash their heads, cut their hair, and patch their shoe leather. Perfectly honorable women, who can be reproached neither for dirtiness nor for ugliness, are in charge of the sick, whom they care for with similar piety. The houses of the sick are illuminated, by day by divine light, at night by lamps that glow

like the light of morning. The sick rest in soft and well-adorned beds. No one leaves before he has recovered his health.[16]

A vault and a funerary chapel near the hospice contradict the last sentence. But the Augustinians of Roncesvalles were past masters in the art of advertising.

The presence of so many establishments was not merely a response to the concern to encourage pilgrimages. The monasteries in charge, in fact, received many donations in return, so much so that they sometimes competed with one another. In 1118, the monks of Villafranca complained of a nearby hospice because it was usurping their rights over pilgrims. Monarchs even guaranteed a monopoly for housing travelers on parts of the road.

The growth of hospitality on the road in the course of the second half of the twelfth century was related to the development of traffic linked to the growth of trade. The poor were not the only travelers, but in the face of the dangers of the mountains all men were equal.

Forests were another area of risk. Hence, from the late eleventh century on, monks, canons, and even laymen formed associations in the forested regions between the Scheide and the Rhine to provide assistance to travelers.

Over the centuries there thus came into being an entire network of hospices, the management of which was frequently entrusted to monks or nuns, most of whom followed the Rule of Saint Augustine. Towns and villages had such hospices, but only major cities had *hôtels-Dieu*, where instead of putting everyone in a common room, it was possible to separate the sick from travelers staying for a few nights and to keep them away from women in labor.

Most deeds establishing *hôtels-Dieu* or donations to support them make reference to the notion of poverty. The traveler far from his country of origin, often lacking in temporal goods, seemed to be the quintessential poor man. The hospice of the Saint-Esprit-en-Grève in Paris had its origin in the poverty of provincial émigrés. A judgment rendered by the personnel of the

---

16. Document quoted by M. Defourneaux.

Requêtes du Palais in 1497 recalled that in 1360, 1361, and 1362, the kingdom of France went through major wars, famines, and great mortality

> because of which many men, women, and children left their country to seek food and other necessities, and such poor people came to Paris in very great number and quantity, and especially many children who went door to door for bread by day, and at night found nowhere to sleep, and for that reason, and especially the girls, they were in great peril of falling into sin.

In 1410–11, the *hôtel-Dieu* of Saint-Gervais in Soissons registered the death of a crossbow man who was passing through with several companions. According to a record of the *hôtel-Dieu* of Paris from 1457–58, various foreigners were frequently received "such as Flemings, Germans, Scotchmen, Englishmen, Spaniards, and people from beyond the mountains."

Illness was mentioned less frequently than poverty. However at Saint-Sauveur in Lille, the canons of Saint-Pierre noted that

> since this hospice was particularly intended for the relief of the sick and bedridden poor, and for the reception of pilgrims and travelers, we are absolutely determined that the said hospice avoid lodging travelers in good health . . . so that the revenues intended for pilgrims and the bedridden sick can be fully reserved for them.

Given the suspicion of diseases that seafarers might bring with them, special hospices and lazarettos were provided for them very early. In Venice, a surgeon named Gualtieri was paid by the authorities to take care of the sick and wounded on galleys. In 1318, he became governor of the Saint-Antoine hospice intended for poor, aged, and infirm sailors.

In France, with the crises that arose in the middle of the fourteenth century, the hospices whose revenues were of agricultural origin experienced marked decay, and in the late Middle Ages, the feeling about poverty was transformed. In the interests of the common good, it was necessary to identify the false poor and the idle in order to drive them off. As for the truly unfortunate, in the good cities of the fifteenth century, activity was undertaken in two directions. It was important to reform the institution of the hospice; since the Church manifested obvious incapacity, there was a secularization of the management of hospices. In the second place, because the hospices could not deal with famines, the authorities took measures to remedy shortages.

In Jerusalem, after a prayer at the Holy Sepulcher, the pilgrims would go to their lodgings. The Italians had a wider choice than other Westerners. The clergy went to the hospice located on the ruins of the hospice of Saint John of Jerusalem, formerly splendid but now notorious for its lack of comfort. In 1480, the laymen who had come on the *Contarina* stayed in a house halfway between the Holy Sepulcher and Mount Zion. Sancto Brascha, a guest of Agostino Contarini, was more comfortably lodged in the monastery of Mount Zion. In fact, custom allowed the captain of the galley to stay there with two passengers. Sancto Brascha noted the well-being he enjoyed and emphasized the quality of the wine served by the brothers. In 1493, the Franciscans secured the abolition of this obligation from the Venetian Senate so that they could choose their own guests. In addition to comfort, the Mount Zion monastery, located outside the walls, benefited from cooler air.

To the free, but uncomfortable hospice, those who were well off preferred a hotel.

In a Hotel

Inns existed in the early Middle Ages, but it was preferable to seek hospitality from a relation or in a monastery. Sidonius Apollinaris—to be sure a high official—declared to Lampridius that only under duress would he go to those places frequented by drinkers, where you have to hold your nose "while grumbling about the smoke from the kitchens where strings of red sausages flavored with wild thyme held on two metal rings spread their odor, mixed with the smoke coming out of the pots, amidst the crashing of dishes." Aside from such drawbacks, there was always the possibility of an attack. The frequently licentious atmosphere of these places made them a target for harsh criticism from moralists.

Hostelry had, of course, long been connected to the road. But in what period of the Middle Ages did it take on the functions assumed by monasteries and put in place specific characteristics? This probably occurred during the urbanization that characterized the twelfth and thirteenth centuries. It has been noted that communal regulations make mention of the innkeeper in the course of the first quarter of the thirteenth century, in Toulouse in 1205.

In England, because the monks were not strict enough and their guests took advantage of this weakness, the Statute of Westminster I in 1275 prohibited the abuse of monastic charity. In addition, because of inflation, large abbeys tried to increase their revenues and established new hostelries to gain a profit from their hospitality. In the fourteenth century, such creations by monasteries and perhaps by lay owners proliferated. For example, when Hinton Charterhouse transferred a fair to Norton Saint-Philip in 1345, a new inn, The George, was built to support the trade in sheep and wool which had made the monastery's reputation.

Travelers' itineraries of the later Middle Ages suggest that there was an entire network of urban, village, and rural shelters.

The number of inns probably reflected the size of the town. The cities of southern France—there were 27 inns in Aix in the first half of the fifteenth century, 28 in Toulouse, around 60 in Avignon in 1370 when the pope was living there—were much less well provided than the major Italian cities—Milan where 150 innkeepers were counted in the late thirteenth century, or Florence where 622 innkeepers were registered in the late fourteenth century. We must obviously take account of the relationship between the number of hostelries and the size of the population, as well as of chronology. Establishments in the cities of Toulouse, Aix, and Rome date primarily from the fifteenth century. In contrast, in the same period, there was a significant decline in Parisian hostelries.

Further, within a single city, the distribution of inns changed. In the thirteenth century in Toulouse, they were located primarily on the rue des Auberges-du-Pont, frequented by pilgrims; then the main street coming from the south increased in importance, which brought about the establishment of inns there. Toulouse showed the coexistence of concentration and dispersion. Hostelries were concentrated essentially in two places, but there were some in every neighborhood. However, the tendency was toward concentration, where the road entered the city, along main roads going through it, and in the center. In Paris, for example, inns were numerous along the road running from north to south through the capital, as well as in the neighborhood off Les Halles, near which many merchants slept in order to be at market early the next morning.

Inns did however exist on the periphery. This location offered a certain number of advantages: space was available for stables and outbuildings; late travelers had an interest in finding shelter when the gates were closed. Thomas Platter writes that, when he arrived in Sommières, "since the gates are closed every night, we stayed at The Crown, on the outskirts, where the best inns happen to be found."

The inn was shown by its sign, by the representation of a symbol, from The Siren to The Wild Man, and including The Black Head, The White Cross, The Image of Our Lady, and The Three Pillars. It generally was an ordinary house that had been converted. Two neighboring houses or even more could be joined together. The stables were often able to hold twenty or thirty horses. The building intended for lodging normally contained a kitchen, a room for taking meals, and a greater or lesser number of bedrooms. The rooms were not numbered but bore names derived from their characteristics (The Painted Room), unless they were placed under the patronage of a saint or a biblical figure, or designated according to no particular rule. They often contained several beds.

The medieval bed bore a strong resemblance to its contemporary counterpart. It contained three elements: the wooden frame; the bed proper which corresponded more particularly to what we call bedding; and finally, the materials set around and above the bed to protect the sleeper from the view of others, from light, and from drafts. Generally, in inns as in private houses, beds were wide enough to sleep two people without difficulty.

The fittings of the bed varied according to the category of the inn. The materials used and the presence or absence of curtains and canopies established an entire hotel hierarchy. An inn in Rouen, for which we have an inventory prepared in 1395, had rooms reduced to the bare necessities: twelve beds and twelve candlesticks intended for twelve travelers. Each guest was given a made-up bed without a panel, a candlestick, two pairs of sheets, four towels, two pillows, and four nightcaps. The latter were very important, for although people slept naked, they wore nightcaps to keep their heads warm, since the rooms were not heated.

Hostelries were differentiated not only by comfort but also by size. Out of eleven inns in Aix in the fifteenth century, only two, with eighteen to twenty beds, could accommodate thirty to forty people; most of them, with seven to twelve beds, were able to shelter fifteen to thirty people; at least three inns had only three or four beds.

Given the investment necessary to set up a hostelry, the innkeeper was often merely a paid employee. Valets and chambermaids helped him in his tasks, and they are characters in literary texts. For example, in the eighteenth of the *Cent nouvelles nouvelles:*

> Not long ago, a gentleman of Burgundy went off to Paris on business and stayed in an excellent inn; it was his custom always to look for the best houses. It did not take him very long, for he wasn't born yesterday, to notice that the chambermaid who was there was a person who was bound to be generous to her fellow man.

Hostelries might house residents for very long stays: students in university towns, men at arms ensuring the defense of the city during troubles, workers involved in major projects. But guests were generally passing through. Following Noël Coulet, let us consider the clients of The Crown in Aix-en-Provence in the late Middle Ages. The clientele included merchants as 20 to 32 percent among those who have been identified, depending on the year. Mule drivers and other carriers stayed elsewhere. The percentage of clergy was between 27 and 32 percent of those identified; these were priests as well as monks and mendicant friars. The abbot of Saint-Victor in Marseille spent the night when he was hunting boar. Administrative and judicial necessities explain the presence of a certain number of court personnel and agents of the count's government, between 16 and 18 percent. Nobles sometimes stopped at this place in the course of a long journey. Most of them—from 17 to 22 percent of the identified clients—were from Provence. They came to Aix for the same reasons as the count's agents and were of course accompanied by servants. This hotel thus received an essentially regional clientele who were motivated by the role of the city of Aix as capital.

The majority of these travelers stayed for only one day. Some merely rested their animals, others arrived at night and left the following morning. Most of them came on horseback, alone or accompanied by one other person. The Crown was one of the best establishments in Aix, if not the best.

Some rich pilgrims had little recourse to monastic hospitality. On February 25, 1488, Jean de Tournai, a merchant from Valenciennes, left his town not to return until March 7, 1489, after going to the three great pilgrimage sites, Rome, Jerusalem, and Compostela, not to mention less celebrated places like Our Lady of Loreto, Saint Nicholas of Bari, or the shrine of Mary Magdalene in the Sainte-Baume. Jean declared himself wealthy enough to stay at good inns and not to rely on hospices. He nevertheless encountered many difficulties, first of all the lack of inns, some of which turned out to be bordellos. Others had no beds. He sometimes had to sleep on straw while he dreamed of a feather bed. One day he was forced to sleep in an attic, and several times in a stable. As for meals, he had to serve himself and prepare his own meat. Because the region was lacking in wood, bread and meat were badly cooked. But when he could, Jean ate well.

Merchants who traveled frequently had their habits. In August 1491, Jean Le Maçon, known as the Norman, and Jean L'Esperon, clothing merchants aged about twenty, went with their merchandise to Saint-Symphorien in the Vendée for the fair to be held on August 22, the festival of the town's patron saint. They stayed at the hostelry of a man named Étienne Dorion. L'Esperon had supper there on Sunday evening while Le Maçon went to amuse himself with a few companions. The next morning they set up their stall and were occupied all day at the fair. "In the evening, very late," they returned to the inn and ate in the lower room with other merchants. Then they sat on a bench near the fireplace and talked to pass the time. But a quarrel about a woman caused them serious trouble.

Hotel keepers provided many services. They supplied mounts for their clients, gave them loans, guaranteed their debts, collected money due them when they were not there, and stored various objects, including sums of money.

Some establishments might create anxiety. In his memoirs, the fifteen-year-old Platter recounts how, on his way from Basel to Montpellier, he spent a night in a shabby inn set in the middle of a forest. He sat at a long table in the company of shifty-looking beggars and Savoyard peasants, who were eating chestnuts and black bread and drinking cheap wine. Fortunately, after staring intently at the travelers' weapons, they started drinking seriously and tipsily went off to sleep before an outside fire.

Letters of remission, of course, emphasize the relatively frequent problems caused by lack of privacy. A letter from February 1470 narrates the adventure of Jean Taillebeuf, a young clothing merchant from Melle, who was twenty-five. He stopped at the hotel of Lucas Rateau, where he usually stayed, with four other merchants. After dinner, they groomed their horses, then returned to the room where they had eaten and conversed until bedtime. Meanwhile, two other guests returned from a wedding. Rateau then decided that four of them would sleep in one bed and three in the other, which the five merchants refused to do. A brawl ensued. When travelers were too numerous, innkeepers not infrequently decided to put men unknown to each other in the same room, at least in inferior establishments.

A much odder adventure happened to Jacques de Belleville. This twenty-five-year-old squire came to Poitiers in October 1462 to carry on a suit against the bishop of Luçon. Arrested on orders of the king's prosecutor in Poitou, then released, he decided to stay in town to settle his affairs. So he took a room in the Mouton. On Saint Luke's Day at around eleven o'clock at night, a certain Hilleret Tondeur, an officer of the town provostship, secretly entered the hotel and came into his room, armed with a large dagger, accompanied by two valets in cloaks, each one of which had a large knife. Terrified, Jacques told Hilleret that this was no time to carry out justice. He got up and sat on the bed, dressed only in a nightshirt. Hilleret put his right hand on his dagger and his left on the petitioner, who tried to flee but fell on the corner of the fireplace and injured his arm and shoulder. The candle was almost out and since it was rather dark in the room, he managed to escape. While looking for the ladder that led up to the room, he found a lantern. Because he was bleeding, while going down the ladder, he cried out: "Murder! Help in the name of the king!"

It was dark at the bottom of the ladder, but he found the open door to the unlit bedroom of the innkeeper. He went in complaining about the outrage that had been done to him. As he heard Hilleret and his valets approaching, he tried to close the door, but was prevented by a roasting spit that was in the way. He then seized the spit and, thinking that the others would try to come into the room, cried out: "Don't come in and beware. I can't see anything!" And he stuck the spit through the open door. He then heard Hilleret say: "Jesus, foul traitor, you've killed me!" He had not seen him, because there was no candle or any other light, and if he struck Hilleret with the spit, it was by accident and not deliberately and in defending himself—or so he said in the letter of remission that recounted the anecdote. The valets finally managed to enter the room and seize Jacques de Belleville.

Much more frequent were drunken quarrels, thefts, and problems of sexual morality. Drunken quarrels were frequent in taverns where men gambled at dice while drinking. And gambling, condemned by both the Church and the civil authorities, led to cheating and violence. Some inns harbored real professionals lying in wait for an unsuspecting player whom they would fleece. On December 24, 1438, the archbishop of Lyon decided to banish four individuals from Savoy who had been staying for three or four weeks in the inn of Jean du Baston living entirely on gambling proceeds.

When there were several people in a single room, it was relatively easy to get hold of a sleeping neighbor's money without being seen. For example, in June 1460, in the hotel of L'Amour de Dieu, on rue de la Barillerie in Paris, in the same room were a man from Dijon, a Norman, one from Nantes, and two others of unknown origin. Alain Robert, the Breton, was caught while taking money from his bedmate's bag.

Love is bound up with night. In Lyon, the house of Benoît Morel was on several occasions involved with matters of adultery. In July 1438, his servant, Colete de Cour, was caught *in flagrante delicto* with a married man. A year later, Benoît Morel asked the court to return to him a bed that the sergeants had confiscated after establishing that it had been used for lovemaking by a widow from Lyon and a citizen of Chalon-sur-Saône.

It was not proper for a single woman to stay at an inn. Jacques Séguin, a blacksmith from Luçon, and several companions, carpenters and tailors, hearing that there was a prostitute at the inn of Colas Giraudeau, went there. They found "the said woman, who was said to be a married woman, who was all alone in the said place in Luçon, where she had come to take care of a trial in which she was involved in the ecclesiastical court of the town concerning some legacies." When she refused to accede to their advances, they dragged her out of the hotel and raped her.

All hotels, however, should not be considered places of ill repute. On the contrary: in 1479, for example, Jean Gadart killed a soldier by hitting him in the head with a shovel while trying to prevent him from stealing the horse of a merchant staying at the inn. Satisfaction leaves few documentary traces.

In the East, caravanserais were established along the caravan routes for lodging travelers and their mounts. The caravanserai was surrounded by an outer wall containing towers and gates that were closed at night, but could be opened by watchmen if a caravan arrived at night. The large internal courtyard contained a fountain or one or more wells. There were buildings to shelter travelers, animals, and goods. The rooms had no furniture, and travelers had to bring blankets and kitchen implements, although they might rent or buy them. Ibn Jubayr provides the following description of the establishment in which he stayed that had been built on the orders of Saladin the sultan of Syria between Homs and Damascus:

> It is a very solid and very handsome building, with a strong iron gate, like other caravanserais on this road. This hostelry has running water: it flows through underground pipes to the inside, forms a kind of pool with orifices through which the water flows into a channel running around the outside of the pool, and is then absorbed by the ground.

Ibn Battuta stayed on many occasions in a *zâwiya*, a building set near the tomb of a holy figure, which served simultaneously as a chapel, a monastery for dervishes, a school, and a hotel. In Delhi, India, a lodging was especially prepared for him and his retinue.

> On arrival at the mansion which had been prepared for my occupation I found in it everything that was required in the

way of furniture, carpets, mats, vessels, and bed. Their beds in India are light and one of them can be carried by a single man; every person when travelling has to transport his own bed, which his slave-boy carries on his head. It consists of four conical legs with four crosspieces of wood on which braids of silk or cotton are woven. When one lies down on it, there is no need for anything to make it pliable, for it is pliable of itself. Along with the bed they brought two mattresses and pillows and a coverlet, all made of silk. Their custom is to use white slips made of linen or cotton as cover for the mattresses and coverlets, so that when they become dirty they wash the slips, while the bedding inside is kept clean.[17]

In the Open

Not everyone could afford a hotel room, even a modest one. Some therefore camped at night in the fields, gathering in groups when the situation seemed dangerous, for example in time of war. At all times, travelers had to deal with bad weather, which seems not to have dissuaded them, to judge from these lines by a fifteenth-century poet:

> Whoever has not slept in wind and rain,
> He is not a worthy companion.

Michault Taillevent, in the same period, recounts his adventures near Beauvais. Overtaken by darkness, he had to sleep on the ground, with only a shrub for a cushion:

> Then he looks at his bed all adorned,
> Its curtains of thistles and thorns,
> And the bed itself hard ground,
> The pillow was a thick root
> And brambles were its blankets.

Silence reigned, but Michault was not reassured. His ear was cocked for fear of wolves. He waited impatiently for church

---

17. *The Travels of Ibn Battuta,* tr. H. A. R. Gibb, v. III, pp. 737–38.

bells, cockcrow, or dogs barking. And so he spent the night full of anxiety, and then went off with his companions, merchants and carters, but bandits seized them.

Sleeping in the open air did have its pleasures, including amorous adventures. On July 24, 1391, Jehannette la Grosse reported to the tribunal of the Châtelet in Paris that the preceding Saturday at around nine o'clock at night, as she was coming back to Paris to sleep—where she usually did, in the old houses in the ditches surrounding the city—she noticed a pile of thatch. Since she needed some for the night, she approached to take some. There she saw a fellow she did not know and had carnal relations with him.

And it was pleasant to sleep under the stars in summer, when the nights were warm and you could admire sunset or daybreak. "Red night and white morning/Are the joy of the pilgrim," runs the saying.

In the desert, it was hard not to sleep in the open, or at least under a tent. Relating his journey to Jerusalem in the late fourteenth century, the lord of Anglure noted on many occasions that he slept "near a fountain."

During his second pilgrimage in 1483, Felix Faber recounts his first night in Gaza. The interpreter led the pilgrims in his group into a courtyard surrounded by a wall that could be closed by a gate. There was no roof over their heads. After lighting torches, the travelers had the camels kneel outside the wall, unloaded them and the donkeys, carried their possessions into the courtyard, and had the camel and mule drivers stay outside. After blocking the gate with stones and wood to prevent any incursion by the Saracens, they lit a fire and cooked pieces of dough. After the meal, they lay down next to a stone and cement trough built along the wall. Those who could find no room near this trough settled where they could. "And so we slept that night in the open air, exposed to the dew from heaven." A little further on, Faber describes the usual nighttime arrangements. When the pilgrims got off their donkeys, they set up the tents under which they slept. However, some of them used their clothing for more protection. The tents and baggage were set together in the middle. On the periphery slept the mule and camel drivers with their animals. It was forbidden to leave the camp.

In Baalbek, a mameluke took Bertrandon de La Broquière along with him, but since he had no tent, the two men stayed in gardens under the trees; and the Burgundian lord noted that he thus learned to sleep on the ground, to drink water without wine, and to sit on the ground with his legs crossed "which was a little hard for me at first."

## PAYING

The record of an overland journey between Manosque and Genoa toward the middle of the thirteenth century gives us some idea of the expenses incurred by travelers.[18] A group of Hospitalers and their servants, traveling with horses and pack animals, went to Genoa in May 1251 to meet Pope Innocent IV and to ask his help for the hospice of Manosque. The author of the account, a certain André, was no doubt not the only "spender"; thus he did not note all daily payments, particularly for food.

Expenses fell under two major categories: transportation, and lodging and food. For the former, we may ignore the repair of Martin's shoes (10 deniers the first time, 1 denier each of the two others), which suggests that he was traveling on foot, but it was also necessary to repair horse collars or a saddle, perhaps to buy a new pack animal, and on several occasions to change the shoes on Brother Jacques's horses and mule. Above all, the animals had to be fed: daily sustenance for a horse came to between 1 and 1.5 sous per day, as much as for a man.

In the matter of lodging, it is difficult to separate men from animals, and the cost was obviously a function of the comfort. Lodging for the servants and the horses of Brother Jacques together came to 22 deniers tournois[19] in Ventimiglia, 40 deniers tournois in San Remo (24 for the horses, 16 for the men), and only 20 deniers in Porto-Mauricio. To nightly shelter itself were added the costs of lighting.

As for feeding the men, it should be noted that the Hospitalers had a cook, for whom they bought earthen pots and wood. But his role was determined by locally available resources. The food was apparently rich and varied, but we do not know its cost.

---

18. According to A. Venturini.

19. The *livre tournois*, an accounting device, was worth 20 *sous tournois* or 240 *deniers tournois* (1 sou was worth 12 deniers). In France, there was no coin worth 1 sou until 1266 (the *gros*), and no coin worth a livre until 1311 (the *agnel*).

To the extent possible, let us compare the cost of this journey by monks in the thirteenth century with the expenses incurred by wealthier people two centuries later.[20] First there were some bourgeois sent by the commune of Poitiers to see the king in Paris in 1449, 1451, and 1454. These embassies included as many as thirty horses or more, which considerably increased expenses. It is appropriate to separate costs for food from those for shelter. A cook appears in the account for 1449. The travelers bought their own food. During the nine days spent in Chinon in 1449, bread accounted for 18 percent of expenses, wine for 22 percent, and the rest for 60 percent. And expenses varied from day to day. On Thursday, September 12, 1454, the nine Poitevins spent approximately 37 sous for food, including bread, wine, mutton, pork, and two capons during the day; bread, wine, two capons, four chickens, a shoulder of mutton, saffron, and spices in the evening. But the following day, a Friday, that is, a day of abstinence, food cost them only 21 sous and 10 deniers for bread, wine, eggs, butter, and cheese. Fish was much more expensive than meat, and for the price of a dish of carp it was possible to purchase seven or eight chickens and two shoulders of mutton.

It is difficult to be precise about lodging expenses, because they were not separately noted, but were included in the costs of supper. However, for the 1449 journey, they accounted for 22 percent of the expenses related to people. Although the travelers slept two to a bed, which was customary, the mayor perhaps had an individual bed, since its cost for one night in 1454 was 20 deniers, or the price of a meal.

An average charge for the horses can be determined, generally 35 deniers each, 10 for lunch and 20 for supper—which included shelter—and 5 deniers for oats supplied in the morning before departure. In Chinon in 1449, the expenses were higher, between 40 and 45 deniers per day, because instead of relying on the innkeeper, they had to buy the food and have the stables cleaned. It cost 30 deniers a day to rent a horse. In 1463, a merchant from Bressuire who wanted to go to Châtellerault rented a horse from an innkeeper in the town for a much lower sum— 20 deniers—but he had not made a good bargain, because it was

---

20. According to R. Favreau.

a nag, and the poor merchant took ten days instead of five to cover the 160-kilometer round trip between the two towns.

At around the same time, Julien Boutaric, host of The Crown, a three-star hotel in the town of Aix, kept account books. For each client, he noted the length of stay, the size of the retinue, and the sum expended. The brevity of these documents makes interpretation difficult. The formula used most frequently indicates the average price of a day "for a man and his horse, 5 gros." However, it is also noted that a horse left alone at the hotel for the entire day cost 3 gros. The traveler's noon or evening meal came to 1 gros, 2 patacs. (A patac was worth 2 deniers, according to the rate published by the *États de Langue d'Oc* in 1487.) The cost of a bed was rarely indicated separately.

A canon of Notre-Dame-la-Grande of Poitiers, named Jean Ferrut, went to Paris three times in six months in the course of 1408, because of a pending trial between the chapter and its abbot. He traveled on horseback. Normally he took five or six days to go from Poitiers to Paris and back, leaving on Monday and returning on Saturday. His daily expenses, which diminished from February to July, were on the order of 4 sous. When he left, he bought a horse that he sold on arriving in Paris, and did the same on his return, which saved him stable expenses. During one journey, the canon had to keep the horse in Paris for six days so that it could recover before being sold: this cost him 2 sous, 3 deniers per day. To these expenses were added those for a blacksmith.

It is difficult to draw conclusions from such notations, except that upkeep for a horse was almost the same as that for a person. Expenses varied as a function of the social condition of travelers. Some events created an explosion in prices, such as the jubilees of 1300 and 1450 that drew hordes of pilgrims to Rome.

To be more fully appreciated, these prices should be compared to the cost of living. A day at The Crown was equivalent to the daily wages of a reaper, not including the expenses for a horse, which doubled the price. In the early fifteenth century, a mason in Poitiers was paid 3 sous per day, a laborer 20 deniers. This amounts to saying that an artisan could hardly afford a horse, even a common one, the price for which, judging by the accounts of Canon Jean Ferrut, varied from about 4 to about 9 livres.

Obviously, questions of money brought about quarrels in inns, particularly when clients did not want to pay, but also because innkeepers interfered in their affairs. Patrick Calendar, the Scottish servant of a king's chamberlain, loaned 2 onzains to Mathurin Pelletier, a relative of the woman innkeeper of The Black Head in Lusignan. He was told that she would answer for it. But when he was about to leave the following morning, she said that she had promised nothing and refused to deduct the amount loaned from the bill.

In 1384, Robinet Tirand, a king's equerry, went to Toulouse, where he lodged with Jacomard de Joye and his wife, who ran a hotel on rue du Temple. He occupied a room on the upper floor, and his servants put under the bed in the room two chests containing money and jewels. Tirand asserted that he had asked for the key to his room in vain; the hostess answered that she would give it to him a little later. During his absence, the chests disappeared. When Tirand accused the hostess of having robbed him, she and her husband declared that they knew nothing of the chests. They said that they had given him a key, and were therefore in no way responsible. They tried to cast suspicion on a certain Jean Denys. Finally, the Parlement ordered them to return the stolen objects or their value to Tirand and to pay for the costs of trial.

What was the budget of a traveler who went by sea? Sancto Brascha, who went to the Holy Land in 1480, provided excellent advice at the conclusion of his narrative in a note entitled *Instructions for those who want to make this holy journey*.[21] He noted in particular:

> Thirdly, he [the pilgrim] should take two purses, one filled with infinite patience, and the other containing 200 Venetian ducats, or at least 150, because you need 100 per person for the journey if you love life and are accustomed to living delicately at home; the other 50 will be for illness and anything that might happen.

---

21. The quotations from Sancto Brasch are drawn from the introduction to the edition of the *Voyage de Pierre Barbatre à Jérusalem en 1480* by Pierre Tucoo-Chala and Noël Pinzuti.

A little further on, after indicating that it is better to sail on a galley reserved for pilgrims, although you can find cheaper passage on a coasting vessel:

> You have to sign an agreement with the captain, who generally asks for 50 or 60 ducats. For this price, he is obliged to provide round trip passage, to give you food (except at port stops), to pay for transport animals in the Holy Land, and to cover all taxes and tributes.

Sancta Brascha, an important personage, was well aware that some pilgrims had only meager resources. He therefore worried about their fate:

> Since I do not wish to discourage poor people, who do not have sufficient resources to allow them to bring enough money, from undertaking this journey, I can tell them as a consolation that when the captain knows that some pilgrims are poor, he is inclined to accept them for 30 or 32 ducats, and for this sum he provides them with passage and pays for transport animals, taxes, and tribute; it is up to them to secure food more economically than those who have greater means; the poor pilgrims have access to the kitchen to cook their food, just like the others.

In an age in which each Italian state coined its own currency, a final piece of advice turned out to be of some use.

> Finally, it is indispensable to have gold and silver coins minted in Venice shortly before departure, because otherwise the Moors would not accept these coins even if they were to weigh 10 grains more; and the captain must be paid in this currency because he is required to use it with the Moors.

It should be added that the shipmaster was more or less greedy. For example, when the 1479 expedition turned out to have incurred a loss, Agostino Contarini, the master of the ship on which Sancto Brascha embarked, needed financial recompense; in addition, he wanted to amortize his very recently built ship as quickly as possible. Pierre Barbatre mentions the numerous ruses he used to increase his profits: he threatened to abandon the pilgrims on the way to get an increase in the price of the journey, and he carried merchandise on his ship, which was forbidden by the regulations. When, because of political events, some pilgrims left the ship in Corfu, hence shortly after sailing from Venice, he returned 10 ducats to each of them, whereas they had paid 55. (The ducat, a gold coin, was worth 40 sous, according to the rate published by the *États de Langue d'Oc* in 1487.)

Wishing to return to Venice, Felix Faber went with other pilgrims to the Venetian dock in Alexandria to discuss their crossing and its cost with the masters of the galleys:

> But we found them greedy and abusive in their demands for the price of sailing, more than the Saracens or the Arabs. Some indeed asked for 50 ducats from each pilgrim. And as we showed ourselves hesitant to accept that price, another master arrogantly declared that for his part he would not accept less than 100 ducats per man. Thus he mocked and humiliated us.

Muslim ship owners seemed just as greedy. Ibn Jubayr notes that the inhabitants of 'Aydhâb—a port on the African coast near the Sudanese border—loaded their ships so much that passengers were piled on top of one another. They thus recovered the cost of building in a single crossing, with no concern for the dangers of the sea, in accordance with the proverb: "We are responsible for the planks, the pilgrims for themselves." Ibn Jubayr spoke from experience, for he had spent twenty-three days in 'Aydhâb, not counting the Monday of his departure, he carefully points out.

Bertrandon de La Broquière writes that in the Holy Land the Saracens wanted to force pilgrims to rent donkeys for 5 ducats that cost only 2 to buy.

The Crusades involved significant expenses. In 1201, in order to deliver Jerusalem, the Crusaders needed ships; an embassy was sent to Venice. An agreement provided for the construction of transport ships to carry 4,500 horses and 9,000 squires and other ships for 4,500 knights and 20,000 foot soldiers; these ships would hold nine months of provisions for men and horses. The Venetians would receive 4 marcs per horse and 2 per man. But all the Crusaders did not go to Venice.

The price of passage was demanded in the army. And there were many who said that they could not pay for their passage; and the barons took those that they could. So they paid the price of passage—at least as much as they could—when they had requested and demanded it. And, when they had paid, they were neither halfway there nor at the end.

Pilgrims drew from their savings, sold their goods, and borrowed particularly from the Templars, who used their own funds and donations not designated for special purposes. In 1135, a couple from Saragossa asked them for 50 *morabetins* to go to the Holy Land; in 1168, Ramon de Castela and his wife, who wished to make the same journey, left their goods as a pledge with the order for an advance of 100 *morabetins*. Officers on missions had their expenses covered by the administration:

> Know all that I, Jean Le Mercier, counselor of the king our lord [Charles V—the document dates from 1377] confess having had and received from François Chanteprime, general collector of assistance destined for the war, the sum of 70 francs which was due me because of the 5 francs that the king ordered me to take and have each day when I ride abroad for the purpose of his work.

Material questions also included the traveler's equipment, his baggage, and his clothing. Let us recall some advice from Sancto Brascha who, it is true, liked his comfort and was making a long journey.

> He should take with him a long and warm piece of clothing for the return, when it is cold; a large quantity of shirts to avoid lice and other unclean things, as much as possible; and also table napkins, towels, handkerchiefs, sheets, cushions, and other things of the kind. . . .
> Then, he should have made a long coat of coarse material with sleeves that can be set on the bridge to sleep in the open; he should buy a thin mat to use as a bed, a large chest, and two casks, one for wine, the other for water.
> Then, take with you a good supply of Lombard cheese [Sancto Brascha was from Milan], sausages and other salted meats of all kinds, biscuit, some loaves of sugar, and several

kinds of preserves and sweets, but not in too great quantity because they spoil rapidly. Above all, you must have with you a large quantity of fruit syrup because it is the only thing you can consume when it is very hot; and also ginger syrup to soothe the stomach when it has been tired out by repeated vomiting; but you must use ginger sparingly, because it heats you up a good deal. It is also good to take a few quinces without seasoning, some seasonings flavored with rose and carnation, and some good products with milk. . . .

When you disembark somewhere, you should supply yourself with eggs, fowl, bread, sweets, and fruit, paying no heed to what has been paid to the captain, for this is a journey during which your purse should not remain closed.

And let the ship sail on!

# knowledge of geography

℣raveling meant covering a certain distance which, if it was small, posed no particular problem. A peasant would go to the fields every day, or to the tavern, and theoretically every Sunday to church. The road was well known, tied to habits acquired in childhood. But when there was a question of venturing beyond the familiar horizon, it was necessary to find out about the roads and possibly to learn how to use maps to get one's bearings.

## THE WORLD IN WORDS

There are passages of geographical interest in many medieval works, including commentaries on the Bible and chronicles. Writers knew that a complete description must encompass the country, the people, and surprising things.

When the Venerable Bede († 735) described Britain at the beginning of his *History of the English Church and People*, he drew inspiration from Pliny's *Natural History* (first century), from the *Collection of Curiosities* of Solinus (third century), and from the *Historia adversos paganos* of Orosius (fifth century).

Britain, formerly known as Albion, is an island in the ocean, facing between north and west, and lying at a considerable distance from the coasts of Germany, Gaul, and Spain, which together form the greater part of Europe. It extends 800 miles northwards, and is 200 in breadth, except where a number of promontories stretch further, the coastline around which extends to 3675 miles.[22]

The same texts were still being used in the late tenth century. In his *History of France*, Richer felt the need to describe the world and Gaul.

Divisions of the world. The habitable surface of the globe is divided, according to the geographers, into three parts: Asia, Africa, and Europe. The first, which extends from north to south in the East, is externally limited by the Ocean; internally, it is separated from Europe from the Riphée mountains to the navel of the world by the Thanaïs, Lake Méotide, and the Mediterranean. From the navel to the south, it is separated from Africa by the River Nile. As for Africa and Europe, they are externally surrounded by the Ocean from south to north. The Mediterranean flowing between them separates them. Their internal borders with Asia are the Nile for one and, as we have said, the Mediterranean, the Thanaïs and Lake Méotide for the other.

Although each one has its own subdivisions, I have thought it proper to indicate the parts of only one country in Europe, Gaul. Its name comes from whiteness, because its native inhabitants are characterized by very white skin.

Divisions of Gaul. Gaul itself is divided into three parts: Belgium, Celtic Gaul, and Aquitaine. The first, Belgium, stretches from the Marne to the Rhine, which, beginning at the Ocean, is the border with Germany, the cradle of many races whose name comes from the word 'germinate'. On its two sides, Belgium is protected by the Pennine Alps and by the sea that flows around the British Isles. Celtic Gaul stretches lengthwise from the Marne to the Garonne; its sides are bordered by the British ocean and the British Isles.

---

22. Bede, *A History of the English Church and People*, tr. Leo Sherley-Price (Baltimore: Penguin Books, 1955), 37.

The region stretching from the Garonne to the Pyrenees is called Aquitaine; its borders are on one side the Rhône and the Saône and the Mediterranean on the other. In summary, we see that the whole territory of Gaul is bordered on the east by the Rhine, on the west by the Pyrenees, on the north by the British sea, and on the south by the Mediterranean.

All the elements of this description come from Orosius, the *Etymologies* of the early seventh-century bishop of Seville Isidore, and from Caesar's *Commentaries*. It would be futile for travelers to seek information in works of this kind.

Works that really dealt with geography were of two kinds. Some were theoretical, dealing with the Image of the World, and the others belonged to a lived geography, that is, narratives by travelers and pilgrims.

The theoretical works dealt with the universe as a whole and consequently were of little interest to the traveler. There were four elements, of which earth was one, the last, enclosed within the others, since philosophers considered the world to be a sphere.

When various countries were examined, they were first grouped together under the heading of the three continents (Europe, Asia, Africa), but soon scattered through thematic chapters studying islands, promontories, mountains, and the like.

The Image of the World, however, was gradually perfected. The first geographers wished primarily to provide lists making it possible to understand the works of Antiquity and the Bible. But some did not restrict themselves to the Mediterranean world of the Ancients. In his history of the archbishopric of Hamburg and Bremen, Adam of Bremen († c. 1081) introduced into the geography of Europe Scandinavia, Iceland, and the Orkney, Faroe, and Hebrides Islands, regions that were part of his episcopal province. The work was not a simple compilation but relied on primary sources. For example, to describe Scandinavia, Adam used accounts by King Svend of Denmark and his advisers and even elements derived from his own experience. After crossing the Danish islands, he writes, travelers reach two immense kingdoms, "practically unknown until now," Sweden and Norway. "I received information about them from the very learned king of the Danes," who assured Adam that he knew them well since he had served twelve years in those countries.

How did Brunetto Latino (*c.* 1220–1294), encyclopedist and Florentine political figure, who composed his masterpiece, *Le Trésor*, in French, imagine the world? The earth, surrounded on all sides by the sea, contains three parts: Asia, Africa, and Europe, but Asia makes up half of it, from the mouth of the Nile to the Ocean Sea and the earthly paradise. The Mediterranean, an arm of the Ocean Sea, separates the two western continents, Europe in the north and Africa in the south.

In Asia, Egypt is watered by the Nile, flowing from the Tigris, which lies between Africa and Asia. Arabia is located between the Tigris and the Nile, near the Red Sea. Syria and Judea make up a large province watered by the Jordan, which flows into the Dead Sea near Jericho. Then comes Palestine and the country of the Amazons. Still further on, there are vast snowy solitudes and deserts. Beyond that live the "Seres" (the Chinese). To India is attached the Caucasus which overhangs a large part of the world and the island of Taprobane in the Red Sea. The earthly paradise, whose climate is always temperate, is located in India, but it has been closed since the first sin.

Europe contains first Italy, with Rome the capital of Christendom. From the mountains that border it on the west flow two rivers, the Po that crosses Lombardy and flows into the Adriatic near Ravenna, and the Rhône which turns toward Burgundy and Provence. Beyond that lies Greece, with Thessaly, and then Macedonia and Mount Olympus, Thrace, Romania, and Constantinople. The Danube, which has its source in the high mountains of Germany, has sixty navigable tributaries. Further on, Scythia is in Asia. Germany stretches to the Rhine and even beyond, since Lorraine is a part of it. France and Spain are bordered on the west by the Ocean Sea. Because of the increase in population, inhabitants crossed a strait and came to a large island called England. Nearby is Ireland. Beyond the island of Thule, the last one in the north, the sea is frozen.

From Spain, through the pillars of Hercules, you reach Africa, the country of the Moors that stretches as far as Egypt. Brunetto mentions Mount Atlas in the middle of the sands, the two Gulfs of Sidra where the sea is very rough, the desert of Ethiopia in the south, and the Tigris.

A new period began, however, in the thirteenth century. The seizure of Constantinople and the ability to reach the Russian steppes through the Black Sea, and the Mongol conquest that made it possible to cross Asia in safety facilitated travel and made it possible for travelers to describe regions that had been practically unknown until then.

The routes that connected the West to Egypt and the Holy Land were followed by a horde of pilgrims. Academic descriptions gave way to lived experience. In a preamble addressed to King James III of Scotland, Jean Adorno writes that his father "did not choose the simplest and shortest route, but a holy and very long pilgrimage in the course of which he visited many holy and celebrated places in Africa, Asia, and Europe."

Next to be opened to western travelers was the interior of Asia, along with its coastal fringes. Around 1220, Jacques de Vitry could still write that his description of Asia owed a good deal to the writings of Pliny, Solinus, and Isidore. In contrast, toward the middle of the thirteenth century, Giovanni del Pian di Carpini and William of Rubruck described a very real continent, with its snowy plains inhabited by Tatars, simultaneously fearsome warriors and peaceful cattle breeders. Marco Polo then revealed to the West a more southerly Asia, with its expanses of sand and high plateaus.

While Asia was being opened up to travelers, Africa appeared to be less well known. Until the middle of the thirteenth century, knowledge of Africa came from the works of late Antiquity, except for the Mediterranean coasts. The desert prevented Europeans from venturing into black Africa, and they were blocked even more by the Muslims' desire to have no competition in trade with the Sahel. Beginning in 1250, missionaries belonging to the mendicant orders traveled to Ethiopia, known indirectly from accounts by pilgrims to the Holy Land. Not only the east, but also the west of the African continent was gradually opened up. But there were countless mistakes and confusions. In a letter sent to a probably Ethiopian King John in 1177, Pope Alexander III calls him "king of the Indies." And the eastern shores of the Indian Ocean still remained quite mysterious.

Western travelers, as opposed to scholars, described the countries that they visited, but did not limit themselves to landscape, also showing interest in the people and their customs. It is not without interest to consider, conversely, the knowledge that Easterners had of the countries of the West. Arab travelers, who wrote copiously about Eastern Europe and the Byzantine Empire, were much less forthcoming about Western lands.

Their works nevertheless contain many detailed observations that made it possible to supplement earlier compilations. For example, Ibrâhîm ben Ya'qûb made a long journey to the West around 965. Although we have only excerpts from his account made by a writer in Damascus who died in 1283, it is possible to reconstruct the journey. From Bordeaux, he went to Noirmoutier and perhaps to Saint-Malo, and then to Ireland; he then made a long tour of the Empire and crossed Italy to reach Sicily, where he embarked in Trapani. According to him, the continental West is comprised of two parts, the "land of the Franks" subject to the emperor (the king of Western Francia is not mentioned), and "the land of the Slavs." The country of the Franks, enormous and with a harsh climate, is rich in grains, fruit, rivers, and cattle. The soldiers are very brave, and the people dirty and deceitful.

Laonikos Chalkokondylis, an Athenian who, it seems, never left the East, but who, of all the Greek writers of the fifteenth century seemed the best informed about France and England, had very limited and frequently mistaken knowledge of geography (according to Alain Ducellier). The northern border of France is supposed to be "upper" Germany. The River Tartèsos separates the two countries. It flows from "Mount Pyrenee" (designating the Alps) and into the "western ocean" opposite the British Isles. On the east, France shares a border with Liguria, on the south with Spain; on the west are located the Ocean and the British Isles. From the "external Alps of Italy" to the Ocean and the country of the Germans is at most a seventeen-day journey, while it takes nineteen to go from Italy itself to the Ocean and from Spain to Germany. One of the British Isles is named Anglia. There are three of these islands, but only at low tide; at high tide they make up a single island. The capital of the country, London, is located on a river that flows into the Ocean opposite France. Ships can go as far as the city at high tide.

A traveler could not be satisfied with names alone. To keep from getting lost, he needed maps.

## THE WORLD IN PICTURES

It is necessary to distinguish the concrete space of the user from the abstract space of the cartographer. For a peasant, a forest was more a collection of rights than an organized surface, which did not prevent him from knowing its shape. A unified vision was the later accomplishment of the forest administration.

The representations produced by the cartographers of the Middle Ages reveal their intellectual and technical capacities. A map is, in addition, conditioned by cultural traditions. It has a fictive character (even if it has scientific pretensions) tied to conventions, such as the location of north at the top of current maps.

With respect to the area represented, there appeared successively, in the early Middle Ages maps in two hemispheres depicting either the entire world or its habitable surface, in the twelfth and thirteenth centuries regional maps, and in the fourteenth maritime maps.

Another variety of map, deriving from a Roman tradition, was that of the itinerary aimed at presenting a network of lines and not grasping a continuous surface. The most famous of these is the Table of Peutinger, prepared in the mid-fourth century, in which various itineraries are represented on a simplified map of the then known world.

Aristotle saw the earth as a globe, about which Greek scientists provided details, recognizing four parts, only one of which, that inhabited by men, was known; within that, they distinguished Europe, Asia, and Africa. The Fathers of the Church were hostile to this conception. How could men live upside down? Moreover, the Gospel had been preached in the four corners of the world. There was a return to the idea of a flat disc on water. But, since Macrobius and Martianus Capella, whose works were read throughout the Middle Ages, adopted the theories of the Greeks and believed that the earth was a sphere, the picture of the terrestrial globe survived.

Schematic maps represented the world as a flat disk on which only the inhabited land was indicated. The disk was divided by two axes in the form of a T, the horizontal indicating the Mediterranean and the vertical the Nile and the Tanaïs (the Don, believed to be a continuation of the Nile). The T marked off three parts: the upper half was Asia, the lower left quarter Europe, and the lower right quarter Africa. In Antiquity and the early Middle Ages, the island of Naxos was placed in the center. But in 1110, shortly after the First Crusade, Jerusalem was for the first time represented on a map as the center of the world, where it remained throughout the Crusades.

After recognizing that medieval geography impoverished the legacy of Antiquity, aimed at confirming the symbolic value of its conceptions, and was notably characterized by opposing categories such as Christian world and pagan world, another kind of interpretation, closer to immediate medieval reality, would place this cartography in the larger context of a culture dominated by theology. Maps did not represent a real world but an allegory of that world, cartographic equivalents, in a sense, to universal chronicles. They could therefore have no possible practical use.

This analysis seems to be accurate with respect to the map of Ebstorf or the map of Hereford, both of which date from the thirteenth century. But a subsidiary document connected to the former states that it can be of use to travelers. And the assertion is not inaccurate insofar as, although no routes are shown, the traveler can find on the map the stages and the end of a journey. It has been possible to recognize on the second the stages on the pilgrimage route to Santiago de Compostela. It is nevertheless quite clear that these maps have to be considered in a theological context. What must be emphasized is that they represented reality for their makers and those who consulted them. It was by looking at a map that Hugh of Saint-Victor became aware, for the first time in the Middle Ages, of geographical phenomena that had not been transmitted by Antiquity.[23]

Two periods seem to have been particularly important in the development of cartography. In the Carolingian era, maps grew out of the teaching dispensed in monasteries. In the twelfth century, contacts with the East through the Crusades showed up in maps, notably the one on which Hugh of Saint-Victor made a commentary. What was new in this period, and the travelers of the thirteenth century were to benefit from it, was the confidence given to maps. Until then, maps had served to recall names and were subordinate to written texts. But Hugh of Saint-Victor's description of the world follows the opposite procedure. It is drawn from the map, attentively examined, so that a much more precise description of geographical realities comes out. After a prologue, in twenty-eight chapters the author treats:

---

23. See particularly the work of Patrick Gautier-Dalché, as well as Paul Zumthor, *La Mesure du monde* (Paris, 1993).

1. The twelve winds
2. The islands of the Ocean Sea
3. The islands of the Tyrrhenian Sea
4. The islands of the Adriatic Sea
5. The cities of the larger islands
6. The islands of the Red Sea
7. The rivers of Asia
8. The mountains of Asia
9. The regions and peoples of southern Asia
10. The provinces and cities of western Asia
11. The provinces of Asia Minor
12. The provinces and cities of northern Asia
13. The names and various things of the sea
14. The part of the world called Africa
15. The monsters of Ethiopia
16. The regions of Egypt
17. Libya and the peoples of the region
18. The part of Africa opposite Spain
19. Europe which is the third part of the earth
20. The provinces and cities of Italy and Greece
21. The cisalpine part of Europe
22. The provinces and cities of Gaul
23. The provinces of Spain
24. The location of Italy
25. The location of Gaul
26. The location of Great Britain
27. The location of Hibernia [Ireland]
28. The location of certain islands.

For the first time with this work we see a map playing a significant role in the knowledge of geography.

From the thirteenth century on, the idea of granting maps priority over documents was constantly reiterated; at the very least, they were to be considered of equal value, as Hugh asserts in his prologue. Roger Bacon declares that a map must come to the aid of perception, because a text does not provide enough clarity. At the beginning of his work on maps, the Franciscan Paulin of Venice writes that the map cannot be separated from the geographic text. Petrarch used maps and claimed they were superior to traveling, while at the same time criticizing mistakes in place names.

This intellectual procedure was followed by practical applications. In the course of the second half of the thirteenth century, authors of plans for Crusades supplemented their texts with maps. For example, Fidentius of Padua added a sketch of the Mediterranean to his *Book of the Recovery of the Holy Land*. In the early fourteenth century, Marino Sanudo asked a maker of maritime maps to illustrate one of his works.

The *portulans* (coastal maps) were the most fully developed form of this way of thinking. The earliest known date from the second half of the thirteenth century. It seems that Saint Louis had a *portulan* for his Crusade of 1270. Contemporary with the maritime expansion of the major Italian cities, the *portulan*, the work of merchants, was a response to economic requirements. It was a coastal map designed for sailors practicing coastal navigation in the Mediterranean, and thereafter in the Atlantic and even in the Indian Ocean. The irregularities and particular places located on a sea journey made up the substance of the document, in which inland territory was given little space. The *portulan* was thus profoundly different from the usual map. It had no enumeration with exhaustive pretensions and no theological context, but a concrete space with comprehensible signs and the essential element of the representation of distances.

Of Italian origin, the *portulan* spread very rapidly, to Catalonia by the fourteenth century and to Portugal and Spain by the fifteenth. By around 1350, an shipmaster under the authority of the king of Aragon had to have two on board.

In addition to the *portulan* providing information on distances, the fifteenth-century pilot used a route chart, a work indicating the nature and depth of the sea bottom, seamarks, and access to ports. One of the best-known route charts is that of the Portuguese Garcia, known as Ferrande, composed in 1483.

On the technical level, the *portulan* presupposed the use of a compass. Probably introduced into the Mediterranean in an archaic form by the Normans around 1200, the compass showed the movement of a magnet on a compass rose with sixteen points. If he knew the speed of his ship, the master or pilot could take soundings and determine his distance from irregularities of the coast. The Mediterranean, whose dimensions had been exaggerated in Antiquity, was thus given more precise measurements. In the absence of a scale, possible mistakes about intervals were corrected by a grid of lines that cut the space into triangles following the rhumb lines (an angle equal to 11°15'). It was thus possible to situate points on the shore in relation to one another. In 1210, Guiot de Provins explained how to use a compass. When the needle has touched the magnetized stone, the sailors place it on a piece of straw that they set in the water. The point then turns to the polar star. When the night is dark, the sailors light up the needle and can thus see their way.

The geographical coordinates of longitude and latitude were very late to appear in the West, even though they were known from tenth- and eleventh-century Arabic translations of treatises on the astrolabe, and from the twelfth century on, from translations of ancient Greek works on astronomy. Roger Bacon writes that because of the lack of precision of the measurements of latitude and longitude, they have to be authenticated by an authority.

In 1480, Eustache de La Fosse from Tours, prisoner on a Portuguese ship, struck up a friendship with the pilot, who showed him "the right methods to sail a ship on the sea and to orient the map so as to go from one country to another and to know how to calculate the moons, and when it will be Lent, Easter, and all at the same time." The Portuguese, who knew the southern constellations, carried out plottings of latitude on the African coast. But, although these plottings made navigation along the east-west parallels possible in both directions, it was not until the eighteenth century that longitude became fully available to navigators.

The great voyages of the fifteenth century excited the curiosity of cartographers, the pride of explorers, and the greed of monarchs, who were thus bound together by common interests. The map maker collected information provided by the navigator and prepared maps that had become ever more useful for the merchant and the prince. Nevertheless, in the late Middle Ages, there remained many uncertainties and even mistakes.

## A MISTAKE OF GENIUS

Technical progress made possible the introduction and growth of ocean navigation at a distance from the Atlantic coasts. The Canaries, islands off Cape Verde, and the Azores were discovered and occupied. These islands provoked feverish imaginings.

Ancient writers had located the Isles of the Blest far out in the western Ocean. The Middle Ages created other legends, and on maps there appeared fabulous islands, such as those of Saint Brendan (who was supposed to have reached an archipelago that was the entrance to the earthly paradise), Brasil, Antilla (also called the Island of Seven Cities), and still further west Cipangu, for the Atlantic Ocean was thought to touch the shores of both Europe and Asia. Cipangu was the Japan described by Marco Polo in the *Divisament dou Monde,* a place he had not seen, although he claimed it had large quantities of gold. The Venetian explorer also spoke at length of Cathay, or China, of the Great Khan, and his capital Khan-balik:

> You may take it for a fact that more precious and costly wares are imported into Khan-balik than into any other city in the world. Let me give you particulars. All the treasures that come from India—precious stones, pearls, and other rarities—are brought here.[24]

But after the establishment of the Ming dynasty in China in the middle of the fourteenth century relations with the Far East had practically ceased. Then, in 1441, the Venetian Niccolò Conti, who had lived for twenty-five years in Cathay, India, and Ethiopia, arrived in Florence. Conti's account made it possible for cartographers to clarify their knowledge of the East, even though they still followed Ptolemy's representation of the world.

In 1472, Christopher Columbus entered into the service of René of Anjou and found himself at twenty-one the master of a galley. He showed himself an accomplished leader and claimed to have changed the compass needle, by magnetizing the wrong end in order to deceive a crew that was afraid to undertake a dangerous expedition. He had little theoretical knowledge but appears to have been a master in the art of sailing by dead reckoning, that is, calculating the approximate position of a ship by estimating the distance traveled using navigation instruments.

---

24. *The Travels of Marco Polo,* tr. Ronald Latham, 130. On Christopher Columbus, see M. Mahn-Lot, *Portrait historique de Christophe Colomb* (Paris, 1960).

After a voyage to Iceland, Christopher Columbus settled in Portugal, which in 1456 had received from the pope plenary powers over the coasts of Africa and beyond, over the way to the Indies. He obtained the *History of Things* of Pope Pius II, a work printed in 1477, and the *Image of the World* of the French cardinal Pierre d'Ailly (1351–1420), printed around 1480. He read Marco Polo, whose description of what is now Japan and China fired his enthusiasm. The world described by Pierre d'Ailly, in agreement with Aristotle's ideas about its small size, could not fail to encourage the navigator to sail west. According to Aristotle, a single ocean touched India and the region of the Pillars of Hercules.

Ever since Aristotle, the learned had believed that the earth was round, with the terrestrial sphere containing 360 degrees. But opinions diverged concerning the length that should be attributed to each degree. For Ptolemy, this distance was fifty nautical miles. But Columbus thought it was forty-five nautical miles, which made his world one-tenth smaller than that of Ptolemy. In addition, according to the latter, Eurasia measured 180° from west to east. But Marinus of Tyre, an ancient cosmographer copied by Pierre d'Ailly, gave the figure of 225°. Columbus, who made detailed annotations of d'Ailly's work, drew from it conclusions of considerable importance: "The extremity of habitable lands in the East and the extremity of habitable lands in the West are fairly close to one another, and in the middle lies a small sea." Because it was necessary to add to the 225° of Marinus of Tyre the 30° of longitude east needed, according to Marco Polo, to reach Japan, Columbus believed that India was not far from Spain.

Cartographers shared these opinions; for example, on a globe made in Nuremburg between 1487 and 1492 by Martin Behaim, Japan is placed at the location of Mexico, on the same latitude as the Canary Islands, a latitude on which Columbus sailed in 1492. Further, when the Portuguese court consulted the Florentine cosmographer Paolo Toscanelli about the possibility of reaching the Indies by sailing west, he is said to have responded in the affirmative and included with his letter a map indicating the distances between Spain, Antilla, Cipangu, and Cathay. Columbus, who had heard of this, is said to have asked for and received copies of Toscanelli's letter and map.

Probably in 1484, the king of Portugal had the Genoese navigator's proposals investigated. But the learned men who were consulted replied that his assertions were based on his imagination or on claims by Marco Polo. John II wished to circumnavigate Africa and thereby find a new route to the Indies. Moreover, three years later, Bartholomeu Dias sailed around the Cape of Good Hope.

Columbus then left Portugal in 1485 to go to the court of Castile. In the next few years he prepared several maps and globes. He obtained a printed copy of Marco Polo's work, as well as the 1484 Latin translation of *The Voyage and Travels of Sir John Mandeville*, who claimed to have reached China in the fourteenth century.

Belief that the earth was round raised a number of questions, in particular about the antipodes. Did the hemisphere opposite the known hemisphere contain land? And if so was it inhabited? According to Saint Augustine, the opposite hemisphere could not contain men, because an insuperable barrier, made up of the Ocean or a torrid zone, made it impossible to evangelize them. This opinion then prevailed in Castile. But Albert the Great asserted that it was difficult, but not impossible, to cross the torrid zone and Columbus noted that the Portuguese sailed in these regions and that they were heavily populated. This referred to the southern antipodes, but Columbus wished to reach the western antipodes.

Showing his globe to the monarchs, Columbus asserted that the distance to be covered in a voyage to the Indies was small, and he managed to persuade them. Finally, in this particular case, a mistake in the estimation of distance played a decisive role and made possible the discovery of new worlds.

# PART TWO

# mentalities

In 1386 or 1387, the English writer Chaucer seems to have had
the idea of presenting a picture of contemporary society, not
only the great, but also the bourgeois, and even simple folk. To
accomplish this, he decided to portray a group of characters on
the road to the cathedral of Canterbury, a major pilgrimage site
holding the remains of Thomas à Becket, assassinated on the
orders of King Henry II. The group of thirty pilgrims comes together at the Tabard Inn on the south bank of the Thames. The
innkeeper offers to lead the journey and since

> For trewely, confort ne myrthe is noon
> To ride by the weye doumb as a stoon,

he suggests that each of them tell a tale on the way there and
back. Before the departure, Chaucer presents the pilgrims.

He begins with the Knight, who has traversed Europe and
fought for his faith, his son the Squire who has accompanied
him, but fights for his lady's grace, and the squire's Yeoman,

> Ful worthy was he in his lordes werre,
> And thereto hadde he riden, no man ferre,
> As wel in cristendom as in hethenesse
>
> . . . . . . . . . . . . . . .
>
> But, for to tellen yow of his array,
> His hors were good, but he was nat gay,
> Of fustian he wered a gypon
> Al bismotered with his habergeon,
> For he was late ycome from his viage,
> And went for to doon his pigrymage.
> With him ther was his sone, a yong SQUIER,
> A lovyere and a lusty bacheler,

With lokkes crulle as they were leyd in presse.
Of twenty yeer of age he was, I gesse

. . . . . . . . . . . .

And he hadde been somtyme in chyvachie
In Flaundres, in Artoys, and Pycardie,
And born hym weel, as of so litel space,
In hope to stonden in his lady grace.

The regular or secular clergy are situated at all levels. There
is the Prioress "that of hir smylyng was ful symple and coy,"
traveling with another nun, her chaplain, and three priests.
There is the Monk

that lovede venerie,
A manly man, to been an abbot able.
Ful many a deyntee hors hadde he in stable.

He thinks Saint Benedict's Rule outdated according to which

a monk, whan he is recchelees,
Is likned til a fissh that is waterlees,—
This is to seyn, a monk out of his cloystre.
But thilke text heeld he not worth an oystre.

He rides a palfrey as brown as a bay. There are rascally
monks: the mendicant Friar who lives off others and turns out
to be capable of exploiting even the poor; the Pardoner or seller
of indulgences who has fabricated bizarre relics; the Summoner,
or clerk of the ecclesiastical court, lascivious and drunk. The
gallery of church figures concludes with the fine image of the
Parson, who visits his parishioners in all weathers.

Wyd was his parisshe, and houses fer asunder,
But he left nat, for reyn ne thonder,
In siknesse nor in meschief to visite
The ferreste in his parisshe, much and lite,
Upon his feet, and in his hand a staf.

Next come members of professions. The Clerk of Oxenford,
who plans to become a priest, does not yet have a living and
rides a nag "as leene as a rake"; with hollow cheeks and a sad

countenance, he wears a threadbare short coat. The very learned Doctor has grown rich from the plague and knows Hippocrates better than the Bible. The Sergeant of the Law, prudent and wise, very able in making land purchases, rides "but hoomly in a medlee cote,/Girt with a ceint of silk, with barres smale." And there is the poet himself, readily accepted by the other pilgrims.

There are tradesmen, beginning with the Merchant "in mottelee, and hye on horse," "sownynge alwey th' encrees of his wynnyng," but still an honest man who hopes that no ill fortune lies in store for him at sea. The Shipman, riding a russet and wearing a coarse gown, has no scruples of conscience.

> If that he faught, and hadde the hyer hond,
> By water he sente him hoom to every lond.
> But of his craft to rekene wel his tydes,
> His stremes, and his daungers hym bisides,
> His herberwe, and his moone, his lodemenage,
> Ther nas noon swich from Hulle to Cartage.
> Hardy he was and wys to undertake;
> With many a tempest hadde his berd been shake.

The Manciple, very adept at acquiring provisions, can serve as an example to buyers. The Cook can "rooste, and sethe, and broille, and frye." Alongside ride the town artisans: the Haberdasher, the Carpenter, the Weaver, the Dyer, and the Tapestrymaker, all wearing the livery of a major guild. Also in the company is the Wife of Bath, a widow of five husbands, not to mention the companions of her youth. She rides a hackney.

> And thries hadde she been at Jerusalem;
> She hadde passed many a straunge strem;
> At Rome she hadde been, and at Boloigne,
> In Galice at Seint Jame, and at Coloigne.
> She koude muchel of wandrynge by the weye.

Peasants are part of the group. The Plowman, a good worker living in peace, rides a mare. The Reeve, thin and ill-tempered, a genial scoundrel, rides a handsome dapple gray stallion and wears a long grey-blue surcoat. The Franklin, owner of a freehold, a gourmand and a great drinker, is generous in his hospitality.

The poet provides a realistic description of this variegated group as it proceeds along the roads of Kent. Of course, in many respects the characters are conventional figures, but the author focuses on their physical characteristics, their costumes, and the way they exercise their professions. They are presented again in the prologues preceding each tale. A portrait is followed by a vivid narrative. The pilgrimage brings together, at least temporarily, individuals of widely different characters.

But many journeys had other than religious motives. For Ibn Rustek—an Iranian who compiled an encyclopedia entitled *Precious Finery* shortly after 903—there were four categories of travelers: sailors and merchants; ambassadors and messengers; pilgrims and missionaries; and finally "the others," who traveled occasionally or for their pleasure. No classification system, however, can account for the complexity of human motivations.

# in the service of oneself

## Acquiring

Medieval men traveled to obtain money and glory, but it was one thing to be a young man attempting in various ways to make a place for oneself in society, and quite another to be established and wishing to improve one's lot, maintain a family, or satisfy greedy instincts.

### The Young

When we examine literary works, and in particular fabliaux, we note that the quintessential traveler, the one who shows to best advantage, is the young man. He is poor and has no profession. With no regular resources, he has no obligations and can travel as he wishes. His age is not indicated, but that is of little importance, for what counts is that he is not among the established.

He immediately solicits sympathy through his good looks, his gaiety, and his boldness. His amorous adventures end well.

The lady gave him 20 marcs;
The clerk then went off.
The next day he said farewell:
I will go to school, he thought.

In the fabliaux, he triumphs over the mature man, despite his experience, wealth, and connections. Did reality corroborate this vision of the writers of fabliaux?

## Nobles

Georges Duby has clearly shown that the term "young" applied in the twelfth century to the sons of the nobility referred to individuals older than eighteen or nineteen, who had therefore been dubbed knights and were adults. These knights seem to have been unstable. Until that point they had lived in the paternal house, and now they were traveling over hill and dale seeking glory and fortune in tournaments and through a rich marriage.

This was primarily a journey of education and the young man, at least at the outset, was accompanied by an older person who gave him advice and completed his education. He usually was part of a group. For example, Robert Courte-Heuse, son of the duke of Normandy, traveled with sons of his father's vassals who were the same age as he.

Groups of young men lived very freely. Their principal occupation was fighting, making war, but especially fighting in tournaments. One day, a group of French knights left the road they had been traveling to visit Clairvaux. Since Lent was approaching, Saint Bernard tried to turn them away from the life of arms, but in vain. They left after drinking to participate in warlike games. This kind of life was a source of danger. In setting out his genealogy in the *Annales de Cambrai* shortly after the middle of the twelfth century, Lambert d'Ardres noted the death of the ten brothers of his grandfather Raoul, killed in a single day of combat.

After wandering for a year or two, when the young man returned home, he felt ill at ease; he had tasted liberty and could no longer do without it. He went off again, sometimes after quarreling with his father who still held authority over the estate. To gain access to revenues—this was even truer for the younger sons—the best solution was to find a rich heiress to marry. Georges Duby provides a remarkable example of this quest for glory crowned by a rich marriage in William Marshal, the flower of chivalry.

His father decided to place him with William of Tancarville, and he left England with a companion and a servant. Eight years later, when he was over twenty, probably in the spring of 1167, he was dubbed a knight. After the ceremony, he and the other new knights were warned that they must hereafter count only on themselves to take care of their needs. They were strongly encouraged to go "turning about the world," hence to travel, not toward a precise goal, but searching here and there. Turning also meant tourneying, going from one tournament to another to attempt to defeat his opponents and grow rich from ransoming them. At the very moment that William was preparing to leave, word arrived of a tournament. William of Tancarville, who was forming his "team," engaged the new knight, who in one day captured four and a half prisoners—one of his companions claimed to have helped him capture one of them, and he shared with him.

Soon thereafter, William returned to England to stay with his maternal uncle Patrick of Salisbury, from whom he hoped to derive great benefit. The sire of Tancarville advised him, and William heeded the advice, not to stay long in England where tournaments were not being held. Thanks to the support of his uncle, William entered the service of the king and returned to the continent at Poitou.

Constituting the household of his elder son, young Henry, Henry II entrusted the young man to William, who became the leader of a troop of varying size, generally consisting of twenty warriors. A life of wandering began. The biography of William describes sixteen tournaments, some of which involved many participants. For example, at Lagny, the most successful, three thousand knights came with their servants. As in real battles, what was sought above all was to unhorse the leaders and to capture them. Negotiations took place in the evening. It was necessary to evaluate and to pay. The victors—and William was obviously always one of them—freely spent the money available and then were once again impecunious. It thus turned out that Marshal did little to enrich himself at the time.

After a period of disgrace, William again became close to young Henry, but the prince died in 1183. With two companions, William had to begin tourneying again. Fortunately he was a

Crusader, and on his deathbed young Henry had asked him to carry his cross to the Holy Sepulcher. After returning to England to take his leave, he left for the Holy Land where he stayed for two years. On his return, he fought in the service of the old King Henry II against the troops of Philip Augustus.

At nearly fifty, however, William wished to settle down and marry a rich heiress. The king gave him his seneschal's daughter (the father having died three years earlier without a male heir), Helvis the "damsel of Lancaster." She was entrusted to him, but she was not yet nubile, and he did not make her his wife. And he set off again to fight in the region of Maine. In 1189, he asked for and received a much better match, Isabel of Striguil. With her he had hit the jackpot. Indeed, whereas Helvis would have brought him only one knight's fief, with Isabel he acquired sixty-five and a half fiefs. But before he could receive the girl, carefully guarded in London, Henry II died, leaving the throne to Richard Cœur de Lion, who fortunately confirmed the will of his father. William immediately left Fontevraud. In two days, he crossed Anjou, Maine, and Normandy, but injured himself leaping into a boat at Dieppe. He hurried on to London, where the girl was handed over to him. At nearly fifty, he had left youth behind. He was to live another thirty years and father at least ten children.

This was an exceptional life. But in the late Middle Ages, journeys still constituted for young aristocrats a kind of apprenticeship, a means of learning about the world and of becoming known. "I have undertaken this journey to exercise my chivalric virtues, which I have the intention of carrying out successfully, with the help of God," declared Leon of Rozmital to Duke Philip the Good of Burgundy. Leon of Rozmital was one of a group of Czech lords who made a long journey of fifteen months (November 1465–February 1467) to Santiago de Compostela, passing through other holy places. In fact, the principal purpose of these young men was to visit the courts of princes to show their worth. The same was true of Pierre de Sainte-Feyre, lord of la Marche, whose first journeys brought him several times to Italy, for military reasons when he went to Naples in 1502–03, for religious motives three years later when he left to visit Our Lady of Loreto and Rome. He was proud to show his courage. When he embarked under the leadership of the count of Nemours, he noted with pleasure that others showed cowardice and dared go no further. But he was also aware of the spiritual or material usefulness of these journeys. He thought that his loyalty to the duke of Bourbon, of whom he was a vassal, would be beneficial to him, and he was not wrong. The count of Nemours granted him the title of captain of the castle of Capua, which brought in 500 ducats a year.

### Sons of Merchants, Artisans, and Peasants

Many young men, in the modern sense of the term, traveled to learn a trade or to find work. In 1341, in a letter sent from Tana to Pignol Zuchello, Niccolò Gata, a Venetian furrier, wrote:

> You know that Niccoleto, the son of Messer Marco Ieriço arrived in Tana on May 11, and he gave me a letter from you . . . and you wrote that I should treat Niccoleto as though he were you. I took him home and treated him as I would treat one of your sons tomorrow.

This passage from a commercial correspondence shows that the sons of Venetian merchants left the paternal roof when they were old enough to travel and thereby complete an education that had been only theoretical up to that point. At first, they had only modest responsibilities, notably on the state's galleys. There they would become familiar with the sea and make trading contacts, since they were allowed to bring along goods for sale. Later, they would travel to distant countries, entrusted by their fathers with management of the freight carried by the family galley. They traveled to the Channel ports in the West or the Black Sea colonies in the East, or else they set themselves up for a time in a distant location and carried on business for themselves, for their families, or for third parties for whom they acted as agents. At around the age of forty, they settled permanently. They might do so in a foreign country, but most of them preferred to return home.

In Florence, where the organization of commerce seems to have been slightly different, the education of the young was also based on experience involving many journeys. After acquiring the theoretical knowledge necessary for his trade, the son of a Florentine businessman would begin as a trainee, receiving no pay for a year. He was then sent to a branch office as an agent, perhaps later to become its director. Some might become associates on a reorganization of the company or leave and establish a new company with other young men. But most of them continued as agents.

The archives of Francesco di Marco Datini shed light on the life of this merchant born in Prato, probably in 1335. He lost most of his family at the age of thirteen. His father and mother and two of their children were struck down by the black plague. Only Francesco and his brother Stefano survived. Their tutor took charge of their small inheritance, and the two children went to live with a good woman of Prato. But Francesco, too active to remain confined, went to Florence as an apprentice thirteen months after the death of his father. There he heard merchants returning from Avignon speak of that populous and prosperous city that was then the residence of the pope. Florence was too small for him. At fifteen, he sold a plot of land for 150 florins and went to Avignon. He continued his apprenticeship with a number of Florentine merchants in that city. Enthralled by business, at twenty-eight, in 1363, using his father's inheritance, he and a compatriot established a company that brought each of them a 200 florin profit within six months. He may have traveled less than the sons of rich merchants, but his family situation made that impossible. But he was not satisfied with his native town, and even Florence was not enough for him. He had understood everything he could gain from the City of the Popes. Indeed, he stayed in Avignon after they left and did not return to Prato until 1383.

The Florentine Buonaccorso Pitti left Florence in 1372, at the age of eighteen. He returned to settle there much later. In the interval, he went twice to London, five times to Bruges, and fifteen times to Paris, following various itineraries.

Northern Europe followed the same pattern. After completing his studies, the son of a Hanseatic merchant would generally make his start under the authority of a relative. He would then go to various trading posts to familiarize himself with his future profession. Two or three years later, he became an agent and began to work for himself during trips carried out on his master's account. He might remain an agent for life, but as a rule he became more or less the head of his own business. Once settled in a city, he traveled less. Some had more adventurous lives than others. When Franz Wessel was only twelve, he was sent to the fair of Scania. Over the course of the next eight years, despite an illness that prevented him from traveling on several occasions, he went to Holland twice, twice more to Scania, to Gotland, and to Riga. At twenty-one, in 1508, he made a perilous journey, but one that was unrelated to his profession, a pilgrimage to Santiago de Compostela, during which he encountered many dangers. When he returned to Stralsund safe and sound, his parents were overcome with joy because they believed he had died.

Young men might even be completely autonomous, provided no real apprenticeship was necessary. For example, in 1464, Guillaume Porchet, an eighteen- to twenty-year-old traveling merchant from the diocese of Nantes, carried cloth to Brittany, Poitou, the Limousin, la Marche, Auvergne, and several other regions of the kingdom of France.

Although a merchant was expected to travel, the same thing was apparently not true for artisans and peasants. An artisan could learn and carry on his trade in the village of his birth or certainly in the nearest town. And yet, the reality was quite different. A letter of remission from June 1453 concerns Léonard Chétif, a journeyman shoemaker in prison in Aulnay for a number of thefts. At the age of sixteen, he had left his native town of Crozant in the region of la Marche to go to Chauvigny in Poitou, where he learned the trade of shoemaking. After staying there for two years, he went to Charroux, in the lower Marche, and since then he had lived in various parts of Poitou and the Limousin.

A study of 582 apprentices mentioned in letters of remission from 1380 to 1490 shows that 27.3 percent of them were apprenticed in their native towns, and 22.5 percent of them traveled fewer than thirty kilometers for their apprenticeship; thus, half of them traveled more than thirty kilometers to be apprenticed. However, whereas a third of the apprentices in the period from 1380 to 1440 were migrants, that is, traveled more than thirty kilometers, the percentage for the years 1440 to 1490 rose to 61.5 percent. A kind of balancing of available manpower among regions took place after French unification. But migrants did not frequently travel great distances, and almost all of them lived in the regions of the langue d'oïl.

When he had no family responsibilities, a young artisan could travel if he had no work, as shown, for example, in a document from April 1469 concerning a Parisian second-hand clothes dealer. Jean Piot le Jeune, married with children, aged twenty-five or twenty-six, declares that he was born in Paris, spent his childhood there, and was apprenticed to a doublet maker, where he stayed until he was eighteen. Having learned his profession, he went on the road and traveled to Bruges, where he stayed for a while. Then he went to work in Arras, where he got married. He had set up shop in Paris with his wife about three years before. Since he did not have enough money to become a master doublet maker, he secured letters from the duke of Burgundy allowing him to exercise the trade of second-hand clothes dealer.

Peasants themselves did not always remain attached to the soil. A father's land might not be enough to support all the children. Farm workers were sometimes forced to leave their village to find work.

Many young women went to towns to find work, particularly as chambermaids. The author of the *Ménagier de Paris* advises his wife to inquire about the past of servants, to send people to find out the region they came from, how long they had lived there, and why they had left. "And know that often women from 'foreign countries' have been rebuked for the way they lived in their country, and this is why they are serving far from home." When they came from modest families, girls were quickly placed as servants on the death of their parents. Documents from Reims in 1422 mention one servant aged six and another aged seven. More frequently, girls were placed between the ages of twelve and fourteen. Many of them probably came from the country.

Marriage, particularly of young women, was another reason for leaving home. Of course, geographical endogamy was the rule. But Church prohibition against marriage between even distant relatives led to the search for partners outside the village. Other causes had similar effects, for example, hard times. In their complaints set down in 1428, the inhabitants of the village of Saint-Christophe-en-Oisans (now in Isère) mentioned the reluctance of young women to get married in the village: "The men of the said parish marry the women and girls of the said parish, and that is where they find their wives, if the women agree, and if not, they remain bachelors."

The young were not always impelled to travel for material reasons. Sometimes, and this was true for many students, they were prompted by the urge to seek knowledge in renowned university centers.

## Students

Student mobility was apparently one of the important characteristics of medieval intellectual life. The young, and the less young—there was no fixed age for learning—went from university to university to receive the teaching of the most eminent masters. Jean Gerson, chancellor of the University of Paris in the early fifteenth century, asserted that his university represented the whole kingdom of France, or indeed the entire world, since people who wished to acquire doctrine and wisdom came there from everywhere. Jacques Verger, one of the finest scholars of medieval university life, qualifies this vision to some degree in works from which the following pages borrow heavily.[25]

Mobility existed before the establishment of universities properly speaking. It seemed unavoidable insofar as the most illustrious cathedral schools, particularly those of Paris and Bologna, acquired renown beyond their own dioceses. In the *Histoire de mes malheurs*, Abelard, who was to become a celebrated teacher and who is best known as the lover of Héloïse, recounts his intellectual travels around the year 1100. Always eager to engage in discussion, he traveled to places where the art of dialectic was honored. This was why he came to Paris. A few years later, when he wished to learn theology, he went to see Anselm of Laon, the reigning authority in the field. Bologna, famous for the teaching of law, attracted not only Italians but students from countries on the other side of the Alps. This influx obviously posed practical problems of housing and public order.

People criticized students who, when they arrived in Paris after a long journey, went to see washerwomen rather than going to confession, and claimed that their minds wandered while they were singing mass. But although they protested against

---

25. See also Léo Moulin, *La Vie des étudiants au Moyen Age* (Paris, 1991).

disturbances, the inhabitants of Paris and Bologna had no hesitation in exploiting foreigners, because only members of the city were under legal protection.

This situation brought about the intervention of superior authorities, the emperor and the pope, eager to develop schooling. For example, between 1155 and 1158, Emperor Frederick Barbarossa showed his concern for students who traveled in order to study and thus left their families, spent a good deal of money, made great efforts, and exposed themselves to many dangers. More concretely, he exempted them from the right of reprisal; that is, the local authorities were not to hold them responsible for violence committed by their compatriots, and he specified that they were subject to the authority only of their lord or of the local bishop. In 1200, King Philip Augustus of France accorded Parisian students the same status, placing them under royal protection and granting them the privilege of ecclesiastical jurisdiction. On the foundation of the University of Heidelberg in 1386, Duke Ruprecht of Bavaria took all measures "to prevent cupidity from weighing heavily on teachers and students."

In the course of the second half of the twelfth century, the religious authorities took similar measures. In 1155, students asserted that they could reside in the center of the city of Bologna, and in 1189, Pope Clement III asked the bishop to prevent prices from rising and to enforce the custom according to which once a room had been rented to a student, it was permanently reserved for that purpose. In 1280, it was provided that even if an owner was guilty of an act punished by the destruction of his house, the sentence would not be carried out if a student was living in it.

Specific guarantees applied to foreign students. Beginning in the late thirteenth century, the king of France ordered that his officers and vassals not obstruct the free travel of students on their way to Paris. Holders of church livings were increasingly excused from residential obligations so that they could continue their studies. And to prevent interruption in those studies, students were allowed to ignore any summons from the judicial authorities of their place of origin.

Because teaching was required to be done in Latin, and because the pedagogical methods used in different universities were theoretically the same, it is understandable that students could move without difficulty from one university to another. This was all the more the case because once a license to teach had been obtained, it was valid throughout Christendom. Obviously, as now, some universities were more renowned than others. Hence, whereas a Parisian graduate could easily teach in a second tier university, the converse was not true, and the equivalence of diplomas was purely theoretical.

Let us look at concrete examples of student travel. Their destinations were about fifteen universities in 1300, the most famous of which were Paris, a center renowned for philosophy and theology, and Bologna, reputed for the teaching of law. There were twenty-eight universities in 1378, at the outset of the Great Schism, principally because of establishments in the south; and sixty-three in 1500, most of the new establishments located in Germanic countries. Students from the region or the country of any particular university did not really feel uprooted. Large-scale mobility affected a much smaller number of people.

Brief manuals helped keep the student from getting lost in the intricacies of university life. The work *On conduct and the way to study,* by Martino da Fano, professor of law in Arezzo and Modena in the middle of the thirteenth century, which, according to the author, every student should own, indicates precisely how to behave: to begin with, find a professor preferably from your own country and have him accept you.

Early on, in the thirteenth century, the two major centers of Paris and Bologna attracted students from all over the West and even from the Latin East. In Bologna, the list of ultramontane nations included fourteen names: Germany, Poland, Hungary, England, France, Normandy, Picardy, Burgundy, Touraine, Poitou, Gascony, Provence, Catalonia, Spain. But Italian students made up a substantial majority. Toward the end of the Middle Ages, in the fourteenth and fifteenth centuries, there was a decline in geographical diversity. In 1403, the local area provided 92 percent of the students in Paris—to be sure, the Great Schism had led to the departure of German, English, and Italian students—and 89 percent in Toulouse. There were several reasons for this: because of new establishments, students could register in a university near home, the troubles of the time made travel more dangerous, the growth of states made getting a diploma from a distant institution of less interest, and incidents between nations proliferated. But perhaps it was less the number than the proportion of foreign students that had declined because of the increase in local numbers.

Hence, students continued to travel. They came primarily from the Empire and from regions to the north (Scandinavia) and the east (Poland, Bohemia, Hungary). For specific reasons, some universities, such as Montpellier and more precisely its medical school, maintained an extended range of recruitment. In 1393 and 1394, the small university of Avignon, one of the pontifical capitals during the Great Schism, received students from 165 dioceses; in 1403, they still represented 101.

As the situation improved, travel increased again in the fifteenth century. Whereas in the past, once a student had completed his studies in a single university he would return to his country of origin, it became fairly common to take courses in several centers. Elisabeth Mornet has analyzed the student journeys of 370 young Danish nobles from 1400 to 1540. The noble contingent represented approximately 20 percent of the total Danish university population. The proportion of young nobles intending to follow an ecclesiastical career diminished from approximately 85 percent for the period from 1330 to 1400 to approximately 65 percent for the period from 1478 to 1540. The desire or the obligation to learn had thus increased among these young travelers.

In the fourteenth century, Paris and Prague both had a modest number of Danish nobles for students, whereas in the fifteenth century they showed a marked preference for German universities. The most frequently attended were Cologne, and especially Rostock, challenged after 1456 by the nearby town of Greifswald. There was thus a retreat to the north as new establishments were created. In the late fifteenth century, however, the university horizon broadened, with students once again going to Paris or Italy, or to recently established universities such as Louvain and Wittenberg. Yet at the time there was a national university in Copenhagen. Despite the efforts of the authorities, this had done little to reduce travel. Thus, young Danish nobles traveled rather far for their studies. In addition, they went to several universities, two for more than a third of them, and 8.5 percent of that third had studied at three or even four centers. Erik Nielsen Rosenkrantz registered at Erfurt in 1465. Having become master of arts in 1470, and then a bachelor of canon law, he was rector of Erfurt in May 1472. He registered at Rostock in early February 1473, and late the same month at Greifswald, where he lived for a time and where he became rector by October. He was also the first rector of Copenhagen in 1479.

Three categories can be distinguished. The first, with a short university stay, includes only a small number of young men intending to follow a secular career who received few diplomas. In contrast were courses of study that lasted more than four years. An extreme case is Hans Axelsen Walkendorff, registered at Greifswald in 1496, not receiving his bachelor's degree until 1500, his master's at an unknown date, and residing in Louvain in 1514, when he wrote to his brother to ask for money so he could continue his studies in Paris. But the average length of studies was between two and three years if the limits of one's ambition were to be a graduate of the faculty of arts.

These nobles entered the university between the ages of fifteen and twenty-two. After several years of study, they were men when they returned to Denmark. Sometimes the process was a veritable initiation. Peder Johanson Oxe, born in 1520, left on a voyage of study at the age of twelve, accompanied by a tutor, Christian Morsing, a renowned humanist. He was in Paris in 1532, and then registered at Montpellier in October 1533. His tutor had probably stayed with him, since both went to Basel in 1534–35, where Peder Oxe took courses in theology. They returned to Denmark in 1537.

The travels of students were related to their social condition. Only those with sufficient resources, nobles supported by their families, clerics with comfortable livings, could travel to distant universities and live there for a while. Of course, there were poor students, but their numbers were limited.

Student life was made easier by a certain number of institutions. The "nations" brought together students from the same regions. In Bologna, the number increased from fourteen to seventeen to which were added four Italian nations. Paris, in contrast, had only four: French, Norman, Picard, and Anglo-German, although there were subdivisions. These nations made their first appearance in bulls of Honorius III in 1219 and 1222; but organized nations at the university of Paris are not mentioned until 1249. Their boundaries and hence their makeup varied over time. For example, in 1356–58, a quarrel broke out between the Picard and English nations over a Dutch student,

J. Mast. For years, he had been a part of the English nation, in which he had received his bachelor's degree. The Picards claimed him for unknown reasons. A commission decreed that the Meuse would be the border between the two nations, and a map was even drawn. The day after the agreement, students met at the La Grange tavern, and the understanding was sealed with hearty drinking.

The "nation" had a multinational character. For example, the English nation was divided into three provinces corresponding to English, German, and Swedish dioceses. The most important role was played by the student's diocese of origin. In Bologna, the major distinction lay between Ultramontanes and Cismontanes.

The nations had freely elected leaders. Each nation was represented by a procurator. Resources came principally from dues from members, students and professors, to which were added taxes such as those paid to obtain an academic title. Particularly from the fourteenth century on, the nation sometimes loaned money to its members when possible. Its money was locked in a safe entrusted to a church. The most frequent expense was for wine, for there were many festivals. They were organized, for example, in honor of patron saints, Saint Denis for France (the Ile de France), Saint Hilaire for Aquitaine, Saint Martin for Touraine, and were the occasion for celebration and feasting. "That day," wrote a chronicler, "more sins are committed than throughout the rest of the year." Everything was a pretext for drinking. The management of finances thus turned out generally to be mediocre and the deficits frequent.

The nations gave their members the consciousness of a certain solidarity, but their importance should not be exaggerated. Colleges created stronger bonds. Frequently, students from the same country as the founder were sheltered in a college. In Paris, students from the northern part of the kingdom had the largest number of places, with 130 reserved for them in ten colleges. Next came the Normans with 120 scholarships in eight colleges. Some houses were particularly intended for foreigners. The college of the Lombards was intended for nine students from Florence, Modena, and Piacenza. In total, there were about fifty houses able to accommodate 680 scholarship recipients, or 20 to 25 percent of the students. Most were foreigners, since except for the Sorbonne and Navarre, there were no colleges intended for the free housing of Parisians.

There were also hotels, frequently owned by foreign inn-keepers. Students often came together in such establishments, also according to their country of origin. In Bologna, Polish and Hungarian students frequently lived in an establishment located near the Sachet Brothers, while the German-speaking Swiss stayed at the A la Bèche, an inn owned by a native of Basel.

Poor students might receive scholarships generally desig-nated by the founder for his compatriots. When money was short, others relied on their families. The nations organized a postal service. In 1470, the German nation protested against its excessive charges. Because a letter had to be persuasive, there were public writers who taught how to compose one. Guillaume Houvet, procurator of the nation of France in 1494, wrote a col-lection of fictitious letters. A student could read and copy: "I have found a very good tutor and in all Paris there is no man more adept at poesy and oratory than he." The conclusion fol-lowed naturally: "I would be grateful if it were to please you to send him something so that he might know me better and know that I was better suited. Farewell."

We have many letters written in Latin. A small collection of letters, attached to a work dealing with the art of composi-tion, probably from Orléans in the mid-thirteenth century, con-tains a letter from two students to their parents. After indicating that they are in good health and that they devote themselves entirely to their work, that they are living in a fine house near the schools and that they have very respectable good friends, they add that they fear the lack of instruments will interfere with their studies and ask to have sent by the bearer of the let-ter enough money to buy parchment, ink, a writing case, and the other things they need. "You will not leave us in want, and you will make sure that we complete our studies properly, so that we can return honorably to our country." The bearer will also pos-sibly carry back shoes and stockings. Finally (courtesy is cer-tainly the order of the day), the parents can give their own news through the same bearer. The latter answered favorably and sent enough money for their two sons to "stay in school properly." Although we may not be sure of the formal authenticity of these documents, their content reflects a plausible context.

The poet Eustache Deschamps, a law student at Orléans, sent the following ballad to his father:

Dear father, please help me.
I fear I have been named excommunicate.
I have neither meat bone nor fish bone.
I have no money for the feast
Of Easter. I will be thrown out of school.
Grant my request.
I ask you for money and salvation.

Many prejudices, not to say xenophobia, were rife in university circles. In the early thirteenth century, Jacques de Vitry mentioned the gossip making the round of the schools. It was said that the English were drunk and cowardly, the French vain, soft, and effeminate, the Germans hot-tempered, the Normans proud and vainglorious, the Poitevins treacherous and greedy, the Burgundians brutal and foolish, the Bretons inconstant, the Lombards stingy and deceitful, the Romans brawlers, the Sicilians arrogant and cruel, the Brabançons arsonists and thieves, and the Flemings prodigal and gluttonous. These judgments on students of other regions were not of the kind that would soothe spirits and incidents often broke out. For example, the Norman nation regularly passed a proposal to arm its strongest members and to attack other nations. In 1356, a violent brawl broke out among French, Picard, and Norman students of the faculty of medicine over the election of deans and examiners.

In a contrary direction, this mixture of very diverse nationalities—which, however, affected only a minority—made students aware of a certain community. University life made it possible for them not only to acquire diplomas, it initiated them into life itself.

## Maturity

When youth, which in the medieval sense might last quite long, as we have seen, came to an end, travels did not necessarily end with it. But they then had the purpose not of education but of the acquisition of material goods.

*Merchants*

In the early Middle Ages, until about the tenth century, the merchant seems to have been rather isolated since he lived in a society that was essentially rural. Commercial activity, moreover, was principally carried on by foreigners, particularly Jews.

However, there was a revival of trade in the early eighth century. Around 800, then, there was a coexistence among Jews and Syrians who continued their activities, itinerant peddlers, and city people who sold locally made products at newly created fairs. The monk of Saint-Gall, who wrote a biography of Charlemagne, full of anecdotes, between 883 and 887, indirectly indicates the frequency of ships used by Jews. When the emperor was visiting a port in Narbonnaise Gaul, Norman pirates appeared in the distance; at first it was believed that Jewish merchants were on the ship. They carried out their trade throughout the Empire and sometimes even beyond its borders.

In the course of the early Middle Ages, they made it possible to maintain trade between Christians and Muslims. Ibn Khordadbeh, master of posts of the Abassid Empire, indicates the itineraries they followed in the ninth century. These merchants, he writes, know Persian, Greek, Latin, Arabic, and the Frankish, Spanish, and Slavic languages. They go from West to East and back, sometimes on land, sometimes on sea. They bring to the West eunuchs, slaves, silk, furs, and swords. Leaving the shores of the Mediterranean, they head toward present-day Port-Saïd where they place their goods on pack animals. At Suez, they take ship again and travel to the regions of Medina and Mecca, then India and China. They bring back musk, camphor, aloe, cinnamon, and other oriental products, and return to the Mediterranean along the same routes. Some sail to Constantinople, others to the country of the Franks.

Jewish merchants sometimes went to Antioch. After three days' march, they reached the Euphrates and Baghdad. Embarking on the Tigris, they arrived at Al-Obollah (a trading center that has now disappeared), and from there went to India and China. These journeys could also be made overland. Leaving from Spain and the country of the Franks, the merchants reached Tangier in Morocco, then Tunisia and Egypt. From there, through Damascus, Baghdad, southern Iran, and the region of the mouth of the Indus, they reached India and China. They might also head for upper Mesopotamia and, crossing the country of the Slavs, reach present-day Astrakhan at the mouth of the Volga, embark on the Caspian Sea, and then reach China through Turkestan.

Jews provoked animosity based on both religious and economic grounds. They could count on little but the protection of the Church. For example, four centuries later, in 1266, learning that they were the victim of abuses, Archbishop Engelbert of Cologne ordered that their liberties be posted. In particular, within the jurisdiction of his archbishopric, they were to be subject to the same duties and tolls as Christians and their goods, and nothing more.

All merchants were not Jews. For example, the pseudo-Frédégaire, author of a chronicle written in the second half of the seventh century, recounts the history of a Frank named Samo, born in the region of Sens or Soignies in Hainaut, who joined with other merchants to trade with the Slavs known as Wends, who probably lived in present-day Bohemia. Because of his bravery, they made Samo their king. The capitulary of Thionville, which dates from 805, deals with merchants traveling to the country of the Slavs or Avars, indicating how far they should go. They are forbidden to bring arms for sale, since they might be used by enemy peoples. If weapons are found, all their goods will be confiscated, half going to the palace, the other half being divided between the *missi* and whoever discovers the fraud.

Speaking of a Frisian from Saint-Goar who sailed up the Rhine toward the Lorelei in the early ninth century, Wandalbert suggests that he was both a merchant and master and captain of his ship, able to handle the tiller. We do not know whether his ship contained a cargo, but he must have been bringing something back because he had a lot of money with him, allowing him to give the gift of one livre to the altar of Saint-Goar.

Let us look more closely at the commercial activity of the Normans, of particular interest because they are usually seen primarily as warriors. After verifying the good condition of his ship and carefully recruiting his crew, a Viking ship owner took care of weapons and merchandise. His ship could not carry heavy objects; he therefore carried precious products: furs and skins, ivory, soapstone, and especially amber. These goods were sold or traded for various products in France, England, the Germanic and Slavic countries, and Byzantium. In his *Travel Narrative*, Ibn Fadlan, an Arab diplomat speaks of the Rus, that is the Varegs or Vikings, probably Swedes, who traveled to the east.

> I saw the Rus who had come to trade. . . . As soon as the ships have been anchored, each Rus disembarks with bread, meat, onions, milk, and a fermented drink, and goes to a large post set there, which has a human face and is surrounded by little idols, themselves ringed by stakes set in the ground. Each Rus then goes up to the great idol and prostrates himself, saying: "Lord, I come from a far country with so many young women slaves and so many marten skins," and he starts to enumerate all the goods he has brought. He then adds: "I offer you this present." Then he lays down his offerings before the post. Then he says: "I wish you to grant me the favor of sending me a merchant covered with many dinars and dirhams, that he buy from me everything I want to sell to him, and that he not disagree with what I say." Then he steps aside.

In the eleventh and twelfth centuries, merchants were still "dusty feet" carrying rare products coveted by nobles. Harsh measures were taken against them, but they resisted. In the twelfth century, statutes began to regulate their trade. It was advisable to treat them well for fear of reprisal. The protection of the prince was obviously not free. It is not certain that a legal system governing merchants was in place by the twelfth century, but the privileges granted by the countess of Flanders in 1252, and the creation of a captain of the king to protect traveling merchants in France in 1288 probably played a greater role than the peace institutions of the eleventh century.

*The Essential Rights of the City of Pavia*, whose central sections were composed between 1010 and 1027, shows the ancient wealth of the Lombard kingdom. "On their entry into the kingdom, the merchants paid, at the crossing points on the roads belonging to the king, a tithe on all goods. . . ." And the document mentions Englishmen, Saxons, Venetians, and people from Salerno, Gaëte, and Amalfi "coming traditionally to Pavia with plentiful goods." Hence, professionals in the town fostered a diversified commerce controlled by the state, which granted them safe-conducts. Some came from abroad, but most from

Italy. Within the borders of the kingdom, the document does not mention merchants from cities linked to Pavia, but the rest of the document indicates that they all were.

In the late Middle Ages, some places presented a genuinely cosmopolitan appearance. Since the island of Cyprus was the last Christian land before the East, the merchants and their ships had to stop there, as did pilgrims. Rudolf, the vicar of Suchen in Westphalia, who went to the Holy Land in the mid-fourteenth century, noted that all the languages of the world were taught, spoken, and read there. Hieronymus Münzer, a German traveler, reports that in the late fifteenth century merchants gathered in the square in front of the Exchange in Bruges. There you could see Spaniards, Italians, Englishmen, Germans, and Osterlins, in short, representatives of all nations. Some streets were reserved for Spaniards, others for Florentines or Genoese.

Some figures emerge from the shadows, such as Benedetto Zaccaria, born around 1248 in a family of the Genoese nobility. In 1259, when he was still quite young, he traveled to the East. Along with his brother Manuel, he obtained in fief the territory of Phocea in Asia Minor, which had significant alum deposits. To reduce the price of this mineral, the brothers built, bought, or rented ships to transport it themselves. When they were not using these ships for their business, they rented them or used them to fight the Aegean pirates. They also imported and exported many other goods in addition to alum. Their business caused them to travel constantly in the Mediterranean and the Black Sea. Benedetto often went to Genoa where he participated in loans to the state and to Constantinople where he owned a house. In addition to his economic activities, he played political and military roles. But he remained a merchant. In 1286, after pursuing Pisan corsairs as far as Tunis, because his term of office had expired, he left the Genoese fleet to take care of his own ships. The political position he held for a time in Syrian Tripoli allowed him to pursue Muslim pirates who were extremely harmful to his business. In return for twelve galleys, the king of Castile granted him as a hereditary fief the town of Puerto Santa Maria, opposite Cadiz. This town was a port of call for his ships in the Atlantic and made it possible for him to do business in Spain. King Philippe le Bel of France named him admiral of his fleet built in Rouen. Zaccaria then returned to the East, where he seized Chios which the emperor granted him as a fief; Chios was the only producer of putty. He returned to Genoa where he died in 1307 or 1308.

After a Genoese, two Venetians. Around 1260, Niccolò Polo and his brother Maffeo decided "to embark on one of their ships, loaded with varied and precious goods; having set sail, they sailed over the deep sea and, with a good wind and the guidance of God, they reached Constantinople with the vessel and the goods." After staying a while in that city, they agreed together to go across the Black Sea with their cargo to increase their profits. "So they bought many jewels of great beauty and price, set out from Constantinople by ship and, sailing into the Great Sea [the Black Sea], they went to Soldanie [Sudak]."

There, the two brothers considered and decided to continue on their way. They set out on horseback. In that way, they reached the court of a Tatar king about one hundred kilometers south of Kazan. They obtained the right to trade on his territories. As they were about to return to Venice, a war broke out and anyone who traveled the roads was taken prisoner. Since Niccolò and Maffeo could not return to Constantinople the way they had come, they decided to go further, to go around the Tatar kingdom on an unknown route, and to return to Venice another way. They crossed the Volga, journeyed for seventeen days through a desert, and reached Bukhara on the silk road, in present-day Uzbekistan. Because of the war, they had to stay there for three years. While there, a messenger came to invite them to come to the Great Khan. They left with him and traveled eastward for an entire year, apparently passing north of the Tien Shan mountains instead of crossing the Pamirs and skirting the desert on the south, as they were to do on their second voyage. After being very well treated by the Great Khan, who sent them on a mission to the pope, the two brothers set off on the return trip.

> They rode day after day until they arrived safe and sound in Ayas, a town on the sea in Lesser Armenia; and I assure you that they were hard put to it to make the journey in three years. This was because they could not ride all the time, but were delayed by stress of weather, by snow and by swollen rivers.[26]

---

26. *The Travels of Marco Polo*, tr. Ronald Latham, 37.

In April 1269, they embarked on a ship and sailed off to Acre where they learned of the death of Clement IV. They expressed bitterness to a legate, who advised them to wait for the election of the new pope. Wishing to see Venice again, the two brothers left Acre for Negropont, and from there they returned to Venice. Niccolò learned that his wife, whom he had left pregnant had died in the interval and that she had given him a son named Marco. Because the election of the Holy Father was delayed, Niccolò and Maffeo stayed in Venice for two years and Niccolò remarried.

Fearing that the Great Khan might imagine that they had abandoned their mission, they went off again, bringing Marco with them, and went to Acre and then Ayas. There, they learned that the legate they had met earlier had been elected as Pope Gregory X. They returned to Acre to see him and then resumed their journey to the Far East. The three Venetians were to be gone for a quarter century, and their commercial aims faded. This is the way, in a rather elliptical style, that Marco Polo narrates the journey of his father and his uncle.

A merchant who wanted to go to Cathay was now no longer setting off into the unknown. In the middle of the fourteenth century, in the *Practice of Commerce,* Francesco Balducci Pegolotti gave him instructions. First he should let his beard grow and not shave. In Tana, he should get good interpreters and at least two servants who know the Comanian language. If he wishes, he may bring a woman from Tana; he will be more respected if he does. Before reaching Astrakhan, he needs to obtain provisions for twenty-five days, that is, flour and salt fish, because he can get meat along the way.

The road from Tana to Cathay is very safe, day and night, according to the travelers who have taken it; but if a merchant dies on the way or in Cathay, his goods revert to the lord of the country in which he dies, unless he has a brother, who then inherits. There is another danger, the death of the lord, for until his successor is designated, the road is not safe. Cathay is a country with many towns and villages. The capital is named Khan-balik, and most trading is done there.

A merchant with an interpreter, two servants, and goods of the value of 25,000 gold florins would spend on the way to Cathay, if he were economical, from 60 to 80 silver *sommi* (one *sommo* is approximately equal to five gold florins). A cart requires only one ox and can carry a load of 10 Genoese *cantares;* a camel cart requires three camels and can carry 30 Genoese *cantares;* a horse cart requires one horse and can normally carry 6.5 *cantares* of silk.

Anyone who wants to travel from Genoa or Venice to Cathay would do well to carry cloth and to go to Urgandzh to buy *sommi* and to take that currency with him, not investing in other goods, unless he can find some bales of very delicate cloth not taking up much space.

In the late Middle Ages, businessmen traveled to distant countries. In Damascus, Bertrandon de La Broquière met several French, Venetian, Genevan, Florentine, and Catalan merchants, among them a man named Jacques Cœur. But these travels were primarily made by young men. Indeed, the company of "travelers of Bergen," organized by the town of Lübeck in 1380, comprised two categories of merchants: one, established in Lübeck, had age and experience; the others traveled frequently to Bergen or other towns.

There were, however, still small tradesmen constantly traveling over regional roads earning a petty living. In May 1494, a letter of remission was granted to Guillaume Pilet and François Ponot, poor merchants and transporters of salt, who had been earning a living for fifteen years "by taking and carrying on land the merchandise consigned to them . . . buying and selling and carrying or having carried . . . all goods and merchandise in various places in our kingdom."

In the 1440s, Jean Olmier from Charroux had his goods stolen by soldiers. In order to be able to support his wife and children, he contracted loans to enable him to carry on trade. He went to Villefranche-en Bourbonnais to sell pigs. There he met a certain Gonin Roland from Montluçon, with whom he decided to travel to Germany. The two companions spent several days in Bruère, Néronde, and Faulquement, in present-day Moselle, where they bought counterfeit money. Leaving Roland in Germany, Olmier came to Bourges, where he acquired lamb and rabbit skins, then went off to sell wine in Orléans and Paris. He made many other business trips in the Bourbonnais, as well as in the nearby regions of Auvergne, Limousin, and Forez. But several people realized that the currency was counterfeit, and Jean Olmier asked the king to pardon him. The man of the Middle Ages thus seems to have been available, willing to leave his family to try to earn a living. This mobility was amplified by the fact that he did not have a very clear conception of time, at least if he belonged to the lower classes.

*Professors*
Wishing to have the young men of the city learn Greek and Latin, the authorities of Florence decided to call on an eminent professor from Byzantium, Manuel Chrysoloras, to whom they addressed an official invitation on March 28, 1396:

> Informed of your competence and your moral character by one of our fellow citizens, in the hope that you will turn out to be as you have been described, and that you will be ready, willing, and able to accept this charge, we have decided to choose you to teach grammar and Greek letters in our city for ten years, with a salary of 100 florins each year, to be paid every six months.

He would find "profit and glory" in Florence. Chrysoloras accepted, and for some years taught not only the young men of the city but also "foreigners," such as Piero Vergerio de Capodistria from Padua, who was drawn to Florence by the reputation of the teacher.

The great Professor Guarino (1374–1460), after stays in Byzantium from 1403 to 1408, in Florence as professor of Greek in 1413–14, in Bologna, and Venice, taught in Verona for ten years from 1419 to 1429. He then settled in Ferrara where he opened a private school, thereafter becoming a tutor to Lionello d'Este, and a teacher in another school.

Chrysoloras and Guarino were not exceptional figures. After attending several universities, brilliant students would teach in various schools, moving from one to another to take more prestigious and remunerative positions. But there might be other reasons for moving.

Albert the Great, born in Swabia in 1206, went to Padua to study natural science in 1222–23. He decided to enter the Dominican Order when he was barely sixteen. As soon as he finished his schooling, he devoted himself to teaching. He taught successively in Cologne (1228), Hildesheim (1233), Freiburg im Breisgau, Regensburg, and Strasbourg; in 1240, he went to Paris for the formal award of a degree. Two years later, he became regent of the Saint-Jacques monastery. In 1248, the order sent him to Cologne as regent of the school that had just been created there. In succeeding years, he assumed positions outside the university: provincial prior of Germany and bishop of Regensburg. But, believing that his duties as bishop risked distracting him from his vocation as a teacher of theology, he resigned and returned to his studies. He went on some missions, refused the position of chancellor of the University of Paris, and returned to teaching in Strasbourg in 1267, and then Cologne in 1270, where he died ten years later.

Mobility of professors was so frequent that universities had future holders of the doctorate take a vow not to leave once they had passed their examinations. Indeed, it was not easy to abandon a position one had accepted. A teacher in Padua, originally from Rotterdam, stated that he needed to return to his homeland and wished to resign; he had chosen two of his students to succeed him, a Batavian from Amsterdam and a Fleming. The lure of wealth and increased prestige overcame many resistances. After teaching in Bologna for ten years for an annual salary of 300 gold florins, a certain Corsetti from Sicily, an eminent professor of canon law, was attracted by an offer from the Doge of Venice to teach in Padua for four years at a salary of 350 florins, with the possibility of an increase. Corsetti was tempted, but he was heavily in debt, and his creditors were alarmed when they learned he might leave. He nevertheless accepted the Doge's proposition. However the senate of Bologna was not pleased that such a brilliant man was leaving the city. The community was not especially wealthy, but it offered him a salary of 400 livres for the next three years, although it finally allowed him to leave for Padua—Corsetti had already signed the contract. He managed to find sureties and left Bologna without difficulty.

Many other members of medieval society traveled to seek wealth. Mercenaries were paid to fight, but many others fought out of duty or because of feudal obligation. One man might travel for many different reasons. For example, Pierre de Sainte-Feyre made about twenty journeys between 1507 and 1526: to Lyon for family banking business; to Montluçon, Poitiers, and Paris for trials; to Paris again for the education and placement of his children; to Tours and Moulins, the capital of Charles de Bourbon; to Périgord for the weddings of his children; and to Notre-Dame d'Hautefaye where he made a final pilgrimage. A human being is diverse, and our account has placed the emphasis on one essential motive, while remaining aware that other reasons also played a role.

## APPEARANCES

Appearances played an essential role from the very beginning of the Middle Ages. Sidonius Apollinaris describes for his friend Domicius the entry of the barbarian prince Sigismer into Lyon in 470 in these terms:

> He was preceded by his horse with a decorative harness; other horses glittering with gems walked before and behind, adding great solemnity to the procession, while he himself went on foot surrounded by his steeds and his retinue, also on foot, dressed in scarlet, shining with gold, glittering in silk as white as milk.

### Rulers

There was a taste for glitter and a need to travel. The court was for a long time itinerant, and monarchs traveled to make use of the resources of their domains, particularly in the early Middle Ages. A biographer of Louis the Pious writes that the king "decided to spend his winters, from year to year, in four different dwellings. . . . Hence, each of these domains, when its year arrived, had enough to supply the king's needs." But the explanation is not adequate. In addition to their military campaigns, kings were constantly traveling to keep track of the proper execution of their orders, to receive homage from the population, thereby strengthening their power by establishing direct contact with their subjects. Charlemagne was often on the road, particularly in Francia and in Germany, much less frequently in Aquitaine, Bavaria, and Italy. During the final years of his reign, he often resided in Aix-la-Chapelle. Although the more sedentary Louis the Pious remained in Francia, his grandson Charles the Bald, intent on securing the obedience of his subjects and on fighting against the Normans, traveled constantly. For example, in 867, he spent the winter in Compiègne, made an appearance on the Loire in spring, celebrated Easter at Saint-Denis, and then traveled to Metz. In May, he was at Samoussy, then Attigny, and went hunting in the Ardennes. He summoned his army to Chartres in August, hosted a Breton prince in Compiègne, and turned up at Saint-Vaast and Orville in September. He went to Troyes in October, then to Reims, returned to Troyes, and spent Christmas in Auxerre.

The journey to Languedoc by Charles VI in 1389–90 provides an example of how the king of France traveled in the late Middle Ages.[27] The monarch brought with him the young princes of his family, the council with many of his favorites, among whom were Olivier de Clisson and Bureau de la Rivière, as well as representatives of the royal administration for justice and finance. The archives of the merchant of Prato mention the presence of "quite a few barons of the kingdom" with their four thousand horses. Wagons were requisitioned to transport supplies. So many people accompanied the king that they did not all stay in the same place. For example, on November 7 and 8, when the king was in Beaucaire, his council was still in Avignon.

The king left Paris on September 3 and Melun, where his escort was assembled, on September 13. The troop traveled slowly, covering at most six or seven leagues a day and stopping frequently. The company rested a week at Nevers and set off again on October 3. It crossed the valley of the Allier, the mountains, and went through the valley of the Saône. The entry into Lyon involved a more elaborate ritual than in the past. The monk of Saint-Denis describes it in his *Chronicle:*

> With what transports of joy did the inhabitants of the city greet their king! First they sent him gifts of sheep, cattle, and wine. The bourgeois came to meet him on horseback, all dressed in the same colors, and after paying him homage on their knees, they placed themselves and their possessions at his disposal. On his entry into the city, he was received by four beautiful and noble maidens richly dressed and covered with precious stones; they carried a canopy of cloth of gold under which they led him with stately steps to the palace of the archbishop.

---

27. See the work of Françoise Autrand.

Still other preparations had been made to perpetuate the memory of this extraordinary celebration. More than a thousand young children had been dressed in royal clothing and distributed on wooden galleries at the different crossroads of the town so that they could make loud acclamations in the king's honor as he passed. On the occasion of this visit that had been so long awaited, the population spent four days in balls and theater diversions. . . . And the king received still more precious jewels on his departure.

The next destination was a meeting with the pope, who prepared to receive Charles VI with great honor. He began by sending the cardinals to serve as an escort, but they could not get through the crowd encumbering the bridge over the Rhône—this was the narrow Saint-Bénézet bridge, nearly nine hundred meters long. They therefore deputed two of their number to greet the king.

The officers of the holy palace then went before him in the midst of a considerable procession of the nobility, and they greeted him with great ceremony outside the town; they led him and a large retinue of his people and those of the palace to the castle, where the pope and my lord cardinals had long been awaiting him in the consistory.

The welcome was followed by a private conversation and a banquet, concluding the first day. The next day, All Saints Day, witnessed the coronation of King Louis of Sicily.

The pope and the king exchanged gifts. Charles VI offered Clement II a blue velvet cope embroidered with pearls and decorated with angels, fleurs-de-lis, and stars. Of course, all these solemnities were only one aspect of the meeting, during which negotiations were also carried on. Some results were achieved, but the king did not win over the local inhabitants. The serious air that Charles had to assume because of his position did not charm the men of the South. Montpellier and Béziers received the king with canopies of cloth of gold—carried by the consuls—fleurs-de-lis, corteges, and songs, but complaints were voiced.

In Toulouse, where they stopped for six weeks, it was possible to work to seek remedies for the problems of the country.

Traveling through the towns and the countryside, he [the king] had seen destroyed and abandoned dwellings. He dismissed all those [corrupt] officials and enjoined on those he put in their place to govern less harshly and to make do with the usual taxes.

In reality, the personal role of the king consisted in receiving ambassadors. He passed the time in playing chess and surveying the region.

After settling his affairs, Charles left Toulouse and turned toward Foix. The count, the celebrated Gaston Phœbus, was the author of books of venery that the king knew. But before the two personages could meet, delicate questions on which diplomats had been working for more than a year had to be settled. In particular, Gaston Phœbus had reached an agreement with the count of Armagnac. But would he swear to peace in the presence of the young king? Finally, the king came to see the old man, who received him with great honor. This was a southern celebration, without a royal entry or an austere liturgy.

> The count, delighted with the honor that had been granted him, following the advice of the nobles of his court, prepared to receive the king with extraordinary splendor. . . . As the king approached the large town of Mazères, one hundred noble knights of the most illustrious families came to meet him and offered him sheep, fattened cattle, and fine horses with silver bells on their necks. These gifts were very pleasing to the king; but the strange manner in which they were offered made him laugh and caused him much merriment. The knights themselves led the animals, dressed in peasant smocks and herdsmen's clothing. This coarse dress made it at first impossible to recognize their noble condition that their fine appearance might have revealed. Then they suddenly appeared in the feasting hall, with musical instruments, dressed in robes dotted with golden fleurs-de-lis, and humbly presented themselves to the king, who was at table. With a satisfied air, the king asked the count who were those people who had just come in; "They are," said the count, "your humble servants who are ready to execute your orders and to obey you in all things, as shepherds and herdsmen would obey their master."

The next day, there was a tournament in which the same knights were asked to joust with lances. The reward for the winner of the contest was a golden crown.

Until then, the king had not engaged in that kind of activity. However, as he took pleasure in it, he joined the competitors several times, surpassed them all in skill and agility, and was judged worthy of the prize by the entire audience. But on this occasion he demonstrated his usual generosity by making a gift of the crown to the knights.

The ceremonies took place on the final day. Gaston Phœbus spoke in praise of the king and then made him a pledge of loyalty.

Charles VI could return to Paris "after assuring himself by this journey of the friendship of the barons and counts of Aquitaine and carrying out many reforms throughout the province." The troop passed again through Montpellier, Avignon, and Lyon, where it stayed from February 6 to 9. For four days in Dijon, the duke of Burgundy produced festivals in honor of his nephew. In Bar, Charles and his brother wagered on who would reach Paris first. They left at the gallop, and Louis won on February 23.

This journey, which lasted nearly six months and cast so many people on the roads of France, could not have been accomplished without the resolution of a number of material problems. Bishops, nobles, and some royal castles provided shelter for the king. It had been necessary to requisition beds and hang the rooms with curtains and tapestries. The administrative accounts contain a minute record of all the hooks needed to accomplish this. In fact, except for hammers and pliers, this was the sole expense paid by the king's men. The right of shelter obliged towns and bishops to supply food, drink, tableware, and fodder; but because it was thought the towns would not have enough, provisions were brought along.

Froissart writes that in his youth, a king should visit his lands, become acquainted with his people, and learn how they are governed. He will thereby acquire great honor and his subjects will love him more. The reception of Charles VI in Lyon was only one of the numerous entries that the king made on his travels through the kingdom to foster monarchical feeling. Whereas this was a very simple ceremony in the early fourteenth century, two centuries later it had become a grandiose spectacle complete with theatrical performances. In addition, several innovations seem to have been designed to exalt the monarchy, such as the canopy under which Charles VI rode in 1389.

When a royal visit was announced, a municipality would begin looking for money, because an entry was expensive. The heaviest expense was for gifts to the king and his retinue. There were gifts of food, but also more personal gifts, and some of them were truly fit for a king. When Louis XI entered Tournai in 1464, the community gave him a gift of the 20,000 golden écus that had been loaned to purchase the towns of Picardy.

Making the canopy was a matter of some concern. First, they made the wooden stretcher, that is, the frame carried by four poles. The cloth, generally blue, to cover it was sometimes bought from far off, because this was precious material, velvet from Bruges, silk, taffeta from Florence, or sumptuous damascene. Around the frame were set fringes of gold and silk. Many fleurs-de-lis were embroidered, sometimes on the underside, usually on the exterior, and painted on the poles.

The town had to put on its best appearance. Roads and bridges were repaired and the streets cleaned. Fountains flowing with hippocras, wine, and water were built. On the streets along the route of the procession, the houses were covered with white or red cloths, sometimes of silk, and even with tapestries. Everything had to contribute to royal glory, and fleurs-de-lis covered the city.

Shortly before the monarch's arrival, a long procession set out to meet him. In the fifteenth century, the king received the keys to the city at the gate, as a sign of obedience. Then the canopy was set over him and the procession entered the town. At his passage, trumpets sounded, bells rang, and choirs of children sang his praises. The procession reached the church and the king went in. Soon thereafter, the procession set off for his residence where he received gifts. And while the most important personages joined him for a feast, the population at large danced and played in the light of torches and bonfires.

Nothing was left to chance in these proceedings. On the entry of Isabella of Bavaria into Paris in 1389, the use of a litter, one's position with respect to it, and whether or not one was on horseback were signs of social importance. The queen left Melun for Saint-Denis where were assembled the lofty and noble ladies of France who were to accompany her and the lords who were to *adextrer* the litters of the queen and the ladies. Clothed in a silken dress all dotted with golden fleurs-de-lis, [she] was seated in a covered litter . . . one could see in painted and gilded carriages the duchesses of Burgundy, Bar, Berry, and Touraine.

At the head of the procession, surprisingly on horseback, was Valentine Visconti, the king's sister-in-law; she had no litter to distinguish her from the others. "At Saint-Lazare, near Paris, the queen and the duchesses placed on their heads crowns covered in gold and silver, and the carriages were uncovered. The principal nobles dismounted to line up on either side of the queen's litter. . . ." Similarly, at her marriage in Bruges in 1429, the young bride Elizabeth of Portugal, in a litter, was accompanied by nobles on foot, except for her brother Don Ferrande and the lord of Roubaix.

There was also a hierarchy among horses. For example, on the entry of Charles VII into Rouen in 1449, according to Mathieu d'Escouchy, the king was on a palfrey; Potron de Saintrailles, the chief equerry who carried the monarch's sword, on a charger; and the leader of the lances on a black charger, a less noble color. Various steeds are also mentioned: a bay mounted by Nevers, a black one by Tancarville, and a dapple by the count of Saint-Pol. On mere "horses" were the bailiff of Rouen and various others, including twenty men at arms.

Looks were drawn by dress more than anything else. Red, the first color in the scale of values, was reserved for the king. At the meeting between King Charles V and Emperor Charles IV in 1378, the princes of the royal retinue wore parti-colored clothing: white and blue for the duke of Bourbon, in the king's favor, but because azure was the color of the house of France, the inferiority was marked. The dukes of Berry and Burgundy, brothers of Charles V whom he favored less, wore black and gray, demeaning colors. Similarly, there were dark colors for people of lesser standing, such as blue for the personal and stable squires. Combined with another color, thus manifesting inferiority, they were used by the masters of arms (blue and red) and by the sergeants of arms (blue and black); red and black indicating the difference in level between these servants.

Let us conclude with the entry of King Louis XI into his city of Paris in August 1461, described by Commynes. The king, who had been crowned at Reims a short while before, reached Saint-Denis where he hunted wild game and birds for a few days. Since it had not been possible to conclude the preparations for a solemn and magnificent reception on time, he delayed his entry into Paris and went off to a residence located near Montmartre. He spent three or four days there, and then "surrounded by a very noble and very magnificent escort," he made his entry into the capital.

It would take too long to describe in detail the magnificent clothing and precious ornaments worn by the princes and the dukes, and those that covered their horses, hanging down to the ground; indeed, some details would seem barely credible to the reader. The procession advanced in groups of twelve, fifteen, or twenty persons and horses, each group separated from the others by a suitable interval, and there were more than twenty of these groups; all the members of the procession were dressed in golden material reaching down to their feet and inlaid with precious stones, as were the horses' caparisons, so that the incomparable brilliance of the gold and jewels, glowing with a thousand flames from the rays of the sun, dazzled the spectators. Countless other groups followed, made up of less powerful nobles, who wore clothing of every color, of crimson cloth or silk, adorned with gold and silver, and riding horses with varied and sumptuous caparisons. Finally came knights in armor and officers of every rank, in an immense crowd difficult to count.

As for the common people, they had flocked en masse to Paris from all the regions of France, drawn by the desire to see with their own eyes the splendors of that solemn entry. There were people of all classes and ages and both sexes, of every condition and from every rank, and we heard a venerable knight who had once served the father and grandfather of King Louis estimate their number at more than three hundred thousand souls, not counting the Parisians. . . .

When a monarch traveled, he brought a large retinue with him. He also carried a quantity of goods.

Isabella of Bavaria had no official residence. She stayed most often at the hôtel Saint-Pol, and made frequent trips to the castle of Vincennes. But she made longer journeys. From May to December 1417, for example, she went to Orléans, Blois, Tours, Vendôme, Bonneval, Chartres, and Troyes.

In this troubled period, it was most important to ensure that the queen ran no risks during the journey. A faithful servant was deputed to ask the bailiffs and priests if the villages to be passed through were affected by an epidemic. He also learned of the condition of the roads and their safety. In addition, because she suffered from agoraphobia, Isabella required that any bridge she had to cross be furnished with solid railings.

The residences that were to receive her had to be put in shape. Masons, carpenters, and painters worked on setting up her apartments. Princely dwellings, rarely inhabited, were not well maintained. Sometimes the queen stayed with a simple bourgeois. In Troyes, she stayed in the home of Jacqueline la Blanchette, where she had some repairs made. "In whose home the queen stayed for a long time, so that she had to repair the halls, the bedroom, and the gardens, and spend money for furniture and provisions."

It was necessary to take baggage, because the dwellings in which the queen stayed had only empty rooms with bare walls. Isabella brought not only her dresses, jewels, and books, but also her tapestries, organs, baths, and furniture. "To Pierre du Fou . . . for a large chest of tawny leather lined with cloth, with straps and locks . . . also a large cabinet to set above this chest . . . to store and carry the bed of Madam the Queen." The chests that arrived at their destination had to be stored safely: "For a wooden lock, with two keys, placed and set in the room in Senlis, in which were money, papers, and writings concerning the chests of the said lady." Isabella's baggage preceded her, forming a long procession of wagons. And when something was forgotten, a servant went back to get it.

Isabella, who preferred to use a litter, did not travel alone. Counselors, priests, and valets accompanied her, and soldiers protected her. Her children and their servants went with her, as soon as they were old enough. Hence, she traveled in short stages of approximately twenty kilometers a day. In covering the distance between Paris and Compiègne, she stopped at Louvres and Senlis. She was also delayed by the solemn ceremonies that marked her entry into a town. Learning of her approaching arrival, on August 17, 1387, the nobles of Chartres immediately sent valets to buy jewels in Paris. Three days later, the captain greeted her before the ramparts and accompanied her to her residence. Minstrels performed at the crossroads. In the house where her apartments had been set up, a Dominican friar played the organ, an instrument that she greatly appreciated.

While the kings of France generally displayed great splendor in the course of their travels, they also attempted to welcome other monarchs lavishly. The arrival of Emperor Charles IV in Paris in 1378 was the occasion for many solemnities. The emperor, old and suffering from gout, had undertaken a long voyage, since from his brand new city of Prague he had to cross Germany that was then the prey of local wars. According to the *Grandes Chroniques,* he wrote twice to King Charles V of France; he informed him that he had set out to pay him a visit and to accomplish a pilgrimage. Even if these reasons did not seem sufficient, such a meeting might be considered a godsend by the king of France, to the extent that it increased his prestige. It was certainly worth minute preparation.

The arrival of the emperor in France obviously posed serious problems of protocol. In 1365, he was welcomed in Chambéry, Avignon, and Arles with full imperial honors. For example, in Avignon, he was on horseback, wearing a crown, under a canopy of cloth of gold, preceded by the imperial sword, globe, and scepter. But he was coming into the kingdom of France. When letters announced his arrival in Paris a week before Christmas, because the king and his advisers did not wish him to display the imperial insignia during the celebration of that festival, they asked him not to enter the kingdom until after Christmas. He readily agreed. In Saint-Quentin, the royal officers, the bourgeois, and the inhabitants of the town came to meet him on horseback and received him with honor. They gave him great gifts of food and drink. But in no town of the kingdom of France did he receive signs of domination reserved for the king alone or his representatives. However, from stage to stage, the processions that came to meet him grew ever more brilliant and were made up of noble figures. He was greeted in Compiègne by the duke of Bourbon, the queen's brother, by a cousin of the king's, by the bishops of Beauvais and Paris, and by three hundred knights; in Senlis by the dukes of Berry and Burgundy, one of the queen's brothers-in-law, the archbishop of Reims, the bishop of Laon, and five hundred knights and squires; in Saint-Denis by many prelates, archbishops, and bishops, led by the abbot of Saint-Denis.

Finally, on January 4, the emperor arrived in Paris. In the morning, between Saint-Denis and Paris, he saw the procession of Parisians approaching: the provost of Paris, the captain of the watch and the sergeants dressed in the same color, followed by the provost of merchants, the magistrates, and bourgeois to the number of eighteen hundred to two thousand wearing parti-colored clothing of white and violet. At La Chapelle, the emperor left his litter and mounted a black horse that the king of France had sent for him. The color of the horse had not been chosen at random. In fact, when he entered cities under his authority, the emperor rode a white horse.

At the same moment, the king left the palace. He mounted a white palfrey whose azure saddle was decorated with golden fleurs-de-lis. His cloak was bright scarlet with ermine fur. The dukes and eleven counts rode with him, along with knights and squires wearing their livery. The prelates in Roman copes followed with their retinue. Each branch of the king's service wore different colors. The two processions converged midway between Moulin-à-Vent and La Chapelle, and turned toward Paris. Charles V rode between the emperor and his eldest son Wenceslas. At three o'clock in the afternoon, the procession arrived in front of the palace, where Charles IV occupied the finest room and his retinue the *piano nobile,* while Wenceslas and his men were on the floor below, and Charles V above.

During his stay, which was to last for two weeks, the emperor passed his time in festivities and diplomatic discussions. His departure took place on Saturday January 16. Charles V accompanied his uncle as far as the hôtel de Plaisance, but the dukes of Berry, Burgundy, and Bourbon escorted the emperor beyond Meaux. After the farewells, on Monday, Charles IV took the road to Germany through Château-Thierry, Reims, and Mouzon. Advisers to the king remained with him until he reached the border. Although a visit like this was expensive—the *Grandes Chroniques* indicate that all the expenses of the emperor and his people were paid by the king, as were the gifts made in the name of towns—it was nonetheless beneficial.

Popes

In order to follow the teaching of Christ, popes should have lived a simple life. But they were also temporal sovereigns, and the character of some of them inclined them to make a display of their power and wealth. The pope was normally accompanied by a large number of people. The registers of the Apostolic Chamber for May 1299 contain the list of those who had been reimbursed for five days, that is, the length of the journey of Boniface VIII from Rome to Anagni, his native town, where he liked to spend the summer. This list provides the names and functions of 194 people. We may note in particular four cooks and seven kitchen boys and servants, the pope's three personal doctors, twenty-two knights, eleven pages, seven cooks of the lesser kitchen, three chefs and two kitchen boys of the lesser kitchen, three butchers and a cattle merchant, six grooms, thirteen chaplains, twenty-six servants, twenty-seven messengers, ten people in charge of the pope's carriages and quadrigae, and eleven confessors. But this list is not complete, because the Chamber did not reimburse some who were obliged to follow the sovereign pontiff. We should therefore add approximately fifteen cardinals—and for each of them about twenty followers—about one hundred procurators, and about fifty composers of papal letters. Also on the journey were prelates who had come to deal with various matters, as well as penitents guilty of grave sins that only the pope could absolve.

The Holy Father rode a white horse or a white mule. Donkeys carried the objects needed for a stay. The court brought eight to twelve carriages. In addition, there were requisitions for the transport of baggage.

On joyous entries, the municipal authorities went out to meet the sovereign pontiff. Relics were set down and blessed, then a great procession went to the cathedral as the bells rang. The pope's white horses, covered in red cloth, were followed by the flags of the town and the people and the red and yellow pontifical pennant. Behind the cross, a mule, traditionally white since the late fourteenth century, carried a monstrance. There followed cardinals two by two; nobles, knights, citizens, and bourgeois all on foot; and the pope on his white horse, with a canopy above his head; behind him came the camerlingo, the patriarchs, the prelates, and the members of the clergy; finally came the pontifical almoner who threw out small coins. Flowers and herbs decorated the streets.

## In the East

The luxury of Oriental courts was legendary. It is therefore not surprising to see monarchs or members of their family displaying great splendor in their travels. In 1184, soon after its departure from Baghdad for Mosul, the caravan in which Ibn Jubayr was traveling was joined by a princess, daughter of Emir Masud and wife of Prince Nuraddin.

> She was carried in a palanquin set on two pieces of wood placed crosswise on two horses walking one behind the other, covered with golden blankets; and they moved as quickly and supply as the breeze. The palanquin had two openings, in front and back, and the princess appeared in the middle enveloped in her veil, a golden diadem on her head. She was preceded by a troop of eunuchs who belonged to her and by her guards; on the right could be seen riding horses and finely bred hackneys; behind her came the procession of her followers mounted on camels and horses with golden saddles; they wore golden headbands, and the breeze made their tresses dance. They came behind their mistress like advancing clouds. The princess had pennants; drums and trumpets sounded when she got in or out of her palanquin. We recognized that the luxury and splendor of this feminine power were such that they shook the earth and proudly dragged behind them the fragments of the world.

When the princess arrived in Mosul, her palanquin was "decorated with wands of soft gold shaped into crescents, dinars the length of a hand, chains, and extraordinary designs; there were so many of them that the palanquin itself could no longer be seen."

In 1334, Ibn Battuta traveled with the khatun Bayalun, the wife of Uzbak, king of the Golden Horde. An emir at the head of five thousand men accompanied the princess.

[T]he khatun's own troops numbered about five hundred, some two hundred of whom were slaves and Greeks in attendance on her, and the remainder Turks. She had with her about two hundred slave girls, most of them Greeks, and about four hundred wagons with about two thousand horses to draw them and for riding, as well as some three hundred oxen and two hundred camels to draw them. She also had ten Greek pages with her, and the same number of Indian pages. . . . She left most of her slave girls and of her baggage in the sultan's *mahalla,* since she had set out with the intention [only] of paying a visit and giving birth to her child.[28]

Great Personages

Ambassadors representing the monarch usually traveled in great style to demonstrate the power of the one who sent them. In the course of the early Middle Ages, and even later, the Byzantine Empire relied more on diplomacy than on war. The appearance of embassies varied according to their object. The patriarchal envoy John Grammatikos went to the caliph of Baghdad in 829 with the difficult mission of impressing the Arabs with the pomp he displayed. As for the embassy that the Pagratid king John Sempad sent to Basil II in 1022, it was led by the Armenian Catholikos accompanied by twelve bishops, seventy monks, two scholars, and three hundred men from the army and the nobility; in addition, it was followed by pack animals carrying significant sums of money.

Information, which is scanty for the early Middle Ages in the West, becomes more detailed as the centuries pass. When an English embassy in the late fourteenth century came to ask King Charles VI of France for the hand of his daughter Isabelle for King Richard, it included "some of the principal knights and lords of his Court."

> The envoys, having obtained a safe-conduct from the king, arrived in France with a retinue of twelve hundred gentlemen and made its entry into Paris with great ceremony. The king recommended to his nobles to receive them with the greatest respect and to prepare magnificent lodgings for them.

---

28. *The Travels of Ibn Battuta,* tr. H. A. R. Gibb, v. II, p. 498.

The power of aristocrats was shown first of all in the size of their escort. The purchase of cloth in 1327–28 suggests that Countess Mahaut of Artois was clothing fifty to sixty knights and as many squires, all of whom probably did not accompany her on her travels. In addition to knights, officers and servants lived at her court. Those who wore livery made up a kind of aristocracy, including noble girls, followers and companions of Mahaut, the clerics in charge of church services, and administrators. An intermediate group was made up of forty-five or forty-eight valets who received wages. At the bottom of the social ladder were the humble people, almost all of them designated by their function, such as Remy of the wine cellar. In all, two hundred people lived with Mahaut, and more than a hundred, perhaps 120 or 130 traveled with her. When she traveled to Burgundy, lodging and food for fifty to sixty-five horses was required; in 1328, seventy-seven horses had to be lodged in Saint-Omer. An escort of this size was not at all exceptional. In May and June 1328, hosting the duke and duchess of Burgundy in her castles in Artois, Mahaut gave gifts to at least ninety-four people, knights and officers not included in this figure.

For travel on land, horses and pack animals, and carriages and wagons played a significant role. Mahaut's carriages were very costly because of repairs and the materials used. Enlivened by painting, covered with rich cloth, with silk cloth for the ceiling, and furnished with rugs inside, they showed the greatness of their owner. Furniture was, of course, taken on the journey, such as a large room that contained at least twelve rugs, that is, twelve tapestries; this was thus not mere bed furnishings, but tapestries used to cover the walls of a room.

On May 15, 1344, Duke Eudes IV of Burgundy left Argilly for a journey to the South. Accounts suggest that he brought with him around 140 people of subaltern rank. To this must be added the heads of his services, as well as nobles, whose numbers must have varied. In all, there were approximately 170 people, including 67 paid valets. The number of horses, 123 at departure, was 110 in Cahors, but when the duchess arrived it reached 223, and at Rouvres went as high as 306.

The number of people included in the household of Isabelle of Portugal, the wife of Duke Philip the Good of Burgundy, was set at 160 in 1438. Since the court moved frequently, it is likely that most of them followed their mistress on her travels. In fact, the duchess always needed her ladies of honor, and people with various duties, such as cooks, carters, and servants to prepare residences for her arrival. Whereas wagons and horses carried clothing and provisions that could be preserved (because there were not enough horses and wagons, some had to be rented), waterways were used for the rest because of the bad state of the roads. For example, in 1447, a ship carried chests, tapestries, and other baggage from Ghent to Bruges.

To what extent were these journeys accompanied with ceremonies and receptions? The rhythm of Mahaut's journeys shifted with the reasons for them. The court carried some of its provisions or had them transported in advance, except for what it bought after arriving. The countess was more often a hostess than a guest, and her hospitality was linked to political motivations, particularly when bourgeois joined the nobles at her table, which happened when she traveled to towns.

Social life depended on the calendar and the itinerary. Although Mahaut gave no great festivities, on some days she did have many guests. While the stable normally housed sixty to eighty horses, during the visit of the duke and duchess of Burgundy in June 1328, there were 326 of them at Mont-Saint-Eloi. The average cost of food was 12 to 15 livres per day, and this rose to 900 livres for the three days of Pentecost in 1328, 682 for Sunday alone, and this did not include provisions for the garrison. These were meals intended to bring together people belonging to the same social group. Mahaut seldom gave luxurious receptions. However, when the duke and duchess of Burgundy came to Hesdin on June 15 and 16, 1328, she treated them very well, sending two valets, one to Bruges and the other to Holland to get sturgeons. Temporary structures were set up on these occasions, because the rooms of the castle could not contain two hundred guests; tables were set under tents. The countess displayed fine pieces of silver and gold plate. She also provided musicians. But there were none of the sumptuous delicacies offered by the dukes of Burgundy in the following century.

Medieval man, even though primarily concerned with his own interests and appearance, could not forget that he had duties to others.

# in the service
# of one's lord

Officials were at the service of a king or a noble, and their principal goal was not to enrich themselves. Because of their functions, some of them were obliged to devote a good deal of time to travel, namely, ambassadors and messengers.

## DIPLOMATS

Negotiations between states were necessary to resolve problems of every kind. To conduct these negotiations, monarchs sent personages invested with more or less extended authority. Sometimes, monarchs themselves traveled, like the four sons of Clotaire I in 561 to settle the problem of his succession. Under the Carolingians, Louis the German and Charles the Bald met at Meersen in 870 to agree on the division of Lotharingia. Popes traveled from Italy to ask for help from foreign princes. In 754, Stephen II went to see Pepin the Short; the meeting concluded with an alliance that later brought about the creation of the Pontifical State. But most of the time, negotiations took place between a monarch's envoys on the one hand, and the head of state himself or advisers representing him on the other.

The Byzantine administration contained a department in charge of sending ambassadors to foreign countries. These ambassadors were seldom professional diplomats. In 781, Empress Irene sent the sacellary (high treasury official) Constantine and the primicier (head chamberlain) Stauriakos to negotiate the marriage of Constantine IV with a daughter of Charlemagne. It was recommended to choose as ambassadors men who were honest, pious, and incorruptible. Before leaving, they went through a kind of examination designed to verify their knowledge of the country to which they were going and their way of acting in different circumstances. They were accompanied by a great number of interpreters and servants and carried gifts for the monarchs they were going to see. They were given credentials and instructions by the emperor. When they were going to a distant country, insofar as possible their retinue contained people native to the region. Valentinus, sent by Emperor Tiberius to a Turkish prince in 576, brought with him 106 Turks who were living in Constantinople.

Permanent envoys, apocrisaries, represented the pope before the emperor of Byzantium. They disappeared in the course of the first half of the eighth century. Thereafter, popes used clergy, called envoys or legates of the Apostolic See, to deal with specific problems. Western monarchs had no similar organization. They called on great personages, secular or ecclesiastical. In 581, Bishop Egidius of Reims, along with the principal nobles of King Childebert of Austrasia, went on an embassy to King Chilperic of Neustria. A conference was held so that the two kings could form an alliance after having taken his kingdom away from King Gontran of Burgundy. Childebert's ambassadors accepted Chilperic's proposal to bequeath his holdings to their ruler, though he would continue in their possession during his lifetime, confirmed it with formal agreements, and returned to their master with great gifts. For his part, Chilperic sent Bishop Leudovald of Bayeux, along with the principal personages of his kingdom, who exchanged oaths of peace and signed agreements. As in Byzantium, embassies to distant countries contained at least one person knowledgeable about the customs and the language, such as the Jew Isaac, who returned alone in 801 from a mission to Harun al-Rashid, because the negotiators had died on the way.

The submission of a letter by ambassadors was usually followed by an exchange of views, accompanied by gifts. Among other gifts, in 802, Harun-al-Rashid sent an elephant to Charlemagne, and five years later a splendid clock. In the East, monarchs engaged in contests of magnificence. More than five centuries after Harun al-Rashid, in exchange for magnificent gifts sent by the emperor of China, the sultan of India sent him even more sumptuous ones: a hundred purebred horses, a hundred white slaves, a hundred dancers and singers, a hundred cotton garments, a hundred pieces of silk dyed in different colors, three hundred pieces of cloth, five hundred of goat wool, a hundred of linen, a hundred cloth dresses, a wall of canvas, six tents, four golden candelabra and six of nielloed silver, four golden bowls with matching ewers, six silver bowls, ten embroidered formal robes, ten bonnets, one adorned with gems, ten embroidered quivers, ten sabers, one with a scabbard encrusted with gems, gloves studded with gems, and fifteen eunuchs.

Immunity was granted to diplomats in all countries, and it seems that breaches of this rule were infrequent, although they did exist. King Childebert of Austrasia sent to King Gontran Bishop Egidius, Gontran Boson, Sigivald, and a number of other personages. But the discussion went badly and the meeting degenerated.

> Another one of the ambassadors replied: "We bid you farewell, oh king, for, since you have not agreed to cede the cities to your nephew, we know that the ax planted in the heads of your brothers is intact. Soon, planted in your head, it will cut it off." And they thus went off causing a scandal. Then the king, outraged by these remarks, had his men throw on the heads of the departing ambassadors horse dung, rotten wood, putrefied straw and hay, and even the fetid mud of the city.

Sometimes ambassadors would stay for a long time in the country to which they were sent, either because the ruler delayed receiving them—in 859–60, the envoy of the Abassid caliph al-Muttawakkil to Emperor Michael III of Byzantium waited for four months—or because the communication routes turned out to be dangerous—in 863, Charles the Bald kept envoys from the emir of Córdoba at Senlis until the political situation improved.

In the course of the central period of the Middle Ages, from the tenth to the twelfth century, more abundant documentation makes possible a better understanding of the machinery of diplomacy. In the West, negotiations in which heads of state participated directly seem to have been more frequent than in the preceding period. There were many meetings, usually prepared by envoys or intermediaries.

There still were no specialized personnel, either in Byzantium or in the West. To be sure, certain personages were used more frequently, but only because of their experience or because of their position in the ruler's favor. Sometimes a person was selected for precise reasons. Emperor Otto I selected Bishop Liutprand of Cremona to lead an embassy to the emperor of the East Nicephorus Phocas in 968, because he knew the Greek language and had already carried out a mission to Constantinople. Otto I wanted his son to marry a Byzantine princess. This alliance, the only one that seemed worthy of the emperors of the West, might facilitate his takeover of the Greek possessions of southern Italy. But Byzantium, then at the peak of its power, was very reluctant. The Venetian Domenico, entrusted with the same mission, had been sent away empty-handed. Would Liutprand be more adept? He set out early in 968. His account reveals a clash between two worlds. The embassy began inauspiciously and was not crowned with success.

If you have not received a letter or a messenger from me sooner, here is the explanation. We arrived in Constantinople on the first nones of June [June 4], and if the shameful way in which we were received is offensive to you, the shameful way in which we were treated was very painful for us; for we were shut up in a vast palace open to all the winds, as little suited to protecting us from the cold as from the heat; they posted armed soldiers as sentinels, charged with keeping my men from going out and anyone else from coming in. In this dwelling there was not a living soul, except for us, its prisoners; the palace was so far away that, forced to go there on foot and not on horseback, we arrived completely out of breath. To crown our unhappiness, Greek wine, a mixture of pitch, resin, and plaster, we found undrinkable. There was not a drop of water in the house, and we were unable even to buy any to quench our thirst. To so many evils, another evil was added in the person of the major-domo, entrusted with daily purchases; to find anyone resembling him, you would have to search not on earth but perhaps in hell; this man poured out on us like a torrent everything he could imagine in the way of calamities, banditry, damage, sorrow, and misery. And over 120 days, not one went by without bringing us reasons for laments and tears.

A third journey, less than three years later, in which Liutprand participated but did not lead, finally obtained satisfaction when Nicephorus Phocas's successor, John Tzimiskes, granted the hand of Theophano to the young Otto II.

The institution of pontifical legates spread from the middle of the eleventh century on. Obviously, given the interweaving of the temporal and the spiritual in the Middle Ages, the missions of these legates did not deal exclusively with religion.

The custom of giving documents to ambassadors began to grow in the West—it was the rule in the East. A distinction must be made between credentials that indicated to the recipient that he could trust what the envoy said, and full authority that allowed the envoy to bargain. Before the rebirth of Roman law, the messenger of the prince could not both negotiate and reach final agreement. If he negotiated, he could not conclude an agreement. If he did conclude an agreement, he had to confine himself to the conditions set out in his credentials. It is thus easy to understand why personal meetings between heads of state were so important at the time. But a change was getting under way. Late in 1200, the leaders of the Crusades met in Compiègne and decided to send a delegation to settle transport problems. Despite the uncertain vocabulary of the documents, it is clear that the members of the delegation had the power to decide. They even had blank parchments with their masters' seals.

The personal immunity of ambassadors remained the rule, but it did not shelter them from occasional snubs. As an illustration, let us return to the relations of Liutprand with the court of Byzantium. One day, Nicephorus Phocas ordered him to be among his guests, but had him seated fifteen places away, without a cloth, and the meal "was very long, obscene, full of drunkenness, seasoned with oil, and washed down with a frightful fishy liquor." During another meal, the bishop was shocked to be placed after a Bulgarian envoy; to soften his bitterness, the emperor took from his own refined menu and sent down to the bishop a fattened kid, marvelously stuffed with garlic, onions, and leeks. Later, they tried to isolate him, and for this purpose lions belonging to the imperial menagerie were put in his house. He was kept for more than two months after his mission had been completed. Finally, on October 2, he was able to leave Constantinople, "that once opulent and flourishing city, now shabby, false, lying, dishonest, rapacious, greedy, avaricious, and vain." He was accompanied by a guide on board a small ship. Then, traveling for forty-nine days on muleback, on foot, and on horseback, suffering from hunger and thirst, he reached Naupaktos. There his guide had him and his companions embark on two small ships and entrusted them to two officers who were supposed to bring them by sea to Otranto. But since the officers had not been given a safe-conduct, they were rejected everywhere, and rather than providing food for Otto's envoys, it was the reverse. Having left Naupaktos on November 23, Liutprand reached the river Fidaris two days later, at the same time as those of his companions who had not been able to embark on ship and had followed the coast. But while he was at sea, a storm broke out and raged night and day. Calm returned after two days, and Liutprand was able to reach Leukas on December 6; there, of course, he was badly received by the local bishop. "In all of Greece, I speak truly, I am not lying, I have never met hospitable bishops. . . . They sit alone at a table without a cloth, before a sea biscuit, and drink, or rather sip a wine drowned in water in a plain glass." On December 14, the grumpy bishop left Leukas. Sailing on their own, because the sailors had disappeared after the storm, he and his companions reached Corfu on December 18, where they were welcomed by the governor, always ready for a laugh but, "as it later turned out, with a diabolical mind." On the way to Byzantium, Liutprand had given the governor's son a shield of great price; on the way back, he gave the father a valuable coat. And what did the governor do to thank him? According to the terms of a letter from Emperor Nicephorus, he was to embark him without delay on a galley. But he kept him for twenty days without paying for food. Liutprand then ran into a person "full of injustice and wickedness." His misfortunes continued, but the document breaks off. The troubles of John of Gorzia were even greater than those of the bilious bishop of Cremona—he was kept in Córdoba for three years before securing permission to see the caliph.

Relations among states increased in the late Middle Ages. While meetings between rulers continued, ambassadors took on the bulk of foreign relations. They came from very varied backgrounds. They were members of the nobility or gentry, the clergy, officials with extensive legal knowledge, or even people of modest extraction. In 1477, a Flemish bourgeois, Olivier le Daim, Louis XI's barber, was sent to the Low Countries by his master. But specialization became increasingly the rule. Under Edward III of England, for example, several members of the upper clergy and the nobility, such as Henry Burghersh the bishop of Lincoln, the count of Huntington, and William of Clinton, were appreciated for their knowledge of the Low Countries and western Germany. Embassies led by important personages frequently included technicians, notably jurists.

Terminology related to envoys remained vague. By the thirteenth century, the Italians were commonly using the term *ambasciator*, which later became widespread. Only the Holy See had a more precise vocabulary. By the time of the reign of Pope Innocent II from 1198 to 1216, the status of permanent legate had become quite unusual. Under Innocent and his successors, we generally encounter legates *de latere*, most frequently cardinals as personal representatives of the pope, who were given important missions and wide authority. Envoys called simply legates, archbishops or bishops, had lesser powers and disappeared around 1460. On the other hand, *nuncii* (nuncios) appeared with increasing frequency. By 1460, they had taken the place of ordinary legates. Among those accredited to the Holy See, a particular place was occupied by the ambassadors or "orators," who were under the authority of sovereign states. Procurators represented parties to legal proceedings. As a consequence of the problems posed by the application of the Treaty of Paris of 1259, many of them traveled from London to Paris to defend the interests of the king of England, and this continued until the eve of the Hundred Years' War. Since most questions involved both legal and diplomatic aspects, these procurators became in the end lower-ranked diplomats. During the Easter mass of 1422, a question of precedence sparked a conflict between the ambassador of Castile and the bishop of Chichester, the envoy of the king of England, which ended in their coming to blows. Pope Martin V granted primacy to the Castilian, because he was an orator and the Englishman a mere procurator.

Permanent foreign missions made their appearance in the fifteenth century. Ambassadors carried documents, notably credentials, which tended to take on a uniform character. Envoys given the task of settling a question were generally given letters conferring full authority on them. In addition, they had a safe-conduct from the ruler to whom they were accredited. This was particularly important when there was a danger of conflict between kingdoms. Froissart notes that after King Edward III of England submitted a challenge to King Philip VI of France in 1337, the latter delivered to the English ambassador Henry Burghersh "a good safe-conduct for him and all his men, thanks to which he passed back through the kingdom of France without danger and returned to England." Finally, written instructions were more and more frequently given to negotiators.

Let us examine the complex course of an embassy, as set out in the *Chronicle* of the monk of Saint-Denis. This took place in 1407, at the time of the Great Schism. Two popes occupied the throne of Saint Peter, one, Benedict XIII, residing in Avignon, the other, Gregory XII, in Rome. After the festival of Easter, the ambassadors of King Charles VI of France set out for Marseille, separately and at a few days' interval. The first to arrive at Villeneuve would wait there for the others. Meanwhile, Gregory had sent to Benedict his nephew the bishop of Modon, Bishop William of Todi, and Antonio de Butrio, a doctor of civil and canon law. Benedict accepted their credentials favorably. The discussion, however, led to a dispute. But discussions resumed for the purpose of designating a meeting place. Each side rejected the other's proposals, and the discussion became heated. Because there were only three envoys from Rome, they asked that only three from the other side participate in the discussions. Benedict named the cardinal of Thury, the bishop of Lérida, and Francisco de Aranda, and an agreement was reached.

> When things had thus been settled by the efforts of the said arbiters, they drew up a memorandum concerning the place and the manner of the meeting, the retinue of persons who were to attend, and the choice of another place, in case some

difficulty should arise for Savona. This memorandum having been accepted by both sides, Monsignor Benedict, at the
request of the representatives of Rome, handed to them the
writing that had been made, and they presented a similar
document to him.

As for the ambassadors sent by the king and Church of France
to seek unity, they arrived in Villeneuve on the last day of April.
They met and took an oath to keep their mission secret and to
follow strictly the instructions they had been given with respect
to the two competitors.

When loyal friends gave several of the ambassadors some
reason to be afraid and pointed out to them that it was customary for those leaving the kingdom not to enter onto the
territory of another ruler without forewarning him, it was
decided to send the lieutenant of the seneschal of Beaucaire to the captain of the pontifical palace to request pass-
ports. . . .

After setting out the bases for the negotiations, the ambassadors held another meeting in Villeneuve on May 2 to deliberate about the terms of the speech that would be addressed to
the pope. They arrived in Aix on May 4. The fatigue of the journey forced them to rest on the eve and the day of the Ascension.
In Marseille, they met Benedict XIII, who delivered a long speech
"so full of obscurities that none of the listeners reported it in the
same way." This is why they decided to ask him the next day,
in accordance with the terms of their instructions, and in view
of the fact that his adversary had accepted the offer of transfer,
to provide them with bulls indicating his intention to restore
peace in the Church through the path of renunciation. Many
conversations took place because of the pope's reluctance. The
ambassadors returned to Aix from Marseille to deliberate as to
whether they should convey to him the decision to reject his
authority. They finally decided to postpone this action. Then
the ambassadors split up into three groups: the largest was to go
to Gregory XII in Rome; The archbishop of Tours and the abbot
of Saint-Michel remained in Marseille to hold the pope to his
good intentions and to inform the king of France of any possible

changes; finally Abbot Philip of Saint-Denis and Master Hugh, the dean of Rouen, were sent to Paris to report.

After hearing the report from his ambassadors, the king of France received Gregory's envoys.

> The king, charmed by what he had just heard, affectionately congratulated Gregory's envoys and, with his customary munificence, ordered that they be well fed at his expense for as long as they pleased to remain in Paris. Finally he made all sorts of gifts to them of gold and jewels, and sent them off with letters addressed to Gregory and his so-called college exhorting them to persevere in the unity of the Church.

Meanwhile, in June, the principal members of the French embassy to Gregory arrived in Genoa, where they were welcomed with great respect. When Gregory's nephew informed them that he could persuade his uncle to advance the date of the meeting if he were provided with ships, the Genoese offered to fit out five galleys. The ambassadors left some of their number in Genoa to speed the preparations along and continued their journey on land. They passed through Lucca and Florence where they were treated magnificently. After securing safe-conducts, they left Florence and on July 1 arrived in Viterbo where they met the cardinal of Ursins and the cardinal of Liège, who informed them that Gregory had been written from Paris to be on guard, not to leave Rome, and not to trust foreigners. They went on to say that Gregory had been very disturbed when he saw the ambassadors' instructions and other documents that he had been sent from Paris, and that he would seek all sorts of subterfuges to evade the treaty.

The ambassadors arrived in Rome on July 5. They obtained an audience the following day. They told the pope that they had no letters for him, but that they were being brought by sea; that they were not authorized to provide a detailed description of the object of the embassy, but that this was the task of their colleagues who would soon arrive. However, they asked him to leave Rome quickly and to start on the journey. Gregory replied that there was no need to hurry. There was another meeting on July 17. To persuade the Roman pope, the ambassadors offered to stay as hostages. But Gregory made use of subterfuges.

After these negotiations and other remarks exchanged by
both sides, as is customary in conferences, they separated,
with the agreement that each side would designate a certain
number of wise men to examine and decide whether, through
the offers that he made, he would faithfully fulfill his promise and his commitments.

It was all in vain. It was impossible to bring Gregory to keep his
word.

As for the ambassadors of Pope Benedict XIII of Avignon,
they gave the bishop of Digne the task of pointing out that they
had on six different occasions requested that Gregory confirm
the treaty signed in Marseille and that they had still received no
reply, although they had been in Rome for twenty-two days.
Finally, Gregory dismissed them with a document in his own
hand for Benedict which was, in effect, a blunt refusal. On hearing this news, the king's ambassadors sent some of their number to Paris to inform Charles VI about what had happened in
Rome; at the same time, others left to go to Benedict.

When most of the French ambassadors had arrived in Genoa,
they decided to send a letter to Gregory to urge him once again
to restore peace to the Church. On August 22, they transmitted
a copy to their colleagues who were still in Rome. Leaving Genoa
the same day, they arrived on the island of Saint-Honorat, where
Pope Benedict had taken refuge to escape the plague raging in
Marseille. Once again, fine speeches were exchanged. At that
point, the monk of Saint-Denis leaves the embassy, to deal with
other events. Indeed, the duke of Orléans was soon murdered,
which had the effect of unfreezing the situation with respect to
Benedict XIII, with whom France was soon to break.

The troubles of princes' envoys were sometimes serious. For
example, a few years later, in 1415, the Council of Constance decided to inform rulers of its decisions, in particular the king of
France. For this purpose, it chose the bishops of Carcassonne and
Evreux, a monk of Saint-Denis, Benoît Gentien, a doctor of theology, and Master Jacques de Spars, a doctor of medicine. But
as they arrived in the duchy of Bar, they were arrested by a fol-
lower of the duke of Burgundy named Henri de La Tour, who
had set up an ambush on their route with some of his men. They
were taken to a fortified castle where they were kept prisoner
and stripped of their money and all their possessions. Fortu-

nately, the duke of Bar learned of their situation and had them released. Diplomatic immunity was thus not always respected. And yet, those who violated it were sometimes harshly punished. For example, in 1340, individuals linked to the curia who had seized an English ambassador to the pope in Avignon were sentenced to death.

Diplomatic activity sometimes approached spying. Bertrandon de La Broquière carried out a spy mission for his master Philip the Good in 1432. He was asked to prepare a travel account useful for a prince wishing to conquer Jerusalem. In order to do this, he carefully studied the military organization and resources of the Turks.

Related to ambassadors were inspectors, sent out by the ruler not to negotiate but to keep watch, and therefore traveled a lot. To take only one example, there were the Carolingian *missi dominici*. Recruited from the great figures, most of the time sent in pairs (a bishop and a layman), they were deputed to watch over a region defined in relation to an ecclesiastical province.

> He [Louis the Pious] designates selected clergy and proven men of religion, people whose habits are known to him and acceptable, to visit the towns of the kingdom, the monasteries, the convents, and to carry out his generous instructions. He says to them: ". . . Now, come, you whom I am sending, apply yourselves to this mission and make your way throughout my empire. . . ."

## MESSENGERS

There were men whose profession was to travel constantly. Once ambassadors had arrived at their destination, they stayed for a while. Messengers, in contrast, often quickly returned to their point of departure. Jean Andry, a rider from the stable of the duke of Burgundy, received a franc "that my lords of the Accounts have granted him for waiting in Dijon from March 8, 1417 to the following day," when they gave him sealed letters to carry to his master.

Correspondence fulfilled many needs, private as well as public. In late Antiquity, the meager facilities provided by the state for individual travel also held true for their mail. The state took care only of the circulation of official documents, only exceptionally of private mail. Individuals could count only on themselves, with the surest method being to have their own messengers, usually taken from among their servants; bishops would select theirs from their retinue. But seldom did people travel only to carry letters. Someone who was making a journey was often asked to do so as a favor. The converse could also happen. Sidonius wrote to his beloved Simplicius: "The bearer of my message insistently requests the favor of carrying a letter from me to you, while in any case I was prepared, had he said nothing, to ask him the same favor, as soon as we knew of his journey."

These messengers, generally of modest extraction, were well received in the name of the sender.

> I think I can already see how new everything will be for this man, whose elegance has nothing that might provoke jealousy, when he is invited . . . a poor man, to your table, and, while he lives here as a common man, with thoroughly unpolished people stuffed with onions to the point of indigestion, he will be treated there with the same politeness as if he had been accustomed to belch in the company of the gourmets of Apicius. . . . Although people of this kind are often contemptible—or nearly so—when it is a matter of cultivating fellowship by exchanges of letters, friendship would have a good deal to lose, if, because of the vulgarity of the messengers, it were to deprive itself of the possibility of more frequent conversations.

But letters did not always reach their destination. Sidonius Apollinaris showed bitterness at the loss of one of them, for the messenger could provide no information. He was reading with his son when his servant came in:

> "What is it?" we asked him.
> "It is the *lector* Constant," he answered, "who is at the door and who has just come back from my lords Simplicius and Apollinaris; he certainly handed over the letter he had been given for them, but he has lost the one he was given in reply."

At these words, the calm of my delight was immediately darkened by the veil of a cloud of sadness, and the annoyance provoked by this news so strongly stimulated my bile that, for a goodly number of days, I forbade this new Hermes, so profoundly stupid, from appearing before my eyes. . . . But when, with time, our anger had gradually subsided, I had the fellow come in to ask him whether, besides the letter, he had received some oral message to give to me. Trembling, prostrate, stuttering, his sight troubled by the awareness of his fault, he finally answered that everything that might inform and please me had been confided to the pages that had disappeared.

The Byzantine Empire had a public postal service, intended to make the ruler's orders promptly known, as well as to transmit information requiring immediate decisions. Its organization seems to have been excellent in the fourth century, but it began to decline under the reign of Justinian. Nevertheless, it functioned properly in the eastern provinces until the Seljuk invasion in the late eleventh century. The Arab Harun ben Jahja, made prisoner around 880, was transported by sea to the port of Attalia, a crucial stage in the public postal system. There, a director was in charge of mail carried by mules and horses as well as baggage transported by sea. On land, it took a week to cross Asia Minor, which suggests that there were organized relays. Harun and his companions took three days to reach Nicaea, then, three days later probably arrived in Malagina, a major mail center. The travelers then walked for two days before reaching the sea where they embarked for Constantinople.

This organization seems no longer to have existed under the Comneni. Routes still survived in the Balkan peninsula, but it was more and more difficult to find messengers. In 1424, John VIII, son of Emperor Manuel II and his associate on the throne, who was in Hungary, wished to inform his father of his return to the capital; he found only one messenger, who knew no Greek, to whom to give the letter.

The Muslim world, following the tradition of the Sassanids, had a postal service that was available to the public. Mail was regularly and quickly carried by dromedaries or mules, mail ships, or even carrier pigeons and light signals. In each center, a postmaster was in charge of the transit of letters and packages.

West of the Euphrates, distances were indicated in miles, to the east in parasanges (a parasange equals three miles). Every two parasanges along the major roads, a relay station made it possible to change horses. Special messengers, who were very fast, carried official dispatches. The Chinese service in the east and the Byzantine service in the west were linked to the Muslim postal service, so that Constantinople merchants could write to correspondents in China and quickly receive an answer.

The postal service in India and China did indeed seem to be well organized. According to Ibn Battuta,

> The postal service in India is of two kinds. The horse-post . . . consists of horses belonging to the Sultan [with relays] every four miles. The service of couriers on foot has within the space of each mile three relays, which they call *dawa*. . . . At every third of a mile, there is an inhabited village, outside which there are three pavilions. In these sit men girded up ready to move off, each of whom has a rod two cubits long with copper bells at the top. When a courier leaves the town he takes the letter in the fingers of one hand and the rod with the bells in the other, and runs with all his might. The men in the pavilions, on hearing the sound of the bells, get ready to meet him and when he reaches them one of them takes the letter in his hand and passes on, running with all his might until he reaches the next *dawa*, and so they continue until the letter reaches its destination.[29]

In China, the state postal system was in existence by the third century B.C. Under the Tang (612–907), a network of roads with relay stations connected the capital to other large cities. Each relay station had a director, employees, many animals, and sometimes ships. Every year, the director gave an accounting to the provincial authorities. As today, mail went at two speeds: slow, carried on foot or by donkey; rapid, carried by messengers on horseback. Thanks to relay stations located approximately every 20 kilometers, a messenger on horseback could cover an average of 100 kilometers a day, while an express messenger could go as far as 320 kilometers. This postal service, which was

---

29. *The Travels of Ibn Battuta*, tr. H. A. R. Gibb, v. III, p. 594.

costly but to which the administration was attached, was further developed by the Sung dynasty from the tenth through the early thirteenth century.

In the thirteenth century, the Mongols extended the system to all the territories that they conquered. During the apogee of the Mongol Empire, more than 60,000 kilometers were equipped with the service, half in China, which represented between 2,500 and 3,000 relay stations. Many roads, says Marco Polo, radiate from Khan-balik, and after 25 miles one finds a posting station.

> At every post the messengers find a spacious and palatial hostelry for their lodging. These hostelries have splendid beds with rich coverlets of silk and all that befits an emissary of high rank. . . . And at each of these posts the messengers find three or four hundred horses in readiness awaiting their command. . . . These posts are found every twenty-five or thirty miles.

When messengers have to cross wild and mountainous terrain where there were no houses,

> they find that the Great Khan has had posts established even in these wilds, with the same palatial accommodation and the same supply of horses and accoutrements. But here the stages are longer; for the posts are thirty-five miles apart and in some cases over forty miles. The Khan sends people to live at these places and till the soil and serve the posts, so that they grow into good-sized villages.

Every three miles between posts, there is a hamlet of about forty houses where runners live who wear very large belts set all around with bells so that they can be heard from a distance. They are required to carry letters as far as the next hamlet, where they are relayed by other messengers. But the Great Khan may have urgent messages to send, and there are express messengers for this purpose. The messenger, who must go very fast, "carries a tablet with the sign of the gerfalcon as a token that he wishes to ride post haste, and if it happens that while galloping on the road, the horse collapses or there is any sort of delay, if he comes across anyone else, whoever he may be, the messenger can have him dismount and take his horse, for no one would dare refuse. . . ." If two of them leave from the same place, they ride two good horses.

> Off they go with all the speed they can muster, till they reach the next post-house twenty-five miles away. As they draw near they sound a sort of horn which is audible at a great distance, so that horses may be got ready for them. On arrival they find two fresh horses, ready harnessed, fully rested, and in good running form. They mount there and then, without a moment's breathing space, and are no sooner mounted than off they go again. . . .[30]

And so they gallop all day long, covering 250 miles in a day. In case of necessity, they even ride at night. "If there is no moon, the men of the post run in front of them with torches as far as the next post." This relay service was for the transmission of state letters, not for those of individuals.

In the West, it seems that the public service survived during the Carolingian era. In the second half of the eighth century in Aquitaine, royal letters authorized the requisition of horses and food for messengers. Appreciable speeds can be observed in the late eleventh century. A letter sent from Rome by Gregory VII to Henry IV on December 8, 1075, carried by three envoys of the king, was read twenty-three days later in Goslar, at a distance of 1,700 to 1,800 kilometers, corresponding to 70 to 75 kilometers covered a day.

For individuals, as in the time of Sidonius Apollinaris, only the most powerful, laymen or clergy, were able to send a member of their retinue or a servant to carry a letter to some correspondent. In 847, Abbot Loup of Ferrières recommends to Abbot Marcward his "new messenger, carrier of this letter; in his way of life, he is thoroughly suited to his condition, except that he cannot yet sleep alone, because, I believe, of his fear of the dark." In 852, the same Abbot Loup asked Abbot Altsig of York to send, by very trustworthy messengers, a certain number of

---

30. *The Travels of Marco Polo*, tr. Ronald Latham, 151, 154.

works that he wanted to have copied. Private postal services came into being because of communities such as universities whose students wished to be able to ask their parents for help.

Businessmen, of course, needed to know of events that might perturb the smooth running of commerce. Because they were more enterprising in Italy than in the other European countries, it was there that the first private postal services made their appearance. Sending a message by horse or on ship was expensive, so merchants came together to share the expense of common messengers to the fairs of Champagne in the thirteenth century. The habit took root. In 1357, seventeen Florentine companies created the fund of Florentine merchants that each week sent a messenger from Florence to Avignon through Genoa and another in the opposite direction. This fund accepted letters from individuals in return for payment of a fee; until the fourteenth and fifteenth centuries, individuals relied on the services of travelers, pilgrims, merchants, or jongleurs.

The time taken by messengers to complete their journeys obviously varied according to region and season, and depended on whether they traveled on foot, on horseback, or by ship. Francesco di Marco Datini writes that one of his employees took three days to go from Florence to Genoa; it normally took six days to go from Florence to Venice. In the same period, Bonaccorso Pitti asserts that he rode from Florence to Padua in a little more than two days, and another time that it took him only nine days to go from Asti to Paris. When a letter had to reach England, it was obviously necessary to wait for the tide and a favorable wind to cross the Channel. Francesco's accounts, however, show that his letters reached his correspondents quickly and without mishap.

An average speed was indicated in manuals of commerce. Here are times given by the Florentine Giovanni di Antonio da Uzzano in 1442 and 1458: Genoa-Paris, 18 to 22 days; Avignon-Paris, 15 to 16 days; Barcelona-Bruges, 22 to 24 days; Florence-London, 25 to 30 days; Florence-Paris, 20 to 22 days. On average then, messengers covered 50 to 80 kilometers a day, when there was only one stage or when man and horse were replaced at each stage. But when a journey involved several stages without relays—these were the most frequent and least expensive—the distances covered were smaller. In fact, at each stage, the messenger had to concern himself with letters that he gave out or received, take care of his horse, eat, and rest. He therefore would travel about 60 kilometers a day, a distance corresponding to the length of journeys provided by Giovanni di Antonio da Uzzano. At sea, the distance covered, calculated as a straight line between point of departure and point of arrival, ranged from 120 to 150 kilometers for a twenty-four hour day.

It was thus private entities, driven by economic considerations, that organized the transmission of news. Following the example of the Florentine companies whose skills they used, the popes established a messenger service in the fourteenth century. Under Innocent IV, the average number of pontifical messengers was between forty-five and fifty, but it declined as a result of the plague. Under Urban V, it rose again to thirty, according to Anne-Marie Hayez. Every two months, these messengers were paid 8 florins, 6 sous, that is, 3 or 4 sous a day, approximately the wages of a laborer. Added to this were certain perquisites, such as travel expenses. Their duties were in part sedentary. Nevertheless, they traveled a good deal and for various reasons. To supply the pontifical court: Dominique de Lucarrel went frequently to the Bordeaux region to purchase cloth and fish. To bring in prisoners or take them to various places: in 1354, with a chaplain and a servant, Bernard Plantat made a five-day journey to Nîmes, Oiselet, and Roquemaure in search of a monk suspected of homicide. To inquire about the dangers created by the Great Companies or to warn the populations: in 1362, Henri de Tongres spent a week going through the villages of the Comtat to warn of the arrival of mercenaries. Finally, to carry the letters of the pope, the chamberlain, the treasurer, and the cardinals went through all of Christendom.

Popes also called on professional messengers, some of whom were self-employed, whereas others were at the service of merchants for whom they worked either directly or through the intermediary of the master of the merchants' messengers. This master asked 18 florins for a six-day journey to Paris, but 25 florins if the trip took only five days. Some pontifical messengers could do as well or even better. Pierre de Ala went from Paris to Avignon in four days for a payment of 22 florins.

Merchants' messengers went to Paris, to Italy, sometimes to Spain, but pontifical messengers were the ones who went to Germany and England. They were not specialized, although some preferred to go long distances while others seldom went far from court, and carried not only letters but other things as well.

Princes had professional messengers who did not all travel at the same speed. Only a few received orders to ride without stopping. Even then, very few traveled on moonless nights. But these messengers who covered impressive distances in little time must have slept badly. The messenger that Charles VI sent to the cardinals to delay the conclave in 1394 took four days to cover the distance between Paris and Avignon. In France, it was only under Louis XI that royal posts were set up on certain routes.

In Hainaut, it seems that the authorities relied increasingly on foot messengers, less costly than horsemen. For example, when Philip the Good published some edicts in February 1438, the bailiff relied on four foot messengers. An ordinary rider of the duke's stable received 3 sous a day when he was at the duke's residence, along with free lodging. He was paid 8 sous for each day traveling, but he had to pay for lodging and the care of his horse. As for the foot messenger, he received 6 sous for each day on the road. Exceptional expenses were scrutinized with great rigor. And anything that saved money was looked on with favor. A single messenger on foot or horseback would carry, without extra pay, letters of different kinds addressed to the same recipient. It was, however, difficult to avoid supplementary expenses: the death of a horse on the road, or the repair of shoes. When messengers brought good news, they often received a gratuity. In 1492, for a letter concerning the peace reached between Maximilian and the Flemings, Arson was given 20 sous. "Tips" were welcome since messengers were badly paid.

The town of Chartres, finding the information that it received inadequate, put in place two services—messages and travels—and it seems to have been more generous. In the late fourteenth century, professional messengers received 5 sous tournois to go to Gallardon (20 kilometers), 10 sous for Châteaudun (44 kilometers), but double if the journey was at night, 20 sous for Paris (90 kilometers), and 60 sous for Le Mans (120 kilometers). Travel expenses varied according to class or social importance. For a journey to the capital a messenger received 5 sous tournois, but a magistrate 1 livre, and the bailiff 7 livres. Sending messengers was still a luxury.

## LEGAL AND FINANCIAL OFFICERS

At the solemn opening ceremonies in 1408, Chancellor de Corbie, aged eighty-three, declared to his colleagues in the Parlement of Paris that the king had ordered that he go to Gien, "which was most grievous for him, given his great age and the times, because the times were now very dangerous." Five years later, he could no longer perform his duties, for he was "so stupid and weak that he could hardly go from place to place." Royal officers generally had to be able to go on frequent travels.

The agents of the king of England in charge of the administration of Gascony were an extreme case.[31] Most of them had no fixed position and traveled frequently between England, Paris, Gascony, and the court of Rome. In England, they oversaw decisions related to the duchy and advised the king and the chancellor. In France, at first procurators of the king-duke for some diplomatic matters and for all legal matters, they later became advisers to the permanent procurators. Maître Bonet de Saint-Quentin was probably one of the most active. Mentioned for the first time in 1271, when he was dean of the royal chapel in Bruges, he was asked to carry out an investigation of Edward's interests in Gascony. In 1275, the king sent him to witness the oath that the inhabitants of Limousin, Périgord, Quercy, and Saintonge owed to the king of France. The business ended in failure, and Maître Bonet went to England to report. He returned during the winter with the mission to seize the holdings of the opposition. In 1276, he had to survey royal rights throughout the duchy. Back in England the following winter, he was confined to Oxford for a while because of illness. In 1277, he failed again to secure the oath, and he traveled again to England and then to France to keep the king informed. Back in England, Maître Bonet received a safe-conduct for a journey "overseas." He was probably in England again in January 1279, and then accompanied Edward I to France. In February 1281, he was a priest in Lincolnshire, but reappeared in Gascony in the spring. From July 1281 to February 1284, he made ten trips between England and France, not to mention a visit to Aragon in the spring of 1282. His travels were

---

31. They have been studied by J. P. Trabut-Cussac.

just as frequent after 1284. Maître Bonet was still alive on May 8, 1290; thereafter, his name disappears from the documentary record.

There were certainly few agents who traveled as much. Nevertheless, from 1297 to 1306, Maître Pierre Eymeric, involved in peace negotiations among London, Paris, and Rome, went to Flanders twice, to Rome four times, to France six times, and stayed in Gascony on three occasions. Generally speaking, travels made by officers of the king of France in connection with their work might take place within their district, between the district and the seat of central authority in Paris, or throughout the kingdom.

Legal matters gave rise to countless travels. On the roads: people involved in trials; offenders being brought to prison; men of the law, as for example, two counselors of the Parlement of Paris who went to Carentan in Normandy to deal with the question of a fief and the guardianship of some minors, and who summoned witnesses to come from a dozen neighboring communities. Some travels were of an exceptional character: an under-sergeant from Evreux went to Vernon in 1398 to get the executioner, because his counterpart in Evreux was incapable of performing his duties by reason of his age and his blindness.

Procurators traveled a good deal. Although they earned less than advocates, their work had certain advantages, namely, travel. On the slightest pretext, a procurator would go to the nearest town to handle his clients' proceedings. In the fifteenth century, one third, one half, and sometimes nearly two-thirds of a litigant's legal expenses were attributable to a procurator's travels. A procurator would be reimbursed for more than he spent. He had various ways of accomplishing this: make a single trip for several litigants and have each one pay the total expense; after the trial, inflate the number of days traveled; request a large sum for each day spent away from home. Even if he were honest, a procurator profited from his travels, for he was normally paid 12 sous parisis or more, while his actual expenses probably did not exceed 3 sous parisis—the sum set by a judge for a day's travel by a procurator in his calculation of expenses owed by a litigant.

In the realm of finance, tax authorities traveled for purposes of establishing rates or farming out certain taxes. In 1368, Étienne

Courvillain went to Chartres and "compelled the submission of the papers, lists, and registers of the collectors who in the past had received and collected the taxes and other obligations of the town." In 1391, Jacques de Jauly, charged with collecting war taxes in the viscounty of Montivilliers and the exempt territory of Fécamp, received 100 sous tournois from Dreux d'Antrain, tax collector, for a journey he had made from Montivilliers to Louviers to see Jean Le Flament, counselor-general to the king on taxes, in order to give an account of the receipts of the preceding and current years, "on which journey I spent, going, staying, and returning, five days, at the rate of 20 sous tournois per day." In 1460, wishing for a better distribution of the taille, the king indicated in a decree: "We wish the supervisors of our finances to go themselves or send deputies to the districts in their charge to be better informed of the capabilities and resources of the people of each region."

The work of a collector, intermediary between the government and the population, occasioned frequent travel. To obtain the funds necessary for the repair of a road near Lamballe, Guillaume Cadet and his assistants had to make many trips in the course of 1466 and 1467:[32] late April 1466, trip to the Chamber in Vannes to describe the situation, but the absence of the president made a decision impossible; June 1466, another trip to Vannes with the estimate and reports; July 1466, third trip to Vannes to obtain authorization to postpone the work until the following spring, because they could not be completed before bad weather set in; March 1467, return to Vannes, but the Chamber was too busy to deal with the question; April 1467, presentation of the file to the Chamber of Accounts, which sent it to the council; May 1467, presentation to the council. The distance from Lamballe to Vannes—more than 100 kilometers—required at least five days round trip; from Lamballe to Nantes—more than 180 kilometers—at least ten. There were thus thirty-five to forty days of travel before the repairs were begun. And travel expenses amounted to more than 14 livres, one quarter of the annual earnings of the collector.

---

32. Chronology established by Jean Kerhervé.

Beginning in 1297 or 1298, district and regional collectors had to go to Paris twice a year to present the receipts and expenses of their jurisdictions to the Chamber of Accounts. Sometimes, things were not simple. The viscount of Ponautou and Pont-Audemer went to the capital during the Easter term in 1405. Because of some extraordinary expenses, his accounts were in deficit, and he did not dare appear before the Chamber, sending a clerk in his place. The Chamber recognized his good faith and reimbursed his expenses for an eleven-day stay in Paris, including the four days he had been in hiding.

Transfers of funds required frequent travel. Carriers provided pack horses, but a royal officer no doubt had to go along.

Of particular interest is the diary of the procurator Dauvet, who was given the task of preparing an inventory of the possessions of Jacques Coeur after his trial and conviction. It shows us the activity of a royal official traveling throughout France for four years, from June 2, 1453 to July 5, 1457. He was in Tours from June 17 to August 14, 1453; in Blois, Orléans, Paris, and Rouen from August 14 to October 3, 1453; in Berry from October 14, 1453 to January 24, 1454 (recalled to Paris because of the illness of his deputy in the Parlement, Jean Dauvet stayed there from December 23 to 30, 1453, before returning to Bourges); in Langres and Languedoc from January 27 to October 18, 1454 (with side trips to Aix and Marseille); in Lyon and the surrounding region from October 29, 1454 to May 22, 1455; in Saint-Pourçain from May 22 to June 7, 1455; in Moulins from June 7 to 20, 1455; again in Berry from June 25, 1455 to January 19, 1456; in Montpellier from January 19 to March 23, 1456; in Gannat, Moulins, and Bourges from May 8, 1456 to February 5, 1457; then, going to see the king, he passed through Moulins, Lyon, and Feurs from February 7 to July 5, 1457. In addition, Jean Dauvet sent others to investigate in other cities of the kingdom, such as Limoges and La Rochelle, and even abroad. Sometimes, the king gave him missions to be carried out immediately, which required rather long journeys; on January 17, 1456, when he was in Saint-Pourçain, the monarch ordered him to be in Montpellier for the opening of the Estates General three days later. Jean Dauvet was thus constantly on the road for several years. Although he observed holidays, he took advantage of the free days of Easter week to study his files.

## SOLDIERS

Fighters sometimes came from distant regions to serve as mercenaries. The French army had soldiers from Wales in the fourteenth century and from Scotland in the fifteenth. Genoese crossbow men were not a negligible quantity. These foreign mercenaries were motivated primarily by money, but sometimes by political reasons.

The profession of soldiering made travel necessary. Under Charles VI, to take possession of the Kingdom of Sicily, the duke of Anjou led a large army. The soldiers set off for Provence in forced marches, burning and pillaging as they went. In the course of seven months, they seized a number of purportedly impregnable places. The duke and his army then crossed, as friends, Lombardy and Tuscany, encountering no obstacles except the inhabitants of the Alps. Overcoming all difficulties, he reached the Kingdom of Naples. Crusades were, of course, even more distant expeditions.

The speed of armies, like that of messengers, varied according to terrain but also according to circumstances. To deal with unexpected attacks from Arabs, Byzantine troops had become very mobile. Starting out from Bulgaria, Basil II crossed Asia Minor in sixteen days to come to the aid of the emir of Aleppo.

Letters of remission make it possible to focus on individual experience. Guillaume (or Regaut) and Jean Balbet, brothers, were in Tournehem in 1369, then joined the troops that reconquered Poitou in 1372 under the command of a marshal of the duke of Berry. After a six-month siege of Lusignan, they went into the service of the duke of Bourbonnais who wanted to relieve fortresses in Auvergne. Jean was also part of the expedition led by Du Guesclin in Tirelle against the duke of Lancaster, near Le Carladès, where he was captured. He was at Châteauneuf-de-Randon when Du Guesclin was killed. Finally, he was under the orders of the king in his Flanders campaign of 1382. Simon Pingreau, from Pozay-le-Vieux, obtained pardon in 1449. This laborer had served the king at Pontoise, probably during the siege begun eight years earlier in 1441, in Tarts, in Germany, and in various other places. He was on his way to the siege of Fougères with two companions when he was arrested. A 1451 letter of remission tells us that Jean Deschamps, archer, from Sainte-Soline in Poitou, had first served as a page to a certain Grégoire who died at the siege of Pontoise in 1441, then as a crossbow man and an archer in the company of the lord of Jaloignes, with whom he had gone to Normandy, and then to Guyenne for the siege of Bergerac in 1450. After spending some time in the garrison of that town, he had made several expeditions on foot and on horseback against the English. These Englishmen had to leave their country to come to fight in France, the site of all the military operations of the Hundred Years' War.

These distances are small compared to those traveled by Johan Schiltberger. Born in Bavaria, he accompanied his master Leonard Richartinger to Hungary. He was only sixteen when he was captured at the battle of Nicopolis in 1396. In the service of the sultan, he appears to have taken part in the siege of Constantinople as well as in several expeditions to Egypt and Asia Minor. At the defeat of Bayezid at Angora in 1402, he fell into the hands of the troops of Tamerlane and went with them to the Middle East and central Asia. After Tamerlane's death in 1405, he served various princes and participated in expeditions to Samarkand, the region of the Oxus, and as far as Great Tartary, where he rode with Prince Cheku, the future leader of the Golden Horde: "The countries described all belong to Great Tartary, and I have been in all of them." He took part in this prince's expedition to Siberia. His adventures continued in various regions of the Caspian, the Black Sea, Egypt, Palestine, and perhaps Arabia. After more than thirty years in Muslim countries, he managed to escape with four other Christians on a ship sailing in the Black Sea. He reached Constantinople after further adventures and finally returned to Bavaria in 1427.

The service of the king involved many travels, but the service of God might lead men even further.

# in the service
# of the lord

$\mathcal{P}$ILGRIMS AND CRUSADERS

Pilgrimage was at first understood as a complete break with the world; the most important thing was to set out, and the goal of the journey turned out to be secondary. Nevertheless, from the earliest centuries A.D., the faithful went to the places where Christ had lived and later to where relics could be found.

The desire to follow the steps of Christ was expressed particularly from the eleventh century on. His power showed itself more clearly, it was thought, in the places where He had lived. The city of Jerusalem thus became the principal destination for pilgrims. In his *Histoires*, relating events between 900 and 1044, the Burgundian monk Raoul Glaber writes:

> At the same time [around 1033], a countless host came streaming from everywhere in the world to the sepulcher of the Savior in Jerusalem; no one had previously foreseen such a crowd. First came the simple people, then the middle classes, then all the greatest kings, counts, marquis, and prelates; finally, and this had never happened, women of the high nobility took the road to Jerusalem in the company of the poorest people.

Adémar de Chabannes, a monk of Saint-Cybard in Angoulême, who was born around 988 and died in 1034, provides the
following account of the pilgrimage of Count Guillaume II Tail-
lefer of Angoulême in 1026–27:

> At that time, Count Guillaume of Angoulême crossed Ba-
> varia on his way to the tomb of the Lord. He was accompa-
> nied . . . by a large cohort of noble persons. . . . He set out
> on the first day of October, reached the Holy City in the first
> week of the month of March, and set out to return to his
> estates in the third week of June. On his return, he passed
> through Limoges, where the entire assembly of the monks
> of Saint-Martial came out to meet him and received him
> with great ceremony. Even better, as soon as the news of his
> arrival reached Angoulême, all the nobles, not only local,
> but those from Poitou and Saintonge, and people of all ages
> and both sexes came running to meet him and were filled
> with joy at his sight.

There was another motivation. The faithful thought that
they would be better situated in Rome, where Saint Peter was
buried, and especially in Jerusalem to await the resurrection of
the dead. After noting the great crowd of people at the tomb of
the Lord, Raoul Glaber writes that "many wished to die before
returning home." And he recounts the story of a Burgundian
named Liébaut who, when he came to the Mount of Olives,
prostrated himself, overcome with tears and an unspeakable
inner joy:

> Lord Jesus . . . I beg that Your almighty goodness will allow
> that, if my soul is to leave my body this year, I may not ever
> leave this place, but that it happen in view of the place of
> Your Ascension. I believe indeed that, as I have pursued You
> with my body by coming here, so my soul will enter safe
> and sound and joyous in Your wake into paradise.

His prayer was answered when he gave up the ghost that very
night.

The Middle Ages accorded particular importance to relics.
They were even stolen to increase a monastery's treasure. The
cult of relics goes some way toward explaining the growth of

pilgrimages in the period. The ill and infirm hoped to be cured by the intervention of the saint whose remains they had come to venerate. An example among a thousand related by Gregory, bishop of Tours from 573 to 594, is one that he was well placed to describe since he was the one who was cured:

> [In 562] I fell ill. Afflicted with malignant pustules and fever, and no longer able to eat or drink, I suffered so greatly that, having lost all hope of living in this world, I no longer thought of anything but the care of my sepulcher. Death constantly besieged me with ferocity and attempted to expel my soul from my body. Then, although very feeble, having invoked the name of the blessed pontiff Martin, I recovered a little, and by slow steps I began to prepare my journey, for I had had the idea that it was necessary to visit the spot where the venerable tomb was found. My desire was so great that I no longer wished to live if I had to further delay going there; so much so that I, who had hardly gotten over the fevers of illness, was enflamed anew by the fever of my desire. No longer delaying and although still very weak, I set out with my companions.

According to the calculations of Luce Pietri, of the pilgrims who at the time traveled to Tours, 20 percent came from the city or the region, 75 percent from other towns in Gaul, particularly from the center, the Loire Valley, the Parisian basin, Normandy, and Brittany (in decreasing order of importance), and 5 percent from outside Gaul, particularly from Italy and Spain. There were powerful lay figures, clergy, and making up 73 percent, people of modest social rank. They were 65 percent adult men, 20 percent adult women, and 15 percent children. Most suffered from illness or an infirmity of the body or the mind. They saw Martin principally as a doctor who healed especially the blind and paralytic, but also the deaf, the mute, the feverish, those afflicted with the plague, or those possessed by the devil. A pilgrim who had been healed sometimes vowed to return every year in order to thank the saint. If he forgot his vow, the saint would remind him by making him ill again.

Pilgrimage, however, had to fulfill certain requirements. Although Saint Peter Damien rebuked Marquis Rainier because he delayed going to Jerusalem, he declared that whoever was living according to a rule should keep to the kind of life which he had adopted. And Raoul Glaber, after narrating the edifying story of Liébaut, added: "Surely, this man was free from the feelings of vanity that make so many people undertake this journey, solely interested in clothing themselves with the prestigious title of pilgrims to Jerusalem."

People required to undertake a penitential pilgrimage were not necessarily infused with piety. In 813, the Council of Châlon-sur-Saône stigmatized false pilgrims of every condition. Churchmen constantly reiterated such condemnations, evidence that they had little effect. Besides, pilgrims were joined by all kinds of dubious elements: heretics, beggars, loose women.

Around 1233, four heretics who were traveling "in the manner of pilgrims" lodged with Géraud Gaillard in Castelsarrasin. But soon thereafter they were arrested and sentenced to being burned. Two men claiming to be pilgrims asked for hospitality from a woman in Castelnau-Montratier in what is now the department of Lot. The next day, they admitted that they were heretics. Heresy, moreover, used the pilgrim roads to grow. For example, in the thirteenth and fourteenth centuries heresy appeared in Galicia, far from any other heterodox center.

Some adopted pilgrim dress to travel through hostile regions without mishap. Giacomo Pecoraria, cardinal-bishop of Palestrina, was sent on a mission to France by Pope Gregory IX. He could not go by sea because of the Pisan fleet, and the supporters of the emperor controlled the roads. Giacomo Pecoraria and a companion left Rome in 1239 concealed under monks' cowls and leaning on pilgrim staffs. They thus reached Genoa without incident.

Pilgrimage by women was disapproved by men. Disputes and scandals frequently occurred on the subject in the late Middle Ages, and it was better not to run around on pilgrimage at every opportunity; above all, young women should do so only in good company. Women were apparently not always guided by piety. Households suffered from the situation, and husbands complained. Geoffroy de La Tour Landry, author of a late fourteenth-century treatise addressed to young women, asserted that pilgrimages were merely a pretext to *take up dalliances and follies*. According to Matheolus, women went on pilgrimage to carry on affairs with the clergy. In his *Miroir de mariage*, Eustache Deschamps wrote:

If I say; keep the house,
She objects with a pilgrimage.
She has to go to Saint-Denis!
There they mock married men.

The eighth of the *Quinze Joies de mariage* provides a no more edifying picture. And the preacher Olivier Maillard harshly criticized women who used pilgrimage as an excuse for amorous encounters: "Are you there, ladies, you who love to run off on pilgrimages? It is neither God nor the saints that you go to seek."

On a pilgrimage, Perrin and other young men began to dance in a church of the Orléans region along with other people of both sexes, among whom was Jeannette, a prostitute. The men then put out the candles and covered Jeannette's mouth so she would not cry out.

In other cases, pilgrimage might be a punishment. A letter of June 1387 pardoned Jean Bigot of Saint-Maurice-des-Noues, guilty of homicide, on condition that he travel to Notre-Dame du Puy and have a hundred masses said for the soul of the deceased. In 1393, remission was granted to two residents of the parish of Azay-le-Brûlé who four years earlier had participated in the murder of a looter and the robbery of a woman, on condition that one go to Notre-Dame du Puy and the other to Santiago de Compostela. As for three characters who had had their valets beat to death a certain Jean Mérigeau, called Caillaut, from la Jarrie, their pardon in 1410 was conditioned on a pilgrimage to Mont-Saint-Michel and a fine.

In the late Middle Ages, there were even professional pilgrims who, for a price, carried out this act of piety for others. For the dead: in 1413, Dino Rapondi, a rich merchant from Lucca, left 40 livres parisis in his will for a horseman to make a pilgrimage from Paris to Santiago de Compostela, the same sum for another pilgrimage from Paris to Rome, and 80 livres parisis for a third pilgrimage from Paris to the Holy Sepulcher in Jerusalem on the same conditions. For the living: Jean Gurguesel, a priest, traveled to Saint-Lomer near Courcy in Normandy in place of Isabella of Bavaria. Around 1374, Yvonnet Warguier, a professional pilgrim, was living comfortably in Paris with his wife Gillete and two young children. But the profession involved frequent absences, of which a wife was likely to take advantage, as evidenced in letters of remission.

The places of pilgrimage were many and various. Three were more prominent than the others: Jerusalem, Rome, and Santiago de Compostela.

There is a long list of those who had gone to Jerusalem from the time of the death of Christ. The upheavals of the second half of the eleventh century and the Muslim advance seemed to foretell persecutions of pilgrims that the Crusades managed to forestall for at least a few generations. The fall of Saint-Jean d'Acre in the late thirteenth century seems to have disrupted pilgrimages. A compromise was reached, however, and in the late Middle Ages, many of the faithful traveled to the Holy Land despite harassment from Muslims and the hazards of the journey.

The tombs of Saint Peter and Saint Paul drew pilgrims to Rome from the very beginning of the Middle Ages. A certain decline occurred in the eleventh century due to the competition from Jerusalem and Santiago de Compostela, the devastation of the city by the Germanic emperors, and disturbances caused by the turbulent Roman nobility. But in the fourteenth century, pilgrimage to Rome resumed in force. Pilgrims came not only to pray at the tombs of Peter and Paul but thought also of all the martyrs, sometimes little known, who were buried in Roman churches and cemeteries. Jubilees organized by the popes drew crowds. In particular, the jubilee of 1300, led by Boniface VIII, had an enormous success. Complete remission of sins was granted to every Roman who, for thirty successive days went to the churches of the apostles Peter and Paul and to every non-Roman who did the same for fifteen days, on condition that he confess beforehand. Hence many Christians, sometimes from distant countries, came to Rome. According to the Florentine chronicler Giovanni Villani, that year the city welcomed 200,000 pilgrims.

Once in the Eternal City, after a journey that lasted between five and seven weeks for the English, the pilgrims had available ever more numerous guidebooks. In the fifteenth century, Stefan Planck published one in Rome written in Middle High German, and it was so successful that it was reprinted twenty-six times before 1500. When they had returned home, pilgrims could display insignia—representing in particular the two princes of the Apostles or the keys of Saint Peter—that proved that they had visited Rome.

The pilgrimage to Santiago could not lay claim to the same antiquity. It began to take shape in the ninth century. Its apogee

took place between the late eleventh and late thirteenth centuries. But many pilgrims carried the shell in the course of succeeding centuries.

Any Muslim who has the means must, at least once in his
life, make a pilgrimage to Mecca. Ibn Battuta traveled there on
four occasions. He arrived the first time in October 1326 and left
the following month. Returning in October 1327, he spent three
years in the holy city. After an expedition to Yemen and East
Africa, he lived there again for nearly a year from late 1331 to
September 1332. He went back for the last time in 1349 after
living for a long time in India and traveling to China.

Through his extravagance on his pilgrimage in 1346, King
Mansa-Moussa of Mali revealed the unsuspected wealth of black
Africa. Ibn Khaldun reports: "Twelve thousand young slaves,
dressed in tunics of brocade and Yemeni silk, carried his possessions. He came from his country with eighty loads of gold
powder, each one weighing three quintals." Of course, as in the
West, most Muslim pilgrims were of modest rank and often
traveled in harsh conditions.

Plenary indulgence, granted for the first time, it seems, in
1095 by Pope Urban II, to those who would deliver the tomb of
Christ, was assimilated by his audience to indulgence earned by
pilgrims who traveled to Jerusalem. Moreover, some Crusaders,
after visiting the tombs of the apostles in Rome in the course
of their journey, returned home thinking they had fulfilled their
vow. When Louis VII undertook the Second Crusade after the
fall of Urfa, he began by going to Jerusalem as soon as he had
arrived in the Holy Land. And his army included a large number of pilgrims. It took the catastrophe of Hattin in 1187 and the
capture of Jerusalem by the Muslims to change such ideas. Crusades and pilgrimages could no longer be identified, for the popes
prohibited visiting the Holy Sepulcher as long as the infidels
occupied the Holy City.

In a celebrated passage, Joinville retraces his departure for
the Seventh Crusade:

> At Easter in 1248, I called together my men and my vassals
> in Joinville. . . . I told them on Friday: "Lords, I am going
> over the sea, and I do not know if I will return. Step forward;
> if I have done you some wrong, I will make reparation to
> each in turn, as I am accustomed to do, to all who wish to

claim something from me or my people." I made reparation to them following the advice of all the people of my land; and in order not to influence them, I left the council, and I followed their conclusions without discussion.

As I did not wish to take with me any money wrongly, I went to Metz in Lorraine and pledged a large quantity of my land. And you should know that on the day I left our country to go to the Holy Land, the land I possessed brought in less than one thousand livres in revenue, for my mother was still alive. And I went there with nine knights, and three of us carried banners. And I remind you of these facts because, if God, who has never failed me, had not helped me, I would have had trouble bearing the situation for as long as the period of six years that I stayed in the Holy Land.

As I was making my preparations for departure, Jean, the sire of Apremont and count of Sarrebrück on his wife's side, sent me a messenger and told me that he had made preparations to go across the sea with nine knights; and he told me that, if I wished, we could join together, he and I, to hire a ship; I gave my agreement; his men and mine hired a ship in Marseille. . . .

After these events [a trip to Paris], I returned to our country; and we made our preparations, the count of Sarrebrück and I, to send our equipment to Auxonne on carts, to embark it on the river Saône and to go as far as Arles, from the Saône to the Rhône. . . .

The abbot of Cheminon gave me my sash and my pilgrim's staff. And then I left Joinville, not reentering the castle until my return, on foot, without hose and my body covered in wool, and I thus went on pilgrimage to Blécourt and to Saint-Urbain and to the other bodies of saints that are there. And as I went to Blécourt and to Saint-Urbain, I never turned my eyes back toward Joinville, for fear that my heart would soften over the beautiful castle I was leaving and over my two children.

My companions and I ate at the Fontaine-l'Archevêque before Donjeux; and there, the abbot of Saint-Urbain (may God absolve him) gave to me and to the knights who were with me a great quantity of beautiful jewels. From there we went to Auxonne; and we went with all our equipment that we had had loaded on ships from Auxonne to Lyon, downstream on the Saône; and the large warhorses were led beside the ships.

At Lyon, we entered the Rhône to go to Arles-le-Blanc. . . .

In the month of August, we embarked on our ships at La Roche de Marseille.

For the Crusader, as for the pilgrim, it was wise to leave everything in order before undertaking a long journey, sometimes the last in this earthly existence. First on the spiritual level, debts were repaid, forgiveness was obtained from those one had offended. On the material level, in order to secure money, the poor relied on charity; others sold or mortgaged land, contracting loans. Achard, lord of the castle of Montmerle, in what is now the department of Ain, pledged property inherited from his father at the abbey of Cluny and received 2,000 sous, in Lyon currency, and four mules. He could theoretically recover his land if he reimbursed his creditor, but the continuation of the document indicates that he hardly believed that possible. In 1197, a Danish knight, Johan Sanuson, borrowed 200 silver marcs from the abbot of Sorö, for which he left in return a piece of land that would become property of the community if he died on the way, and that is what happened. Guibert de Nogent could write: "As everyone was eager to take the path of God, they hurried to convert into currency everything that might be useful for the journey." Great nobles needed large sums for, even when they went on pilgrimage, they were accompanied by an escort that sometimes contained several hundred people, which demonstrated their power and ensured their safety. Modest pilgrims, for that very reason, seldom traveled alone, sometimes grouping together along regional lines: sixty pilgrims from Vézelay embarked on a ship on the Loire in the late twelfth century to go to Saint-Martin de Tours. People from different places but going to the same sanctuary might also travel together. The Crusade was, by definition, a collective enterprise.

The journey exposed them to many dangers. Hence, the pilgrim benefited from a special legal status. His person was protected and whoever attacked him was harshly punished. He was exempt from customs duties and tolls. The relatives and possessions that he left behind benefited from the protection of the Church as well as that of customary law. As for the Crusader, a constitution of the Fourth Lateran Council in 1215 indicated that his vow was obligatory. Prelates would force those who hesitated to leave, if necessary by excommunication of their persons and an interdict on their lands. Spiritual and temporal privileges were now clearly defined.

> It is right that those who enter into the service of the King of Heaven enjoy special prerogatives, and the time before departure is scarcely more than a year; hence, the Crusaders will be exempt from tailles and other taxes. From the moment that they take up the cross, we take their persons and their possessions under the protection of Saint Peter and our own . . . so that their possessions may be totally and peacefully preserved until we are completely assured of their return or their demise. . . .
>
> If, among those who are leaving, some have sworn to pay interest, we also order their creditors to hold them harmless from their oath and to refrain from collecting interest. . . .
>
> We grant full forgiveness of their sins to all who will undertake this task in person and at their own expense, provided that, for those sins, they have had a true and heartfelt contrition and that they have confessed those sins, and we promise them the increase in eternal salvation promised as a reward to the just. To those who do not go in person, but send at their expense, according to their capacities and their rank, other fitting persons, and to those who, even though at the expense of others, go in person, we grant full forgiveness of their sins. We also wish to have participate in this remission, according to the quality of their assistance and the ardor of their devotion, those who contribute their wealth, in an appropriate manner, to the help sent to the Holy Land, or else who appropriately offer their counsel and their assistance.

The Crusade sometimes turned out to be particularly trying. The *Histoire anonyme de la première croisade* provides a realistic depiction of the agonies of the German and Lombard Crusaders besieged in Zerigordon in 1096. Before perishing under the arrows of the Turks, they suffered so much from thirst that they opened the veins of their horses and donkeys to drink the blood; some threw rags into the latrines to absorb a little liquid; others, after digging in the damp soil, lay down and spread the dirt over themselves.

It is easy to imagine that enthusiasm was not universal. Was this distant journey full of perils really necessary to gain eternal life? At the time of Saint Louis, the trouvère Rutebeuf tells of two knights, one of whom has taken up the cross, while the other refuses to do so. Each one sets out his arguments. The non-Crusader explains his attitude by saying that he has no intention of abandoning his possessions, of borrowing money from some usurer, and leaving his children without protection. It is up to the prelates to avenge God's shame since they are living off His revenues. As for him, he prefers to amuse himself with his neighbors. He causes no harm to anyone, and carries on friendly relations with those around him. Hence, he deems it preferable to remain at home.

Rutebeuf of course grants victory to the Crusader. Faith was still vigorous. It did not prevent a certain melancholy among those who had left their native land, such as the poet Tannhaüser, a Minnesänger born in southern Germany, who participated in Emperor Frederick II's crusade in 1228.

> I live in constant torment; I cannot stay in one place; I am here today and there tomorrow. If I have to go on leading this life, how many cares will I have, night and day, despite the joyous songs I sing! Where will this storm carry me? How can I save my life on water and on dry land? How can I prolong my life to the appointed hour? If people pity me in my miserable clothes, I still must bear all the anguish of the journey. There is one thing I should think about while I still have the strength: I cannot escape from my host, the world; in a single day I will have to return to him everything he has loaned me.

Joinville refused to join the Crusade in 1270 and criticized Saint Louis for leaving his kingdom. He answered the king of France and the king of Navarre who placed him under heavy pressure that their subordinates had impoverished his men. "And I told them that, if I wanted to work according to the will of God, I would stay here to help my people and defend them." And he went on: "I believed that everyone who advised this journey were committing mortal sin, because, as France now stood, the whole kingdom was at peace within and with all its neighbors; and, since he has left, the state of the kingdom has only gotten worse."

In any event, a great number of people, of all social conditions and all ages, set out on the roads. While Urban II, at the Council of Clermont in 1095, thought of a well-supplied army, the poor were the first to leave, because the nobles took time to equip themselves. And if for the nobles this was a military expedition, the humble intended to stay in the Holy Land. Guibert de Nogent depicts peasants having their horses shod and leading their families off in wagons. In 1212, young people left at their own initiative from various regions of northern France. They were joined by the poor, male and female servants, abandoning their tools and their herds when the young passed by. Their intention was to deliver the Holy Sepulcher, to succeed where the powerful had failed. The expedition obviously ended in failure. But the earthly journey of these unfortunates had led them to God. And was that not the most important thing?

## MEN OF THE CHURCH

In the Middle Ages, the temporal and the spiritual were closely intertwined. The pope, vicar of Christ, was also the ruler of the Papal States. In what follows, we will examine only travels that were primarily in response to moral and spiritual needs.

Councils were frequently held bringing together the principle dignitaries of an ecclesiastical province, of a country, or even of the entire universe, in the case of ecumenical councils. After the rebellion of the nuns of Sainte-Croix in Poitiers under the leadership of Princess Chrodielde, a synod took place in November 589. The princess defeated the bishops who had excommunicated her. "On learning of this," writes Gregory of Tours,

> King Childebert sent an embassy to King Gontran to arrange for a meeting of the bishops to repress the acts that were being committed by a canonical sanction. This is the reason for which King Childebert ordered our modest person, as well as Eberegisèle of Cologne and Bishop Marovée of Poitiers itself to go there; for his part, King Gontran summoned Godégisile of Bordeaux and the bishops of his province because he was the metropolitan of the city [of Poitiers].

A second council therefore met in Poitiers in the spring of 590.

Between 1120 and 1130, legates and metropolitans held twenty-three councils in France, in addition to four councils on the schism of Anaclet. This occasioned the travel of many bishops and abbots, obviously accompanied by clergy and servants.

Here are two examples. The Council of Clermont was held in 1095. Pope Urban wished to examine all outstanding questions during his journey to France at the time. In August, he was in Valence, and then traveled to Le Puy, where he met Bishop Adhémar of Monteil, who had gone to the Holy Land a few years earlier. It was probably as a result of their meeting that the plans for a council and a crusade took on concrete form. It was decided to confer the leadership on Count Raymond of Saint-Gilles, on whom Urban II paid a visit. Before the meeting of the council, scheduled for late November, he traveled to Cluny through the valleys of the Rhône and Saône and then to Autun, where he met Bishop Aganon, who had also made a pilgrimage to Jerusalem. Many prelates went to Clermont for a council that was neither general nor national, although most of them were French. A few Italians came with the pope. Also present were the bishops of Metz and Toul, the only representatives of the German episcopate, and a few Spanish bishops, including the primate of Toledo and the archbishop of Tarragona. In all, there were thirteen archbishops and 205 bishops, according to Bernold of Constance. Orderic Vital mentions thirteen archbishops and 235 bishops, in addition to abbots and members of the laity.

The Council of Constance was held almost three centuries later. The Church had become three-headed. It was important to put an end to the Great Schism. On October 30, 1413, Emperor Sigismond announced that a council would open in Constance one year later. Although the popes balked, and Venice indicated that it would decide depending on the circumstances, many states responded favorably, beginning with France and England. Assemblies of the clergy were held in Paris and London to secure the sums necessary to support the delegates. Members of the English embassy, designated by the king, numbering about twenty with three prelates and a retinue of eight hundred horses, did not arrive until the end of January. The French also took their time. Some managed to arrive before the end of 1414, Pierre d'Ailly in November and Mauroux in December. The latter was criticized for his lavish style of life. Cardinal d'Ailly's retinue contained only forty-four people. The ambassadors of the king of France reached Constance in March. Duke John the Fearless of Burgundy had named his own ambassadors. In February, the twenty-two first deputies of the University of Paris were still making preparations. Also arriving in January after the opening were the Danish and Polish delegates, the archbishop of Mainz with two hundred knights, German bishops, and representatives of the Greek Church. Of course, the city of Constance was overcrowded, resulting in a rise in prices. Courtesans flocked to the scene.

In the other direction, bishops went to see their flock on pastoral visits. Indeed, they were expected to visit the parishes and monasteries in their dioceses. For example, Simon de Beaulieu conducted his first inspection in 1283, two years after his elevation to the see of Bourges. His regular visits, usually annual, lasted between a month and a month and a half. He would go to one, two, three, perhaps five dioceses, never to all the dioceses in the province in a single year. Inspections normally took place in spring, between March and May, with secondary tours taking place in the fall.

Most of the time, Simon de Beaulieu arrived during the day and left on the following day. He stayed several days, for the most part, only in episcopal cities. Usually traveling on horseback (although sometimes he had to go by water), he covered daily between two and thirty-two kilometers. He was accompanied by a substantial escort the exact size of which is unknown. In 1284, in the diocese of Clermont, his retinue must have reached at least thirty, because the prior of Teilhède refused to receive more than thirty horses, but some of these were probably pack animals. In order to protect monasteries from excessive expenses, the Lateran and Saintes Councils, in 1179 and 1182, limited the escort to fifty knights. The itineraries followed covered both plains and mountains. Simon was generally well received. According to the scribe, there was even sometimes a holiday atmosphere. But thirteen establishments showed little zeal, refusing to receive the archbishop or to pay an indemnity, and sometimes both.

Monasteries were not controlled exclusively by bishops. Indeed, some of them came under the direct authority of the Holy See. The Cluniac order contained a principal monastery, the abbey of Cluny and twenty other abbeys, some depending directly on the abbot of Cluny, while the others enjoyed a certain autonomy. These monasteries themselves had a power of direction and control over their priories. At the annual general chapter, two visitors were elected for each province. They were charged with verifying the condition of the various monasteries. For example, in 1286, Guillaume de Sansmur and Brother Richard, designated for the province of Auvergne, inspected seventeen monasteries in the space of twelve days. On April 18, 1286, they were in Mozac, near Riom; on April 22 in Saint-Flour, 125 kilometers away; on April 23 in La Voulte, 38 kilometers further; and on April 25, another 56 kilometers on, in Sauxillanges. Inspections were thus carried out at a rather rapid pace.

Some figures seem to have been constantly traveling, not merely surveying, but reforming or even creating religious establishments. Abbot Hugh of Cluny, who came from one of the first families of Burgundy, a monk at fifteen and appointed chief prior at twenty, carried out many missions for the pope and the emperor. He was twice named apostolic legate, for Aquitaine by Nicholas II in 1059, and by Gregory VII in 1078. During his first term of office he held two councils, in Vienne and Toulouse. The second time, he co-chaired with Hugh of Die a council in Langres that was charged with judging two bishops. In the course of his diverse missions, he founded or restored many monasteries in France. He made many journeys during his term as abbot, which lasted no less than sixty years, from 1049 to 1109. He was present in Canossa in 1077 to serve as an intermediary between the pope and the emperor. He attempted another mediation in Rome in 1083, but without success. He attended the Council of Clermont in 1095. He was in contact with William the Conqueror and King Philip I of France, and established close ties with Alfonso VI of Castile.

When we examine the life of Saint Bernard of Clairvaux, we are struck by the dynamism he demonstrated throughout his existence. In spring 1112, a young nobleman, Bernard de Fontaines-lès-Dijon, escorted by thirty companions, arrived at the monastery of Cîteaux. After three years of monastic life, at the age of twenty-four, Bernard became the head of the establishment at Clairvaux. Ten years later, his sanctity having been recognized, the greatest figures of the age, clergy such as Peter the Venerable, Suger, and Norbert, and laymen such as the counts of Champagne and Poitou, King Louis VII, and the emperor sought him out for his advice. Following the schism created at the death of Honorius II in 1130 by the election of two popes, Innocent II and Anaclet II, the Council of Étampes placed Bernard at the head of the supporters of Innocent. For eight years, while continuing to work for his order, he traveled around Europe in the service of Innocent II. He traveled through parts of France and Germany to secure the support of King Louis VI of France and Henry I of England; he went to Italy three times, to Pisa and Genoa in 1133, to Milan in 1135, and to see Roger II of Sicily in 1137. Entrusted with preaching the Second Crusade by Pope Eugenius III, he stirred the crowd at Vézelay on March 31, 1146. And then to find recruits, he traveled through various French provinces. In 1146 and 1147, he preached in Flanders and then in Germany.

More characteristic was Étienne of Obazine, a reformer of lesser stature, who made many shorter journeys. According to his biographer, who knew him very well, Étienne was never still. He often went to the monastery of Dalon, almost nine miles distant, traveling at night according to the custom of the time. He frequently visited the monasteries in the area to draw examples from them. When he learned of the reputation of the Carthusian monks, he decided to visit them. On the way, he suffered a good deal from hunger and cold. "He made the journey on foot, sometimes barefoot, and carried no provisions." He traveled to the region of Cahors, which took three days of walking, several times to Limoges, nearly a hundred kilometers from Obazine, to Pleaux in the canton of Mauriac, "constrained by the necessities of the journey," and he participated in the chapter of Cîteaux. When he was about to leave this world, learning that an abbey was without a priest, he decided to fill the place according to the rules.

He traveled so frequently that his biographer devotes a chapter to his way of traveling. When he left, he would bless the monks and ask the sick to pray for him. He took some worthy people with him. In every monastic farm, he examined everything and circulated everywhere. Fatigue was no obstacle to his visiting those who were working far away or living in the pastures.

There were countless clerics on the roads. According to the Rule of Saint Benedict, monks who worked far from the monastery and could not return to the chapel at the appointed hour were supposed to celebrate the Work of God at the very spot where they were working. Those who were traveling had to do the same. Another chapter dealt with monks traveling on some business or other who were expected back the same day. Leaving aside wandering monks, who were obviously contravening the prescriptions of the Rule, let us consider a particular aspect of monastic travel. When someone for whom a "roll of the dead" was planned to be put into circulation died and was buried, the librarian would write a letter recounting his life and asking for prayers on his behalf; this letter was carried from monastery to monastery. A monk who had been given the list of monasteries to visit would present the letter to the librarian of the first, who would prepare a response on a strip of parchment sewn to the bottom of the letter. Each monastery would do the same. When the messenger returned, he sometimes had a very long roll. The first of these rolls date from the ninth century, and the custom persisted in France until the sixteenth century.

The roll of a dead person concerned an important figure who had died in a monastery linked by an association of prayers to other religious establishments, sometimes more than a hundred. This suggests the length of the journey the bearer might have to make, which could last several months. It was made all the more difficult by the fact that monasteries were often located in remote places.

Around 1050, Guifred de Cerdagne, who fourteen years earlier had retreated to Saint-Martin-du-Canigou near Ripoll, died. The monks of the abbey that he had established wished to secure many prayers for their benefactor. But the messenger did not leave until two and a half years after the death. Was this a problem of money? Benedictine hospitality made it possible to travel with little expense. Perhaps they spent a good deal of time composing the letter, unless private wars had made an immediate departure too dangerous. Guifred's roll contains 103 responses. Having crossed the Loire, the messenger traveled to Paris, Reims, and, after making the rounds of the religious establishments of Liège, he reached Aix-la-Chapelle. He then went through Metz and Toul, and turned toward Cluny, Sauxillanges, and Le Puy. On the last day of 1053, after nine months of walking, he returned to Saint-Marin-du-Canigou.

Mathilde, daughter of William the Conqueror and abbess of a convent founded by her parents, was given a roll containing 253 responses and measuring almost 21 meters in length. Aside from apparently inevitable places such as Paris, Reims, Soissons, and Angers, the possessions of the King of England made up an essential part of the roll. The territory covered by the messenger was immense: southern and central England (fifty-seven responses), Normandy, Brittany, Anjou, the Limousin, Beauce, the Sénonais, Champagne, and Burgundy as far as Vézelay, but not including Cluny although it was nearby.

Councils that issued regulations and settled disputed questions, pastoral visits, and inspections aimed at reforming abuses led bishops and abbots, accompanied by a more or less numerous retinue, to travel within Christendom. But Christ had asked that the good news be carried to the pagans. The Church could therefore not avoid its missionary duty. The length of journeys tended to grow as populations were converted.

*England*. Pope Gregory the Great, who undertook the evangelization of the country, sent a mission led by Augustine, prior of his own monastery of Saint-André, whom he also asked to bring along priests from neighboring countries. Augustine landed at the mouth of the Thames at Easter 597, and in June of the same year secured the conversion of King Ethelbert of Kent, chief of the Anglo-Saxon confederation. Augustine returned to Arles to be ordained as a bishop, which would allow him to lead the new Church of England. After the first successes, Gregory gave him instructions in a letter addressed to Abbott Mellitus whom he had sent in support. Evangelization later extended throughout the island, though its path was not always smooth.

*Bavaria*. The evangelist Saint Emmeram succeeded where Eustasius the disciple of Columbanus had failed. Learning that the people of Pannonia served idols, Bishop Emmeram of Poitiers decided to travel to the region. After installing a successor in the bishopric of his city,

> the intercessor and patron saint, together with an escort, crossed the Loire, on his way passed through various regions of Gaul distributing the seeds of faith, crossed the river Rhine, where Germany begins, and thus approached more remote regions. Once he had entered Germany, whose language he did not know, it was with the help of an interpreter, a monk named Vitalis, that he divinely planted the excellent words of the holy doctrine, while continuing on his way. . . . He left these provinces behind him and soon entered southern Germany, going as far as the river Danube, in the country of the Bavarians. Following the river, he reached Regensburg. . . .

At this time, a dispute broke out between the Huns and the Bavarians, so that at the approaches to the Enns, the towns seemed depopulated and the countryside almost deserted, and the savage beasts were so numerous that it was easy to understand that fragile humans hesitated to go in any direction. . . . It was then that the duke of the Bavarians, Theodo, proclaimed that he was at war with the Avars and for that reason [the saint] should not go into that region; he humbly begged such an eminent father rather to remain with him and his people.

Unable to obtain authorization to travel to the Avars in Pannonia, Emmeram remained in Bavaria.

From Lyon, where a council was in progress, Pope Innocent IV sent four ambassadors to meet the Tatars. The Franciscan Dominique of Aragon was to travel to the Armenians. The French Dominican André de Longjumeau was entrusted with letters to Muslim princes and the bishops of the Eastern Christian Churches. Another Dominican, Ascelino of Cremona, was sent to the Mongols, but got no further than the Baku region. A fourth, Giovanni da Pian del Carpini, was supposed to attempt to make an alliance with the Russians, but he was the one who traveled the farthest into mysterious Asia.

Carpini, a Franciscan, and provincial successively of Germany, Spain, and Saxony, countries located at the borders of Christendom, had traveled a good deal. On his journey to the Mongols, he was accompanied by two monks, Stephen of Bohemia and Benedict of Poland. Leaving Lyon in April 1245, he went to Prague to seek information, passed through Breslau in Silesia, and continued east with a group of merchants. His next stop was in the region of Warsaw. He met Vasilko of Russia and in his company reached Kiev in early February 1246. He stayed only a day or two in the city and rode hard to reach the Volga two months later. By late July 1246, he was in Karakorum.

We made the whole of this journey at great speed, for our Tartars had been ordered to take us quickly. . . . And so we started at dawn and journeyed until night without a meal, and many a time we arrived so late that we did not eat that night but were given in the morning the food we should have eaten the previous evening. We went as fast as the horses could trot, for the horses were in no way spared since we had fresh ones several times a day, and those which fell out returned . . . and so we rode swiftly without a break.[33]

Carpini learned a good deal from Russians and Hungarians who spoke Latin and French, from Russian priests and other foreigners living among the Tatars. Some had fought with them and shared their life for thirty years. Others had been living with them for ten or twenty years. All these informants told the Franciscan what he wanted to know.

Carpini learned that the Great Khan wished to send him a Mongol embassy, which he thought inopportune. He feared that the spectacle of dissension among Westerners would encourage the Tatars to attack them, that the Great Khan's envoys would turn out to be spies, and that they would be assassinated or captured by his compatriots. Finally, the embassy would have no purpose but to transmit letters entrusted to it. Carpini was back in the West early in 1247. He later continued his Eastern travels and died as bishop of Antovori in Dalmatia in 1252.

Another expedition was that made by William of Rubruck, which was decided by the pope, but inspired by Louis IX, then living in the Holy Land. Originally from Flanders, William was a monk in a monastery on Cyprus when the French Crusaders arrived in 1248, and was in Constantinople in April 1253. He left the city in early May, along with another Franciscan, a clerk belonging to the retinue of the king of France, a not very competent interpreter, and a slave. He sailed on the Black Sea to Crimea and then went through the territory of the Comans to the Volga. After crossing the plateaus of Turkestan, he arrived in Caracorum on April 5. He left the town on July 10. On the return trip he traveled further north. Through Georgia and Armenia, he reached Ayas in southern Asia Minor and then his monastery in Nicosia on the island of Cyprus. Because his superior forbade him to go to Paris, he reported by letter and did not go to France until much later.

Rubruck apparently considered settling among the Mongols to evangelize them. In the course of his journey, he took an

---

33. John of Plano Carpini, *History of the Mongols*, in *The Mongol Mission*, ed. Christopher Dawson (New York: Sheed and Ward, 1955), 60–61.

interest in the fate of Westerners who had been deported to the empire. He met "a great crowd of Christians . . . Hungarians, Alans, Russians, Georgians and Armenians,"[34] deprived of the sacrament since their capture and for whom he celebrated mass on Maundy Thursday and Easter Day. He baptized on several occasions and gave the last rites to a Parisian goldsmith. He taught the Mongols about Christian faith, participating in a discussion in which he had to prove the existence of God to Buddhists.

> Then they [the priests of the Iugurs] asked me somewhat mockingly: "Where is God?"
> To which I replied, "Where is your soul?"
> "In our bodies," they said.
> "Is it not everywhere in your body," I asked, "and in complete control of it, and yet is not to be seen? In this way God is everywhere and governs all things, while being invisible, because He is wisdom and understanding." But at this point, when I wanted to argue further with them, my interpreter, who was tired and incapable of finding the right words, made me stop talking.[35]

He discussed religion with the Khan and initiated negotiations with the Nestorian prelates of the court. He was especially concerned with the Chaldeans of central Asia.

While members of the Cistercians and the Premonstratensians had introduced Christ to the Baltic and Slavic peoples, in the twelfth and early thirteenth centuries Dominicans and Franciscans seemed to exercise a monopoly in the missionary realm. In 1336, Pope Benedict XII addressed a bull to the Franciscans that emphasized the training of missionaries whose faith and knowledge were to be verified before being sent out. In addition, knowledge of Eastern languages was necessary. The problem could be resolved by bringing to the West young men from the countries to be evangelized to study theology. Scholarships were even created for them in the University of Paris. But more fre-

---

34. William of Rubruck, *The Mission of Friar William of Rubruck*, tr. Peter Jackson (London: The Hakluyt Society, 1990), 213.
35. *The Travels of Marco Polo*, tr. Ronald Latham, 155–56.

quently missionaries learned the language after reaching the country to be evangelized. For example, Pascal de Vittoria, a young Spanish Franciscan, member of a mission sent to Tartary, declared in a letter written in 1338:

> I was rather eager to go with him [my companion], but after getting some advice on the subject, I decided first to learn the language of the country. And with the help of God, I learned the language of the Comans and Iugur writing; this language and writing are commonly used through all the kingdoms and empires of the Tatars, Persians, Chaldeans, Medes, and of Cathay. . . . This is why, my fathers, once I had acquired mastery of the language, thanks be to God, I have often preached without an interpreter both to Saracens and to schismatic and heretical Christians.

From his accession in 1260, Kubilai Khan made Beijing, then called Khan-balik, his capital. And missionaries went to China.

As Jean Richard has shown, the papacy's policy became more active in the fourteenth century. A Franciscan from the province of Salerno, Giovanni de Montecorvino, was sent to Kubilai Khan, who had several times expressed the wish to meet Western religious men. He left Rieti in July 1289, bearing letters from the pope which called on Mongol princes to convert and on Christian monarchs, such as the king of Armenia, to join in church union. With a companion who died on the way, he reached Tabriz. Because of the war ravaging the country, he took the route of the Persian Gulf with a Dominican and a merchant. He became archbishop of Beijing in 1307.

In the early fifteenth century, Archbishop John of Sultanieh composed a work that provides a general picture of the Latin missions. He mentions the successes achieved in Tartary and points to the many Catholics living in Cathay despite the probable lack of priests. In Georgia, the mendicants have achieved many conversions, but the invasion of Tamerlane has dealt a harsh blow to the Catholic religion. The mission to Ziquia has produced excellent results. There are Catholics in Baghdad and Kurdistan. Ethiopia maintains diplomatic relations with the Holy See. Reports of pilgrims testify to the expansion of Christianity. In 1404, Catholic Christians from India who had visited Jerusalem landed in Sicily on their way to Rome and Compostela.

The regions under the rule of the sultan of Cairo, deserted by missionaries since the fall of Acre, were recovering some religious activity. Many Western captives lived in Egypt. Under Boniface VIII, five Franciscans went there to bring spiritual comfort to these unfortunates. But monks going to Egypt most often could merely minister to merchants, because of their precarious position. In Syria, by contrast, where pilgrims, who were a source of revenue, needed priests to celebrate services, the context appears to have been better.

In his autobiography composed early in the twelfth century, Guibert de Nogent, after noting the damage caused by a lightning strike to a wall of the cathedral of Laon, writes: "There then began, following a custom which is worth what it is worth, the circulation of reliquaries and relics of saints, in order to collect money. . . . A magnificent reliquary was carried on these travels along with another that was rather mediocre." On a second tour, the cortege, on its way to Touraine, passed through the town of Buzançais. A deaf-mute boy of twenty began to hear and speak. In Angers, a woman who could not remove a wedding ring that she had put on when very young was able to remove it. In the same diocese, the priests brought the relics to a lady who had urgently requested them, and she was cured of a serious illness. A third journey took place during which a stop was made at the castle of Nesle. Then the troop decided to go abroad. To cross the English Channel, it embarked on a ship with some rich merchants. The relics allowed them to escape from pirates. In England, they were welcomed in Winchester and Exeter.

Traveling collections that might involve the display of relics began shortly after the middle of the eleventh century. These practices took place principally in the region between the Schelde and the Loire; they were used only by cathedrals and monastic communities.

At the beginning, the spiritual aspect was incontestably foremost. *Miracles de saint Marcoul* relates how the monks of the priory of Corbeny-en-Laonnais attempted to find the sums needed for the restoration of their establishment in 1102. Under the leadership of the provost, several of them gathered around the reliquary containing the remains of their patron saint. They traveled first to Reims, where they were received by the canons of the cathedral; the relics were placed in the basilica of the consecration. All night long, the faithful venerated them. The next morning, the monks of Saint-Remi placed the reliquary in their own church. Then the cortege moved on, stopping in Châlons, Épernay, Soissons, Noyon, and finally Péronne. The reliquary was installed in the collegiate church of Saint-Fursy.

When the monks wished to leave the next day, the crowd asked them to stay for a while. The precious reliquary was displayed in the parish church of Saint-Jean Baptiste. The ill and infirm were miraculously cured. The canons of Saint-Quentin, who were carrying the relics of their patron saint, then passed through the town and installed them next to those of Saint-Marcoul. After a transfer at Saint-Fursy, the monks returned to their priory.

In a study of the travels of relics in the eleventh and twelfth centuries, Pierre André Sigal mentions journeys of between 200 and 2,000 kilometers. The reasons for travel obviously had an influence on the distances covered. When it was a matter of affirming a challenged property right, it was enough to transport the reliquaries to the property in dispute or to the seat of the authority that would decide the question. According to *Translation de saint Vivian,* relics were brought to a peace council in Auvergne to reinforce the decisions of the bishops. Divine authority added to or even replaced human authority. When offerings were to be collected, there was greater freedom. Of course, the region near the monastery that knew the saint was likely to be more generous, but other considerations entered into play. Hermann de Laon notes that in 1113 the relics of Notre-Dame de Laon were sent to England because of the prosperity of the country. In addition, there were good relations between the clergy of the Laon cathedral and the English bishops. As for the duration of the journeys studied by Sigal, they lasted from 15 to 162 days. The distance covered daily ranged from nine to fourteen kilometers; this was, of course, an average. Sometimes stops lasted for several days: the canons of Laon had to wait two weeks for favorable winds, and spent a week in Winchester and ten days in Exeter. On the other hand, some days relics could travel over thirty kilometers. Stops took place for various reasons: an impossibility to go from one town to another in a single day and hence the need to stop in a village in between; the wish of residents in one place to keep the relics longer than had been planned; personal relations, such as the presence of former students of Laon in some English towns. In short, there were four

kinds of stops: towns, villages, lands dependent on the origi-
nating church, and monasteries.

More and more, however, the material prevailed over the
spiritual. In the beginning, the members of the community
themselves solicited the generosity of the faithful, and the custom lasted until the middle of the fifteenth century. But outside
priests were soon recruited. As early as 1094, the collection for
Saint-Faron of Meaux was farmed out to a priest who, in return
for 120 livres a year, agreed to display the relics of Saint Faron
in the province of Reims for nine years; the alms collected would
be turned over to the community. A contract was drawn up in
which the priest pledged his own possessions. Traveling collections disappeared shortly after 1550.

Pilgrims and Crusaders were moved principally by religious
concerns. But, in going to Jerusalem, they went through foreign
countries that they could contemplate and admire, although
this was not their principal purpose. Some travelers, on the
other hand, were driven principally by the desire to see new
countries.

# EIGHT

# Öiscovering the wide world

## TOURISTS

Lorenzo the Magnificent tasted fully of the joys of traveling with friends in the Florentine countryside. Politian recounts one of his rides to San Miniato in April 1476: "Leaving Florence last night, we sang all along the way. . . . When we reached San Miniato in the evening, we started to read Saint Augustine, but we soon gave that up to make music." The happy group traveled around the country. In winter, Lorenzo frequently stayed in Pisa, or in his rural estates near the sea and in the heart of a region full of game. He often left Florence to go to the nearby villa of Careggi. In spring, he traveled to his lands in Mugello. In 1477, he bought what would become his preferred residence, a villa belonging to the father-in-law of his sister Nannina, in Poggio a Cajano.

The men of the Middle Ages had travel accounts, guide-books which, even though not designed for that purpose, allowed them to look at and appreciate the beauties of nature and especially the works of man. We have had occasion to allude to some of these guidebooks, one by Aimeri Picaud intended for pilgrims to Santiago de Compostela, and one by Stefan Planck describing the wonders of Rome. To be sure, they were intended for a religious use, but their interest for tourists was obvious. Let us consider just two examples, Arles and the cathedral of Compostela.

> There is a suburb near Arles, between two arms of the Rhône, called Trinquetaille, where there is a very tall magnificent marble column set on the land behind the saint's church. . . . From there you should go to visit the cemetery near Arles, in a place that is called Aliscamps . . . which is a mile wide and a mile long. In no other cemetery anywhere can be found so many marble tombs, nor such large ones, aligned on the earth. They are of varied workmanship, have ancient inscriptions carved in Latin letters, but in an unintelligible language. The more one looks in the distance, the more one sees the line of sarcophagi stretching out. In this cemetery, there are seven churches. . . .

The writer then advises a visit to the tomb of Saint Gilles. Behind its altar is a great golden reliquary that is described in great detail.

As for the cathedral of Compostela, the goal of the pilgrims' journey, its description would not be out of place in one of today's *Guides bleus*.

> The basilica of Santiago measures in length 53 times the height of a man, from the western door to the altar of the Holy Savior; in width 40 times less one, from the door of France to the southern door; as for the internal height, it is as high as 14 men; but no one can measure the length and height of the building on the outside. . . .
>
> The church includes nine naves in its lower part and six in the upper part and a head [chapel] larger than the others where the altar of the Holy Savior is located, a crown [ambulatory around the choir], a body [nave] and two members [arms of the transept] and eight other small heads [chapels]; in each of them is an altar. . . .
>
> The western portal, with its two entries, surpasses in beauty, grandeur, and the workmanship of its decoration the other portals. It is larger and more beautiful than the others and has even more admirable workmanship; it is reached from outside by many steps; it is flanked by columns of

various kinds of marble and decorated with varied figures and ornaments: men, women, animals, birds, saints, angels, flowers, and ornaments of all kinds. Its decoration is so rich that it cannot be described in detail. We should, however, point out high up the Transfiguration of Our Lord, as it occurred on Mount Tabor, which is carved with magnificent artistry. Our Lord is there in a glowing cloud, His face as radiant as the sun, His clothing as white as snow and the Father above speaking to Him; and you can see Moses and Elijah who appeared at the same time speaking of the fate that was to befall Him in Jerusalem. There too is Saint James, with Saint Peter and Saint John, to whom, before all others, Our Lord manifested His Transfiguration. . . .

Enthusiastic descriptions of religious monuments were also provided by Arab travelers, notably Ibn Jubayr, who was very interested in the mosques of the towns he visited, for example, the mosque of Harran.

The venerated mosque is adjacent to these markets; it is old, has been restored, and is very beautiful. It has a large courtyard in which three raised pavilions are set on marble pillars, each one over a well of fresh water. Also in the courtyard can be seen a fourth enormous pavilion set on ten marble pillars of nine empans [an empan is the distance from the thumb to the little finger] in circumference enclosing in the center a large marble pillar 15 empans around. This pavilion is of Byzantine construction. The upper part is hollow, resembling a solid tower. . . . This venerable mosque has a ceiling made of arcades and transversal beams that are enormous and have the length of the nave, that is, fifteen feet; it has five naves. We have never seen a mosque with such wide bays. The wall adjacent to the courtyard where the entry is located is cut with nineteen doors, nine to the right, nine to the left, and the nineteenth is a large door in the center of the other eighteen, with an arcade that curves from the top to the bottom of the wall. Its appearance is so marvelous and it is so perfectly constructed that it might be mistaken for the gate of a great city. All these doors have wooden panels superbly detailed and carved, and they are as closely fitted as the doors of a reception room in a palace.

We were able to admire the splendor of the architecture of this mosque and the arrangement of the adjoining markets, a marvelous spectacle.

Let us consider two German travelers in Provence and in Dauphiné in the late fifteenth century. In examining what drew their attention or distracted them from the straight road, we may learn about the centers of interest for Westerners of the Middle Ages. Hans van Waltheym was a patrician from the Saxon city of Halle. Born in 1422, he was relatively old when he undertook a journey to Provence in 1474–75. He remained away from February 17, 1474 until March 19, 1475. He was both a pilgrim and a traveler taking advantage of his trip for a little tourism.

Born around 1437 in the Vorarlberg, Hieronymus Münzer, after completing his studies, practiced medicine in Nuremberg, except during times of plague, when he was on the road. For example, in 1484, he fled the epidemic and traveled to Italy. He visited Rome and went as far as Naples. When the plague once again threatened in 1494, he left his city with several companions, who kept him from solitude and served as interpreters. On August 2, he set out for Switzerland. From Geneva, he went to Lyon and then down the Rhône as far as Avignon. His devotion to Saint Mary Magdalene drew him to Provence. After crossing the Pyrenees, he spent nearly five months in the Iberian peninsula. Through Toulouse, Tours (which he greatly appreciated), Bruges (that dazzled him with the beauty of its monuments), Ghent (where he was enthusiastic over the retable of the Mystic Lamb), and Cologne, he returned to Nuremberg. Münzer was above all a traveler, we might say a tourist.

Hans van Waltheym admired beautiful gardens, the royal gardens in Aix, but also the bourgeois gardens of Basel and Constance. Guided by a procurator, he visited the palace of the king of Sicily.

It [the dining room] is very large and very pleasant. It has two large fireplaces, and he led us into a closed room where the king dispenses justice. He also led us into a pleasant room in which the king is accustomed to hold council. The rooms and halls were covered in a beautiful green tapestry. Then, he led us over the ditch into the king's garden, which is very large and very beautiful.

The garden is laid out as follows. When you enter, there are two walls about 240 meters long separated by a path of 18 meters.

> The two walls are filled with earth for their entire height. On both sides are planted vines guided over arches so that as they grow they come together above and are rounded as a vault, and they have grown together so densely that you can walk beneath and no ray of sun can reach you, and in the earth between the walls, at the foot of the vines, there are all sorts of aromatic herbs and many fragrant flowers as varied as the world can offer and of such strange shapes that they cannot all be described or even named. . . . [T]hrough the garden flows a cool stream that makes the mill turn and beside the water King René of Sicily had built pleasant palaces and summer houses. . . .

In front of these palaces, the king has built a garden 20 meters high covered by wire. "Inside, there are low trees and in this aviary the king has all kinds of varied and foreign birds, whatever he has been able to get from various places."

Hans van Waltheym paid attention to the solidity of urban walls; he pointed out castles remarkable for their location in town or their size, such as Burhausen in Bavaria. The Palace of the Popes in Avignon, with three great towers, is very large. "It also has great solid and thick walls, large refectories and rooms, and many large vaults that I crossed through and saw with my own eyes."

Waltheym and Münzer both visited Arles. Münzer in particular was interested in ancient monuments, in arenas made "of large, square, and very hard stones," and inhabited by poor people who "have little houses inside the vaults and arcades." Both travelers saw the Aliscamps. Münzer speaks of "countless sepulchers," "square urns, carved in very hard stone, such that each one could contain ten or fourteen bodies, and closed by stone doors."

Waltheym was concerned with economic life. He seems to have seen the glassmaker's workshop located in the village where he stopped between Aix and Saint-Maximin. He describes the production of salt near Marseille and in the Camargue. In Marseille, he writes, the sun transforms sea water into salt four months in the year.

And the manufacture of salt takes place in this way: near the city, they have made compartments with planks each of which is ten or twelve ells long and the same width. Then there is a plank in the sea: they raise it and let the sea enter the compartments so that it covers several acres. There are about one hundred to one hundred and fifty compartments and when they are full to the depth of one hand, they let the plank drop and thus the sun draws the salt from the sea water. And when it has then become salt, they cart it away in barrows and make great piles of it as we make piles of hay. And when the salt has been collected, they let the sea enter the compartments again. Thereafter, the salt is carried off on large ships.

He traveled to an enterprise in Thuringia where copper was separated from silver. In the Baden region, he visited a tapestry workshop and admired the tapestries decorating the owner's bedroom.

Travelers' interests as tourists seem to have been aroused especially by cities. This was true of Paris, famously praised by Guy de Bazoches in 1175:

Two suburbs are spread out to the right and left, the least of which excites the envy of other cities. Each suburb projects two stone bridges toward the island. . . . The bridge known as *Grand*, which is broad, rich, and commercial, bubbles, breathes, abounds in ships, wealth, countless goods. . . . In the middle of the island arises the dominating height of the royal palace.

Jean de Jandun admired the same palace in the fourteenth century: "Its impregnable walls enclose a space so wide and long that it can contain countless people."

On his journey to the Holy Land, Adorno devoted a large part of his account to the cities he went through.

Genoa is situated on the shores of the Mediterranean and is much longer than it is wide. It is decorated and beautified by many very tall marble houses with gates of iron; it is full of basilicas of admirable beauty. . . . The city is surrounded by two walls, old and new. Water from a spring that has been artificially channeled flows like a stream on the top of the walls throughout the city. Each square and each street has a structure in the shape of a fountain which receives this water and distributes it through pipes. . . . The port of the city, astonishingly large and deep, harbors great quantities of the largest ships in the world up to the very edges of its moles. . . . There is nothing in this city that does not help to beautify it, except perhaps for the narrowness of its streets, which does not contribute to its beauty but is useful for its defense. No city in Italy is as strong. This is why the Italians call it Genoa the superb, the magnanimous, and the strong, just as they speak of Milan the populous and great, Venice the rich and admirable, Naples the elegant and noble, and Ravenna the ancient. The squares are of small size, but they are very clean. Indeed, throughout the year, even in winter, there is no trace of [mud].

Pierre Barbatre provided a similarly detailed description of Venice when he sailed from there.

Tunis provides another example. Following his custom, Jean Adorno first considers the external appearance of the city and the strength of its fortifications, then treats places of worship, secular aspects (castles, squares, streets), and the inhabitants. The passage on Sicily is principally devoted to cities. Similarly, on the voyage from Rhodes to Brindisi, the principal attractions of the islands seem to have been castles and cities.

When speaking of nature, travelers note especially its useful or surprising aspects. Around 1430, the poet Michault Taillevent, a servant of Duke Philip the Good of Burgundy, was sent by the duke on a mission that brought him to the Jura. The first impression of this man of the plains was surprise at the height of the mountains stretching beyond the horizon, the gigantic mass of enormous blocks. The ascent was harsh and dangerous because of the precipices.

In a work entitled *La Salade,* Antoine de La Sale relates the climb he made in the Apennines on May 18, 1420. First he remarks on the beauty of the vegetation and the colors of the flowers. But he seems not to have been a very good mountaineer, because he emphasizes the difficulties, the frightening chasm, and stones falling with a terrifying noise.

While giving a privileged place to cities, the Arab Ibn Jubayr nevertheless expresses his admiration for some landscapes.

Noting in Ra's al-'Ayn, a city on the Khabur, a tributary of the Euphrates, the presence of a madrasa (a school providing instruction in theology and law), he writes:

> Nowhere in the world have I seen a site more beautiful than that of this madrasa; indeed, it is located in an island of greenery enclosed by the river on three sides, with a single means of access; it is surrounded by orchards in front and behind and looks out on a noria that pours water into the gardens set higher than the level of the river. This spot is marvelous.

The island of Hispaniola seemed so beautiful to Columbus that he could not bring himself "to leave so many beautiful things, nor the songs of birds both small and large." And he went on: "I am never weary of admiring this beautiful vegetation that is so different from ours." Felix Faber seemed even more sensitive to the beauty of the desert, a region in which most travelers principally described difficulties.

> Among other things, what makes walking in the desert tolerable is, in the first place, that every day and even almost every hour, you come into new regions that differ in climate and soil—and new mountains that differ in shape and color—from everything that man has been able to admire before and from everything he might wish to see thereafter. There is always something new to fill you with admiration: the appearance of the mountains, the color of the earth and the variety of rocks and pebbles, the very excess of the landscape, its sterility and size, all things appealing to the curious. I must myself confess that I have experienced more delights in the immensity and sterility of the desert and the frightful spectacle it presents to view than I ever did in the midst of the fertility of Egypt, its wealth, and its captivating beauty.

It seems that tourism in the modern sense of the word did not exist in the Middle Ages. People traveled for religious or economic reasons and not for pleasure. But, in the course of their travels, they could not prevent themselves from being attracted by monuments or even sites. They would momentarily turn away from the original goal and satisfy their curiosity. There was tourism then as part of a journey that had other aims. We might even wonder, when a pilgrim is advised to visit one church or another, whether he followed the advice out of piety or curiosity. The author of the guide for the pilgrims to Santiago de Compostela writes:

> On this road, you should also visit, on the banks of the Loire, the venerable body of Saint Martin, bishop and confessor. . . . The reliquary in which his precious remains repose, near the city of Tours, glitters with a profusion of gold, silver, and precious stones, and it is renowned for frequent miracles.

A little further on, he declares: "In the city of Poitiers, what must be visited is the very holy body of the blessed Hilary, bishop and confessor. . . . The tomb in which his venerable and very holy bones lie is decorated with a profusion of gold, silver, and precious stones." Thus the guide emphasizes not only the relics of saints but the splendor of their tombs.

Is it possible to speak of tourism when people revisit places linked to their childhood or adolescence? Froissart landed in England in July 1395. For what reasons? The first "was that in my youth I had been nurtured in the court and the home of the noble Edward, of blessed memory, and of the noble Queen Philippa his wife, among their children and the barons of England, who lived there at the time. For I had found in them all honor, generosity, and courtesy." And the chronicler adds a little further on: "And it seemed to me in my imagination that if I saw it [the country], I would live longer because of it. For, for twenty-seven full years, I had held myself back from going there and if I did not find the nobles I had seen and left there on my departure, I would see their heirs, and that would do me great good."

An anecdote told by Raoul Glaber is worth dwelling on. "A little fellow, a citizen of Marseille, one of those people who travels through countries never tiring of learning or of seeing new places, came to pass through there," that is, "the remote regions of Africa" (for Glaber the sense of the term is quite vague), where there lived a hermit. The traveler ended up finding the anchorite. When the hermit asked him whether he had seen the monastery of Cluny, he answered that he knew it very well.

To what extent are we dealing with a tourist, a traveler going throughout the world to see as many places as possible, a pilgrim principally concerned with visiting religious establishments and meeting holy persons, or an explorer, for "he confronted that desert region that was consumed by the heat of the sun, and he long insisted on making the attempt to discover it"?

## EXPLORERS[36]

### Marco Polo's Asia

Central Asia had been opened to Europeans by missionaries. With the Mongol expansion, the Far East in turn became available. Now, to deal with the Great Khan, it was no longer enough to go to Mongolia, it was necessary to go to China, and that was what Marco Polo did.

As we have seen, after a first journey, Niccolò and Maffeo Polo set out again with their son and nephew Marco, whose book *Divisament dou Monde*, is far from an exact description of the expeditions. Marco Polo does not provide a description of his itineraries. He gives information about the countries he has traveled through and those more or less nearby that he has heard about. It seems that on the journey out (the text of the *Divisament* is not clear) the travelers followed the usual road going from Ayas to Erzerum and Tabriz, and then went south of the Caspian.

The route across central Asia seems easier to grasp. Beginning southeast of the Caspian Sea, it took the travelers to Shibarghan, then, after crossing a desert, to the salt mines of Talikhan south of the Amu Darya. After crossing the plateaus of the Pamirs, Marco and his companions reached Lop, where they rested for a time before crossing the Gobi desert. "This desert is reported to be so long that it would take a year to go from end to end; and at the narrowest point it takes a month to cross it. It consists entirely of mountains and sand and valleys. There is

---

36. See Jean-Paul Roux, *Les Explorateurs au Moyen Age*, Paris, 1985. Michel Mollat, *Les Explorateurs du XIIIe au XVIe siècles. Premiers regards sur des mondes nouveaux*, Paris, 1984.

nothing at all to eat."[37] It is not wise to cross the desert with a group larger than fifty. There are twenty-eight watering-places with good water for drinking, though not very plentiful, and three or four with bitter and brackish water. Beyond the desert to the south lies the province of Tangut. From Etzina, in an oasis in the Gobi on the border of Mongolia, a road goes north toward Karakorum, the first capital of the Mongols. "In this city [Etzina] the traveler must take in a forty days' stock of provisions; for . . . he has forty days' journey ahead of him across a desert without house or inn, where nobody lives except among the valleys and mountains in summer."[38] Then crossing Kansu province, after five days the traveler arrives at Erguiul (present-day Liangchau) which is also part of the province of Tangut and lies at the foot of the Great Wall. The traveler journeys eight days to the east to reach Kalachan. Finally, the road crosses a loop in the Yellow River and leads to Khan-balik, that is, Beijing.

The route taken by Marco Polo does not match that of the missionaries, later used by merchants, that went to the north of the Caspian. Did the Polos wish to explore unknown routes? Perhaps, as Jacques Heers has suggested, Marco, in order to more fully captivate his readers, chose to describe not the real road taken but an imaginary one.

Marco Polo, who was to stay in China for sixteen years, speaks little of himself, except as an observer; it is thus difficult to get a sense of his life at the time. After an apprenticeship in the Mongol language and the customs of the court, he traveled to Yunnan in southwestern China, probably in 1277–78.

> It came about that Marco, the son of Messer Niccolò, acquired a remarkable knowledge of the customs of the Tartars and of their languages and letters. . . . Observing his wisdom, the Khan sent him as his emissary to a country named Kara-jang, which it took him a good six months to reach. The lad fulfilled his mission well and wisely. . . . When Marco went on his mission . . . he paid close attention to all the novelties and curiosities that came his way, so that he might retail them to the Great Khan.[39]

---

37. *The Travels of Marco Polo*, tr. Ronald Latham, 84.
38. Ibid., 92.
39. Ibid., 40–41.

Marco Polo was probably in Beijing during the events following the assassination of Kubilai Khan's finance minister in 1282. For three years, he occupied a position that might have been connected to the salt tax, in the city of Yang-chau. Finally, he was sent on a mission to Ceylon, perhaps in 1284, and to the kingdom of Chamba in Vietnam, in 1288 or later.

But the years were passing. Despite the desire of the Polos to return home, they could not secure authorization to leave. The opportunity finally offered itself in 1291. Arghun, the Mongol lord of the Levant, wished to find a successor for his dead wife from the same lineage, and sent an embassy to the Great Khan. The young woman was selected, but carrying her to her future husband posed difficult problems. Indeed, the descendants of Genghis Khan who dominated central Asia were in revolt against their sedentary cousins who ruled over Persia and China. Marco Polo proposed a solution to the benefit of all. Because his missions had made him acquainted with the southern oceans, he could serve as guide for a sea voyage. The Khan accepted. The return voyage would last from 1291 to 1295. The Great Khan gave the Polos safe-conducts and entrusted them with messages for the pope and the various kings of Christendom. Fourteen four-masted ships were fitted out. The travelers, supplied with provisions and money for two years, left China, reached Java three months later, and then sailed over the Indian Ocean for eighteen months. Marco Polo provides the detail that they were six hundred when they embarked, not counting the seamen. Almost all died on the voyage.

The very brief prologue does not provide a clear idea of the return route, so we must look at the *Divisament* itself. It is generally agreed that the ships sailed from Zaiton, around 200 kilometers north of Hong Kong. Each ship, very precisely described, had a bridge generally containing sixty small rooms. It had a rudder, four masts, and four sails. Often, two masts were added, raised and lowered with their sails according to the weather. The itineraries of Marco Polo show that he was above all an explorer, joining with merchants only for sea voyages. His travels were generally made in the style of a functionary of the Khan provided with relay horses and escorts.

After the port of Chamba, 1,500 miles from the point of departure, and the islands of Condur, Sondur, Borneo, and Java, the ships arrived in Sumatra, where Marco Polo made a long stay. "In this kingdom I myself Marco Polo spent five months [probably from May to October, during the monsoon], waiting for weather that would permit us to continue our voyage."[40] The ships sailed on and came to the city of Kayal at the southern tip of India, "the port of call for all ships trading with the west . . . for horses and other goods."[41] In India, the travelers passed through Quilon in Kerala, at the southern end of the western coast. From there, they sailed up the Malabar coast as far as Gujarat, in which Marco names only a few ports. Pirates were a danger in this region.

> [M]ore than 100 ships cruise out every year as corsairs, seizing other ships and robbing the merchants. For they are pirates on a big scale. I assure you that they bring their wives and little children with them. They spend the whole summer on a cruise and work havoc among the merchants.[42]

After making port at Kech-Makran, Marco Polo reached Hormuz. There he learned of the death of King Arghun who was to have married the young woman he was escorting. The son of the dead king married her. Through Trebizond and Constantinople, Marco Polo returned to Venice in 1295.

Because events lived through are seldom mentioned, there is some uncertainty about the regions he actually visited. Marco Polo's work is indeed a *divisament*, a book of wonders, much more than a precise travel account. Nevertheless, the explorer could assert with some justification that "there has been no man, Christian or Pagan, Tartar or Indian, or of any race whatsoever, who has known or explored so many of the various parts of the world and of its great wonders as this same Messer Marco Polo."[43]

But the road to the east was soon closed off. The Great Khan was dethroned by the Ming in 1368. The immense Mongol Empire no longer existed. The Ming were probably less hostile to foreigners than has been said, but Europeans no longer had a

---

40. *The Travels of Marco Polo,* tr. Ronald Latham, 254.
41. Ibid., 285.
42. Ibid., 290.
43. Ibid., 33.

base for traveling east. Saint-Jean d'Acre had fallen in 1291 and the Holy Land had been lost. Hostile Mamelukes occupied Egypt and Syria, although pilgrimages returned to life in the late Middle Ages. In the north, the Golden Horde had converted to Islam. Between the two, the emirates had taken the place of the Seljuk Empire. The empire of the Ottomans, masters of the Balkans through the victory of Kossovo in 1389, confined the Byzantine Empire to Constantinople. A wall had risen, and only a few adventurers managed to cross it.

Ibn Battuta's Africa

Contrasted to Asia, which received missionaries, merchants, and explorers, was an Africa that was unknown, at least as far as the interior of the continent was concerned. At most, we know the points of departure and arrival of the largest caravans: in the east, Ghadamas, on the border of Tunisia; in the west, Tlemcen, the terminus of Sudanese commercial routes. The trails leaving from Tlemcen ended in the south in Iwalatan in southeastern Mauritania, where Saharan caravans gave way to those of the blacks. The traffic was entirely in the hands of Muslims.

After 1250, indirect relations through pilgrims and Crusaders going to the Holy Land gave way to direct encounters with Ethiopia by Franciscan and Dominican missionaries. Raymond Lully, born in Palma de Mallorca in 1232, eager to convert the infidels, a great traveler who went on several occasions to Tunis where he was stoned in 1315, mentions caravans of camels loaded with salt traveling toward the region of the sources of the Nile and beyond Ghana where the men are black and worship idols. Indeed, both eastern and western parts of the continent gradually became known to Europeans. Expeditions organized in Mallorca set out for the Isles of the Blest.

During this period, a great traveler, perhaps the greatest of the Middle Ages, explored not only Asia, like Marco Polo, but also Africa. He was Ibn Battuta, born in Tangiers in 1304 in a large middle-ranking family. He left for Arabia in 1325 in order to carry out the ritual pilgrimage to Mecca, but, driven by an insatiable curiosity, he was never to stop wandering throughout the wide world. He returned to Fez in 1349, but soon was back on the road. He traveled to Grenada and then returned to settle permanently in Tangiers, or so he thought. His travels lasted twenty-four years, one year fewer than those of Marco Polo, but because of detours, he had covered many more kilometers, perhaps as many as 120,000.

Soon, his ruler sent him to the center of the African continent. This journey took only twenty-two months, but it has provided us with the first serious document on black Africa; it was written not by Ibn Battuta himself, but under his dictation by a man of letters, Ibn Djuzayy.

Leaving Fez, the indefatigable traveler reached the country of the blacks. At Sijilmasa, he bought camels and had them fattened for four months. Then, on February 18, 1352, he set out with some merchants. After a journey of twenty-five days, the caravan reached the village of Taghaza, where there was nothing but sand and salt, used by the blacks as currency. The stay turned out to be very unpleasant because of the brackish water and the many flies. This was where water was taken on before crossing the desert, a journey of ten days.

At the beginning, Ibn Battuta and his companions went ahead of the caravan in order to be the first to find a suitable spot to graze their animals, and they did this until a man got lost in the desert. "After that, I did not go ahead or fall behind the caravan."[44] The travelers arrived in Tasarahla, a watering-place where they stopped for three days to rest, repair the skins, and fill them with water. Scouts were sent ahead from there to rent houses in Iwalatan and ask that the caravan be met four days away with supplies of water. If the scout lost his way in the desert, the members of the caravan risked dying of thirst. On the seventh day, the travelers saw the torches of the inhabitants of Iwalatan coming to meet them. They could then water their horses. To cross a torrid desert, they traveled at night and stopped during the day. In early April, after a journey of two months, they finally arrived in Iwalatan, in the first province of the country of the blacks.

The way in which the sultan's officer treated the merchants shocked Ibn Battuta, who was always full of his own importance. "At this I was sorry I had come to their country, because of their bad manners and contempt for white people."[45] When

---

44. *The Travels of Ibn Battuta*, tr. H. A. R. Gibb, v. IV, p. 948.
45. Ibid., p. 950.

the customs official invited the members of the caravan to a meal, Ibn Battuta at first refused, but finally accepted at the urging of his companions. The meal consisted only of a gruel made of millet, honey, and curdled milk served in a half gourd. "Those present drank and then left. I said to them: 'Is it for this that the Blacks invited us?' They said: 'Yes. For them, it is the greatest hospitality.'"[46] Disgusted, Ibn Battuta wanted to leave with the pilgrims, but finally decided to go to visit the capital of the king of the blacks. He stayed for around fifty days in Iwalatan, where the heat was extreme.

To reach Mali, which was at a distance of twenty-four days of fast traveling, he hired the services of a guide, since it was not necessary to travel in a caravan because the country was safe. Large trees shaded the road. The traveler carried neither food nor money, but pieces of salt, glass trinkets, and a few spices. When he arrived in a village, he bought the products he wanted from the women. After ten days' journey, Ibn Battuta arrived in Zaghari, inhabited by black merchants and a few whites. Then, passing through the town of Karsakhu on the banks of the Niger, after crossing the river Sansara, he reached Mali, capital of the king of the blacks, on June 28, 1352. He left again on February 27, 1353, in the company of a merchant and riding on a camel because of the high price of horses. On the banks of a channel of the Nile, he saw enormous animals that provoked his astonishment: they were hippopotami. After a stop not far from the lake, in a large village administered by a black who had made the pilgrimage to Mecca with Sultan Mansa Musa, and another in Mima, he reached Timbuktu. There he embarked on a pirogue carved out of a single tree trunk. He stayed in a town whose name he had forgotten, then went to Kaukau [Gao], one of the most beautiful and largest cities of the country, before heading for Takadda with a large caravan of people coming from Ghadamas. Ibn Battuta arrived in the territory of the Bardama, a Berber tribe, where caravans could not travel except under their protection. Although ill because of the extreme heat, he made a forced march to the town of Takadda, all of whose inhabitants were merchants. Every year they went to Egypt and brought back fine cloth and other merchandise. There, Ibn Battuta re-

---

46. *The Travels of Ibn Battuta*, tr. H. A. R. Gibb, v. IV, pp. 950–51.

ceived the order to return home. He immediately bought two saddle camels, took grain supplies for seventy days, and left with a large caravan on September 12, 1353. After the territory of Kahir, the travelers entered a desert and arid region that was crossed in three days, continued through a desert but not arid territory, that they took fifteen days to cross, and arrived at the crossroads of the Ghat road leading to Egypt and the Tawat road. After ten days' travel, they arrived in the Hoggar Mountains where men wore veils. It took them a month to traverse this stony and sparsely vegetated region. After a few days in Buda, they headed for Sijilmasa, which they reached on December 29, 1353. It was the season of extreme cold, and snow blocked the road. He finally reached the end of his journey in Fez.

In the fifteenth century, Genoese and Venetian sailors working for Portugal undertook an exploration of the African coasts and the islands off them. In 1455, Uso di Mare reported that his caravel was in the vicinity of Guinea and that, having discovered the mouth of the Gambia River, he was sailing up it because he knew that gold and pearls could be found in the region. He was forced to retreat because of the hostility of local fishermen. Seventy leagues further on he encountered a black prince and stated that this place was only three hundred leagues from the borders of the kingdom of Prester John. And he encountered a compatriot whom he believed to be a descendant of the sailors from the crew of the galleys of the Vivaldi brothers, leaders of an expedition in the late thirteenth century.

Arriving in the same region, a noble Venetian Ca' da Mosto, expressed his admiration of Cape Verde, stretching into the sea between two mountains and surrounded by huts inhabited by blacks. Although he had traveled often both east and west, Ca' da Mosto had seen nothing more beautiful.

As for the interior of the African continent, the only information available to Westerners came from accounts by Arab travelers or Jews such as the Mallorcan cartographers, the Cresques, makers of the 1375 map known as the map of Charles V. On it were mentioned the cities of Timbuktu, Mali, and Gao; in the center of the Sahara there reigned a black king. It was not until the middle of the fifteenth century that Westerners really crossed the Sahara. In 1447, the Genoese Antonio Malfante wrote from Tawat to a correspondent in Genoa. He wrote that after landing at Sijilmasa, he and his companions had first traveled south in a caravan for twelve days. For seven days they saw no houses, nothing but plains of sand and, as at sea, they had to direct themselves by the sun during the day and the stars at night. In the country of the blacks, inhabitants that Malfante called Philistines lived in tents like Arabs. They were whites, with veils covering mouth and nose. Enemies of the Jews, they had adopted the religion of the blacks. Further south were territories inhabited only by idol-worshipping blacks, who were constantly at war with one another. These regions were crossed by a very long river which flowed over the neighboring land every year, passed near Timbuktu, crossed Egypt, and watered Cairo. This country was twenty-five days from Tunis, thirty from Tlemcen, and twenty from Fez.

The king of Portugal even intervened in the affairs of African monarchs. In 1483, he sent eight people to the upper Niger, including a squire of his household, a valet named Pero Reinel, a bowman of the court, and other officers. But they succumbed to disease, except for Pero Reinel who, according to the document relating the incident, was accustomed to travel in the region, an indication that this was not his first journey.

Although mercantile and political and religious considerations might play a role, it is nevertheless true that many travelers were impelled by the desire to know other peoples. João Fernandez willingly had himself set on shore. Many details were of no commercial interest. For example, Ca' da Mosto reported that the Azanagi could get through a day on a bowl of barley meal. They always wore a handkerchief around the head, one end of which was used to cover the mouth and part of the nose. They were thin and every day used fish oil on their hair which was curly and hung to their shoulders.

On July 8, 1497, Vasco da Gama left Lisbon with four small and sturdy ships. After rounding the Cape of Good Hope, he arrived in Calcutta on May 20, 1498. The Asia that Marco Polo had explored was now reached by circumnavigating Africa. A few years earlier, another great explorer, also believing that he was sailing to the Indies, discovered America.

America and Christopher Columbus

Sailing from Iceland in the tenth century, Eirik the Red reached Greenland.

Eirik put out to sea past Snæfels Glacier, and made land near the glacier that is known as Blaserk. From there he sailed south to find if the country were habitable there. He spent the winter on Eiriks Island, which lies near the middle of the Eastern Settlement. In the spring he went to Eiriksfjord, where he decided to make his home. That summer he explored the wilderness to the west and gave names to many landmarks there. He spent the second winter on Eiriks Holms, off Hvarfs Peak. The third summer he sailed all the way north. . . . That summer Eirik set off to colonize the country he had discovered; he named it *Greenland,* for he said that people would be much more tempted to go there if it had an attractive name.[47]

According to an Icelandic saga, Leif the son of Eirik explored the coasts of Labrador and settled in a region he called Vinland, supposedly located near the Bay of Saint Lawrence.

The Scandinavian settlements faded away by the fourteenth century, but the memory of them survived. In 1476, the king of Denmark sent an expedition to Greenland. Hence, Europeans had a more or less vague sense that there were lands in the western Atlantic. One can understand that Columbus had the idea of reaching the East by crossing that ocean.

Columbus left Palos on August 3, 1492. He sailed to the Canaries, which belonged to the crown of Castile, and from there he truly set sail. After repairing some damage to the *Pinta,* on September 8, he headed west. For ten days, the wind was steady and the air mild. On September 19, Columbus surveyed his position. He thought he had covered four hundred leagues and was between islands. He reached the Sargasso Sea. Contrary winds began to blow which, Columbus noted, comforted the crew who were afraid they would be unable to return.

Difficulties began after September 25. On that day, Martin Pinzón, who had borrowed from Columbus a map showing islands, asserted that the ships must be near them. He even thought he could see land. But this was a mirage. The crew began to mutter. The crew had seen no land for three weeks, and

---

47. *The Vinland Sagas,* tr. Magnus Magnusson and Hermann Pálsson (New York: New York University Press, 1966), 77–78.

made nervous by idleness, became threatening. On October 10, matters worsened. Discontent came close to mutiny. During the trial of 1512, some old sailors testified that several pilots and some members of the crew wanted to return home. It seems that Columbus was asked to turn back and that he managed to get them to accept a few more days' sailing.

On October 11, they saw traces of nearby land: a tree branch with flowers and a board. That evening, when the crew had assembled for prayer, Columbus asked them to keep a sharp lookout. At ten in the evening he saw a light, but it was too faint to be certain. A little later, a sailor saw the same light from another part of the ship and cried out: "Land!" But the planned cannon shot was not fired because there had already been false sightings. Two hours after midnight, Rodrigo of Triana, who was in the forecastle of the *Pinta*, saw a white strip of sand and cried out: "Land, land!" Martin Pinzón then ordered the cannon fired. At sunrise on October 12, 1492, they dropped anchor facing the beach that was the western end of the coral isle Guanahani in the Bahamas. They took formal possession of the island with unfurled banners, and Columbus gave it the name San Salvador, which it still bears today.

But he understood that this was not Cipangu, for the island had no palaces with golden roofs. Since Marco Polo had mentioned many islands near Japan, and because Indians indicated by signs that to the south there was a king with golden vessels, the ships set sail again on October 14. They sailed through the Bahamas archipelago for two weeks. Columbus thought he was in or near the Indies. According to his log-book of October 21, he prepared to sail to another large island which must be Cipangu from what the Indians said, although they called it Colba (Cuba). Then he would go to the mainland and would deliver the letters from his sovereigns to the Great Khan. On October 28, the ships anchored off the north coast of Cuba, but there was no sign of the expected activity. In early November, Columbus sent messengers to the king of the country, for he thought he was off the coast of Asia, but without results. After visiting the coast, he left Cuba on December 4 to head for Babeque where, his guides had informed him by signs, gold could be gathered at night. The next day, unfavorable winds brought him to Haiti which astonished him and which, because of its resemblance to Spain, he named Hispaniola. On Christmas Day the *Santa Maria* ran aground on a coral reef. Columbus set sail again on the *Niña* with half his men on January 2. Four days later, they were rejoined by the *Pinta,* which, under the command of Martin Pinzón, had deserted the two other caravels on November 22. With the wind driving the ships to the northeast, the direction home, they had only to recross the ocean.

Columbus landed in Lisbon and sent a letter to Ferdinand and Isabela.

> I write to inform you how in thirty-three days I crossed from the Canary Islands to the Indies, with the fleet which our most illustrious sovereigns gave me. I found very many islands with large populations and took possession of them all for their Highnesses; this I did by proclamation and unfurled the royal standard. No opposition was offered. . . .
>
> The inhabitants of . . . all the [islands] that I discovered . . . go naked, as their mothers bore them, men and women alike. . . . They have no iron or steel or arms and are not capable of using them, not because they are not strong and well built but because they are amazingly timid. . . .
>
> In another island, which I am told is larger than Hispaniola . . . there is a vast quantity of gold, and from here and the other islands I bring Indians as evidence.[48]

Thus were opened to Westerners three continents whose exploitation would enable them to dominate the world. But the difficulties were enormous, not only in the material conditions of travel, but also in the psychological and emotional problems that travel produced. Ibn Battuta did not travel without regret: "My parents being yet in the bonds of life, it weighed sorely upon me to part from them, and both they and I were afflicted with sorrow at this separation."[49] Far from their families, the great travelers felt nostalgia for their country of origin and feared they would be unable to return home. For example, the Polos, Marco, his father, and his uncle,

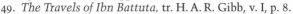

48. Christopher Columbus, *The Four Voyages* (London and New York: Penguin Books, 1969), pp. 115, 117, 122.

49. *The Travels of Ibn Battuta,* tr. H. A. R. Gibb, v. I, p. 8.

began to say among themselves that they would like to return to their own country. Although they were very rich in jewels of great price and in gold, a very great desire to see their own country again was always in their hearts; and although they were honored and favored, they thought of nothing else.

## A New World

Central Asia had been crossed and China reached. But notions gathered in the course of these travels remained fragmentary. The Indies, at least for Europeans, remained almost as little known as before. With respect to Africa, Ibn Battuta believed that the Niger and the Nile were one and the same river. It was easy to describe the country seen. It was much more difficult to know what was the exact course of the river crossed or to reconstitute a mountain range that had been traversed. Marco Polo saw that the island of Ceylon did not have the dimensions attributed to it by ancient writers. What did he do? Instead of doubting their word, he came up with a fanciful hypothesis to explain the change.

> It has a circumference of some 2,400 miles. And I assure you that it used to be bigger than this. For it was once as much as 3,500 miles as appears in the mariners' charts of this sea. But the north wind blows so strongly in these parts that it has submerged a great part of this island under the sea. That is why it is no longer as big as it used to be.[50]

But were explorers really concerned with geography, and indeed, could they be?

They reported what was accessible to them, what presented itself to their view, although they were necessarily selective. Rationalism was not the predominant characteristic of medieval mentality. The wondrous was accepted and a critical spirit was often lacking. It is nonetheless true that concrete facts could be observed and that medieval explorations contributed useful information about people and their ways of life.

---

50. *The Travels of Marco Polo*, tr. Ronald Latham, 258–59.

One example was the city of Khan-balik (Beijing) that Marco Polo knew well. Chinese sources confirm his assertions. Khan-balik was indeed an enormous city whose walls enclosed a rectangle 7.5 kilometers long and 6.5 kilometers wide, that is, a surface of 5,000 hectares, not including the suburbs and the city to the south which alone contains 1,700 hectares, whereas the largest cities in the West were no larger than 500 hectares, less than the size of the palace of the Great Khan. Marco Polo admired not only the size of the city but the activity of its inhabitants. Khan-balik, he writes, contains a multitude of houses and people, both within and without the walls. There are as many suburbs as there are gates, that is, twelve, and they are so vast that they run together. Indeed, these suburbs contain more inhabitants than the capital and buildings that are as beautiful as those of the city itself. That is where merchants and all those who come on business live. Each category of people has its own caravanserai.

The Great Khan forbids burial in the city. Corpses are carried to a distance and burned if they are idolaters, and buried if they are of other religions, such as Christians and Muslims.

All the prostitutes live in the suburbs, and they are very numerous, 20,000, if Marco Polo is to be believed. They do not lack for work because of the great number of foreigners and merchants who come and go every day. They have a captain general and a chief for each hundred and each thousand. When ambassadors come to the Great Khan and are housed at his expense, the captain general is called upon to provide a prostitute for each ambassador and one for each member of his retinue. They are changed every night and receive no payment, for this is the tax they pay to the ruler.

No city in the world receives more merchants or imports more precious things. From India come precious stones, pearls, silk, and spices; choice and costly products also come from Cathay, Manzi, and other neighboring provinces. This is because the ruler lives in the city, along with great numbers of lords and ladies, and many soldiers are stationed in the environs. Each day, more than 1,000 cart-loads of silk enter the city; much cloth of gold and silk is woven there. This is not surprising, for the surrounding regions produce no flax, so that everything must be made of silk. However, some places supply cotton and hemp, but in insufficient quantities. Around the city of Khan-balik are more than two hundred other cities, near or far, and the inhabitants of those cities have no hesitation in traveling two hundred miles to the capital to buy what they need. When the court is in Khan-balik, many of them come to sell their wares. It is thus not surprising that it is a great trading center.

Marco Polo devotes a subsequent passage to currency, demonstrating the cleverness of the Great Khan in the matter. Men take the bark from mulberry trees which are plentiful in the region. From the fine bast between the bark and the wood, they make sheets of paper that are cut into various sizes worth, respectively, half a small tornesel, an entire tornesel, half a silver groat, an entire silver groat, equal in value to a silver groat of Venice, two, five, and ten groats, one, three, and as many as ten gold bezants. These sheets are made with great care, several officers writing their names on each piece of money. When everything is properly completed, the chief dips the seal assigned to him in cinabar and stamps it on the money. Any counterfeiter is punished by death. There is such a quantity of money that it could purchase all the treasure in the world, and it costs nothing. Indeed, we have for this period all the details for the issuance of paper money, which dates from the Tang dynasty (618–905), even the quantity issued each year. This money, distributed throughout all the provinces and kingdoms under the rule of the Great Khan, takes care of all payments, and no one dares refuse it on pain of losing his life. Several times a year, many merchants come from India with precious goods that they give to the ruler. He has them examined by twelve experts, who estimate their value and have the merchants paid with paper money that they can use to buy whatever they wish. When the papers are torn and frayed they are brought to the mint and changed for new ones at a discount of three percent. Neither gold nor silver is used as currency.[51]

In the face of unknown countries, whereas missionaries displayed a certain simplicity, merchants had a tendency to show pride. Rubruck wondered anxiously whether he was behaving well like the wise man of whom Ecclesiastes speaks. Marco Polo constantly boasted of his own merits. "[H]e had mastered four languages with their modes of writings. He was wise and

---

51. *The Travels of Marco Polo*, tr. Ronald Latham, 147–48.

farsighted above the ordinary, and the Great Khan was very well disposed to him because of the exceptional merit and worth that he detected in him."[52]

Relations with others posed problems of communication. Unlike Marco Polo, most explorers had to rely on interpreters. But, to judge from Carpini and Rubruck, interpreters were often incompetent. From the outset of his journey, Rubruck declares that his interpreter, a Turk hired in Crimea, is "without intelligence or ability to speak." He soon notices that the interpreter is transmitting the opposite of what he says, so that he decides to keep silent. Moreover, this individual is often drunk and speaks unintelligibly. And he refuses to translate the Franciscan's statements about religion. Hence, Rubruck and his companion are very happy to find unexpected interpreters among Armenians, Russians, or Western prisoners. Although Columbus had taken precautions by bringing along a converted Jew, who knew Hebrew, Chaldean, and a little Arabic (even though he thought he was going to India), he experienced the same difficulties, for he could neither understand nor make himself understood by the Indians. Indeed, black Africa and America forced expression by gesture, signs, and mimicry.

In the end, traveling led explorers, or at least some of them, into a state of questioning, for they observed that a large portion of the inhabitants of the earth did not know Christ and that Europeans were not in the center of the world.

## WANDERERS

Wandering was the lot of many people who traveled here and there following their desires or impelled by events, not really knowing what would become of them. The knight errant, a kind of model for these men, belongs as much to myth as to reality. Aren't the real travelers, as Baudelaire said, those who leave in order to leave? You cannot find adventure by staying confined within four walls. "It happened more than seven years ago that, solitary as a peasant, I went seeking adventure, armed with all my armor, as a knight should be," says Calogrenant, one of the

---

52. *The Travels of Marco Polo*, tr. Ronald Latham, 40.

knights in *Yvain, le Chevalier au lion*. For knights without resources, errancy was also a means of subsistence. "They went
in search of plunder," writes Chrétien de Troyes of three knights
who come across Erec and Enide and covet their equipment. But
there were not only highway robbers. Some of these travelers
belonged to powerful lineages (Erec is the son of a king) and had
no need to travel. It cannot be claimed that the aim of such wandering was to find a wife: Yvain and Perceval have no hesitation
in leaving fair ladies to continue their quest. Most frequently,
the hero is a man younger than twenty. Errancy perhaps represents a sort of rite of passage, a way of entering the adult world.
Traveling without a goal makes it possible to escape from idleness uncongenial to adolescents and particularly to encounter
adventures and thus to excel, to win glory, by accomplishing
deeds of arms sometimes for a noble cause, but especially for the
pleasure of combat. The young nobles whom we have already
mentioned set out as much for pleasure and the need to wander as in order to find the means to establish an estate.

Errancy often lasted for only a short time. The knight, after
winning glory or fortune, or both, if he does not die in battle,
and the explorer, after seeking new worlds and crossing unknown regions, return to their community of origin. There were
however figures whose essential characteristic was to wander.

## By Inclination

There were clergy who decided to give up the service of God and
wander through the world. Because of their nomadic life, they
were called *clercs vagants* or *vagants*. They were of all origins.
Among them were monks who, unable to bear a life that was
too harsh, had fled their monasteries and traveled about the
country. In particular, in the early twelfth century, there were
men and women who followed preachers and then sought out
solitude. But soon put off by the difficulties of their new existence, they regretted vows pronounced in a moment of enthusiasm. Not wishing to return to their old communities out of a
sense of shame, they traveled on the roads.

Monks, however, did not make up the bulk of the troop.
Much more numerous were clergy from the schools. Mistakes
had made some outcasts. There were some who wanted to study,
but were unable to because of their poverty. Indeed, many schools

established by bishops and monastic orders beginning in the eleventh century, with great teachers on their faculties, attracted poor students who wanted to rise in society through their learning. Very often their hopes were disappointed. What good was it to know the Scriptures if you could not secure a place in the Church? Students accused Rome of preferring flattery to talent. There was nothing left for them but to beg. They now used the knowledge they had acquired in school to present agreeable solicitations, to call upon the generosity of the rich. But they came up against the avarice of both clergy and laity.

These wanderers were not only people to whom fate had been unkind. Many of them had been unable to submit to the laws governing society, and their reputation was deplorable. *Vagant*, goliard, and drunk became synonyms. The origin of the word "goliard" is unknown. Fanciful etymologies trace the word to Goliath, incarnation of the devil, to the Latin *gula* (mouth, throat) or to the Provençal *gualiar* (to deceive), to make them into enemies of God, gluttons.[53]

Although they did not beg, the goliards became jongleurs, or wandering minstrels. The Church identified them as jesters and condemned them. Favoring stability, it could only stigmatize these men who did not stay put and as clergy (or considered to be clergy) presented an unfavorable image of the Church. The *Carmina Burana* tell us what the goliards sought, in the first place, love;

> It is almost impossible to conquer your nature,
> To have pure thoughts at the sight of a girl,
> We young men cannot follow so harsh a law,
> Nor give up our bodies full of vigor.

and then gambling and drinking:

> I plan to die in the tavern,
> Where wine is close to the mouth of the dying.
> And the choir of angels will sing joyously:
> "May God grant help to this drinker!"

---

53. According to E. G. Fichtner, the word "goliard" derives from the Germanic root *goljan* (to shout, sing, perform incantations) and the suffix *-ard*.

Many of the poems emphasize pleasure and criticize the established order. The Church, for which the search for pleasure was to be proscribed because Christ had saved us through his suffering, and which did not appreciate having its wealth stigmatized, could not accept the goliards' words or the life they led. This is why the Councils of Rouen and Château-Gontier in 1231, and the Council of Sens in 1239 ordered wandering clerics to hide their tonsures, the sign of their status. The councils decided that bawdy clerics would be shorn and shaven, so that no trace would be left of their religious tonsure. The goliards disappeared toward the end of the thirteenth century; the final condemnations came from the Councils of Salzburg and Mainz in 1310. The term later came to be used in the sense of deceitful or, in legal language, to indicate the owner of a house of prostitution.

With these goliards can be associated the jongleurs who, as Edmond Faral has shown, constantly traveled in search of subsistence. They provided diversion for people where strollers could most easily gather, in squares, on bridges, and at street corners. Celebrations, and particularly marriages, could hardly do without them. Meeting some squires accompanying a woman on the road to Lagny, Hervi, in an eponymous romance, thinks that she is a young bride, and is surprised not to see a jongleur. Fairs might attract merchants, but they also brought entertainers. In Provins on market night, there was a kind of torchlight retreat in which the sergeants paraded carrying torches accompanied by jongleurs playing various musical instruments.

Artisans and bourgeois were too busy to listen to entertainers for long and too stingy or too poor to pay them well. Hence, jongleurs preferred to go to noble courts, enticed in particular by the reputation for generosity of Italian nobles. According to the chronicler Salimbene, Florence enjoyed such prosperity around 1283 that it attracted jesters from all Italy. And when Genoa organized great festivities to celebrate a victory in 1217, entertainers arrived from Lombardy, Provence, Tuscany, and all the nearby regions. All countries showed the same infatuation for jongleurs, who were constantly on the move from castle to castle. They were usually well received, because they brought information and good humor to a rather tedious life. But nobles soon developed a preference for domestic jongleurs. A wandering minstrel might delight a bourgeois, but a great personage owed it to himself to maintain in his household people who had the duty to cheer him up.

Entertainers had a bad reputation. The term *lecheor* (libertine) became a synonym for jongleur.

> You have used up all your flesh
> In the tavern and the bordello

declares a jongleur to a rival in a play entitled *Les Deux Bordeurs ribauds*.

The *Roman de Renart* contains an episode in which the hero appears in the guise of a jongleur. Unrecognizable, because he has fallen into a dyer's vat and is dressed in yellow, he approaches Ysengrin, whom he addresses in crude French. "You were not born in France. Where are you from?" asks Ysengrin.

> No, lord, but in Brittany.
> I lost all I had
> And I looked for a companion.
> Found nobody to teach me.
> Through all of France and all of England
> I looked for a companion.
> Stayed so long in this country
> That I took all of France.
> But I want to go back
> And I don't know where to find him.
> But I have gone to Paris
> And learned all of French.

Troubadours were great travelers.

From the great gulf of the sea, from the troubles of the port, and from the dangers of the beacon, I have escaped, thanks be to God. So I can tell and enumerate how many evils and torments I have suffered. And since it pleases God that I may return with happy heart to the Limousin I left in sadness, I thank Him for this return and the honor He has granted me,

declares Gaucelm Faidit. According to the narrative of his life, Marcabru was "renowned and listened to throughout the world, and feared for his tongue." For so many of his works to have survived, he must have traveled to many regions. Peire d'Auvergne was perhaps in Montpellier in 1148, stayed for some time at the court of Raymond V of Toulouse, went to the court of Sanche of Castile, and then that of his father Alfonso VII. In 1159, he was with Raymond Bérenguer IV of Barcelona; in 1162, he was living in Narbonne; around 1173, he is said to have been in Puivert; thereafter, information is lacking. Another Auvergnat, Peire Rogier, seems to have wandered as much. A canon of Clermont, he decided to leave the clergy to become a jongleur. He was received by many courts: those of Ermengarde of Narbonne, Raimbaut of Orange, Alfonso VIII of Castile who had just married a daughter of Eleanor of Aquitaine, and Alfonso II of Aragon, the troubadour-king. He was with Raymond V of Toulouse, and finally retired to a monastery.

The wanderings of Guiraut de Bornelh were not limited to Spain. He went as far as Italy, which became more and more frequent. He stayed there from 1193 to 1196, it seems, at the court of Boniface of Montferrat. Two years later he was in Hungary where he probably accompanied one of the daughters of Alfonso II who had come to marry King Emeric. He lived again in Italy, notably in Genoa, at the end of his life.

The life of Uc de Saint-Circ, son of a poor vassal of Quercy, depicts him as an indefatigable traveler. His older brothers, wishing to make him a cleric, sent him to Montpellier. But he spent little time on the study of letters, preferring songs and poetry. He lived for a long time in Gascony, traveling sometimes on foot, sometimes on horseback. He stayed for a long time with the countess of Benauges through whom he formed a connection with Savary of Mauléon. He traveled to Poitou and the neighboring regions, and then to Catalonia and Aragon in Spain, as well as to Provence, Lombardy, and la Marche.

## From Necessity

While *vagants* wandered if not always for their pleasure, at least without being absolutely forced to do so, others, in contrast, were driven from home by invasions and wars that cast them onto the roads in search of a place of refuge.

Chronicles of the Carolingian period tell of monks obliged to leave their monasteries bearing the precious relics under their care. According to the *Miracles de saint Philibert*, fleeing from the Normans who had become masters of the towns they went through without resistance, the monks reached Cunault, a locality of Anjou on the banks of the Loire that Charles the Bald had given them as a refuge before the fall of Angers, while the body of Saint Philibert remained in the monastery of Déas (now Saint-Philibert-de-Grandlieu in the department of Loire-Atlantique). A few years later a large fleet of Norman ships sailed up the Seine. The year 857 witnessed many civil and foreign wars. But the monks still hoped to return to their monastery and, while their flight brought them to stay in various places, the body of Saint Philibert remained where it was, for lack of the certainty of a safe asylum, until they installed it in Cunault, and then brought it to Messay (in present-day Vienne) in 862.

In the late Middle Ages, economic difficulties, epidemics, and the Hundred Years' War (during which truces were as fearsome as periods of combat because of idled mercenaries) brought about the temporary or permanent abandonment of many villages. For example, the community of Castellet-lès-Sausses (Alpes-de-Haute-Provence) was severely depopulated in 1343 when a census was taken for tax purposes. Forty-one households had disappeared.

> Wishing to understand the cause of this diminution, they [the investigators] questioned on this subject the said men [the notables] who answered with one voice that the village and its territory had been devastated by storms and that, for this reason, the population had been deprived of its normal harvests for several years, that some could no longer maintain themselves and their families, that they became indebted to the Jews, and that in the end, after selling their possessions, they left the said village for good.

People did not leave immediately after bad harvests. The inhabitants tried to overcome difficulties by borrowing money. When they finally left, it was because they could not repay their debts. There were other motivations of lesser importance. Three of those who had left had married outside the village and were living with their wives. Eight owned nothing and thus seem to have been very mobile.

In the region of Chartres, movements away of very varied duration, sometimes permanent, might be local, between regions, or international. Colin Gayet from Bois-Rouvray settled in the parish of Saint-Saturnin in Chartres, about twenty kilometers from his original home. There was a significant immigration of Bretons, augmented in the second half of the fourteenth century by Normans and Limousins. Residents of Guyenne forced into exile by poverty were generally, for want of other skills, confined to heavy labor for the municipality. Once the war was over, in the second half of the fifteenth century, migrants became more numerous, probably to cultivate land that had been left fallow. For many, the Chartres region was only a way station on the way to a larger town.

Indeed, the rural exodus to cities was particularly notable. Between 1350 and 1450 in France, out of 1,100 hiring or apprenticeship contracts in the city of Toulouse, 27 percent were for young men of the town, 17 percent came from the surrounding territory, but 56 percent came from provinces such as the Albigeois, or relatively distant regions such as Limousin. Immigrants who were not apprentices even came from as far as Brabant and Flanders. The same observations hold true for the town of Puy-Saint-Front-de-Périgueux where, alongside many immigrants who had traveled less than fifty kilometers, there were others from Limousin, and even from Burgundy and Picardy.

Migrations sometimes took place over a much larger geographic space. In the late eleventh and early twelfth centuries, the Flemings and the Dutch, wishing to leave regions that were already overpopulated, were among the first to head east. Sometime between 1106 and 1113, Archbishop Frederick I of Hamburg made a contract with colonists from the Low Countries. The rather elongated plot of land they were given was to have a size of forty-eight hectares. According to the chronicler Helmold, in 1159 or 1160, Albert the Bear sent emissaries to Utrecht and the neighboring Rhine region as well as to inhabitants living near the sea, in Holland, Zeeland, and Flanders. He settled the newcomers in the towns and strongholds of the Slavs. Dutch colonists thus began to populate the southern reaches of the Elbe.

Another example is Albanian emigration.[54] On the way to Venice, the migration involved several stages through Greece or Dalmatia. Migrants did not always intend to settle in Venice.

---

54. See the work of Alain Ducellier.

But, having the occasion to stay there in the course of their travels, since they were frequently hired as sailors, they recognized the advantages of permanent settlement in a city where there was more work than in their native country. Because work as a sailor was very hard, they preferred finding easier work on land. One sign that showed the extreme poverty of some of them was that they agreed to become something close to slaves, although the term was not used. To cover the costs of their journey, they could either pay 6 ducats or agree to work as unpaid servants for four years. Conditions later became harsher with the sum to be paid increased by 2 ducats and the length of obligatory service increased by two years. Although there was some state protection with respect to wages, the situation changed in the course of the second half of the fifteenth century. The advance of the Turks produced a massive exodus, and both Venetians and Turks forcibly impressed Albanian sailors.

The journey to the Marches or to Apulia differed from that to Venice in the sense that it generally involved the choice of a country known for its prevailing freedom, and the newcomers were not made temporary slaves. The following anecdote illustrates this as well as showing the wandering of many immigrants. On June 2, 1435, in the port of Ancona, a ship docked whose commander had bought from a pirate in Apulia three young children who had been captured on the other side of the sea; two of them were from Durazzo. The merchant obviously intended to sell them in Ancona, but a group of Albanians gathered in the port to protest and had their disapproval officially registered.

Albanians informed themselves about the places where they would be most welcome, for they were obviously afraid of being more or less driven off. They appreciated Recanati, a small market town in the Papal States, from which they could later travel to the cities of the interior. On April 22, 1436, the communal council of Recanati was called to a meeting by the pontifical treasurer, who declared: "In view of the fact that three hundred sick and plague-stricken Albanians have arrived in Ancona and are on their way here, and in order that the town not be infected, let them be expelled and forbidden to come." In the course of the discussion, a councilor stated that he had learned that twelve of these Albanians had already died and that the newcomers should be repelled, without touching already settled inhabitants who had come from the Balkans. Since his speech received the approval of the other members, the council decided to expel only those Albanians who had arrived during the last six days. If these Albanians had left Ancona for Recanati, this was probably because they had been very badly received in the first town.

These unfortunates came principally from northern Albania, less frequently from the center, and never from the south. Very often, they could think of no way of surviving but wandering in search of work as they had in their native country. They were accused of offenses that shows them to have been unstable and ill adapted to a region governed by rules that had to be respected. For example, a certain Giorgio ended up first in Parma, where he said everything had been stolen from him, then in 1410, with eight small children, he was in Fano, where he accidentally set fire to stubble fields.

In addition to political and economic reasons, which might go together as in the case of the Albanians, there were sometimes religious reasons for migration. In this period where tolerance did not exist, heretics tried to avoid sometimes very serious troubles, particularly after the establishment of the Inquisition. Among them were some of the followers of Catharism. After the fall of Montségur in 1244, many of them found refuge in Catalonia, Sicily, and especially in Lombardy. They belonged to all social categories, but the majority was probably made up of merchants and artisans. The nobles tended to go into hiding, hoping sooner or later to recover their castles.

In the years between 1260 and 1280, many Cathars wished to see the exiled *Parfaits* again. They sold their possessions and went off wandering, abandoning their families whom they left without resources; a smuggler refused to take one man because his children needed him. During the persecution of 1308, Bernard Marty of Montaillou, his wife Guillemette, and their two sons fled to Catalonia, where they wandered from village to village, never staying very long in the same place. Bernard Marty died between two moves. While he had still been alive in Juncosa, the next year he died in Orta. Guillemette and her two sons, who were now almost adult, then settled in San Mateo. One of the noble ladies of Châteauverdun left her home even though she had a young child. But she did not leave without regret, finding it hard to abandon her baby.

Clandestine journeys were not without difficulty. Smugglers generally included a certain number of believers. A group led by Pierre Maurel left from Saint-Martin-la-Lande. While the group was staying in a house situated at the edge of the village, their guide went to get other heretics, three women and a child. Then they took the road to Béziers, where four other people joined the company. Through Beaucaire, the travelers headed toward Lombardy, stopping first in Achonia. Pierre Maurel in the meantime had changed his name to Pierre Gailhard. From Achonia, they traveled to Asti, and then to Pavia, where they stayed with a Lombard. They went to Mantua, where they met two men from Limoux, then to Cremona and Milan, and they returned to Coni, from which they reentered France and went to Castelnaudry. This journey took place in 1271–72. There were difficulties, but also dangers, for the Inquisition was on the watch and robbers took advantage of the situation.

People who wandered for various reasons sometimes ended up living a truly marginal existence. The *Registres du Châtelet de Paris* tell the stories of many offenders who had long been wanderers before being captured, imprisoned, and harshly punished for their thefts. Margot de La Barre said that she was born in Beaune-en-Gâtinais, that she left home when she was around fifteen with a companion who did as he pleased with her body and prostituted her "both in the good cities of the kingdom where she went, in one town and another, and in the country where she stayed for a long time with other women living the life of sin."

This kind of existence seemed destined, from the beginning, to lead to crime. Sometimes, wandering was provoked by an event. In 1415, Marion decided to leave the marital home. She had been living in Courtomer, in the jurisdiction of Caen, and had met her lover at a fair. He was a surgeon who lived in a neighboring town. The lovers traveled to Falaise, fifty kilometers to the north. Standard language gives way to a vocabulary more suited to their situation.

And he told her that it would be the next day and that Tuesday evening he would come to get her and they wandered all night and all day Wednesday they were in a hotel whose name he does not know and from there to another place and the next Friday went to Falaise where he left her and went

273

to work in another place where he stayed two weeks before coming back to her.

On his return, they once again set out to find a place to settle; from Falaise, they went to Goulet near Argentan. To find work, the lover had to return to the villages where his clients lived. He was finally sighted by the husband in a village less than five kilometers from Couromer.

In this instance, the wandering was in a limited geographical area, but it might lead men far from their place of origin. The trial of Jean Stulembrot took place in April 1464. He was originally from Liège and was a furniture maker in Condrieu, in the Lyon region. He was accused of killing a carpenter of the town. After hearing the sentence condemning him to be hanged, Jean Stulembrot confessed a crime committed seven years earlier in Hérenthals, near Malines, in Brabant. This is why, he declared, he had left that town and crossed the Oise to the Lyon region. This was not an unusual case. Distances seemed to matter little for migrants drawn by large towns, where they hoped to find work or to be able to hide after committing crimes in the areas they had gone through.

Overall, there is an impression of a certain instability, although the sources, penal records concerning criminals, do not completely reflect reality. An investigation that was opened in 1528 against Guichard Barbier, suspected of stealing a horse, has made it possible for Nicole Gonthier to retrace his movements over the course of the preceding three years. Born in Frans, in the Dombes, he lived for two years in Fontaines-sur-Saône as a servant of Guillaume de Venauges, then he worked for a year in Quincieux for a certain Compayn. There was nothing of note until then, except that he did not like to serve the same master for any length of time. But he admitted not participating in harvests. What could he have been doing during that summer? He said that he had returned to do plowing for Compayn, then that he went to Frans, where his mother was still living. Around mid-October, he was hired by Lespine, in Collonges-au-Mont-d'Or, for the grape harvest. He worked from Monday through Thursday evening; late in the week he helped on the wine press for other masters in Saint-Cyr. In addition, he had also traveled between Fontaines and Saint-Fortunat. Was this wandering? It was at least instability, close to wandering. Of the people imprisoned in the Châtelet from 1389 to 1392, 82 percent were wage laborers and servants characterized by frequent changes in occupation, place of work, and employer. For example, on April 9, 1390, there appeared before the tribunal Perrin Michel, called Pontigniau, who lived in Guérard (a district of Coulommiers in the department of Seine-et-Marne), suspected of homicide. The prisoner declared that he was born in Paris where he had been a shoemaker. But he had not stayed in the city and, to earn his living, had traveled to Soissons, Laon, Noyon, Rouen, Meaux, and the surrounding areas. Two years earlier, he had married a woman from Guérard. He said nothing of having begged, but his work life had involved much travel and probably periods without work.

Taste or necessity? This is the question raised by the life led by the small shepherds in the records of the inquisitor Jacques Fournier studied by Emmanuel Le Roy Ladurie. When a private war broke out between two nobles, they had to lead their flocks away from the scene of battle. Some of them changed grazing grounds, and sometimes went into hiding as the result of a dispute. Jean Maury was involved in a fight with shepherds from Razès. He was injured and, unable to secure justice, he left Montaillou for Puigcerda, where he hired himself out as a shepherd. Guillaume Maurs belonged to an honorable family of farmers in Montaillou. His father and brothers were arrested, but Guillaume managed to escape. He wandered from mountain to mountain from Foix to Catalonia and back. Jean Pellissier became a herdsman between the ages of twelve and fourteen; his parents, who lived in Montaillou, apprenticed him far from their village, in Tournon in the present-day department of Aude. At about eighteen, an experienced shepherd, he returned home where he lived for a while with his mother and four brothers. But he could not stay in one place. Again leaving his mother's house, he became a shepherd in Niort, also in Aude, for two years, and then in Mompret for a year. Short-term employment was frequent, with employers and workers seeming to agree to join up and separate quickly. After his stay in Mompret, Jean Pellissier returned again to Montaillou, where he was hired by Bernard Maurs. When the Inquisition went after the Maurs family, Jean left it for Prades d'Aillon, one league from his native village.

Unfortunately, his new master was also a victim of the Inquisition. After wandering for a long time, Jean Pellissier ended up settling in Montaillou.

The career of this small shepherd unfolded within a network of interconnected families. By contrast, the career of Pierre Maury involved long journeys. He was born in Montaillou in 1282 or 1283, and was first a shepherd in Montaillou itself. At the age of eighteen, he left home to go to the Aude region. Transhumance was common, particularly between the Aude valley and the Ariège mountains. At the age of twenty, he was working as a shepherd for Raymond Pierre, who lived in Arques. Every week, he briefly left the local pastures where he was keeping his sheep and those of Raymond, to get bread from his employer. Because of fear of trouble with the Inquisition, he returned to Montaillou in 1305, and then hired himself out as a shepherd for a breeder in Ax-les-Thermes. His new master, who was engaged in transhumance across the Pyrenees, sent him to keep his flock in the pastures of Tortosa in Catalonia. From then on, Pierre Maury shuttled among Spain, the kingdom of France, and the countship of Foix. He was not yet twenty-five.

Pierre Maury was a happy shepherd, who had given up establishing a family, but enjoyed the freedom of going where he liked. To those who wanted him to marry and settle down, he answered that his fate was "to go over hill and dale, and everywhere to have changing companions and girls."

# PART THREE
# the imaginary

# NINE

# here below

Some travelers gave free rein to their imagination, describing journeys they had not really taken.

## THE MARVELOUS

### A Favorable Mentality

Finding extraordinary things is one of the charms of travel. In his prologue, Marco Polo asserts that "it would be a great pity if he did not have a written record of all the things he had seen and had heard by true report." This taste for the strange was as widespread in the East as in the West. Sent as a messenger by the Great Khan, the Venetian "paid close attention to all the novelties and curiosities that came his way, so that he might retail them to the Great Khan."[55]

Explorers felt a certain intoxication on discovering unknown worlds, not because they had never been talked about—the Ancients had mentioned them—but because they had never been visited. Rubruck asked the Northern Tatars about "the monsters or human freaks that are described by Isidore and Solinus,

---

55. *The Travels of Marco Polo,* tr. Ronald Latham, 33, 41.

but was told that such things had never been sighted, which makes us very much doubt whether [the story] is true."[56]

In the Middle Ages, "nothing was more natural than the supernatural," and men were then very sensitive to magic. Marco Polo constantly asserts that Easterners are master magicians.

> You must know that, when the Great Khan was staying in his palace and the weather was rainy or cloudy, he had wise astrologers and enchanters who by their skill and their enchantments would dispel all the clouds and the bad weather from above the palace so that, while bad weather continued all around, the weather above the palace was fine.

The power of these enchanters did not stop there.

> [W]hen the Great Khan is seated in his high hall at his table, which is raised more than eight cubits above the floor, and the cups are on the floor of the hall, a good ten paces distant from the table, and are full of wine and milk and other pleasant drinks, these *Bakhshi* contrive by their enchantment and their art that the full cups rise up of their own accord from the floor on which they have been standing and come to the Great Khan without anyone touching them. And this they do in the sight of 10,000 men. What I have told you is the plain truth without a word of falsehood. And those who are skilled in necromancy will confirm that it is perfectly feasible.[57]

While living in Delhi, Ibn Battuta was invited to visit the sultan. He was with some close friends and two yogis whom he asked to do extraordinary things.

> One of them squatted on the ground, then rose from the ground into the air above our heads, still sitting. I was so astonished and frightened that I fell to the floor in a faint. The Sultan gave orders to administer to me a potion that he

---

56. *The Mission of Friar William of Rubruck,* tr. Peter Jackson, 201.
57. *The Travels of Marco Polo,* tr. Ronald Latham, 109–10.

had there and I revived and sat up. Meantime this man remained in his sitting posture. His companion then took a
sandal from a sack he had with him, and beat it on the
ground like one infuriated. The sandal rose in the air until
it came above the neck of the sitting man and then began
hitting him on the neck while he descended little by little
until he sat down alongside us. The Sultan said to me: "The
man sitting is the pupil of the owner of the sandal." Then
he said: "If I did not fear for your reason I would have ordered
them to do still stranger things than this you have seen." I
took my leave but was affected with palpitation and fell ill,
until he ordered me to be given a draught which removed
it all.

In China, Ibn Battuta witnessed phenomena that were just
as improbable.

That night a conjuror . . . was present. The amir said to him:
"Show us some of your tricks." He took a wooden ball in
which were holes through which were long cords. He threw
it up and it rose till it disappeared from sight, for we were in
the (courtyard) in the middle of the citadel. . . . When only
a little of the cord was left in his hand he ordered an apprentice of his to cling to it and climb up till he disappeared. The
conjuror called to him three times and he did not answer.
Then he took a knife in his hand as if he were infuriated and
climbed up the cord till he too disappeared. Then he threw
down to the ground the youth's hand, then his foot, then
his other hand, then his other foot, then his trunk, then his
head. Then he came down, panting and his robe bloodstained.
He kissed the ground in front of the amir and spoke to him
in Chinese. The amir told him to do something and he took
the youth's limbs, attached them to each other, kicked him
with his foot, and he stood up intact. I was amazed at this and
suffered palpitation of the heart like what I had had with the
king of India when I had seen the same kind of thing.[58]

<hr />

58. *The Travels of Ibn Battuta,* tr. H. A. R. Gibb, v. IV, pp.790 and
903–4.

One of the guests tried to reassure the traveler. The man had not risen into the air, he said, had not come down again, and had not cut his apprentice's limbs. These were illusions. Ibn Battuta remained troubled, but fortunately another medicine turned out to be effective.

Travelers thus moved through a universe in which magic played a considerable role. They therefore feared being enchanted. During Christopher Columbus's fourth voyage, the elements unleashed such fury that the sailors wondered if these torments were of supernatural origin. "While I was sailing in these parts, at the price of so much suffering, some of my men imagined the heresy that we had been enchanted and they remain persuaded of that to this day."

Magic was an art that came from the devil. According to Marco Polo, enchanters commanded devils although they made people believe that their power came from God. Speaking of magicians who ate living scorpions and snakes, Ricol da Monte Croce added that they could do nothing useful: "All they know how to do is to act and behave like the Antichrist and the forerunners of the Antichrist."

In these circumstances, how could travelers not encounter all sorts of monsters, and how could they avoid embroidering, adding imaginary elements to real facts?

## And Propitious Places

The marvelous appeared essentially in regions located beyond our usual horizons. Rubruck reported that after seeing the Tatars, it seemed that he had entered into another world. A certain number of places seemed favorable to the flourishing of such imaginings.

*The ends of the earth.* Pierre d'Ailly notes that, according to some, the polar regions harbor evil spirits, devils, and beasts harmful to man.

*Deserts.* After showing how difficult it was to cross the Gobi Desert, because of its immensity and the scarcity of fresh water, in short for rational reasons, Marco Polo does not hesitate to write:

> The truth is this. When a man is riding by night through this desert and something happens to make him loiter and

lose touch with his companions, by dropping asleep or for some other reason, and afterwards he wants to rejoin them, then he hears spirits talking in such a way that they seem to be his companions. Sometimes, indeed, they even hail him by name. Often these voices make him stray from the path, so that he never finds it again. And in this way many travellers have been lost and have perished.[59]

Marco Polo seems to share these beliefs. "These things are hard to hear, and what these spirits do is hard to believe. And yet, it is as I have said, and even more surprising." These were optical and auditory illusions that have since been described, but Marco Polo attributed supernatural causes to the natural phenomena that he encountered in crossing the Gobi desert.

*Mountains.* Jourdain de Séverac relates that no one has ever been able to walk on the snow on the top of Mount Ararat, because animals pursued by hunters turn around when they reach the snow and surrender to their pursuers.

*Islands*, worlds turned in on themselves, and particularly the Isles of the Blest. Isidore of Seville asserts that they are not to be confused with the earthly paradise, but that they enjoy near-felicity. His description was frequently repeated. Medieval cartography shared his state of mind. The Catalan map prepared for King Charles V of France indicates in a legend that "in the sea of the Indies, there are 7,548 islands, the marvelous riches contained in which we cannot detail here, both gold and silver as well as spices and precious stones." In reality the document mentions only four, including Ceylon and Sumatra. On his return voyage by sea, Marco Polo encounters many islands overflowing with wealth. The inhabitants of the island of Socotra have magical powers:

> They can make the wind blow from whatever quarter they may wish. They can calm the sea at will, or raise a raging storm and a howling gale. They are masters of many other marvellous enchantments; but I think it better not to speak of these in this book, because these enchantments produce

---

59. *The Travels of Marco Polo*, tr. Ronald Latham, 84.

effects which, were men to hear of them, might set them marvelling overmuch.[60]

The southern hemisphere seemed particularly to favor the extraordinary. Antipodeans were all the stranger because it was not possible to enter into communication with them. This opinion was to last until the fifteenth century, when the Portuguese sailed along the western coast of Africa. In the land of the Antipodes, everything occurred upside down because it was the underside of the world.

From the Real

Travelers wished to persuade their readers that they were objective. At the beginning of his book, Marco Polo forcefully asserts:

> There is also much here that he has not seen but has heard from men of credit and veracity. We will set down things seen as seen, things heard as heard, so that our book may be an accurate record, free from any sort of fabrication. And all who read the book or hear it may do so with full confidence, because it contains nothing but the truth.[61]

Similarly, Odoric claims as true only those events that he saw. He reports nothing, unless he has heard it from men worthy of belief who come from the country; he then indicates that his assertions are based on oral testimony.

Voyagers tried to inform themselves. In Tatar country, Rubruck met a priest from Cathay (probably a Tibetan lama) wearing a magnificent red robe. When he asked the origin of the color, the priest answered that it came from the blood of strange creatures, who were of human form but no taller than a cubit, covered with hair, and living in caves that could not be approached. Thus they had to be put asleep by pouring intoxicating liquor into the hollows of rocks where they came to drink. Once they were asleep, three or four drops of blood were drawn from a vein in the neck, and this blood made it possible to make

---

60. *The Travels of Marco Polo*, tr. Ronald Latham, 298.
61. Ibid., 33.

the dye used for the robe. Rubruck seems to have been convinced, but he refused to believe the rest of the priest's narrative. He told him that beyond Cathay there was a country where men, whatever their age when they entered, stayed that age forever. Not everything was seen as likely, but what was the basis for accepting a story?

Myth and reality were so interwoven at the time that it was difficult for travelers to distinguish between them, to sort out what belonged to each realm. They would certainly have agreed with Pierre d'Ailly when he asserted that the "country of Tingitanian Mauritania produces savage beasts, monkeys, dragons, and ostriches."

How did a Westerner familiar with the reality of gold and women consider them when he entered into unknown worlds? Struck by the wealth of many countries of the East, Marco Polo writes of China that "the walls of the halls and chambers [in the palace of the Great Khan] are all covered with gold and silver. . . . The ceiling is similarly adorned, so that there is nothing to be seen anywhere but gold and pictures."[62]

The island of Cipangu (Japan) contains so much gold that the inhabitants don't know what to do with it.

> They have gold in great abundance, because it is found there in measureless quantities. . . . I can report to you in sober truth a veritable marvel concerning a certain palace of the ruler of the island. You may take it for a fact that he has a very large palace entirely roofed with fine gold. Just as we roof our houses or churches with lead, so this palace is roofed with fine gold. And the value of it is almost beyond computation. Moreover all the chambers, of which there are many, are likewise paved with fine gold to a depth of more than two fingers' breadth. And the halls and the windows and every other part of the palace are likewise adorned with gold. All in all I can tell you that the palace is of such incalculable richness that any attempt to estimate its value would pass the bounds of the marvellous.
>
> They have pearls in abundance, red in colour, very beautiful, large and round. They are worth as much as the white

---

62. *The Travels of Marco Polo,* tr. Ronald Latham, 125.

ones, and indeed more. . . . They also have many other precious stones in abundance. It is a very rich island, so that no one could count its riches.[63]

And more gold and diamonds:

You must know that in the kingdom [of Motupali on the northern Coromandel coast] there are many mountains in which the diamonds are found, as you will hear. When it rains the water rushes down through these mountains, scouring its way through mighty gorges and caverns. When the rain has stopped and the water has drained away, then men go in search of diamonds through these gorges from which the water has come, and they find plenty.[64]

The inhabitants also get diamonds another way. They throw pieces of flesh steeped in blood into a deep valley. The flesh picks up the diamonds that become embedded in it. When eagles see it, they carry it off to another spot, where the men follow them. The eagles fly off leaving the diamonds embedded in flesh. Sometimes, the eagles reach a spot where no one can follow. When they eat, they swallow diamonds that come out in their droppings, and they can also be collected.

The Church condemned all sexual relations outside marriage. In the conjugal relation, pleasure was to be avoided; at most, it was tolerated, with reservations, by certain theologians. Marco Polo was interested in the sexual habits of the peoples he encountered, apparently with a degree of envy.

He writes that the Great Khan has four wives, but also many concubines, from a Tatar tribe where the women are very beautiful and have excellent manners. Every two years, messengers select the one hundred most beautiful young women. After they arrive at the great palace, the Great Khan has them evaluated by other judges, and chooses thirty or forty for his chamber.

These are first allotted, one by one, to the barons' wives, who are instructed to observe them carefully at night in their chambers, to make sure that they are virgins and not blem-

---

63. *The Travels of Marco Polo*, tr. Ronald Latham, 244.
64. Ibid., 272.

ished or defective in any member, that they sleep sweetly without snoring, and that their breath is sweet and they give out no unpleasant odour. Then those who are approved are divided into groups of six, who serve the Khan for three days and three nights at a time in his chamber and his bed, ministering to all his needs. And he uses them according to his pleasure. After three days and nights, in come the next six damsels. And so they continue in rotation throughout the year.[65]

Marco Polo does not conceal the fact that the mores of the inhabitants of Tibet (in reality the western mountainous portion of Sichuan) offer many advantages. In this country, no man wants a virgin for a wife, saying that she is worth nothing if she has not already slept with other men. This is why, when strangers pass through the region and set up their tents near a village, women who have daughters to marry off bring them for the travelers to sleep with. When they leave, the travelers generally give the girls a jewel or a token. With these gifts, when they get married they can prove that they have had lovers. Marco Polo concludes: "So much, then, for this marriage custom, which fully merits a description. Obviously the country is a fine one to visit for a lad from sixteen to twenty-four."[66]

Arab travelers adopted a slightly different attitude toward sexuality. It is true that their religion did not require that relations be limited to a single wife. Although Ibn Battuta was offended by the dress or the nudity of the women of certain regions, his travel narrative shows that he was able to satisfy his desires with complete legality.

My wife suffered severe pains and wanted to return to al-Mahal. However, I repudiated her and left her there. I wrote to the vizier to inform him of the situation, because she was the mother of his son's wife. I also repudiated the woman whom I had married temporarily and I sent for a slave whom I loved. . . . I stayed for seventy days on this island [Muluk, not far from al-Mahal] and married two wives there.

---

65. *The Travels of Marco Polo*, tr. Ronald Latham, 122.
66. Ibid., 173.

To the Fantastic

The medieval traveler was interested in what was different, surprising, or even dreadful. The other, which he feared that he
might resemble, was the monster, which played a much larger
role in the medieval imagination than in other periods. We need
only look at the sculptures and miniatures of the time. Since
these were extraordinary creatures, it was only fitting that they
live far from the everyday world.[67]

The monster was first of all the absolute opposite of man,
in the sense that he did not perform certain actions indispensable for the survival of a normal being. According to Jourdain
de Séverac, "in that part of India and in Lesser India, there are
men who live far from the sea, underground and in the woods;
they have a totally infernal appearance; they neither eat, nor
drink, nor clothe themselves, unlike those who live near the sea."

Much more frequently, the difference from man lay in the
strangeness of an essential organ. Odoric of Pordenone notes that
in one region "it is so hot that the sexual organs of the men hang
down to their knees or to the middle of their legs." Sometimes
the abnormality consisted in the presence of a single limb. Giovanni da Pian del Carpini reports:

> Cirpodan proceeded south against the Armenians. When the
> Tartars were crossing a desert, they came upon certain mon-
> sters, so we were told as a certain truth, who had a human
> shape, but only one arm with a hand, in the middle of the
> breast, and one foot . . . and they ran at such a rate that
> horses could not keep on their track, for they ran by hopping
> on their one foot and, when they grew tired with this method
> of progress, then they got along on the hand and foot turn-
> ing cart-wheels.[68]

Monstrosity might result from the largeness or smallness of
the body. According to Rubruck, in Albania "Isidore says that it

---

67. There is a very thorough study by Claude Kappler, *Monstres, Démons et Merveilles à la fin du Moyen Age,* from which most of the illus-
trations that follow are taken.
68. Carpini, *History of the Mongols,* 31.

contains dogs so large and ferocious that they attack bulls and kill lions. What is true, I learned from tales I heard, is that towards the Northern Ocean dogs are used, on account of their great size and strength, to draw wagons, like oxen."[69] And Marco Polo reports that in the province of Kara-jang "live huge snakes and serpents of such a size that no one could help being amazed to even hear of them."[70]

Some men lived very long. Marco Polo reports that in the province of Lar there are Brahmans who "live longer than anyone else in the world. This is due to their light feeding and great abstinence. . . . Among them are certain men living under a rule who are called *Yogis*. They live even longer than the others, as much as 150 or 200 years. And their bodies remain so active that they can still come and go as they will. . . ." This longevity is due not only to their frugality but also to a mixture that they drink twice a month from childhood on: "And certainly those who live to such a great age are habituated to this drink of sulphur and quicksilver."[71]

Sometimes, different natural kingdoms were mixed together. For example, Odoric mentions a vegetable lamb, "a great wonder that I have heard of from trustworthy people but that I have not seen."

The sexes might be separated; Marco Polo speaks of male and female islands.

> You must know that the men of Male Island go over to Female Island and stay there for three months, that in March, April, and May. For these three months the men stay in the other island with their wives and take their pleasure with them. After this they return to their own island and get on with their business.[72]

This may be compared with Christopher Columbus's belief in the island of the Amazons.

---

69. *The Mission of Friar William of Rubruck*, tr. Peter Jackson, 130.
70. *The Travels of Marco Polo*, tr. Ronald Latham, 178.
71. Ibid., 278–79.
72. Ibid., 295.

The Indians told him that if he continued in that direction he would not fail to find Matinino Island, which they said was inhabited by women without men. The admiral would have been very happy to land there in order to be able to present a half-dozen of these women to the Catholic sovereigns. . . . He said at least that it is certain that these women really exist.

Monstrous births appear often in medieval literary works. It is therefore not surprising that travelers encountered hybrid creatures in distant countries, humans with animal heads. According to Marco Polo, the men of the island of Andaman "have heads like dogs, and teeth and eyes like dogs; for I assure you that the whole aspect of their faces is that of big mastiffs."[73] Carpini adds that the cynocephales (men with dogs' heads) also have the feet of cattle and that they mix human words and dog barking. The *Images du monde,* in particular that of Gossuin which dates from around 1245, assert that men and animals in the Indies have eight toes. In this region live men with dogs' heads who bark; Cyclops who are faster than the wind, with one foot whose sole is so broad that they use it as a shield and an umbrella; men with a single eye in the middle of the forehead; others with their face and mouth in the middle of the chest, one eye at each shoulder, the nose extending into the mouth and bristles on the snout. On the basis of these fabrications, Pierre d'Ailly reports that there are in India mountains of gold that are inaccessible because of dragons, griffins, human monsters, men with reversed feet with eight toes, and others with dogs' heads who bark.

The wild man was characterized both by his way of life and his physique. The inhabitants of the kingdom of Basman have their own language, "but they are without a law, except such as prevails among brute beasts." Marco Polo clearly distinguishes these men from the "pygmy men of the Indies," that is, stuffed monkeys in "the likeness of a man." From the wild man to the cannibal, there is only one step. Arriving in the kingdom of Fuchau [Fukien province], Marco Polo speaks of the cannibalism

---

73. *The Travels of Marco Polo,* tr. Ronald Latham, 258.

of the inhabitants. The fact that the cannibal is a monster leads the traveler to attribute really monstrous elements to him. "The Indians said that it was a large island inhabited by men who had a single eye in the middle of the forehead, and by others called cannibals who seemed to have frightful skin," writes Columbus.

Travelers thus found themselves confronted with monsters, posing a problem with respect to the idea of the harmony of the world. The monsters had a dual nature, wonders because they emanated from the Creator, but also maleficent powers.

## Fictitious Journeys

To tell of the wonders they had seen or heard of, travelers relied on memory and notes. However, some narratives were the work of people who had never traveled or who had at least never seen the countries they described.

John Mandeville is an enigma for historians. His name appears in many places because of the great success of his book: 250 manuscripts, the oldest of which, in French, is from 1371. In the prologue, he declares that he was born in England, that he crossed the sea in 1322, that since then he has traveled widely and seen many lands, provinces, regions, and islands, and that he has gone "through Turkey, Greater and Lesser Armenia, Tartary, Persia, Syria, Arabia, Upper and Lower Egypt, Libya, a large part of Ethiopia, Chaldea, Amazonia, Upper, Lower, and Middle India, and through many diverse peoples, diverse laws, and diverse customs."

Having presented himself in this way, four times in his book he mentions sojourns in foreign lands. The first was in Egypt, where he says that he long served as a soldier in Sudan during the wars against the Bedouins. The second was in China, where he was part of the Great Khan's armies for fifteen months. He also claims to have crossed, with great difficulty, the Valley of the Devil and to have drunk at the Fountain of Youth in India. "I drank three or four times and it still seems to me that I am the better for it." But age and its miseries having come, he is now at rest in spite of himself, and he is now an old man of fifty or sixty (according to the dates of the text composed thirty-five years after his departure) taking pleasure in thinking back over the past while mistrusting his lapses of memory. In addition,

John Mandeville knows classical Latin, but he prefers to write in vulgar Latin in order to be better understood. This is all the author tells us of himself.

Toward the end of the fifteenth century, a fiction was created according to which Mandeville was an English knight, but also a doctor, who had made many voyages before spending his final years in Liège where he set down his memories in writing. He fell into obscurity in the eighteenth century. But in the nineteenth, beginning in the 1830s, textual criticism uncovered the sources used by Mandeville and the reality of his travels was called into question. In short, the name Mandeville in a manuscript is a signal that the text is essentially a compilation.

The text contains two major divisions: a description of the Holy Land and the roads leading to it; and a description of Asia, Asia Minor, Central Asia, India, China, and the islands of the Indian Ocean, as well as of a part of Africa (North Africa, Libya, and Ethiopia). The book begins as a pilgrimage narrative, but changes into an itinerary and a book of wonders.

As Christiane Deluz has shown, a comparison of the work of John Mandeville with works of the same genre and of around the same time, that is, the books of pilgrimage by William of Boldensele and James of Verona for the first division, and the *Divisament dou Monde* of Marco Polo and the *Description of Eastern Regions* by Odoric of Pordenone for the second, reveals both similar organization and similar importance granted to the various countries. For example, the writer spends much more time on the Holy Land than on Egypt, more on China than India, and says very little about Africa.

But examination of the work does reveal some kind of general structure. The passages concerning the various countries are connected to one another in such a way as to present a map of the world. Moreover, Mandeville does not allow himself to be confined within the framework of the "climates" derived from Antiquity, since he locates "the islands and the land of Prester John far outside the climates."

Mandeville sees himself not as a traveler or a pilgrim but as a geographer. He claims to have received permission from the sultan to go everywhere. He took an astrolabe along and was thus able to establish the location of the antarctic pole. He knows that the circumference of the earth is 9,000 leagues, and that he has covered nearly one fifth of it. When he entered the service of the Great Khan, it was to study the mores of the Tatars. Mandeville was in fact an imaginary explorer who displays his knowledge rather than his experience.

To speak of wonders, Mandeville uses his sources judiciously. He sometimes even reworks texts to make them more evocative. Where Brunetto Latino speaks of a country in which "no star is used" except "a large bright one named Canope," emphasizing the utilitarian aspect, Mandeville prefers to dwell on a sky with glittering stars: "On this island you see no star that can glow brightly, except one very bright one called Canope. And you do not see the moon in all seasons, except when it is in the quarter."

Finally, it was generally agreed that Mandeville's journeys were unreal, except perhaps for the one to the Near East. This did not prevent his work from being appreciated, and many writers referred to it.

The genre of imaginary journey also existed in the East. Abu Dulaf Mis'ar, a poet and mineralogist who frequented various Muslim courts between 940 and 990 and traveled frequently, composed two narratives, one concerning the Turks and incidentally India and Malaya, the other Iran and Armenia. The second is personal, the first a compilation. When he wishes to please a patron, he relies on the works of predecessors to describe, following a fanciful itinerary, the different countries he claims to have visited. Unlike Mandeville, who suppresses the "I" of his sources, Abu Dulaf does not hesitate to use it, even to narrate improbabilities like pepper plants shriveled by the wind. But in general, he imposes on the reader a relative feeling of strangeness, in order not to be unmasked. Thus, for a single man, the geography of travel includes both evidence of direct experience and the elements of a culture.

The imaginary journey might take on allegorical form. Philippe de Mézières, born around 1327, first followed a military career and was with Bernabo Visconti in 1345 and then with Andrea of Naples. He traveled to the East where he fought at Smyrna in 1346. The following year, he undertook a pilgrimage to Jerusalem. In 1348 or 1349, he returned to Europe and served in Spain and France. Returning to Cyprus, he entered the service of Peter I, king of Cyprus and then of Jerusalem. When the

king began a long voyage of two years in 1362, he brought Philippe in his retinue. In 1365, Philippe was present at the capture
of Alexandria. In 1367 and 1368, he is said to have visited Aragon
and Castile, Portugal, and Italy. The kingdom of Cyprus experienced terrible troubles, and Peter I was assassinated in 1369. Philippe de Mézières then entered the service of Charles V whose
confidant he became. After the king's death, he withdrew to the
Celestine cloister in Paris, where he spent the last twenty-five
years of his life. It was there that he wrote the *Songe du Vieil
Pèlerin*, which dates from 1389.

The work, which includes a prologue and three books, begins in the cell of the Celestine cloister in Paris. Divine Providence appears in a dream and tells the author that he is going
to undertake a pilgrimage: he must seek Charity, Wisdom, and
Truth, and return with them so that they can reform the world.
The pilgrim travels to the earthly paradise and returns with
Queen Truth, Justice, Peace, and Mercy, so that these ladies may
judge the worth of the inhabitants of our planet.

The journey takes place in a framework that corresponds to
the geographical knowledge of the time. After crossing Nubia,
whose king is lord of Lesser India and Ethiopia, the travelers
head toward Greater India, about which the old pilgrim, according to Mézières, has gathered information from a merchant who
lived there for fifty years. They then go on to the country of
Prester John which is under the domination of the Great Khan
of Tartary. After Cathay, Persia, Babylon, Armenia, and Syria,
the ladies reach the Holy Land where they visit Jerusalem. They
then cross Ethiopia, Tunisia, and Morocco, before reaching Constantinople. Led by Ardent Desire, the queen and her ladies visit
Bulgaria, and Russia until they reach the borders of Tartary.

Ardent Desire then leads Queen Truth and her companions
to the city of Marienburg, founded by the Teutonic Order. The
queen presides over a consistory in which, while admiring the
Rule of the Order, she warns the knights against pride, lust, and
avarice. Philippe de Mézières was familiar with Germany and
the Nordic countries, where he had attended meetings of the
Teutonic Order. He had also traveled in northern regions, Livo-
nia, Norway, Sweden, and Denmark, where the narrative continues. He describes with great charm how herring fishing takes
place, something he had been able to observe in an arm of the

sea between Norway and Denmark. The fishing takes place in September and October, when large numbers of fish move from one sea to another. The journey continues in Westphalia, Holland, Zeeland, Frisia, Saxony, and Bohemia. After crossing Swabia and Bavaria, the queen reaches Austria and then Hungary. According to Philippe de Mézières, the evils suffered by the country are caused by the sins of the inhabitants and a bad government. From there, flying over the mountains, the travelers reach Venice where they are welcomed with great honor.

Until this point, the journey has unfolded at a rapid pace. Led by Ardent Desire and Good Hope, the queen and her ladies have traveled over the greater part of the world without encountering a place capable of receiving them worthily. They are to spend a long time in Western Europe.

Mézières knew Italy well. Thanks to the queen's journey, he can set out the struggles between the various cities and especially speak of the Great Schism and the moral decline of the clergy. He prefers Venice to the other cities of the peninsula and writes in praise of it. "It is one of the noblest and freest cities in the entire world and marvelously situated, that is, in the sea about a league from the mainland." Leaving Venice, the travelers go to Brindisi where they embark for Sicily, see Salerno, and then passing through Naples, arrive in Rome. They then visit the different regions of Italy embroiled in civil wars: Tuscany, Lombardy, and Piedmont. Queen Truth and her ladies preside over a consistory in Genoa, and then go on to Avignon. The author can thus, for the third time, describe in detail not landscapes, but the troubles the Church was then suffering. If ecclesiastical dignitaries in Rome have the features of animals, in Genoa the pope appears as an accused criminal before his judges. In Avignon, the Vices come before the Papal Court to show their influence in the world, particularly among the upper clergy.

The journey continues in the South of France and then in Spain. Heading toward the north, Queen Truth and her ladies pass through Béarn and Normandy to London, where they preside over an assembly in the cathedral, in the presence of the young King Richard II. After Ireland and Scotland, they cross the sea, come to Flanders, and finally go to Paris. The final tableau represents the apotheosis of King Charles VI transformed into Moses.

At the beginning of the work, Divine Providence had given the old pilgrim the task of bringing the sovereign queens to earth. At the end, it returns to his cell to console him for having failed.

An imaginary journey might have a properly scientific interest. Nicolas Oresme who, like Philippe de Mézières, frequented the court of Charles V, imagines that Plato goes around the world heading west, while Socrates walks at the same speed toward the east. In relation to Peter who remains stationary, Plato will be one day behind and Socrates one day ahead. We must distinguish, says Oresme, among the natural day of twenty-four hours, the day of the traveler heading east or west, and the artificial day, that is, the time included between the rising and the setting of the sun. The day is longer for someone going west and shorter for someone going east. A reader of *Around the World in Eighty Days* by Jules Verne will think of the final scene in which Phileas Fogg believes that he has lost his bet, but has in fact won it because he took one day less than planned by heading east.

Imaginary journeys, finally, were connected to superstition and to religion. In the early eleventh century, in book XIX of his *Decree,* entitled *Healer or Doctor,* Bishop Burchard of Worms writes:

> Have you shared the belief of many women of the retinue of Satan? That during the silence of the night . . . you have the power, corporeal as you are, to go out through a closed door, to fly through space with other women like you? That you have the power to kill with invisible weapons Christians who have been baptized and redeemed by the Blood of Christ, and to cook and eat their flesh?

Until the thirteenth century, the educated refused to believe in the nocturnal witch, while the people continued to be credulous. The Englishman Gervaise of Tilbury, in a work composed around 1211, considers the idea widespread that men and women fly over great distances at night, an idea that doctors, he says, attribute to nightmares.

The nocturnal flight of certain women appears in another popular belief. In the early tenth century, Reginon of Prüm, provided the text of a canon destined for great success entitled *Episcopi:*

Have you believed or have you participated in a superstition
to which villainous women, minions of Satan deceived by
diabolical fantasies, claim to give themselves? At night,
with Diana, the pagan goddess, along with a crowd of other
women, they ride on animals, cover great distances in the
silence of deep night, obey the orders of Diana their mistress, and put themselves at her service on certain specified
nights. If only these witches could perish in their impiety
without bringing many others down with them to their
doom! In fact, many people led into error believe that these
rides with Diana really exist, and they separate themselves
from the true faith, and fall into the error of the pagans in
believing that there can exist a divinity or a goddess outside
of the only God.

Two ancient beliefs in nocturnal journeys thus coexisted.

Beginning in the thirteenth century, the previously incredu-
lous clergy imagined that these were devils who had taken on
human form. In the fourteenth and fifteenth centuries, no longer
making a distinction between nocturnal witches and devils of
the night, they came to join them in the same condemnation.
And some imagined that groups of witches went to the witches'
sabbath at night, paid homage to Satan, and had sexual relations
with him. The witches' sabbath was no longer a deceptive dream,
it was now considered a reality.

Some believed that the earthly paradise still existed on our
planet. In the sixth century, Cosmas Indicoleustes, a former
merchant and traveler who later lived in Alexandria and had
perhaps become a monk, wrote that the habitable earth is surrounded by an ocean beyond which an outer earth includes the
paradise in which Adam and Eve live. After the Original Sin,
Adam and his descendants remained on this outer earth, but in
an arid spot. And it was only at the time of the Flood that Noah
and his family reached our earth. Since then, men have been
unable to cross that ocean. Nevertheless, the two earths are connected by the four rivers that the Old Testament has coming
from paradise. In discussing Asia, Isidore of Seville declares that
it includes many regions, among which is paradise. Peter Lombard, bishop of Paris, who died in 1160, wrote in his *Somme des
sentences* that "paradise is found in the eastern part of the world,
separated by a large stretch of land or water from the regions

inhabited by men." And speaking of the source of the Nile in his narrative of the Seventh Crusade, Joinville writes:

> We must first speak of the river which comes into Egypt from the earthly paradise. . . . At a point before the river enters Egypt, people whose custom it is cast their opened nets into the river in the evening; and when morning comes they find in their nets products that are sold by weight that are brought into that country, that is, ginger, rhubarb, aloe wood, and cinnamon. And it is said that these products come from the earthly paradise, for the wind blows them down from the trees in paradise, as the wind in our country blows dry wood down in the forest.

Christopher Columbus, while doubting the locations of the earthly paradise indicated by his predecessors, shared the traditional opinion on the subject. Thus, relating his third voyage in 1498, during which he reached South America near the mouth of the Orinoco, he writes:

> Holy Scripture testifies that Our Lord made the earthly Paradise in which he planted the Tree of Life. From it there flowed four main rivers: the Ganges in India, the Tigris and the Euphrates in Asia . . . and the Nile, which rises in Ethiopia and flows into the sea at Alexandria.
> I do not find and have never found any Greek or Latin writings which definitely state the worldly situation of the earthly Paradise, nor have I seen any world map which establishes its position except by deduction. . . . I believe that, if I pass below the Equator, on reaching these higher regions I shall find a much cooler climate and a greater difference in the stars and waters. Not that I believe it possible to sail to the extreme summit or that it is covered by water, or that it is even possible to go there. For I believe that the earthly Paradise lies here, which no one can enter except by God's leave.[74]

---

74. *The Four Voyages*, 220–21.

In these circumstances, it is easier to understand the *Voyage de saint Brendan,* a poem in French composed in the first quarter of the twelfth century by an Anglo-Norman poet. It recounts the seven-year odyssey undertaken by an Irish abbot and seventeen monks in the sixth century. "Now, a desire arose in him: he often prays to God that He will show him paradise, the first home of Adam, our inheritance from which we were dismissed." The boat drifts for years, with ports such as the back of a large fish that the sailors believed was a small island, the isle of birds who are guilty angels in a kind of purgatory, an abbey outside time and material contingencies. Dangers threaten them. A griffin plunges from the sky and tries to seize the pilgrims, but it is killed by a dragon. The monks can continue their journey. After seven years, they arrive in sight of hell, represented by a mountain with a black slope. Then, led by an angel, they approach paradise.

> They first see a wall rising to the clouds, with no crenelles, nor parapet, nor bartizan, nor turret of any kind. None of the monks knows, truly, of what material this wall is made, but it is even whiter than snow: the heavenly king erected it. He did it without the slightest effort, all in one piece and without a gap. It is sprinkled with gems that give off a great glittering light: choice chrysolite spotted with gold in great quantity; the wall blazes, glowing with topaz, chrysoprase, hyacinth, chalcedony, emeralds, and sardonyx; on the edges, jaspers and amethysts glimmer brightly; there are also brilliant jacinth, crystal, and beryl that reflect light on each other: the artist who set these stones had great talent. They reflect the great brilliance of their colors among themselves and colors blend one with another. The sea laps against the high mountains of hard marble that stretch far out from the wall; and above this chain of mountains rises another mountain entirely of pure gold. At the summit of this mountain rises the wall that encloses the flowers of paradise. It is this wall, set in a dominant position, which [had it not been for Adam] should have been our shelter.

But the entry is guarded by dragons. Fortunately, a very handsome young man arrives, a messenger of God, who welcomes the monks and leads them into paradise.

They see a very fertile land with fine woods and prairies. The meadows, splendid and always in flower, are in fact a garden. The flowers smell very sweetly, as is fitting for a place inhabited by saints, a spot where the trees and flowers give delight to those who see them, and where the fruits and the aromas are of incalculable richness. Neither brambles, nor thistles, nor nettles grow there profusely; there is no tree or plant that does not give off a pleasant aroma. The trees are always full of fruit and the flowers always in full bloom regardless of the season, which does not change; it is always summer and the temperature is always mild. The fruit is always ripe on the trees, the flowers constantly produce their pollen; the woods are always full of game, and all the rivers have excellent fish. There are rivers in which milk flows. This abundance is everywhere: the rose bushes exude honey because of the dew descending from heaven. All of the mountains are of gold and every stone is worth a fortune. The sun never stops shining with all its brightness, and no wind, no breath of air disturbs the slightest hair, and no cloud in the sky blocks the light of the sun. Whoever lives there will suffer no harm, he will feel no storm, he will be sheltered from heat, from cold, from affliction, from hunger, from thirst, from privation. He will have everything he wants, in abundance. He is sure of never being deprived of what he desires the most; he will always have it at hand.

Brendan follows the young man onto a mountain as high as a cypress from which he sees wonders. Then, his guide says to him: "You may know no more before your return; for here, where you have come in flesh and blood, you will soon return in spirit." And indeed, many journeys in the Middle Ages took place in the beyond.

# TEN

# the beyond

Until the seventh century, journeys to the beyond appeared infrequently,[75] because the Church tried to suppress folk culture which it considered to be allied with paganism. In contrast, the following period, from the seventh to the tenth century, saw the flourishing of visions, particularly under the influence of monasticism. The development of folk elements, due in particular to the rise of secular culture in the twelfth century, was later countered by a learned culture that rationalized the beyond. In 1300, Dante constructed a detailed and precise geography of hell, purgatory, and paradise.

## THE ITINERARIES

The visionary sometimes begins his journey in a state of wakefulness. In a vision probably written shortly before his death in 888, Emperor Charles the Fat reports that the event occurred after the singing of nocturn, when he was about to go to sleep:

> During a holy Sunday night, after celebrating the holy office of nocturn, while I was going to lie down to rest and I wanted to sleep and have a nap, a voice spoke to me in a fearsome tone: "Charles, your spirit will soon leave you and a vision

---

75. The "medieval imagination" is the subject of many works by Jacques Le Goff.

will reveal to you the just judgment of God and some predictions concerning you; but your spirit will return to you within the hour."

Most frequently, tormenting devils would appear during sleep and then the journey would begin.

On November 4, 824, a monk named Wetti died in Reichenau; on the eve of his death, he reported a vision he had had and his narrative was transcribed by Heito, the abbot of the monastery. Soon thereafter, the poet Walahfrid Strabon, abbot of Saint-Gall, composed a version in verse. Wetti was ill and resting when an evil spirit, who was very ugly, appeared holding instruments of torture in his hands; this was followed by a troop of evil spirits. Fortunately, magnificent men wearing monastic habits dispersed the devils. An angel of incredible beauty then conversed with the monk. Thus ended a first vision. Night fell and Wetti awoke and asked the monks to pray that God would forgive his sins. He fell asleep and the same angel appeared and congratulated him for having found refuge in the Lord, then led him away.

Dante found himself somewhere on earth, first during the night between Thursday and Good Friday, April 7 and 8, 1300, then on Good Friday morning.

> Midway on our life's journey, I found myself
> In dark woods, the right road lost . . .
>
> . . . though how I came to enter
> I cannot well say, being so full of sleep
> Whatever moment it was I began to blunder
>
> Off the true path. But when I came to stop
> Below a hill that marked one end of the valley
> That had pierced my heart with terror, I looked up
>
> Toward the crest and saw its shoulders already
> Mantled in rays of that bright planet that shows
> The road to everyone, whatever our journey.[76]

---

76. *Inferno*, tr. Robert Pinsky (New York: Farrar, Straus and Giroux, 1994), I, 1–15.

After resting, Dante starts again across the wilderness. Virgil appears and proposes to guide him through hell and purgatory, to be succeeded by Beatrice in paradise. But how was the other world to be reached?

The first way was by ascension, which was favored by early writers, as Claude Carozzi has shown. Saint Fursy was an Irish monk who died in Mazerolles in 649 or 650, whose life seems to have been written by one of his disciples shortly after his death. Fursy's soul is borne off by angels who allow him to cross a region filled with devils. This is an obscure region where angels fight against indistinct forms shooting flaming arrows that are deflected by shields. Fursy is then invited by one of his companions to look at the world which appears to him in the form of a dark valley. This is a vertical trajectory that can be compared to the flight of the soul.

The vision of Barontus, which takes place in 678 or 679, also comes from the monastic world. Barontus was a noble layman who had withdrawn to an abbey for his final years. After a day and night of apparent death, he reported his adventure, which was immediately transcribed. The hero's soul is borne off toward heaven by Saint Raphael despite the efforts of devils pulling it downward. It passes near hell before beginning the ascent to paradise. The structure of the beyond seems to be vertical: hell is underground, paradise celestial; between the two, in the air, devils try to intercept souls.

Between the eighth and eleventh centuries, notably in the Carolingian era, the journey into the beyond becomes "terrestrial." In his *History of the English Church and People,* the Venerable Bede (†735) reports, among others, the vision of Drycthelm. He was a devout layman, the head of a family, who died one night after a serious illness. At daybreak he returned to life. After dividing his property, he retired to an isolated place to do penance. He described his adventure in the following terms. After his death, a guide appears and leads him on foot toward the east. First they cross a valley with flames on the left and ice on the right. A little further along, they see a chasm, the location of hell. They change direction and walk on. They see a tremendous wall, behind which are fields filled with flowers, but this is not yet the kingdom of heaven. In this vision, the four locations, the place of purgation, hell, the earthly paradise, and the kingdom of heaven are set in a continuous landscape with two directions.

This pattern is found in most Carolingian visions, but the geography of the beyond was diversified. Wetti's guide shows him very high mountains of incredible beauty. A very broad river in which the damned are immersed surrounds them. The monk also sees a building in the shape of a castle made of wood and disordered stones, made indistinct by the darkness. Further on, a dwelling without an enclosing wall has become uninhabitable, for two counts are washing themselves nearby and giving off an unbearable stench. In contrast, paradise contains magnificent palaces. Writers did not seek to connect the various elements. At most, we can observe that they are describing a world close to our own.

With the eleventh century, the journey through the air returns. For example, between 1148 and 1158, Rainier related the vision of his master Jean, a monk of Saint-Laurent in Liège. During an illness, the monk visits the beyond, guided by his patron saint. He feels the sensation of an ascension. At the level of the lunar circle, he sees beneath him a zone filled with darkness in which larvae seem to be stirring. Toward the east, men with sad countenances are seated, out of reach of the devils. Jean then arrives before a temple from which issue music and singing. As he comes back down, he notices corpses tormented by devils. In the end he returns to his body.

The theme of ascension appears in the *Book of Muhammad's Ladder,* the original Arabic text of which is lost, although there is a Latin translation from the thirteenth century. The book describes the extraordinary journey of the Prophet, carried into the beyond by the angel Gabriel who appears to him as he is falling asleep. The movement through the air from Mecca to Jerusalem takes place on a winged horse, Al-Buraq, "larger than a donkey and smaller than a mule. It had a human face and its coat was of pearls, with tufts of emeralds, and its tail of rubies; its eyes were brighter than the sun. It had the legs and hooves of a camel." After praying in the Temple, Muhammad is led outside by Gabriel, who shows him

a ladder that came from the first heaven down to earth where I was standing. This ladder was the most beautiful thing that had ever been seen. Its foot touched the stone near which

I had at first dismounted. This is how its rungs were made: the first was ruby, the second emerald, the third the purest white pearl, and each of the others was made of a different precious stone, all enhanced with pearls and the purest gold, so richly that no human heart could imagine it. It was covered with green velvet brighter than emerald, and completely surrounded by angels guarding it. It was so bright that a man could barely look at it. Gabriel took me by the hand and, raising me from the ground, placed me on the first rung of the ladder and said: "Climb, Muhammad!" I climbed and Gabriel climbed with me. All the angels who were assigned to guarding the ladder accompanied me.

Dante's itinerary through the three places of *The Divine Comedy* seems much more complex. Following Virgil, the poet visits thirty regions, ten in each place. Hell is an immense cone situated in the northern hemisphere of the earth with its point in the center. It forms a circle on the surface, one point of which is the entry gate. The cone contains two parts, upper hell with a vestibule and five circles, and lower hell with four circles; between the two are walls. The centers of these ten subdivisions are on a straight line, the vertical axis of the cone, that passes through Jerusalem. Their diameters progressively diminish as the torments of the damned increase. To move from one circle to another, it is necessary to descend, except for the fifth and sixth circles between which there is no difference in level.

Dante and his guide go on foot to the banks of the Acheron, which they cross in an unknown way. The journey continues in the same way, with some modifications. To cross the Styx, the travelers use the boat of Phlegyas

> Bow never drove
> Arrow through air so quickly as then came
> Skimming across the water a little skiff
>
> Guided by a single boatman at the helm:
> "Now, evil soul," he cried out, "you are caught!"
> "Phlegyas, Phlegyas—you roar in vain this time,"
>
> My lord responded. "You'll have us in your boat
> Only as long as it takes to cross the fen."
> (*Inferno* VIII, 13–20)

Dante is sometimes helped during the rest of the journey. For example, the seventh circle contains three zones: a river of blood that he crosses on the back of the centaur Nessus; a forest; a desert of burning sand over which a path must be followed to avoid burning the feet. The descent continues on the back of the monster Geryon, for they cannot go on by natural means. The visit to the eighth circle takes place on bridges and dikes and in ditches. When the travelers reach a pit, they need the help of the giant Antaeus to descend. Crossing the ninth circle, a frozen river, they reach Lucifer, whose lower parts are in the southern hemisphere.

> "But night is rising again, and it is time
> That we depart, for we have seen the whole."
> As he requested, I put my arms round him,
>
> And waiting until the wings were opened full
> He took advantage of the time and place
> And grasped the shaggy flank, and gripping still,
>
> From tuft to tuft descended through the mass
> Of matted hair and crusts of ice. And then,
> When we had reached the pivot of the thighs,
>
> Just where the haunch is at its thickest, with strain
> And effort my master brought around his head
> To where he'd had his legs: and from there on
>
> He grappled the hair as someone climbing would—
> So I supposed we were heading back to Hell.
> "Cling tight, for it is stairs like these," he sighed
>
> Like one who is exhausted, "which we must scale
> To part from so much evil." Then he came up
> Through a split stone, and placed me on its sill,
>
> And climbed up toward me with his cautious step.
>                                    (*Inferno* XXXIV, 67–85)

The descent takes about twenty-four hours, and the ascent of purgatory twenty-two.

Virgil, who knows the way in hell, seems a little disoriented in purgatory; on many occasions, he has to ask souls for directions. One hour before sunrise on Easter Sunday, April 10, 1300, he and Dante arrive on the island where the mountain of purgatory is located. After the guardian gives them some rather vague advice, they walk east to the foot of the mountain which is too sheer to be climbed at that spot. Retracing their steps, they discover a track so steep that they need both hands and feet to climb. They reach a terrace and sit down.

> We made our upward way through rifted rock;
> along each side the edges pressed on us;
> the ground beneath required feet and hands.
> When we had reached the upper rim of that
> steep bank, emerging on the open slope,
> I said: "My master, what way shall we take?"[77]

Virgil instructs Dante that fatigue diminishes as they ascend.

The travelers set out again. But because it is not possible to climb after sunset, they turn toward a valley to spend the night. When he awakes, Dante is surprised to find himself at the gate of purgatory, where he has been carried in the arms of Saint Lucy. The travelers reach the first cornice at around nine in the morning. Now all they need do is to go on to each terrace, always heading to the right; the mountainside is thus on the left and the abyss on the right. They reach the next terrace by flights of stairs. At the top of the last stairway is the earthly paradise. The ascent of purgatory, begun on Easter Monday at nine or ten in the morning, concludes after sunrise on Wednesday.

Dante and Virgil, accompanied by the poet Statius, who has been delivered, head toward the east. They arrive at the stream of Lethe. Suddenly, the forest brightens, and a mystical procession appears on the other side of the river surrounding a cart onto which Beatrice descends from heaven. Dante wishes to speak to Virgil, but he has disappeared. When Beatrice reproaches him for his sins, he faints. Coming to, he crosses Lethe and

---

77. *Purgatorio*, in *The Divine Comedy*, tr. Allen Mandelbaum (New York: Alfred A. Knopf, Everyman Library, 1995), IV, 31–36.

follows the procession. Reaching the source of both Lethe and Eunoë, he drinks the waters of remembrance. He can now go on to paradise.

Like hell and purgatory, paradise contains ten regions: the nine moving heavens and the Empyrean. The ascent is in a straight line from one heaven to the next. Dante arrives on a planet, accompanies it briefly in its rotation, and then moves on to the next highest heaven. He recognizes his change of location by the increase in the beauty of Beatrice, for he has no awareness of his movements.

Travelers into the beyond, often at the price of great difficulties, thus traverse various places. Fortunately, they have guides to show them the way and support them. Sometimes, as for Charles the Fat, a trick makes it easier for them to resist the devils. His guide, holding a ball of bright wool in his hand, orders him to take a thread and tie it firmly to his right thumb. Devils try to grasp the thread with hooks, but the reflection of the rays makes that impossible. When they then try to hook Charles and hurl him into a pit of sulphur, his guide throws a thread from the ball of wool over his shoulder, wraps it around him, and draws him vigorously behind him.

The return to earth is far from pleasant. When he is on the point of being buried, Saint Salvi returns to life, "shakes himself, as though he were waking from a deep sleep, then opens his eyes, raises his hands, and cries out: 'Oh merciful Lord, what have you done to me to allow me to return to this dark place which is the dwelling of the world when your mercy in heaven was better for me than the hateful life of this world?'" In the course of his vision, he has in fact seen the glory of the blessed. Barontus takes a guide, Brother Frammoald, to return to earth; he promises that he will pray at his tomb and will sweep it every Sunday. But his return is full of pitfalls; after the disappearance of his guide, he has no help, and it takes a violent wind for his soul to return to his body. He can then wake up. Many are troubled by the weight of their bodies that they have forgotten for a few moments. Opening his eyes, Wetti calls the monks who have watched over him during the night. Moved by his vision and full of anxiety, he tells them what he has seen and asks that as soon as the father abbot arrives his words be taken down. When he is told that the monks, absorbed by their nocturnal meditation, do not dare break silence, he tells them to imprint on wax what he has just told them, for he fears that he will no longer be capable of relating what he has seen and heard. He must set out his vision for the common good and risks severe punishment if he fails to do so. Moreover, holy virgins have interceded with God on his behalf to grant him a long life; but does this mean eternal life or life on earth? When the abbot comes to see him, he tells him and the four monks with him, in speech and writing, everything he has seen and heard. He asks that they pray for him, for he will die the next day. For that whole day and night, and the following day until the evening, he spends his time expressing his anguish, worrying, moaning, and sighing. When night comes, he asks his brother monks to sing psalms for him. He dies after receiving the last rites.

As Raoul Glaber notes: "We must not forget that when obvious wonders strike the eyes of men still inhabiting their bodies, whether they come from good or evil spirits, those men do not have much longer for the life of the flesh after seeing those things."

Once they reached the beyond, what did travelers find?

## HELL

Even if Pope Gregory the Great was not the first to evoke the world beyond the earth, his text is of great significance because many later narratives refer to it. After leaving his body, a soldier returns to life and recounts his adventures.

> He said that there was a bridge, and under this bridge a river flowed with waves of sinister blackness, exuding a mist with an unbearable stench. . . . This bridge was the bridge of an ordeal. If an evil person tried to cross it, he fell into the dark and malodorous river. . . . The soldier claimed to have recognized Étienne on this bridge. He tried to cross, but he stumbled. Half his body was already hanging over the bridge. Hideous black men rose up from the river, pulling him down by the legs. Very handsome white men drew him upward by the arms. During this struggle, with the good spirits pulling upward and the evil pulling downward, the visionary returned to his body and did not know the outcome of the battle.

In hell are set the proud, the lustful, the avaricious, the liars, the envious, and the infidels, who all burn together. This is a corporeal fire, according to Gregory, for infernal punishments are not only eternal, but real. And he tries to show that a corporeal fire can torture an incorporeal soul. Did the soul of the evil rich man not pray to Lazarus to give him water? But Gregory qualifies his thinking. Thus, the soldier's vision represents in allegorical form the good or evil deeds accomplished on this earth by men who have now left it. Nevertheless, there is a kind of geography with an underground hell. "It is in those islands [in Sicily]," he writes, "that the furnaces of torment are open, spewing forth fire."

Valerio of Bierzo seems to have been the first to provide a description of hell, in the last quarter of the seventh century. Bonellus, who has first been led to paradise, is thrown into the abyss of hell, from a mountain top through a rift in the earth. At the bottom of the abyss, he sees the devil, with the head of an iron bird and in chains, as well as an enormous fire and a sea of burning pitch. Nearby, in the lower pit, the damned suffer the most terrible punishments. He meets three devils. Archers shoot arrows at him. Hell thus really becomes established.

The most precise description is provided by *The Divine Comedy*. Dante contemplates harsher and harsher punishments as he goes on and the sins to be expiated grow more serious. Let us then traverse hell in his company. In the vestibule are the neutral and cowardly spirits. These are the many humans "[w]hose lives earned neither honor nor bad fame." "Hapless ones never alive, their bare skin galled/By wasps and flies, blood trickling down the face"(*Inferno* III, 31, 54–55). After crossing Acheron, which separates the vestibule from hell proper, we arrive in upper hell. Limbo houses unbaptized virtuous spirits, that is, pagans and infidels, suffering no punishment but the permanently unsatisfied desire to contemplate God. The second circle is reserved for the lustful, swept along by a violent wind. Dante faints and awakes in the third circle, "a realm of cold and heavy rain—"

A dark, accursed torrent eternally poured
With changeless measure and nature. Enormous hail
And tainted water mixed with snow are showered

Steadily through the shadowy air of Hell;
The soil they drench gives off a putrid odor.
*(Inferno* VI, 6–11)

This is the punishment of the gluttons lying in the mud. In the fourth circle, spenders and hoarders roll rocks while exchanging insults. Dante arrives at the Styx, where he sees the wrathful

Within that bog, all naked and muddy—with looks
Of fury, striking each other: with a hand
But also with their heads, chests, feet, and backs,

Teeth tearing piecemeal.
*(Inferno* VII, 97–100)

In lower hell are the sinners guilty of malice. First are the heretics who occupy the sixth circle. In a vast plain, their tombs make the ground uneven:

among the graves were flames
That made the sepulchers glow with fiercer heat
Than a smith could need. Among these catacombs

The lids were raised, with sounds of woe so great
Those within surely suffered horrible pain.
*(Inferno* IX, 106–110)

Lower hell exudes a horrible stench, and Virgil therefore advises Dante to delay the descent to get used to the fetid air.

The seventh circle contains the violent. Those who have been cruel to their fellow men are immersed in a river of boiling blood. The violent against themselves are made up of suicides and willful spendthrifts. The former are transformed into trees:

I reached my hand
A little in front of me and twisted off

One shoot of a mighty thornbush—and it moaned,
"Why do you break me?" Then after it had grown
Darker with blood, it began again and mourned,

"Why have you torn me? Have you no pity then?
Once we were men, now we are stumps of wood."
(*Inferno* XIII, 29–35)

The latter are torn to pieces by bitches.

Behind them, eager as greyhounds off the leash,
Black bitches filled the woods, avid and quick.
They set their teeth on the one who stopped to crouch,

And tore his limbs apart; and then they took
The wretched members away.
(*Inferno* XIII, 2118–22)

The violent against God are stretched out on the sand and a rain of fire comes down on them. The violent against nature, that is, the sodomites, run beneath this rain; in contrast, the usurers are seated.

While the seventh circle harbors those who have caused harm by force, the eighth receives those who have done wrong by fraud. They are contained in ten ditches called bolgia. Seducers and panders, whipped by devils, run ceaselessly backward. Flatterers are immersed in a river of shit. Simoniacs have their heads in circular holes while flames burn the soles of their feet.

From each hole stuck
A sinner's feet and legs: the rest of him,
From the calf up, inside. They twitched and shook

Because the soles of both feet were aflame—
So violently, it seemed their joints could burst
Rope or snap withes.
(*Inferno* XIX, 19–24)

The diviners walk with their heads turned backward. The barrators are immersed in burning pitch. The hypocrites wear golden cowls that are lined with lead. Thieves who have stolen God's property are bitten by snakes, become ashes, and then resume human form.

Amid this horde, cruel, grim, and dense,
People were running, naked and terrified,
Without a hope of hiding or a chance

At heliotrope for safety. Their hands were tied
Behind their backs—with snakes, that thrust between
Where the legs meet, entwining tail and head

Into a knot in front. And look!—at one
Near us a serpent darted, and transfixed
Him at the point where neck and shoulders join.

No *o* or *i* could be made with strokes as fast
As he took fire and withered away,
Sinking; and when his ashes came to rest

Ruined on the ground, the dust spontaneously
Resumed its former shape.

*(Inferno* XXIV, 91–104)

Other thieves are turned into snakes. Flames surround the false
counselors. A devil's sword pierces the schismatics.

No barrel staved-in
And missing its end-piece ever gaped as wide
As the man I saw split open from his chin

Down to the farting-place, and from the splayed
Trunk the spilled entrails dangled between his thighs.
I saw his organs, and the sack that makes the bread

We swallow turn to shit.

*(Inferno* XXVIII, 22–28)

Scabs cover the counterfeiters of metals who scratch themselves
constantly. The impersonators have become mad and tear their
companions to pieces. The counterfeiters of currency suffer cru-
elly from thirst. Raging fever torments the perjurers.

The journey concludes with the ninth circle, which holds
the traitors, in four subdivisions. They are all held fast in the

ice. They have betrayed their families, their country or their party, their guests, or their benefactors. Lucifer devours the guiltiest: Judas, Brutus, and Cassius, who betrayed the Church and the Empire.

> The teeth of each mouth held a sinner, kept
> As by a flax rake: thus he held three of them
>
> In agony. For the one the front mouth gripped [Judas],
> The teeth were as nothing to the claws, which sliced
> And tore the skin until his back was stripped.
>
> (*Inferno* XXXIV, 56–60)

## PURGATORY

Jacques Le Goff situates the birth of purgatory in the twelfth century, although he points out that the idea of a place in which punishment is not permanent existed well before. We have only to read the visions of the early Middle Ages. After the painful journey to the damned, let us turn to this place of expectation and hope, though still generally full of harshness. Drycthelm, whose journey beyond the grave is narrated by the Venerable Bede, comes to a broad valley where he sees many souls blown from one side to the other by the wind. When he believes that he is in hell, his guide tells him that he is mistaken. A similar mistake occurs when he thinks he recognizes the kingdom of heaven in the meadow where men dressed in white are walking. His guide explains:

> "The valley that you saw, with its horrible burning flames and icy cold, is the place where souls are tried and punished who have delayed to confess and amend their wicked ways, and who at last had recourse to penitence at the hour of death, and so depart this life. Because they confessed and were penitent, although only at death, they will all be admitted into the Kingdom of Heaven on the Day of Judgement. . . . This flowery place, where you see these fair young people so happy and resplendent, is where souls are received who die having done good, but are not so perfect as to merit

immediate entry into the Kingdom of Heaven. But at the Day of Judgement they shall all see Christ, and enter upon the joys of His heavenly Kingdom."[78]

Drycthelm has visited a place intended for purgation. More precisely, he has seen two places, one close to hell, the other to paradise, and not a veritable intermediate place.

The vision of Charles the Fat in the late ninth century describes a place distinct from hell, a place that it is possible to leave. His uncle Lothaire says to Charles: "I know that you have come through a place of expiation where your father, my brother, has been set in a heated bath intended for him; but the mercy of God will soon deliver him from that punishment."

After his visit to hell, Dante arrives at the foot of the mountain of purification on a shore with only one inhabitant, Cato, the guardian of purgatory. This is where souls land and pass through rapidly. Any who stop are subject to stinging rebukes.

> "What have we here, you laggard spirits?
> What negligence, what lingering is this?
> Quick, to the mountain to cast off the slough
> that will not let you see God show Himself!"
> (*Purgatorio* II, 120–23)

Dante and Virgil imitate the troop that immediately stops singing and runs toward the slope.

The lower part of the mountain is a place of waiting, where the indolent spend some time before reaching the place where they will suffer their punishments. On the way, the poet meets various kinds of indolent people. Some neglected to obtain forgiveness from the Church, although they repented. Sinners have died violent deaths without receiving absolution, having repented only at the last moment. The last category includes princes who were taken up by public matters and left too late the salvation of their souls.

The angel guarding the gate to purgatory allows Dante and Virgil to enter. The two poets will now climb the seven cornices devoted to the seven deadly sins. One by one they meet those

---

78. Bede, *A History of the English Church and People*, 287–88.

who have succumbed to them. The proud, with heads lowered, their chests down to their knees, and crushed by burdensome stones, are condemned for their arrogance; they walk slowly, reciting a paraphrase of the Our Father. The envious, wearing coarse hair-shirts and their eyes sealed by iron wire, are seated; those who, during their life on earth, constantly cast jealous glances at the happiness of their fellows, can see nothing. They ask the saints to take pity on them, while they had often had no pity for others. The angry walk in a thick smoke that prevents them from seeing, analogous to the sin that blinded them. They pray to the Lamb of God, representing the gentleness for which they had contempt. Those whose sloth has removed them from spiritual good run without ceasing, the only inhabitants of purgatory who do not pray. At this point, Virgil explains to Dante the nature of love and how it is linked to free will. The covetous and the prodigal, condemned to the same punishments, are stretched on the ground face down, immobile, bound hand and foot. During their earthly life, there were interested only in the things of this world; cupidity did not allow them to respond to the love of God. The gluttonous, pale and thin, come and go before fruit and water that they may not enjoy. They weep while proclaiming the glory of God. They now know that the mouth is intended not only to assuage bodily appetites. On the last cornice, the lustful sing in flames. They form two processions, for some have merely violated natural law, while others have committed excesses and perversions. Virgil and Dante are gradually drawing nearer to the earthly paradise and the heavenly paradise, for the organization of purgatory is the opposite of that of hell. In hell, sins are ranked in order of increasing severity, while in purgatory their gravity diminishes as they climb. The poet has now reached the earthly paradise. The angel of chastity tells him that to go on, he must cross a wall of fire. Virgil disappears to be replaced by Beatrice.

Dante has a dynamic vision of purgatory. The future blessed are purified, climbing a mountain that allows them to reach heaven. The ascent is steep "and the peak so high it is beyond sight."

Fire is a major presence, to the point that Dante believes he has returned to hell. He is terrified by the fire into which the lustful are plunged.

There, from the wall, the mountain hurls its flames;
but, from the terrace side, there whirls a wind
that pushes back the fire and limits it;
thus on the open side, proceeding one
by one we went; I feared the fire on
the left, and on the right, the precipice.
(Purgatorio XXV, 112–17)

He looks with fear on the wall of fire that separates him from
the earthly paradise. Fortunately, Virgil reassures him:

Be sure: although you were to spend a full
one thousand years within this fire's center,
your head would not be balder by one hair.
(Purgatorio XXVII, 25–27)

The journey through purgatory thus in no way resembles a
pleasant stroll. But the fire of hell and the fire of purgatory are
very different: "My son, you've seen the temporary fire/and the
eternal fire" (*Purgatorio* XXVII, 127–28)

The ascent of the mountain of purification is a march toward
the light. Between the darkness of hell and the brightness of
paradise, purgatory is a zone that gradually becomes brighter. In
the earthly paradise, heavenly light is already anticipated: "Darkness fled in all directions."

## PARADISE

Paradise provided much less inspiration than hell for writers of
visions. It is in fact relatively easy to imagine torments, but
much more difficult to show the experience of joy. The people
of the Middle Ages, who appreciated light, imagined it as having reached its greatest intensity in their attempt to make the
heavenly dwelling palpable. Bede writes that a nun who was
about to die asked that the candles be put out, for she found
them dim in comparison to the light she had already glimpsed.

Another characteristic of these visions was the presence of
precious metals. Gregory the Great indicated the presence in a
large meadow of men dressed in white living in a house made of
golden bricks. Wetti sees arches of gold and silver. Paradise not

only delights the eye but also the sense of smell. Saint Salvi breathes a sweet aroma that provides him food and drink for three days.

God manifests Himself through light and through language. Saint Salvi reaches a place above which "was suspended a cloud more luminous than any light. There you could see neither sun, nor moon, nor any other star, but more splendidly than them all, it shone with a natural brightness, and a murmur came from the cloud that resembled the murmur of flowing water. . . . You heard only the voice; for the one who spoke was absolutely impossible to see."

Following Muhammad and Dante, let us now journey into paradise.

After crossing the eight heavens, Muhammad has encountered God. Returning, he joins Gabriel again who leads him through paradise. They approach a wall whose stones are of gold, silver, and rubies. The mortar holding them together is made of musk and amber dissolved in rose water with an exquisite odor. Gabriel explains to Muhammad that behind this wall is an orchard. "And you must know that to say that there is only one paradise is true, because paradise means only place of delights; but God has distributed these delights in a great number of forms and gives them to His people according to each one's deserts." The seventh paradise is higher than the others and from there they can all be seen. God stays there when He wishes to see the paradises.

Muhammad provides details about the different paradises, first about the one set higher than the others.

An orchard overflowing with all the delights that a human heart could imagine. The walls of this paradise are all of ruby, as are the towers and the houses within; but the beds and their posts, the stairways leading to the terraces, and all the dishes, as well as the doors of these houses are of pearl. Inside, there are very loving maidens, one hundred thousand times more beautiful and pleasant than those I have already told you about. There are also tents, some of ruby, others of emerald, still others of pearl or precious stones of every kind. . . . They are set above fountains that flow with water and wine of all the colors and flavors that a human heart could imagine. There are also marvelous sweet songs from the damsels seated beneath the trees that are there, all made of precious stones, like their fruits that are sweeter and tastier than anything. There is also music from instruments that are so sweet to hear and so pleasant that no human heart could imagine it. Beneath this orchard, there were two others, one surrounded by precious stones, within and without, and the other made of very pure red gold.

This paradise is made up of vast terraces to the number of one hundred, made of gold and silver or of precious stones. The narrator goes on at length about the happiness of the blessed (five hundred wives, four thousand virgins, eight thousand servants), and then begins again with a similar description. God comes to visit the blessed and to make sure of their satisfaction.

Muhammad's paradise, like Dante's, contains several parts, but it seems principally devoted to material pleasures.

In the heavens of the seven planets, Dante contemplates the souls of the blessed whose beatitude grows as they are further from the earth. The poet looks at Beatrice, who in turn looks at the sun, the image of God; together they go to the first heaven, the heaven of the Moon. There are found those who did not completely fulfill their vows. The breathtaking ascent resumes:

> and even as an arrow that has struck
> the mark before the bow-cord comes to rest,
> so did we race to reach the second realm.[79]

The heaven of Mercury is reserved for the souls who have done good from love of glory. In the heaven of Venus appear those who in their earthly life have been subject to love, even profane love, on condition that they have repented. The heaven of the Sun is attributed to spirits inspired by wisdom. Eleven theologians and philosophers occupy the first crown. The eleven wise men of the second crown dance and sing. A third crown appears. Then the ascent continues to the fifth heaven, the heaven of Mars, home of the souls who have fought for the faith; they form a

---

79. *Paradiso*, in *The Divine Comedy*, tr. Allen Mandelbaum (New York: Alfred A. Knopf, Everyman Library, 1995), V, 91–93.

luminous cross. They sing and then fall silent. The poet learns
that he will be exiled and that his mission will be to say everything.

> Nevertheless, all falsehood set aside.
> let all that you have seen be manifest,
> and let them scratch where it may itch.
> For, if at first taste, your words molest,
> they will, when they have been digested, end
> as living nourishment.
> (*Paradiso* XVII, 127–32)

In the heaven of Jupiter, Dante contemplates the princes who
have fought for justice. In the heaven of Saturn, the heaven of
the contemplative, Beatrice smiles no longer, for her smile would
be too bright for a mortal. A golden ladder leads from Saturn to
the Empyrean.

> I saw a ladder rising up so high
> that it could not be followed by my sight:
> its color, gold when gold is struck by sunlight.
> I also saw so many flames descend
> those steps that I thought every light displayed
> in heaven had been poured out from that place.
> (*Paradiso* XXI, 28–33)

This image of the ladder is found in a number of medieval texts
concerning paradise. The original source is the ladder seen by
Jacob in his dream in Genesis. The eighth heaven, or heaven of
the stars is devoted to the triumph of Christ; the ninth or Pri-
mum Mobile, to the angelic hierarchies. The tenth, or Empyrean, is the domain of the heavenly court, the angels and the
blessed. In the first three heavens, Moon, Mercury, and Venus,
the blessed spirits still possess a recognizably human form, but
this diminishes as Dante ascends; in the upper heavens, beginning with the Sun, he sees only light.

## GHOSTS

While humans made journeys into the beyond, inhabitants of
that realm made the reverse journey, and came back momen-

tarily from their other-worldly dwelling to this planet which they had, in principle, left for good. "How is it surprising," wrote Saint Augustine, "that the dead, knowing and feeling nothing, are seen in dreams by the living, and that they say things that are recognized as true when we awake?" The early Middle Ages provide few ghost stories, but they become quite frequent between the tenth and twelfth centuries, principally in monastic literature.

Ghosts might travel in groups. This is the case for the *Mesnie Hellequin,* first mentioned by Orderic Vital, a monk of Saint-Evroult in the diocese of Lisieux and author of an *Ecclesiastical History* of the Normans, written principally between 1123 and 1137. He narrates the abuses committed by Robert de Bellême. This cruel man hated the protector of Saint-Evroult, Hugues de Grandmesnil, to whom he laid siege in Courcy in 1091. It is in this context that a monk saw the *Mesnie Hellequin.*

Orderic Vital heard the story from a witness who was returning home after visiting a sick parishioner on the night of January 1, 1091. When he is alone in the deserted countryside, he hears an enormous noise that he at first thinks is the army of Robert de Bellême heading for Courcy. Hidden behind some medlar trees, he sees a veritable troop parade before his eyes.

A first group contains a crowd of people on foot along with pack animals loaded with baggage. They hurry on groaning, and among them the priest recognizes some recently dead neighbors. They are followed by gravediggers carrying stretchers on which dwarves are lying. Two Ethiopians carry a tree trunk to which is strapped a man screaming in pain; a devil is torturing him by striking him with burning spurs. He is being harshly punished, because he has killed a priest, and he died before repenting. Then comes a countless crowd of women on horseback, sitting on saddles armed with burning nails; the wind constantly lifts the women up, and they come down again; other burning nails pierce their breasts. Among them the priest recognizes several noble ladies who have led a lustful existence.

Next come priests and monks leading bishops and abbots. They ask for prayers. Among them are some esteemed figures, but God alone knows what sinners must be subjected to purification.

There follows an army of knights, black and spewing fire. Mounted on large horses, they press forward as though riding to war. Some of them, recently dead, are known to the priest. Walchelin—that is his name—recognizes that he has just seen the *Mesnie Hellequin*. To make sure that what he says will be believed, he tries to capture a black horse without a rider. After a vain attempt, he manages to grasp a horse, but he has to let go. Then four knights come up, hurl violent reproaches at him, and order him to follow them. But one of them intervenes, because he wants to give the priest a message. When Walchelin says that he does not know him, the knight introduces himself and confesses that he dishonestly took possession of a mill. The priest is to ask his heirs to make restitution. When Walchelin refuses, the furious knight seizes him by the throat where he leaves a mark. He loosens his grip when Walchelin calls on the Virgin Mary and because another knight comes to the rescue. This is the priest's brother, whom he does not at first wish to recognize, but he finally agrees to do so. He thus learns that this brother, because he tried to take possessions from the dead, must suffer the same punishment as they do.

Following this vision, the priest fell ill. After a week, he was able to report what he had seen to Bishop Gilbert of Lisieux. Since he lived for fifteen more years, Orderic Vital was able to question him and to see the mark on his throat.

As Jean-Claude Schmitt has shown, the dead in this vision fall into three groups that can be related to the three estates of society. The first and most disparate group corresponds to the third estate and does not communicate with Walchelin. Similarly, the second, which recalls the order of priests and monks, has no contact with the witness. The third, a homogeneous group, in contrast, enters into a relationship with him, but contact is really established only within the family.

The dead might appear individually. This is still in the realm of the marvelous to the extent that a person is surprised by phenomena of whose cause he is ignorant. In contrast, miracles are attributed to divine intervention, as, for example, in a long narrative by Gervaise of Tilbury.

In his *Book of Wonders* sent to Emperor Otto IV late in 1214 or early in 1215, Gervaise narrates the apparitions of a young man who has died to his cousin, a virgin girl of eleven, in Beaucaire in the year 1211. "To satisfy those who do not believe and who justify, not their ignorance, but their stubbornness, by the near impossibility of a return to this world after death, I am going to recount in detail something new that has recently come to light among us: at its novelty, hearts should marvel, minds should wonder, and bodies tremble."

Guillaume, a native of Apt exiled to Beaucaire for violent behavior, was killed in a brawl. He died as a Christian after receiving the sacraments of the Church and forgiving his killer. Three to five days after his death, he appears to a young cousin, for they loved each other dearly and chastely. As she has asked him to come back, insofar as possible, to tell her about his fate, she is expecting him. They have a conversation, but her parents, who are awake, hear only the words of their daughter. Guillaume reappears seven days later, while the parents have gone to pray for the repose of his soul; he is indeed beginning to feel the beneficial effects of their action. He is accompanied by a devil "horned, black, spewing flames, and breathing fire," who disappears when sprinkled with holy water,

Word spreads about these apparitions. The girl then serves as an intermediary to question the dead man. A layman learns that Guillaume is aware of an act of charity that he has accomplished in secret. The prior of Tarascon asks many questions of Guillaume, who is now accompanied by Saint Michael and wearing his former clothes that his aunt had given to the poor. A belt of fire causes him pain, but this stops when the belt, stolen from an inhabitant of Apt, is restored to its owner. Jean-Claude Schmitt notes a correspondence both between good actions on earth for the benefit of the dead and the remission of sins in the afterlife and between material objects and their imaginary equivalents. Shortly thereafter, "a priest, a learned man, who lived virtuously, was a good priest, and feared God," begs the girl "to suggest to the apparition to talk directly to him, the priest, if that is possible." The request is accepted and the priest questions the ghost closely. A little later, Bishop Guillaume of Orange, unable to come himself, sends a whole series of questions by messenger, and Guillaume knows their substance in advance.

After death, we learn, souls wander for four or five days. After this period, souls that are neither sanctified nor damned go to purgatory, which is in the air. There are two other temporary places in the air. The damned stay in a hell in the air, and will go to the underground hell after the Last Judgment. Similarly, the just occupy a paradise in the air before the true paradise.

Ghosts have superhuman faculties. Souls know everything that takes place on earth and know the future. Through his cousin, Guillaume is able to tell his uncle and the uncle's son that their enemies are planning to kill them. He appears in a dream and wakens the dozing priest, while simultaneously visiting his cousin to tell her that the priest will be late.

Thus, it was thought that souls traveled, if only because of their wandering after death, an idea that the Church would attempt to banish in the late Middle Ages. Questioned by Bishop Jacques Fournier of Pamiers, the peasants of Montaillou expressed the belief that the dead had invisible bodies and were encountered everywhere, near the village and on the roads. In particular, they visited the churches containing their tombs. Only the damned were carried into ravines by devils. On All Saints' Day, souls traveled to a calm place where there were no punishments, and they would go to paradise at the Last Judgment.

What was the meaning of space for the dead? Since body and soul were separated at the moment of death, it was normal that the dead could sometimes appear far from their bodies. Spirits were freed from the constraints of space and time.

# CONCLUSION

What have we discovered in the course of this study? Stability was the normal condition in a largely peasant world in which roads and means of communication experienced little progress. But there was also constant movement in a world in which the idea of the nation was not yet firmly established and in which, for this reason, coexisting with village roots and the resulting immobility were large transnational networks, particularly in the intellectual and religious realms, that prevailed over countries and nations. But this movement, for almost all the men of the Middle Ages, involved not so much journeying as necessary travel.

The medieval world was thus rather close to our own, although usually for opposite reasons. Indeed, the development of technologies such as radio and television able to replace travel, the extreme ease of means of communication, the extensive exploration of the earth, and extreme urbanization have brought about a way of life that is very confined for some and extremely mobile for others.

Nevertheless, contemporary stability and movement turn out to be different from those of the Middle Ages because of the contrast between their infrastructural causes. Sedentary village life cannot be compared to the individual isolation of large metropolises. Because of their routine character, their proliferation, and their speed, present-day journeys are not really seen as journeys. Above all, there is today a frenzy of travel, but travel has lost its character, becoming nothing but a frantic flight from the self, a reflection of the inability to live fully in everyday activities that have indeed become unbearable, and a reflection as well of the aspiration for another world. "All the misfortune of mankind comes from a single thing, our inability to stay quietly in a room," wrote Pascal. In the Middle Ages, travel was essentially movement linked to certain necessities or, for a few adventurers, a quest, an opening out, but not a flight from the self.

To be sure, travel sometimes provoked nostalgia, even for those who had chosen it voluntarily. Then what of those who were banished, condemned to exile? Such complaints were rarely heard. Ovid's *Tristia* were not imitated until the sixteenth century in the *Regrets* of Joachim du Bellay. In paradise, Dante expresses his love for his native land.

> You shall leave everything you love most dearly:
> this is the arrow that the bow of exile
> shoots first. You are to know the bitter taste
> of others' bread, how salt it is, and know
> how hard a path it is for one who goes
> descending and ascending others' stairs.
> And what will be most hard for you to bear
> will be the scheming senseless company
> that is to share your fall into this valley;
> against you they will be insane, completely
> ungrateful and profane; and yet soon after,
> not you but they will have their brows bloodred.
> Of their insensate acts, the proof will be
> in the effects; and thus your honor will
> be best kept if your party is your self
>
> (*Paradiso* XVII, 55–69)

But the poet tries to give a meaning to this exile, and his fate is tied to the fate of the city.

Further, on this earth, is it not appropriate for the apostle to leave his country in order to convert his brothers? To be sure, Saint Benedict strongly recommends stability in his Rule, adopting a way of thinking that goes back to the Fathers of the Church, and yet, Christ and his apostles never ceased their peregrinations. According to Matthew, "Jesus went about all the cities and villages teaching." And when He sent His disciples out as missionaries, according to Luke, "they departed, and went through the towns, preaching the gospel, and healing everywhere." Thus, there were many saints on the roads, Saint Martin in the fourth century, Saint Columbanus in the early seventh century. In the twelfth century, not only monks, but priests went from town to town, such as Robert d'Arbrissel, the founder of Fontevraud. Before founding the Premonstratensians and becoming archbishop of Magdeburg, Norbert led the life of a traveling preacher from 1118 to 1120. His life, written around 1160, tells us that when he came to the village of Huy, he gave all his possessions to the poor and that, dressed in rags and barefoot, he went to Saint-Gilles despite the bitter cold. There he found Pope Gelasius, who gave him full authority to preach.

> Norbert and his companion traveled to castles, villages, and fortified towns, preaching and reconciling enemies, calming hatreds and ending the most persistent wars. He asked nothing of anyone, but everything he was offered he gave to the poor and the lepers. He was absolutely certain of receiving through the grace of God what was indispensable for his existence. Because he thought that he was a simple pilgrim, a traveler on earth, he could be tempted by no ambition, for all his hope lay in heaven.

"A simple pilgrim, a traveler." Do the terms not apply to all men whose earthly existence is but a brief interlude before eternal life? The Epistle to the Hebrews, moreover, reminds Christians that they should consider themselves as "strangers and pilgrims on the earth." Bernard of Clairvaux, writing around 1130 in praise of the new order founded by the Templars, is drawn toward beatitude. What is important is not the earthly, but the heavenly Jerusalem.

In the late Middle Ages, the image of the human pilgrim appears in plays as well as sermons or theological works. William Langland, at the end of *Piers Plowman,* written in 1362, shows the knight Conscience taking up the pilgrim's staff in search of Truth. Gerson wrote a *Testament of the Pilgrim on the Way to Paradise* in Latin, but also in French, providing for the laity a view that had theretofore been restricted to monks. On the occasion of the jubilee of 1400, a short English work told the faithful who were unable to go to Rome how to make an authentic spiritual journey out of the fifty days that the trip to Rome would require.

Throughout the Middle Ages, men were attached to the world in which they lived. But, exiled children of Eve, "moaning and crying in this vale of tears," although they may not have traveled through space, they made a journey in time that led them to God.

# BIBLIOGRAPHY

Primary Sources

*L'An mille. Œuvres de Liutprand, Raoul Glaber, Adémar de Cha-bannes, Adalbéron, Helgaud.* Trans. Ed. Pognon. Paris, 1947.

Anglure. *Le Saint Voyage de Jherusalem du Seigneur d'Anglure.* Ed. F. Bonnardot and A. Lognon. Paris, 1878.

Beaumanoir, Ph. de. *Coutumes de Beauvaisis.* 2 vols. Ed. A. Salmon. Paris, 1899.

Bede. *A History of the English Church and People.* Trans. Leo Sherley-Price. Baltimore: Penguin Books, 1955.

*Beowulf.* Trans. E. Talbot Donaldson. New York: Norton, 1966.

Bertrandon de La Broquière. *Voyage d'Outre-Mer de Bertrandon de La Broquière, premier écuyer tranchant et conseiller de Philippe le Bon, duc de Bourgogne.* Ed. Ch. Schefer. Paris, 1892.

Boldensele, Guillaume de. *Liber de quibusdam ultramarinis partibus.* Ed. Ch. Deluz. Paris, 1972.

Brandan. *Les Voyages merveilleux de saint Brandan à la recherche du Paradis terrestre (XIIe s.).* Ed. Fr. Michel. Paris, 1878.

Carpini, Giovanni del Pian di. *History of the Mongols.* In *The Mongol Mission,* ed. Christopher Dawson. New York: Sheed and Ward, 1955.

Caumont. *Voyage d'Outre-Mer en Jérusalem par le seigneur de Caumont, l'an 1418.* Ed. Marquis de Lagrange. Paris, 1858.

Chastellain, G. *Œuvres.* 8 vols. Ed. Kervyn de Lettenhove. Brussels, 1863–66.

Chaucer, Geoffrey. *The Canterbury Tales.* In *The Complete Poetry and Prose of Geoffrey Chaucer.* New York: Holt, Rinehart and Winston, 1977.

329

Chrétien de Troyes. *Erec and Enide*. Trans. Burton Raffel. New Haven, Conn.: Yale University Press, 1997.

*Chronique du religieux de Saint-Denis contenant le règne de Charles VI de 1380 à 1422*. 3 vols. Ed. and trans. F. L. Bellaguet. Paris, 1994 [1839–52].

Columbus, Christopher. *The Four Voyages*. Ed. and trans. J. M. Cohen. London and New York: Penguin Books, 1969.

Dante. *Inferno*. Trans. Robert Pinsky. New York: Farrar, Straus and Giroux, 1994.

———. *The Divine Comedy*. Trans. Allen Mandelbaum. New York: Knopf (Everyman), 1995.

"Deux voyageurs allemands en Provence et en Dauphiné à la fin du XVe siècle. Le pèlerinage de Hans von Waltheym en l'an 1474. L'itinéraire de Jérôme Münzer en l'an 1495." Ed. Noël Coulet. *Provence historique* 41 (1991): fasc. 166.

Eudes Rigaud. *Journal des visites pastorales d'Eudes Rigaud, archevêque de Rouen. MCCXLVIII–MCCLXIX*. Ed. Th. Bonnin. Rouen, 1852.

Faber, Felix. *Fratris Felicis Fabri Evagatorium in Terrae Sanctae*. 3 vols. Ed. C. D. Hassler. Stuttgart, 1843–49.

———. *Voyage en Egypte de Félix Fabri, 1483*. 3 vols. Trans. J. Masson and G. Hurseaux. Cairo, 1975.

Froissart, Jean. *Chroniques*. 15 vols. to date. Ed. S. Luce, G. Raynaud, and L. and A. Mirot. Paris: Société de l'Histoire de France, 1869–1975.

———. *Chroniques*. 26 vols. Ed. Kervyn de Lettenhove. Brussels, 1870–76.

Gervais de Tilbury. *Le Livre des Merveilles. Divertissement pour un empereur* (part three). Trans. A. Duchesne. Paris, 1992.

Gregory of Tours. *History of the Franks*. Trans. Lewis Thorpe. Harmondsworth: Penguin Books, 1974.

———. *Miracula et opera omnia*. Ed. B. Krusch. In *Monumenta Germaniae historica, Scriptores rerum merovingicarum*, vol. I, 2. 1885.

———. *Les Livres des miracles et autres opuscules*. 4 vols. Ed. and trans. H. Bordier. Paris, 1857–64.

Guenée, B., and F. Lehoux, eds. and trans. *Les Entrées royales françaises de 1328 à 1515*. Paris, 1968.

*Le Guide du pèlerin de Saint-Jacques-de-Compostelle*. Ed. and trans. J. Vielliard. Paris, 1938.

Hariulf. *Chronique de Saint-Riquier*. Ed. F. Lot. Paris, 1901.

Heito. *Visio Wettini*. Ed. Duemmler. In *Monumenta Germaniae historica, Poetae latini medii aevi*, vol. 2, pp. 267–75.

Ibn Battuta. *The Travels of Ibn Battuta*. 4 vols. Trans. H. A. R. Gibb and C. F. Beckingham. Cambridge and London: The Hakluyt Society, 1958–94.

Ibn Khaldun. *Histoire des Berbères*. 4 vols. Trans. G. de Slane. Paris, 1925–56.

*Itinéraire d'Anselme Adorno en Terre sainte (1470–1471)*. Ed. and trans. J. Heers and G. de Groes. Paris, 1978.

*Itineraria et alia geographica*. Turnholt, 1965.

Joinville, Jean de. *The Life of St. Louis*. Trans. René Hague. New York: Sheed and Ward, 1955.

Joos van Ghistele. *Voyage en Egypte. 1482–1483*. Trans. R. Bauwens-Préaux. Cairo, 1976.

Loup de Ferrières. *Correspondance*. 2 vols. Ed. and trans. L. Levillain. Paris, 1927–35.

*Love Lyrics from the Carmina Burana*. Trans. P. G. Walsh. Chapel Hill: University of North Carolina Press, 1993.

Mandeville, Jean de. *Voyage autour de la terre*. Trans. Ch. Deluz. Paris, 1993.

Mézières, Philippe de. *Le Songe du Vieil Pèlerin*. 2 vols. Ed. G. W. Coopland. Cambridge, 1969.

Mollat, M. *Les Affaires de Jacques Cœur. Journal du procureur Dauvet, procès-verbaux de séquestre et d'adjudication*. 2 vols. Paris, 1952–53.

Oderic of Pordenone. *Les Voyages en Asie du bienheureux frère Oderic de Pordenone, religieux de saint François*. Ed. Ch. Schefer. Paris, 1891.

Paris, Matthew. *Chronicles of Matthew Paris*. Trans. Richard Vaughan. New York: St. Martin's Press, 1984.

Pegolotti, F. B. *La Pratica della mercatura*. Ed. A. Evans. Cambridge, 1936.

Polo, Marco. *The Travels of Marco Polo*. Trans. Ronald Latham. New York and London: Penguin Books, 1958.

*Purgatoire de saint Patrice*. Trans. in J. Marchand, *L'Autre monde au Moyen Age*. Paris, 1940.

*Recueil des documents concernant le Poitou, contenus dans les registres de la Chancellerie de France*. Ed. P. Guérin in *Archives historiques du Poitou*, vols. 11, 13, 17, 19, 21, 24, 26, 29, 32. 1881–1909. Ed. P. Guérin and L. Celier in ibid., vol. 41. 1919. Ed. L. Celier in ibid., vols. 50 and 56. 1938 and 1958.

*Registre criminel du Châtelet de Paris du 6 septembre 1389 au 13 mai 1392*. 2 vols. Ed. H. Dupplès-Agier. Paris, 1861–64.

Richer de Reims. *Histoire de France*. 2 vols. Ed. and trans. R. Latouche. Paris, 1930–37.

Rubruck, William of. *The Mission of Friar William of Rubruck*. Trans. Peter Jackson. London: The Hakluyt Society, 1990.

Salimbene. *Chronica fratris Salimbene de Adam*. Ed. O. Holder-Egger. In *Monumenta Germaniae historica, Scriptores*, vol. 32, pp. 1–652. 1905–13

Sidonius Apollinaris, Saint. *The Letters of Sidonius*. 2 vols. Trans. O. M. Dalton. Oxford: Clarendon Press, 1915.

*Terrae incognitae*. Vols 2–4. Trans. into German by Richard Hennig. Leiden, 1937–39.

*Vie de saint Etienne d'Obazine*. Ed. and trans. M. Aubran. Clermont-Ferrand, 1970.

Villehardouin, Geoffroi de. *Memoirs of the Crusades by Villehardoui and de Joinville*. Trans. Frank Marzials. London: Dent, 1915.

*The Vinland Sagas*. Trans. Magnus Magnusson and Heermann Pálsson. New York: New York University Press, 1966.

*Vision de Barontus* (678–679). In *Monumenta Germaniae historica, Scriptores rerum merovingicarum*, vol. 5, pp. 377–94.

*Les Visites pastorales de Simon de Beaulieu, archevêque de Bourges: 1283–1291*. Ed. M.-Th. de Fornel. Typescript. Limoges, 1982.

Voisins, Philippe de. *Voyage à Jérusalem de Philippe de Voisins, seigneur de Montaut*. Ed. Ph. Tamizey de Larroque. Paris and Auch, 1883.

*Le Voyage de Hieronimus Monetarius à travers la France 17 septembre 1494–14 avril 1495*. Ed. E. Ph. Goldschmidt. *Humanisme et Renaissance* 6 (1939): 55–75, 198–220, 324–48, 529–39.

*Le Voyage de Pierre Barbatre à Jérusalem en 1480*. Ed. P. Tucoo-Chala and N. Pinzuti. *Annuaire-Bulletin de la Société de l'Histoire de France*, pp. 73–172. 1972–73.

*Voyageurs arabes. Ibn Fadlân, Ibn Jubayr, Ibn Battûta et un auteur anonyme*. Trans. Paule Charles-Dominique. Paris: Gallimard, Bibliothèque de la Pléiade, 1995.

Wace. *Le Roman de Brut (XIIe s.)*. 2 vols. Ed. I. Arnold. Abbeville and Paris, 1938–40.

Several collections of texts have been used for references and some documents.

Brunel, G., and E. Lalou, eds. *Sources d'histoire médiévale, IXe–milieu du XIVe siècle*. Paris, 1992.

Guyotjeannin, O. *Le Moyen Age. Ve–XVe siècle*. Paris, 1992.

La Roncière, Ch.-M. de, Ph. Contamine, R. Delort, and M. Rouche. *L'Europe au Moyen Age*. 3 vols. Paris, 1969–71.

SECONDARY SOURCES
*(Works most utilized are indicated by an asterisk)*

Alphandéry, P., and A. Dupront. *La Chrétienté et l'idée de croisade*. 2 vols. Paris, 1954–59.

André, J.-M., and M.-F. Baslez. *Voyager dans l'Antiquité*. Paris, 1993.

*Assistance et assistés. Actes du 97e Congrès national des sociétés savantes, Nantes, 1972*. Paris, 1979.

Aubrun, M. "Caractères et portée religieuse et sociale des *Visiones* en Occident du VIe au XIe siècle." *Cahiers de civilisation médiévale* (1980): 109–30.

Autrand, F. *Charles V le Sage*. Paris, 1994.

\*———. *Charles VI. La folie du roi*. Paris, 1986.

Bachelard, Gaston. *The Poetics of Space*. Trans. Maria Jolas. New York: Orion Press, 1964.

Badel, F. *Un Evêque à la diète. Le voyage de Guillaume de Challant auprès de l'empereur Sigismond. Cahiers lausannois d'histoire médiévale* 3 (1991).

Balard, M., ed. *Etat et Colonisation au Moyen Age et à la Renaissance*. Lyon, 1989.

Baltrusaitis, J. *Le Moyen Age fantastique. Antiquités et exotismes dans l'art gothique*. Paris, 1955.

Bar, F. *Les Routes de l'autre monde. Descentes aux Enfers et voyages dans l'au-delà*. Paris, 1946.

\*Barrière, B. "Itinéraires médiévaux du Limousin à l'Aquitaine." In *Les Moyens de communication en Limousin de l'Antiquité à nos jours. Actes du Colloque régional de Limoges, 1990*. Travaux d'Archéologie limousine, 1990, supplement 1, pp. 121–42.

\*Bautier, R.-H. "La route française et son évolution au cours du Moyen Age." Académie royale de Belgique. *Bulletin de la Classe des Lettres et des Sciences morales et politiques* 73, 1–2 (1987): 70–104.

\*———. "Le voyage au Moyen Age." In Institut de France, *Séance publique des cinq académies*, pp. 11–22. 1982.

\*———. "La Circulation fluviale dans la France médiévale." In *Recherches sur l'économie de la France médiévale. Les voies fluviales. La draperie. Actes du 112e Congrès national des sociétés savantes, Lyon 1987*, pp. 7–36. Paris, 1989.

\*Bernard, J. *Navires et Gens de mer à Bordeaux (v. 1400–v. 1550)*. 3 vols. Paris, 1968.

\*Bienvenu, J.-M. "Recherches sur les péages angevins aux XIe et XIIe siècles." *Le Moyen Age* 12 (1957): 209–40, 437–67.

Blachère, R. *Extrait des principaux géographes arabes du Moyen Age*. Paris, 1932.

Boiteux, L. A. *La Fortune de mer, le besoin de sécurité et les débuts de l'assurance maritime*. Paris, 1968.

\*Bottineau, Y. *Les Chemins de Saint-Jacques*. Paris, 1983.

\*Boyer, R. *La Vie quotidienne des Vikings (800–1050)*. Paris, 1992.

\*———. *Les Vikings*. Paris, 1992.

Braunstein, Ph. "Toward Intimacy: The Fourteenth and Fifteenth Centuries." In *A History of Private Life*, II: *Revelations of the Medieval World*, ed. Georges Duby. Trans. Arthur Goldhammer. Cambridge, Mass.: Harvard University Press, 1988.

\*Brehier, L. *Le Monde byzantin*, vol. 2, *Les Institutions de l'empire byzantin*. Paris, 1949.

Carolus-Barré, L. "Aventure de mer et naufrages en Méditerranée au milieu du XIIIe siècle." In *Compte rendu de l'Académie des inscriptions et belles-lettres*, pp. 612–26. 1974.

*Carozzi, C. "La géographie de l'au-delà et sa signification pendant le haut Moyen Age." In *Settimane di studio del centro italiano di studi sull alto medioevo, 29, 1981*, pp. 423–83. Spoleto, 1983.

———. *Le Voyage de l'âme dans l'Au-delà d'après la littérature latine (Ve–XIIIe siècle)*. Rome, 1994.

Céard, J., and J. C. Margolin, eds. *Voyager à la Renaissance*. Paris, 1987.

Champion, P. *François Villon. Sa vie et son temps*. 2 vols. Paris, 1913.

Charbonnier, P. "L'entrée dans la vie au XVe siècle, d'après les lettres de rémission." In *Les Entrées dans la vie. Initiations et apprentissages. 13e Congrès de la Société des historiens médiévistes de l'Enseignement supérieur public, Nancy, 1981. Annales de l'Est* 1–2 (1982): 71–104.

Chartres, J. A. "Les hôtelleries en Angleterre à la fin du Moyen Age et aux temps modernes." *Flaran 2, 1980* (1982): 207–28.

Chaunu, Pierre. *European Expansion in the Later Middle Ages*. Trans. Kattarine Bertram. Amsterdam: North Holland, 1978.

Chelini, J., and H. Branthomme. *Histoire des pèlerinages non chrétiens. Entre magique et sacré: le chemin des dieux*. Paris, 1987

Chénerie, M.-L. *Le Chevalier errant dans les romans arthuriens en vers des XIIe et XIIIe siècles*. Geneva, 1986.

*La circulation des nouvelles au Moyen Age. 24e Congrès de la Société des historiens médiévistes de l'Enseignement supérieur publique, Avignon, 1993*. Paris and Rome, 1994.

Cloulas, I. *Laurent le Magnifique*. Paris, 1982.

Combes, J. "Hôteliers et hôtelleries de Montpellier à la fin du XIVe et au XVe siècle." In *Hommage à André Dupont*, pp. 54–81. Montpellier, 1974.

Commeaux, C. *La Vie quotidienne chez les Mongols de la conquête (XIIIe siècle)*. Paris, 1972.

Contamine, Ph. *La Vie quotidienne pendant la guerre de Cent Ans. France et Angleterre (XIVe siècle)*. Paris, 1976.

Coquery, C., ed. *La découverte de l'Afrique. L'Afrique noire atlantique des origines au XVIIIe siècle*. Paris, 1965.

Coste-Messelière, R. de La, and G. Jugnot. "L'accueil des pèlerins à Toulouse." In *Le Pèlerinage. Cahiers de Fanjeaux* 15, pp. 117–35.

Coulet, N. *Aix-en-Provence: espace et relations d'une capitale*. Aix-en-Provence, 1988.

*———. "Les hôtelleries en France et en Italie au bas Moyen Age." *Flaran 2, 1980* (1982): 181–205.

*Craecker-Dussart, C. de. "L'évolution du sauf-conduit dans les principautés de Basse-Lotharingie, du VIIIe au XIVe siècle." *Le Moyen Age* 80 (1974): 185–243.

Defourneaux, M. *Les Français en Espagne aux XIe et XIIe siècles*. Paris, 1949.

Delaruelle, E., E.-R. Labande, and P. Ourliac. *L'Eglise au temps du Grand Schisme et de la crise conciliaire (1378–1449)*, vol. 2. Paris, 1964.

Delort, R. *Le Commerce des fourrures en Occident à la fin du Moyen Age*. 2 vols. Rome, 1978.

Delumeau, J. *Une histoire du paradis. Le jardin des délices*. Paris, 1992.

Deluz, Ch. "Indifférence au temps dans les récits de pèlerinage (du XIIe au XIVe siècle)?" *Annales de Bretagne et des pays de l'Ouest* 83 (1976): 303–13.

*———. *Le Livre de Jehan de Mandeville. Une "géographie" au XIVe siècle*. Louvain-la-Neuve, 1988.

———. "Pèlerins et voyageurs face à la mer, XIIe–XVIe siècles." In *Horizons marins, itinéraires spirituels*, vol. 2 *Marins, navires et affaires*, ed. H. Dubois, J.-C. Hocquet, and A. Vauchez, pp. 277–88. Paris, 1987.

———. "Sentiment de la nature dans quelques récits de pèlerinage du XIVe siècle." In *Actes du 102e Congrès national des Sociétés savantes, Limoges, 1977, Section de philologie et d'histoire*, vol. 2, pp. 70–80. Paris, 1979.

Denifle, H. *La Guerre de Cent Ans et la désolation des églises, monastères et hôpitaux en France*, vol.1: *Jusqu'à la mort de Charles V (1380)*. Paris, 1899.

Dinzelbacher, P. *Vision und Visionsliteratur im Mittelalter*. Stuttgart, 1981.

*Dollinger, Ph. *La Hanse (XIIe–XVIIe siècles)*. Paris, 1964.

Doresse, J. *L'Empire du prêtre Jean*. Paris, 1957.

*Dossat, Y. "Types exceptionnels de pèlerins: l'hérétique, le voyageur déguisé, le professionnel." In *Le pèlerinage, Cahiers de Fanjeaux* 15, pp. 207–25.

Dubois, H., J.-C. Hocquet, and A. Vauchez, eds. *Horizons marins, itinéraires spirituels. Etudes réunies en l'honneur de Michel Mollat*, vol. 2 *Marins, navires et affaires*. Paris, 1987.

Dubois, H. *Les Foires de Chalon et le commerce dans la vallée de la Saône à la fin du Moyen Age (vers 1280–vers 1430)*. Paris, 1976.

———. "Techniques et coûts des transports terrestres dans l'espace bourguignon à la fin du Moyen Age." *Annales de Bourgogne* 52 (1980): 65–82.

Dubost, F. *Aspects fantastiques de la littérature narrative médiévale (XIIe–XIII siècles)*. Paris, 1991.

*Duby, Georges. *William Marshal: The Flower of Chivalry*. Trans. Richard Howard. New York: Pantheon, 1985.

———. "Les 'jeunes' dans la société aristocratique de la France du Nord-Ouest au XIIe siècle." *Annales ESC* 19 (1964): 835–46.

Ducellier, A. "La France et les Iles Brittaniques vues par un Byzantin du XVe siècle: Laonikos Chalkokondylis." In *Economies et Sociétés*

*au Moyen Age. Mélanges offerts à Edouard Perroy*, pp. 439–45. Paris, 1973.

*Ducellier, A., B Doumerc, B. Imhaus, and J. de Miceli. *Les Chemins de l'exil. Bouleversements de l'est européen et migrations vers l'ouest à la fin du Moyen Age*. Paris, 1992.

Dufourq, Ch.-E. *La Vie quotidienne dans les ports méditerranéens au Moyen Age (Provence-Languedoc-Catalogne)*. Paris, 1975.

Dupâquier, J., ed. *Histoire de la population française*, vol. 1. Paris, 1988.

Duparc, P. "Les cols des Alpes occidentales et centrales au Moyen Age." In *Actes du colloque sur les cols des Alpes dans l'Antiquité et le Moyen Age*, pp. 183–96. Orléans, 1971.

Dupront, A. *Du Sacré. Croisades et pèlerinages. Images et langages*. Paris, 1987.

Ertzdorff, X. von, and D. Neukirch, eds. *Reisen und Reiseliteratur im Mittelalter und in der Frühen Neuzeit*. Amsterdam and Atlanta.

*Espaces du Moyen Age. Médiévales* 18 (1990).

*L'Europe et l'Océan au Moyen Age. 17e Congrès de la Société des médiévistes de l'Enseignement supérieur public, Nantes, 1986*. Nantes, 1988.

*Faral, E. *Les Jongleurs en France au Moyen Age*. Paris, 1910.

Favier, J. *Le Commerce fluvial dans la région parisienne au XVe siècle: le registre des compagnies françaises, 1449–1467*. Paris, 1975.

———. *Les Grandes découvertes d'Alexandre à Magellan*. Paris, 1991.

———. *Gold & Spices: The Rise of Commerce in the Middle Ages*. Trans. Caroline Higgitt. New York: Holmes & Meier, 1998.

*Favreau, R, "Voyages et messageries en Poitou à la fin du Moyen Age." *Bulletin de la Société des Antiquaires de l'Ouest* 13 (1975): 31–53.

Fournial, E. *Les Villes et l'économie d'échange en Forez aux XIIIe et XIVe siècles*. Paris, 1967.

Ganshof, F.-L. "L'étranger dans la monarchie franque." In *Recueils de la Société Jean Bodin*, vol. 9: *L'Etranger*, pp. 5–36. Brussels, 1958.

*———. *Le Moyen Age*, vol. 1 of *Histoire des relations internationales*, ed. P. Renouvin. Paris, 1968.

Gardiner, Eileen, ed. *Visions of Heaven and Hell before Dante*. New York: Italica Press, 1989.

Gatto, G. "Le voyage au paradis. La christianisation des traditions folkloriques au Moyen Age." *Annales ESC* (1979): 929–42.

*Gautier-Dalché, P. *La "descriptio mappe mundi" de Hugues de Saint Victor*. Paris, 1988.

*———. "Un problème d'histoire culturelle: perception et représentation de l'espace au Moyen Age." *Médiévales* 18 (1990): 5–15.

———. "Tradition et renouvellement dans les représentations de l'espace géographique au IXe siècle." *Studi medievali* 24 (1983): 121–65.

Gauvard, Cl. *"De grace especial." Crime, Etat et Société en France à la fin du Moyen Age*. 2 vols. Paris, 1991.

Geremek, Bronislaw. *The Margins of Society in Late Medieval Paris.* Trans. Jean Birrell. New York: Cambridge University Press, 1987.

Germain, R. *Les Campagnes bourbonnaises à la fin du Moyen Age, 1370–1530.* Clermont-Ferrand, 1987.

Gilles, H. "Lex peregrinorum." In *Le pèlerinage, Cahiers de Fanjeaux* 15, pp. 161–89.

Ginzburg, Carlo. *Ecstasies: Deciphering the Witches' Sabbath.* Trans. Raymond Rosenthal. New York: Pantheon, 1991.

Gonthier, N. *Délinquance, justice et société dans le Lyonnais médiéval de la fin du XIIIe siècle au début du XVIe siècle.* Paris, 1993.

*Gorce, D. *Les Voyages. L'hospitalité et le port des lettres dans le monde chrétien des IVe et Ve siècles.* Wépion-sur-Meuse and Paris, 1925.

Grandeau, Y. "Itinéraire d'Isabeau de Bavière." In *Bulletin philologique et historique (jusqu'à 1610). Actes du 89e Congrès national des Sociétés savantes, Lyon, 1964,* pp. 569–670. Paris, 1967.

Guértet-Laferté, M. *Sur les routes de l'empire mongol. Ordre et rhétorique des relations de voyage aux XIIIe et XIVe siècles.* Paris, 1994.

Harley, J. B., and D. Woodward, eds. *The History of Cartography,* vol. 1. Chicago: University of Chicago Press, 1987.

*Hayez, A.-M. "Les courriers des papes d'Avignon sous Innocent VI et Urbain V (1352–1370)." In *La Circulation des nouvelles au Moyen Age,* pp. 49–62.

Heers, J. *Christophe Colomb.* Paris, 1981.

* ———. "La cour de Mahaut d'Artois en 1327–1329: solidarités humaines, livrées, mesures." In *Publications de l'université de Buenos Aires, faculté de philosophie et de lettres.*

* ———. *Marco Polo.* Paris, 1983.

Heliot, P., and M. L. Chastang. "Quêtes et voyages de reliques au profit des églises françaises du Moyen Age." *Revue d'histoire ecclésiastique* 59 (1964): 789–822 and 60 (1965): 5–32.

*Hocquet, J.-C. *Voiliers et commerces en Méditerranée 1200–1650.* Lille, 1970.

———, ed. *Les Hommes et la mer dans l'Europe du Nord-Ouest, de l'Antiquité à nos jours.* Lille, 1986.

*L'Homme et la Route en Europe occidentale au Moyen Age et au Temps Modernes, Centre culturel de l'abbaye de Flaran, 1980.* Auch, 1982.

Huschenbett, D., and J. Margett, eds. *Reisen und Welterfahrung in der deutschen Litteratur des Mittelalters.* Wurzburg, 1991.

*Jehel, G. *La Méditerranée médiévale de 350 à 1450.* Paris, 1992.

Joris, A. "Suivez le guide!" *Le Moyen Age* 98 (1992): 5–15.

Jugnot, G. *Autour de la "Via Podiensis" du Guide du pèlerin de Saint-Jacques-de-Compostelle (Xe–XVe siècle).* 2 vols. Paris, 1979.

————. "Les chemins de pèlerinage dans la France médiévale." In *L'Homme et la Route*, pp. 57–83.

Jusserand, J.-J. *La Vie nomade et les routes d'Angleterre au XIVe siècle.* Paris, 1884.

*Kahn, J.-Cl. *Les Moines messagers. La religion, le pouvoir et la science saisis par les rouleaux des morts XIe–XIIe siècles.* Paris, 1987.

*Kappler, C. *Monstres, démons et merveilles à la fin du Moyen Age.* Paris, 1980.

Kappler, C., et al. *Apocalypses et voyages dans l'au-delà.* Paris, 1987.

Kerhervé, J. *L'Etat breton au XIVe et XVe siècles: les ducs, l'argent, les hommes.* 2 vols. Paris, 1987.

Labande, E.-R. "Recherches sur les pèlerins dans l'Europe des XIe et XIIe siècles." *Cahiers de Civilisation médiévale* (1958): 159–69, 339–47.

*Langlois, Ch.-V. *La Connaissance de la nature et du monde du XIIe siècle au milieu du XIVe siècle.* Paris, 1927.

Larmat, J. "Prières au cours des tempêtes." In *La Prière au Moyen Age.* *Sénéfiance* 10 (1981).

La Roncière, C. de. *Histoire de la découverte de la terre.* Paris, 1939.

Lebecq, S. "Ohthere et Wulfjtan: deux marchands-navigateurs dans le Nord-Est européen à la fin du IXe siècle." In *Horizons marins, itinéraires spirituels* vol. 1, ed. H. Dubois et al., pp. 167–81.

*————. *Marchands et navigateurs frisons du haut Moyen Age.* 2 vols. Lille, 1983.

Leclercq, J. *Monachisme et pérégrination.* In *Aux sources de la spiritualité occidentale*, pp. 35–90. Paris, 1964.

*Le Goff, Jacques. "Aspects savants et populaires des voyages dans l'au-delà au Moyen Age." In *L'Imaginaire médiéval*, pp. 103–19. Paris, 1985.

————. "Un étudiant tchèque à l'université de Paris au XIVe siècle." *Revue des études slaves* 24 (1948): 143–70.

————. "Contacts et non-contacts dans l'Occident médiéval." In *Culture et travail intellectuel dans l'Occident médiéva*, ed. G. Hasenohr and J. Longère, pp. 9–79. Paris, 1981.

*————. *The Birth of Purgatory.* Trans. Arthur Goldhammer. Chicago: University of Chicago Press, 1984.

————. *Time, Work & Culture in the Middle Ages.* Trans. Arthur Goldhammer. Chicago: University of Chicago Press, 1980.

*Le Roy Ladurie, Emmanuel. *Montaillou: The Promised Land of Error.* Trans. Barbara Bray. New York: George Braziller, 1978.

Lestoquoy, J. "La navigation fluviale au IXe siècle: les flottilles monastiques." In *Etudes d'histoire urbaine. Villes et abbayes. Arras au Moyen Age*, pp. 80–83. Arras, 1966

————. "Note sur certains voyages au XIe siècle." In *Etudes d'histoire urbaine. Villes et abbayes. Arras au Moyen Age*, pp. 118–21. Arras, 1966.

*Mahn-Lot, M. *Portrait historique de Christophe Colomb*. Paris, 1988 [1960].

Major, A. "Vision externe sur l'Empire vénitien: les voyageurs méridionaux au XVe siècle." *Le Moyen Age* 98 (1992): 213–26.

Marignan, A. *Etudes sur la civilisation française*. I: *La Société mérovingienne*. II: *Le Culte des saints sous les Mérovingiens*. Paris, 1899.

Martin, H. *Mentalités médiévales XIe–XVe siècle*. Paris, 1996.

*Mazaheri, A. *La Vie quotidienne de musulmans au Moyen Age. Xe au XIIIe siècle*. Paris, 1951.

Medeiros, M.-Th. de. "Voyage et lieux de mémoire. Le retour de Froissart en Angleterre." *Le Moyen Age* 98 (1992): 419–28.

*Merindol, Ch. de. "Le prince et son cortège. La théâtralisation des signes du pouvoir à la fin du Moyen Age." In *Les Princes et le pouvoir au Moyen Age, 23e Congrès de la Société des historiens médiévistes de l'Enseignement supérieur public, Brest, 1992*, pp. 303–23. Paris, 1993.

*Merrien, J. *La Vie quotidienne des marins au Moyen Age, des Vikings aux galères*. Paris, 1969.

Mesqui, J. "Le pont de pierre au Moyen Age. Du concept à l'exécution." In *Artistes, artisans et production artistique au Moyen Age*, vol. 1: *Les Hommes*, ed. X. Barral i Altet, pp. 197–215. Paris, 1986.

Micheau, F. "Les itinéraires maritimes et continentaux des pèlerinages vers Jérusalem." In *9e Congrès de la Société des historiens médiévistes de l'Enseignement supérieur public, Dijon, 1978*. Paris, 1979.

*Miquel, A. *La Géographie humaine du monde musulman jusqu'au milieu du XIe siècle. Géographie et géographie humaine dans la littérature arabe des origines à 1050*. Paris and The Hague, 1973.

Mollat, M. *Le Commerce maritime normand à la fin du Moyen Age*. Paris, 1952.

———. *Grands voyages et connaissance du monde du milieu du XIIIe siècle à la fin du XVe siècle*. Paris, 1966.

*———. *Les Explorateurs du XIIIe au XVIe siècle. Premiers regards sur des mondes nouveaux*. Paris, 1984.

*———. *La Vie quotidienne des gens de mer en Atlantique (IXe–XVIe siècle)*. Paris, 1983.

Monfrin, J. "Etudiants italiens à la fin du XIVe siècle." In *Mélanges d'archéologie et d'histoire*, Ecole française de Rome, 63 (1951): 195–280.

*Mornet, E. "Le voyage d'étude des jeunes nobles danois du XIVe Siècle à la Réforme." *Journal des savants* (1983): 298–318.

*Moulin, L. *La Vie des étudiants au Moyen Age*. Paris, 1991.

*Le Navire et l'Economie maritime du Moyen Age au XVIIIe siècle principalement en Méditerranée. Travaux du Deuxième Colloque international d'histoire maritime, 1957*. Paris, 1958.

Öhler, Norbert. *The Medieval Traveller*. Trans. Caroline Hillier. Wood-bridge: Boydell, 1989.

Origo, Iris. *The Merchant of Prato: Francesco di Maro Datini*. New York: Knopf, 1957.

Oursel, R. *Les Pèlerins du Moyen Age: les hommes, les chemins, les sanctuaires*. Paris, 1963.

Paravicini, W. *Die Preussenreise des europaïschen Adels*, vol. 1. Sig-maringen, 1989.

*Paravicini Bagliani, A. *La Cour des papes au XIIIe siècle*. Paris, 1995.

Parias, L. H., ed. *Histoire universelle des explorations*, vol. 1: *De la Préhistoire à la fin du Moyen Age*. Paris, 1955.

Parks, G. B. *The English Traveler to Italy*, vol. 1: *The Middle Ages (to 1525)*. Stanford, Calif.: Stanford University Press, 1954.

Pastoureau, M. *La Vie quotidienne en France et en Angleterre au temps des chevaliers de la Table ronde*. Paris, 1976.

*Le Pèlerinage. Cahiers de Fanjeaux* 15 (1980).

Petit, E. *Itinéraires de Philippe le Hardi et Jean sans Peur (1363–1419)*. Paris, 1888.

———. *Séjours de Charles V*. Paris, 1888.

———. *Séjours de Charles VI*. Paris, 1894.

Peyer, H. C., ed. *Gastfreundschaft, Taverne und Gasthaus im Mittel-alter*. Munich and Vienna, 1983.

Prescott, Hilda Frances Margaret. *Jerusalem Journey: Pilgrimage to the Holy Land in the Fifteenth Century*. London: Eyre & Spottiswoode, 1954.

*Les Récits de voyage*. Paris, 1986.

*Renouard, Y. *Les Hommes d'affaires italiens du Moyen Age*. Paris, 1968.

———. "L'Occident médiéval à la découverte du monde. A propos de deux grands anniversaires Marco Polo (1254–1324), Amerigo Ves-pucci (1454–1512)." In *Etudes d'histoire médiévale*, pp. 661–75. Paris, 1968.

*———. "Routes, étapes et vitesses de marche de France à Rome au XIIIe et au XIVe siècle d'après les itinéraires d'Eudes Rigaud (1254) et de Barthélémy Bonis (1350)." In *Etudes d'histoire médiévale*, pp. 677–97. Paris, 1968.

———. "Les voies de communication entre pays de la Méditerranée et pays de l'Atlantique au Moyen Age. Problèmes et hypothèses." In *Etudes d'histoire médiévale*, pp. 719–26. Paris, 1968.

Richard, J. *Croisades et Etats latins d'Orient. Points de vue et docu-ments*. Aldershot, 1992.

———. *Croisés, missionnaires et voyageurs. Perspectives orientales du monde latin médiéval*. Aldershot, 1983.

———. *Orient et Occident au Moyen Age. Contacts et relations (XIIe–XVe siècles)*. Aldershot, 1976.

\*———. *La Papauté et les Missions d'Orient au Moyen Age*. Ecole française de Rome, 1977.

\*———. *Les Récits de voyages et de pèlerinages*. Turnhout, 1981.

———. *Les Relations entre l'Occident et l'Orient au Moyen Age*. Aldershot, 1977.

———. "Transports par eau et péages de Chalon à Avignon, à propos des fournitures de poisson à la cour des papes." In *Recherches sur l'économie médiévale. Actes du 112e Congrès national des Sociétés savantes, Lyon, 1987*, pp. 37–44. Paris, 1989.

———. "Voyages réels et voyages imaginaires, instruments de la connaissance géographique au Moyen Age." In *Croisés, missionaires et voyageurs*, pp. 211–20.

\*Richard, J.-M. *Mahaut, comtesse d'Artois et de Borgogne (1302–1329)*. Paris, 1887.

\*Riché, P. *La Vie quotidienne dans l'Empire carolingien*. Paris, 1973.

Rocacher, J. *Rocamadour et son pèlerinage*. 2 vols. Toulouse, 1976.

Roncière, M. de La, and M. Mollat. *Les Portulans, Cartes marines du XIIIe au XVIIe siècles*. Freiburg, 1984.

\*Rouche, M. "L'héritage de la voierie antique dans la Gaule du Haut Moyen Age (Ve–XIe siècle)." *Flaran* 2, pp. 13–32.

Roux, J.-P. *Les Explorateurs au Moyen Age*. Paris, 1961.

\*Schmitt, Jean Claude. *Ghosts in the Middle Ages: The Living and the Dead in Medieval Society*. Trans. Teresa Lavender Fagan. Chicago: University of Chicago Press, 1998.

\*Sigal, P.-A. *Les Marcheurs de Dieu. Pèlerinages et pèlerins au Moyen Age*. Paris, 1974.

Sommé, M. "Les déplacements d'Isabelle de Portugal et la circulation dans les Pays-Bas au milieu du XVe siècle." *Revue du Nord* 52 (1970): 183–97.

Sottas, J. *Les Messageries maritimes de Venise aux XIVe et XVe siècles*. Paris, 1938.

Stanesco, M. *Jeux d'errance du chevalier médiéval*. Leiden, 1988.

Tanaka, M. *La Nation anglo-allemande de l'Université de Paris à la fin du Moyen Age*. Paris, 1990.

Tattersall, J. "*Terra incognita*: allusions aux extrêmes limites du monde dans les anciens textes français jusqu'en 1300." *Cahiers de civilisation médiévale* 24 (1981): 247–55.

*Les Transports au Moyen Age. 7e Congrès de la Société des historiens médiévistes de l'Enseignement supérieur public, Rennes, 1976. Annales de Bretagne et des pays de l'Ouest* 85, 2 (1978).

Tuilier, A. "Un conflit entre un étudiant croate et l'Université de Paris au XVe siècle. *Mélanges de la Bibliothèque de la Sorbonne* 7 (1986): 37–104.

Udovitch, A. L. "Time, the sea and society: duration of commercial voyages on the southern shores of the Mediterranean during the high Middle Ages." In *La Navigazione mediterranea nell'alto medioevo. Settimane di studio del centro italiano di studi sull'alto medioevo* 25 (1977), pp. 503–46. Spoleto, 1978.

*Venturini, A. "Un compte de voyage par voie de terre de Manosque à Gênes en 1251." *Provence historique* 45 (1995): 25–48.

Verger, J. "Les étudiants slaves et hongrois dans les Universités occidentales (XIIIe–XVe siècles)." In *L'Eglise et le peuple chrétien dans les pays de l'Europe du Centre-Est et du Nord (XIVe–XVe siècles)*, pp. 83–106. Rome, 1990.

———. "Les étudiants méridionaux à Paris au Moyen Age: quelques remarques." *Annales du Midi* (1990): 359–66.

*———. "La mobilité étudiante au Moyen Age." *Histoire de l'Education* 50 (1991): 65–90.

———. "Le recrutement géographique des universités françaises au début du XVe siècle d'après les suppliques de 1403." *Mélanges d'archéologie et d'histoire*, Ecole française de Rome, 82 (1970): 855–902.

*Viajeros, peregrinos, mercadores en el Occidente Medieval.* Gobierno de Navarra, 1992.

*Vicaire, M.-H. "Les trois itinérances du pèlerinage aux XIIIe et XIVe siècles." In *Le Pèlerinage. Cahiers de Fanjeaux* 15, pp. 17–41.

Villain-Gandossi, Ch. "La mer et la navigation maritime à travers quelques textes de la littérature française du XIIe au XIVe siècle." *Revue d'histoire économique et sociale* 47 (1969): 150–92.

*Voyage, Quête, Pèlerinage dans la littérature et la civilisation médiévales. Sénéfiance 2, Cahiers du Cuerma.* Aix, 1976.

*Voyages et voyageurs à Byzance et en Occident du Vie au XIe siècle. Actes du Congrès de Liège, 1995.* (forthcoming).

*Voyages et voyageurs au Moyen Age. 26e Congrès de la Société des historiens médiévistes de l'Enseignement supérieur public, Aubazine-Limoges, 1995.* Paris, 1996.

Wolff, Ph. *Commerces et marchands de Toulouse (vers 1350–vers 1450).* Paris 1954.

———. "Les hôtelleries toulousaines au Moyen Age." In *Regards sur le Midi médiéval*, pp. 93–106. Toulouse, 1979.

Wunderli, P., ed. *Reisen in reale und mythische Ferne. Reiseliteratur in Mittelalter und Renaissance.* Düsseldorf, 1993.

Zoubov, V. P. "Un voyage imaginaire autour du monde au XIVe siècle." In *Congresso international de historia dos descobrimentos*, pp. 1–8. Lisbon, 1961.

*Zumthor, P. *La Mesure du monde.* Paris, 1993.

# INDEX

345

JEAN VERDON is professor emeritus of literature and humanities at Limoges University. He is the author of *Night in the Middle Ages,* published by the University of Notre Dame Press.